Easy Everyday
Gluten-Free
Cooking

Easy Everyday
Gluten-Free
Cooking

Includes **250** delicious recipes

Donna Washburn & Heather Butt

Easy Everyday Gluten-Free Cooking
Text copyright © 2013 Donna Washburn and Heather Butt
Photographs copyright © 2013 Robert Rose Inc.
Cover and text design copyright © 2013 Robert Rose Inc.

Most of the recipes in this book appeared in *125 Best Gluten-Free Recipes* and *The Best Gluten-Free Family Cookbook* published by Robert Rose in 2003 and 2005.

For complete cataloguing information, see page 371.

Disclaimer

The recipes in this book have been carefully tested by our kitchen and our tasters. To the best of our knowledge, they are safe and nutritious for ordinary use and users. For those people with food or other allergies, or who have special food requirements or health issues, please read the suggested contents of each recipe carefully and determine whether or not they may create a problem for you. All recipes are used at the risk of the consumer.

We cannot be responsible for any hazards, loss or damage that may occur as a result of any recipe use.

For those with special needs, allergies, requirements or health problems, in the event of any doubt, please contact your medical adviser prior to the use of any recipe.

Design and Production: Kevin Cockburn/PageWave Graphics Inc.
Editors: Carol Sherman and Sue Sumeraj
Proofreaders: Karen Campbell-Sheviak and Sheila Wawanash
Recipe Tester: Jennifer MacKenzie
Cover Photography: Colin Erricson
Associate Photographer: Matt Johannsson
Cover Food Styling: Kathryn Robertson
Interior Photography: Mark T. Shapiro
Interior Food Styling: Kate Bush
Props Styling: Charlene Erricson

Cover image: Thin Pizza Crust (page 110) with Roasted Vegetable Pizza Topping (page 113)

We acknowledge the financial support of the Government of Canada through the Book Publishing Industry Development Program (BPIDP) for our publishing activities.

Published by Robert Rose Inc.
120 Eglinton Avenue East, Suite 800, Toronto, Ontario, Canada, M4P 1E2
Tel: (416) 322-6552 Fax: (416) 322-6936
www.robertrose.ca

Printed and bound in USA

1 2 3 4 5 6 7 8 9 CKV 21 20 19 18 17 16 15 14 13

Contents

We dedicate this book
to those who live with gluten intolerance
and to your families.
Over the years
your friendship has been important to us.

Acknowledgments

This book has had the support and assistance of many from its inception to the final reality.

Our thanks to the following for supplying products for recipe development: Doug Yuen, Dainty Foods, for jasmine and basmati rice, white and brown rice flour and rice bran; George Birinyi Jr., Grain Process Enterprises Ltd., for arrowroot, potato and tapioca starches, xanthan gum and sorghum, garbanzo-fava, white and brown rice flour, chickpea and yellow pea flours; Kingsmill Foods for Egg Replacer®; Jim Grey, Casco, for corn syrup and cornstarch; Faye Clack, Marketing & Communications Inc., for California walnuts and Southern U.S. Trade Association pecans; Compass Food Sales for arrowroot, tapioca and potato starches; Elizabeth and Peter Riesen, El Peto Products Ltd., for rice bran, amaranth, quinoa, sweet rice and flaxseed flours; Maplegrove Foods for Pastariso rice mini-elbows, Mac & Cheese and Pastato potato pasta elbows; Howard Selig, Valley Flaxflour Ltd., for flax flour and flaxseeds; Dennis Gilliam, Bobs Red Mill, for introducing us to sorghum flour and providing this and other gluten-free products; the employee-owners of King Arthur Flour Company for nut flours, dried fruit, xanthan gum, English muffin rings, hamburger and hotdog baking pans and bread machine yeast; Margaret Hudson, Burnbrae Farms Ltd., for Naturegg Simply Whites, Break Free and Omega Pro liquid eggs; Wendi Hiebert, Ontario Egg Producers, for whole shell eggs; Michel Dion, Lallamand Inc., for InstaFerm® (fermipan®) yeast; and Joyce Parslow of the Canadian Beef Information Center for sambal oelek.

Thank you to the many manufacturers of bread machines who continue to supply the latest models to our test kitchen; Zojirushi, Breadman, Cuisinart, Hamilton Beach and Toastmaster.

A huge thank you to the members of our focus group who faithfully and tirelessly tasted and tested gluten-free recipes and products from the beginning to end of recipe development. Your comments, suggestions and critical analysis were invaluable and helped make this a better book. Thanks to Susan Crapper, Rita Purcell, Carol Coulter, Debra Rice, Jim Morton, Larry Bomford, Barbara Wahn, Sue Jennett, Deanna Jennett, Ron Pyatt and Henk Rietveld, and to Lorraine Vinette, RD, Kingston General Hospital, for the nutritional analysis of the Carrot Apple Energy Bars. You'll be pleased to see we listened and incorporated your suggestions.

We want to express our appreciation to photographer Mark Shapiro and Colin Erricson; food stylists Kate Bush and Kathryn Robertson and prop stylist Charlene Erricson. Thank you for making our gluten-free photographs so enticing. Once again, we enjoyed baking for the photo shoot.

Bob Dees, our publisher; Marian Jarkovich, Sales and Marketing Manager, National Retail Accounts; and Nina McCreath, Manager, Corporate Accounts and International Sales at Robert Rose, deserve special thanks for their ongoing support.

To Kevin Cockburn, Daniella Zanchetta and Joseph Gisini of PageWave Graphics, thank you for working through this cookbook's design, layout and production.

To Carol Sherman and Sue Sumeraj, our editors and Jennifer MacKenzie, our recipe tester.

To Magda Fahmy Turnbull, RD, for the nutrient analysis.

Thank you to our families — you help bring balance to our lives when we became too focused on our work.

And finally, to you, who must follow a gluten-free diet, we sincerely hope these recipes help make your life easier and more enjoyable. We developed them with you in mind.

— Donna J. Washburn and Heather L. Butt

About the Nutrient Analysis

The nutrient analysis done on the recipes in this book was derived from the Food Processor SQL Nutrition Analysis Software, version 10.9, ESHA Research (2011). Where necessary, data was supplemented using the following references:

1. Shelley Case, *Gluten-Free Diet: A Comprehensive Resource Guide*, Expanded Edition (Regina, SK: Case Nutrition Consulting, 2006).

2. USDA National Nutrient Database for Standard Reference Release 25 (2012). Retrieved March 2013, from the USDA Agricultural Research Service website: www.nal.usda.gov/fnic/foodcomp/search/.

Recipes were evaluated as follows:

- The larger number of servings was used where there is a range.
- Where alternatives are given, the first ingredient and amount listed were used.
- Optional ingredients and ingredients that are not quantified were not included.
- Calculations were based on imperial measures and weights.
- Nutrient values were rounded to the nearest whole number.
- Defatted soy flour, 25% reduced sodium stock, 1% milk, light cream cheese, light sour cream and brown rice flour were used, including where these ingredients are listed as soy flour, stock, milk, cream cheese and sour cream.
- Calculations involving meat and poultry used lean portions without skin.
- Canola oil was used where the type of fat was not specified.
- Recipes were analyzed prior to cooking.

It is important to note that the cooking method used to prepare the recipe may alter the nutrient content per serving, as may ingredient substitutions and differences among brand-name products.

Introduction

If you have just been diagnosed with gluten intolerance or have decided to eliminate gluten from your diet, have we got the book for you! You will find all the basic recipes you need to begin. This book will introduce you to several new nutritious flours and grains that are now readily available at grocery and health food stores or through mail order or online. Amaranth, quinoa, sorghum and bean — both the grains and the flours — and buckwheat flakes are products that will increase the variety and nutritional value of your diet.

Your emails and letters tell us you are sharing the foods you prepare from our baking chapters with the rest of the family. Our aim was to develop recipes the whole family could enjoy. Our greatest reward came by email. We had delivered a cake to a local person with celiac disease and she wrote, "I did not get to taste the Gingered Pumpkin Snacking Cake — my non-celiac husband ate the whole thing and left me a note pronouncing it 'very good.' "

Although you may find a specific combination of flours and starches repeated in several recipes, we have not developed recipes around a "flour mix," but instead have developed each on its own to give us the taste and baking qualities we desired. This means you'll need to have a greater variety of flours available in your kitchen and you'll have two or three more measurements to make, but you tell us it is worth it. We have included three mixes to save you time. The muffin mix has five variations, the cookie dough has six and the pancake mix has four.

We have met so many terrific people as we take our cookbook to gluten-free trade shows, celiac conferences and chapter meetings in both the U.S. and Canada. Thank you for sharing your successes, your recipes and your suggestions for recipes with us. We have adapted several, which are in the book: Macaroni and Cheese, an energy bar, an oil-based pastry and quick and easy dinner ideas, just to mention a few. We look forward to meeting you as we travel and share our knowledge and experience.

Some of our recipes have been inspired by meals we had at restaurants or while traveling. These include a Sticky Date Pudding with Toffee Sauce just like the sticky toffee pudding Donna tasted in a small village in Wales, and a Chocolate Lover's Hazelnut Surprise that's even better than the volcano cake with a runny chocolate center we shared in a chain restaurant. We have kept up with the latest information on gluten-free ingredients, gluten-free food products and food trends, and we're delighted to pass these tips on to you, along with easy-to-prepare recipes.

We have tested recipes together for many years, and we still enjoy every bite. As professional home economists, we look at every food from nutritional, food safety and quality angles. We can assure you that every recipe has been tested and tested and tested in our test kitchen. We even researched and purchased new pans, another heavy-duty mixer and several modern kitchen tools, as ours have seen many decades of use and abuse. What a good excuse to re-equip our kitchens!

Celiac friends and focus group members have evaluated the tastes, textures and carrying properties of the baked goods and have prepared the foods to make sure the recipe instructions made sense. We've put the same amount of care and time into this cookbook as we have with our other cookbooks. Check them out by visiting www.bestbreadrecipes.com.

— *Donna J. Washburn, PHEc & Heather L. Butt, PHEc*
Quality Professional Services
1655 County Road 2, Mallorytown, Ontario, K0E 1R0
Email: bread@ripnet.com
Website: www.bestbreadrecipes.com

The Gluten-Free Pantry

There is an ever-widening variety of gluten-free flours readily available today in major grocery stores, health food stores and bulk stores, by mail order and on the web.

Flours and Starches

We have introduced several new gluten-free flours into our baking repertoire in this cookbook and are enjoying these more nutritious selections. They are fun to work with and lend themselves to tender, delicious products without the gritty texture and starchy aftertaste of some GF products.

The major flours and starches we baked with are described here, and several others are described in the Ingredient Glossary at the back of the book. Unless otherwise specified, store all flours in airtight containers away from heat and light. For more prolonged storage, freeze. They will keep at room temperature for up to 1 month and in the freezer for 1 year.

Amaranth flour is milled from one of the oldest grains, amaranth, called a "super food" by early Aztecs. It is high in protein, fiber, calcium and iron. It has a light, creamy color, a fine texture and a slightly sweet toasted flavor. Store in the refrigerator for up to 1 month. Products high in amaranth may take slightly longer to bake, as it forms a crust on the outside of the product before it is completely baked. Recipes may require less liquid than some other flours.

Arrowroot is the starch made from the roots of a tropical South American plant with large leaves and white flowers. It blends well with all common gluten-free flours. It is referred to as arrowroot starch, as arrowroot flour and as arrowroot starch flour. We use it in berry sauces, as it thickens below the boiling point, giving a warm, clear shine. It must be mixed with a cold liquid before it is added to hot liquids.

Bean flours are high in fiber and calcium, and higher in protein than rice flour. There are several varieties, including garbanzo bean (chickpea), garbanzo-fava (garfava), which combines garbanzo beans and fava beans, and whole bean flour, made from Romano (cranberry) beans. There are both light and dark bean flours: use the dark with chocolate and the light for fruit breads and cakes, or in place of soy flour. Molasses and brown sugar help balance the stronger flavors.

> Amaranth flour is milled from one of the oldest grains, amaranth, called a "super food" by early Aztecs.

Our recipes were developed with whole bean flour, but all bean and pea flours are interchangeable in recipes. Beans are frequently "micronized" to reduce their flatulent effects before being ground to flour. Bean flours can be used in place of rice flour to make cream soups, cream sauces and gravies. Store in the refrigerator for up to 1 month.

Cornstarch is a flavorless, dense white powder from the endosperm of corn. It thickens to a shiny, clear finish, perfect for fruit sauces and glazes. However, cornstarch lumps easily, so it needs to be added to a small amount of cold liquid to make a paste before using. Cornstarch and corn flour are two different products and are not interchangeable.

Nut flour (nut meal) is a flour made by finely grinding nuts such as almonds, hazelnuts or pecans. All nut flours are interchangeable in recipes. Nut flours increase the fiber in a recipe and add a nutty flavor and richness of texture to baked products. Their high fat content aids in browning. Store in the refrigerator for up to 1 month. To make any of the nut flours, see Techniques Glossary, page 370.

Pea flour is high in fiber. It is available in both yellow and green and can be substituted for whole bean flour in baking. Store in the refrigerator for up to 1 month.

Potato starch cannot be interchanged with **potato flour**; they are two distinctly different products. As potato starch lumps easily, sift it before measuring. Potato starch adds moistness to baked goods. Potato flour is too heavy in texture to use in large amounts as a flour substitute in gluten-free recipes.

Quinoa flour is the finely ground cream-colored flour made from the most nutritious grain available. Quinoa (pronounced keen-wah) is the ancient grain of the Incas. It is high in protein, calcium and iron, and is higher in unsaturated fats and lower in carbohydrates than other flours. The grain has a nutty taste and can be eaten as a cereal or used as a rice replacement or a thickener in salads, casseroles or desserts. The small seeds, which look like millet, are naturally coated with a bitter tasting saporin that protects them from birds and insects. Modern processing removes the saporin, and rinsing may not be required (check with the manufacturer). Quinoa flour, used in small amounts, results in a moist product with good keeping qualities. Store in the refrigerator for up to 1 month.

> Nut flours increase the fiber in a recipe and add a nutty flavor and richness of texture to baked products.

Rice flour used to be the major flour used in gluten-free baking; however, it cannot be used alone but must be used in combination with starches such as corn, potato or tapioca. The products were frequently gritty, crumbly and dried out quickly. *Brown rice flour* has a grainy texture and provides more fiber than white rice flour. It is a creamy brown in color and we use it in all recipes requiring rice flour. Store in the refrigerator for up to 1 month. *Rice bran and rice polish* are the two outer parts of the rice kernel that have been removed during milling for white rice flour. Rice bran is the outermost layer. When added in small amounts to recipes, they increase the fiber content. Bran and polish are interchangeable in recipes. Store in the refrigerator for up to 1 month to prevent rancidity. *Sweet rice flour* is also known as glutinous rice flour, sticky rice flour or sushi rice flour. It is made from high-starch, sticky short-grain rice, and contains more starch than brown or white rice flour. There are two grades: one is beige, grainy and sandy-textured; the other is white, starchy, sticky and less expensive. The latter works better in recipes. It can be used as a thickener, or to dust baking pans or fingers for easier handling of sticky doughs.

Sorghum flour is made from a millet-like grain, milo (sorghum). It is high in fiber, starch and protein. The round seeds are a little smaller than peppercorns and can be red or white. Rich in fat-soluble and B vitamins, it has a slightly sweet taste; therefore, you are able to decrease the sugar content in recipes with sorghum flour. White sorghum produces flour that is quite white, with tan undertones. Stone-ground sorghum flours brown quickly as they cook. The slightly nutty, savory, very earthy flavor is slightly stronger than that of some gluten-free flours, but used in combination with whole bean flour or amaranth flour, sorghum flour bakes delicious chocolate-, pumpkin- and fig-based treats. We like its thickening properties, and have used it for gravy with success. Sorghum flour is unique, and we have found no substitutes.

Soy flour, high in protein, is a yellow-beige in color and has a slightly nutty flavor. Soy is high in protein, calcium, iron and magnesium. You will notice its strong aroma in a batter, but this disappears when the product is baked. The higher-fat variety browns very quickly, so products may need to be tented with aluminum foil during baking. Store in the refrigerator for up to 1 month.

> Rich in fat-soluble and B vitamins, it has a slightly sweet taste; therefore, you are able to decrease the sugar content in recipes with sorghum flour.

Tapioca starch (tapioca flour) is a slightly sweet, powdery product made from the cassava root. Use small amounts to sweeten breads made with rice and millet (corn) flours. Sauces require twice the amount of tapioca to thicken as cornstarch, but it continues to thicken as it cools.

Handling Gluten-Free Flours and Starches

- Purchase flours and starches from reliable sources for consistent quality and to ensure that there is no risk from cross-contamination. Once you succeed with a particular product, either brand or quality, stick with it.
- Store flours and starches in plastic containers rather than the bags they are purchased in. Select square, stackable, airtight containers with wide tops and tightly fitting lids to allow for ease of measuring these powdery ingredients.
- Label all containers with easy-to-read permanent markers. It is impossible to tell the difference between some of the white starches by feel or appearance.
- Sift all flours and starches as you fill the containers rather than spending the time each time you bake. Stir with a spoon or fork just before measuring.
- Organize a baking corner where you keep a variety of dry ingredients (store in the refrigerator only those that need to be there). This could be a deep drawer or an overhead cupboard. Keep a set of dry ingredient measures and spoons, a metal spatula, a large metal spoon, a heat-resistant spatula, a set of your most commonly used baking pans and a cooling rack within easy reach.
- Occasionally, you might require a pan previously used for baking a wheat flour recipe. Wash it carefully, as small particles can get trapped in corners. Be especially cautious with pans with ridges, such as the rim of a springform pan.
- Wear a mask if handling gluten-containing flours. They can become airborne, and inhalation can lead to problems.

> **Label all containers with easy-to-read permanent markers. It is impossible to tell the difference between some of the white starches by feel or appearance.**

Thickening Using Gluten-Free Flours

- Gluten-free flours can be used to thicken gravies, cream sauces, soups and stews when a dull, opaque appearance is desired.

- Either dissolve the GF flour in some cold liquid or cook it in hot fat or drippings for 1 to 3 minutes before adding the remaining cold liquid.
- For more information about thickening with GF flours, see the appendix "Thickener Substitutions" on page 358.

Thickening Using Gluten-Free Starches

- Gluten-free starches can be used to thicken fruit sauces, coulis, custards, Asian food and fruit pies when a clear, glossy appearance is desired.
- Always dissolve the GF starch in cold water, using twice as much liquid as starch, before adding to hot or cold liquids. Liquids may be water, GF stock, milk or juices.
- Do not overcook.
- For more information about thickening with GF starches see the appendix "Thickener Substitutions" on page 358.

Gluten Cross-Contamination in the Kitchen

"Cross-contamination" is the transfer of biological, chemical or physical contaminants to food while processing, preparing, cooking or serving it. Such transfers usually occur when people handle the food. Bacterial cross-contamination can occur when you handle raw then cooked meats, or cut raw meats then vegetables on the same board with the same knife.

If your kitchen is not completely gluten-free, here are a few extra points to help you avoid cross-contamination:

Crumbs can hide in silverware and utensil drawers, as well as in baking dishes and cooling racks.

1. Remember, crumbs can hide in silverware and utensil drawers, as well as in baking dishes and cooling racks.
2. Keep a separate cupboard and work area for GF baking supplies and utensils.
3. Purchase a toaster, frying pan, colander, spatula, microwave and bread machine baking pan to use exclusively for GF foods.
4. Purchase and label separate peanut butter, jam, cream cheese and butter to prevent wheat crumbs from contaminating them when a non-GF family member dips in.
5. Purchase squeeze bottles for mustard, GF mayonnaise, relish and GF barbecue sauce.

6. Keep the top shelf in the refrigerator for GF products, so wheat crumbs can't drop in. Be sure to cover all foods in the refrigerator, whether GF or not.

7. If you use a knife block, ensure that all knives are washed well and rinsed before storing. Better yet, keep separate knives and cutting boards for exclusive GF use.

8. Be extra cautious when using wooden cutting boards, and when serving foods in wooden salad bowls, serving dishes or trays.

9. Wipe counters frequently, rinsing and changing cloths between each task to prevent cross-contamination.

Speaking Our Language: Are We All on the Same Page?

1. *"GF" means "gluten-free," such as GF sour cream, GF mayonnaise, etc., when both gluten-free and gluten-containing products are available. We recommend that you read package labels every time you purchase a GF product. Manufacturers frequently change the ingredients.*

2. Our recipes were developed with the following products: large eggs, liquid honey, fancy (not blackstrap) molasses, bread machine (instant) yeast, fruit juice (not fruit drinks), salted butter and 2%, 1% or nonfat milk, yogurt and sour cream (but our recipes will work with other levels of fat). We know you'll get the same great results if you bake with these; expect slightly different results if you make substitutions.

3. Unless otherwise stated in the recipe, eggs and dairy products are used cold from the refrigerator.

4. If the preparation method (chop, melt, dice, slice, etc.) is listed before the food, it means you prepare the food before measuring. If it is listed after the food, measure first, then prepare. Examples are "melted butter" vs. "butter, melted"; "ground flaxseed" vs. "flaxseed, ground"; "cooked brown rice" vs. "brown rice, cooked."

5. Select either metric or imperial measures and stick to one for the whole recipe; do not mix.

6. Use measuring spoons for small amounts. New sets on the market include smidgeon, pinch, dash, $1/8$ tsp, $1/2$ tbsp, 2 tsp and 2 tbsp, in addition to the traditional

Select either metric or imperial measures and stick to one for the whole recipe; do not mix.

¼ tsp, ½ tsp, 1 tsp and 1 tbsp. The metric small measures are available in 1 mL, 2 mL, 5 mL, 15 mL and 25 mL sizes. There are also sets of long-handled, narrow spoons made especially to fit into spice jars. These are accurate and fun to use.

7. We use the "spoon lightly into the correct dry measure, heap the top and level once" method of measuring dry ingredients for accuracy and perfect products.

8. Use a graduated, clear liquid measuring cup for all liquids. Place on a flat surface and read at eye level.

9. If in doubt about a food term, a piece of equipment or a specific recipe technique, refer to the glossaries located on pages 368 to 371.

10. All foods that require washing are washed before preparation. Foods such as onion, garlic and bananas are peeled, but fresh peaches and apples are not.

Mixing Methods

Are the terms "cream," "cut in," "fold in" and "whisk" foreign to you? They really are need-to-know terms when you're baking. The wrong speed on the mixer, or an incorrect mixing technique, can result in a completely different product.

Your heavy-duty mixer "use and care" manual will have a chart that explains which numbers or speeds you need to select for the following techniques:

Your heavy-duty mixer "use and care" manual will have a chart that explains which numbers or speeds you need to select.

- **Mix, Stir or Combine.** To gently mix ingredients together. (Use the lowest setting or number on the dial.)
- **Cream.** Cookie and cake recipes often begin with "cream the butter and sugar until light and fluffy." Choose the paddle attachment of a heavy-duty electric mixer for the best results. (Use a medium-low setting or number on the dial.)
- **Beat.** This technique usually involves a handheld or heavy-duty electric mixer. (Use a medium-high setting or number on the dial.)
- **Whip.** To beat ingredients vigorously to increase volume and incorporate air. This method typically uses the wire whisk attachment. (Use the highest setting or number on the dial.)

Recipes also often use the following hand techniques:

- **Cut in.** Usually found in biscuit or pastry recipes, this term refers to mixing hard, cold fat with dry ingredients. Choose a special piece of equipment called a pastry blender, or use two knives. The purpose is to cut the fat into small pieces, coating each small particle with dry ingredients. The resulting dough should be the size of small peas or coarse meal, with some slightly larger pieces. This technique ensures tenderness when the dough is baked.
- **Fold in.** To combine two mixtures of different textures. For example, you fold fruit into whipped cream or GF flours into stiffly beaten egg whites. The tricky part is keeping the air that you have incorporated into the cream or egg whites. Select a large rubber spatula to gently lift and spread the lighter ingredients. Repeat until evenly mixed.
- **Whisk.** To incorporate air quickly, or to blend ingredients in a sauce to prevent it from burning as it cooks. Select a multi-tined wire whisk of a convenient size.

Choosing Baking Pans

We recommend using shiny, light-colored metal pans, as they reflect heat away from the baked product so it doesn't brown too much before it is baked.

- Baking pans are now available in a wide variety of materials: nonstick, aluminum, tin, stainless steel, ceramic and silicone. There are different quality levels of each type. For evenly risen and uniformly browned baked goods, purchase the best quality you can afford.
- We recommend using shiny, light-colored metal pans, as they reflect heat away from the baked product so it doesn't brown too much before it is baked.
- Darker pans absorb more heat and can leave edges crisp and over-browned. When using dark pans, check for doneness 5 minutes before the low end of the recommended baking time. For example, if a recipe says to bake for 35 to 45 minutes, check for doneness after 30 minutes.
- Glass baking dishes and metal baking pans with a nonstick finish conduct and retain heat, causing foods to bake more quickly; therefore, reduce the oven temperature by 25°F (20°C). For example, if a recipe says to bake at 350°F (180°C), bake at 325°F (160°C) instead. When we baked cheesecakes using a dark, nonstick finish, glass-bottomed springform pan, we were much happier with the results we got baking them at the lower temperature.
- For best results, it is important to use the size of pan specifically called for in the recipe.

Using an Instant-Read Thermometer

When we bake gluten-free, it is important to use a thermometer to test foods for doneness because it is more difficult to tell when they are baked: the outside of the bread or cake may look browned enough when the inside is still raw. The indicators you may be used to looking for when baking with wheat may not be reliable because gluten-free foods often have a different appearance. A thermometer is the only accurate way to be sure the food is done.

Purchasing

The best thermometer for this purpose is a bimetallic stemmed thermometer often called an instant-read or chef's thermometer. It has a round head at the top, a long metal stem and a pointed end that senses the temperature. There are both digital and dial versions available. Check the temperature range to be sure it covers the temperatures you need. Instant-read thermometers are widely available in department stores, some grocery stores, specialty shops and big box stores, and can also be purchased online.

Use

To test baked goods for doneness, insert the thermometer into the center of the product. With thin or small products, it may be necessary to insert the stem horizontally. Some can be stacked. (Some of the newer thermometers only need to be inserted to a depth of $3/4$ inch/2 cm, so check the manufacturer's instructions.) Gluten-free baked goods, whether breads, cakes or muffins, are baked until an instant-read thermometer registers 200°F (100°C). Do not leave the thermometer in the product during baking, as the plastic cover will melt, ruining the thermometer.

Clean the probe thoroughly after each use and store the thermometer in the plastic sleeve that came with it. Some of the more expensive ones (but not all) are dishwasher-safe. Read the manufacturer's instructions.

How to Calibrate Your Thermometer

It is important to make sure your thermometer is reading temperatures accurately, so you'll want to test it periodically.

> **Gluten-free baked goods, whether breads, cakes or muffins, are baked until an instant-read thermometer registers 200°F (100°C).**

There are two ways of doing this and either will work, though we prefer the boiling-water method.

- **Boiling-water method:** Bring a pot of water to a boil. Insert the thermometer probe into the boiling water, making sure it doesn't touch the pot. It should read 212°F (100°C). (Be careful not to burn yourself on the steam; we hold the thermometer with needle-nose pliers.)
- **Ice-water method:** Fill a container with crushed ice and cold water (mostly ice; just use water to fill the gaps). Insert the thermometer probe into the center of the ice water, making sure it doesn't touch the container. It should read 32°F (0°C).

  If the temperature reading is not exact, hold the calibration nut (found right under the round head) with a wrench and rotate the head until it reads the correct number of degrees.

Healthy Choices for Eating Out — or In!

Today, eating out is a challenge for everyone, but even more so for the celiac. You have to worry not only about individual menu items, food preparation methods and cross-contamination in the kitchen, but also about the nutritional content of your selections. To make wise menu choices, follow these suggestions:

1. **Lower-fat or healthy fat items:** Salmon or shellfish, or a stir-fry is always a good choice. Order skim or nonfat milk, ask for GF dressings on the side and remove all visible fat from meat and skin from poultry.
2. **Nutritious choices:** Select dark green salads, roasted vegetables and skim or lower-fat milk rather than mayonnaise-dressed coleslaw, fried vegetables and carbonated beverages. Order a baked potato or a salad instead of french fries (to avoid contamination, ask the wait staff not to cut open the baked potato). Substitute fresh fruit for a heavier dessert.
3. **Method of preparation:** Choose steaming, poaching, grilling and broiling, where individual portions can be prepared on a "super-clean" (no gluten) surface. Avoid

pan-frying, deep-frying and braising, where extra fat is added.

4. **Portion size:** Restaurants use huge serving plates, so keep these serving sizes in mind. Meat should be the same size as a deck of cards. Vegetables should occupy three-quarters of the plate, and each individual vegetable portion should be the size of a computer mouse. Fruit should be the size of a baseball, cheese a 9-volt battery, pasta a tennis ball, and muffins a yo-yo.

5. **Balance:** Don't starve yourself all day and then overeat that evening. Ask for a doggy bag, leave some on your plate or, better yet, ask for a half-portion. Order an appetizer such as steamed mussels as an entrée and share a GF dessert.

Traveling Gluten-Free Safely

More and more families are carrying food from home when they travel by car, plane or train as a result of new, convenient, car-friendly GF foods, the elimination of GF meals on many airlines and the uncertain availability of gluten-free foods along the way. According to a survey by the American Dietetic Association and ConAgra Foods Foundation, 97% of car travelers take food along. Of these, 67% pack sandwiches, 66% take chips and dip, 65% bring fresh fruits and vegetables and 28% pack meat and/or cheese in prepared lunches. Thirty percent leave food unrefrigerated for 3 to 4 hours, and 15% leave food at room temperature for more than 4 hours.*

At home, it is easier to be conscious of food safety and cross-contamination. Remember to follow the same safety rules you follow at home when you're on the road:

At home, it is easier to be conscious of food safety and cross-contamination. Remember to follow the same safety rules you follow at home when you're on the road.

1. Wash hands with soap and water for 20 seconds before preparing foods and when switching tasks, such as from handling raw meat, fish or poultry to cutting raw vegetables or from working with wheat products to handling those that are gluten-free.

2. Make sure food preparation areas are clean.

3. Pack moist towelettes so you can wash your hands before eating.

4. Carry perishable food in a cooler containing ice or ice packs. Stow the cooler in the back seat of an air-conditioned car, not the trunk. Include a refrigerator

thermometer, and check periodically to make sure the temperature stays below 40°F (4°C). Perishable food left at room temperature for more than an hour is a food safety hazard. If you travel frequently, purchase a cooler that plugs into the cigarette lighter of the car.

5. If stopping along the roadside to grill, watch final cooked temperatures. Hamburgers should reach 160°F (71°C), chicken 170°F (78°C), pork 160°F (71°C) and fish 155°F (68°C). Pack raw meats in the cooler in a well-sealed container separate from other foods.

6. When flying, pack food in small travel cooler bags that fit under an airplane seat. Freeze juice boxes to keep individual insulated lunch bags cool. Freeze bottles of water and drink them as they melt.

7. Carry-out or fast food is also susceptible to food poisoning. If you don't eat or refrigerate it within 2 hours, throw it out. Better yet, refrigerate it promptly.

8. Use the mini-bar refrigerator in your hotel room or ask for an efficiency unit. Request use of the kitchen refrigerator.

* "Beware the En Route Smorgasbord," American Dietetic Association and ConAgra Foods Foundation, March 2004.

Nutritious School Lunches

Between kindergarten and Grade 12, school-children eat approximately 2,400 lunches. Eating healthy meals is equally important for both the celiac and non-celiac child. During the afternoon, students concentrate better and have a higher energy level if they have had a nutritious lunch, resulting in a happier, less stressful learning environment.

Creating healthy, interesting lunches is a constant challenge for every parent. Follow these tasty tips for more nutritious packed lunches:

1. Involve your children in both planning and preparation. They know what is cool to eat. Set some guidelines — one food from each group. Check out the recipes in the box below (see the index for page numbers).

2. Get organized. Keep lunch bags, insulated containers, colorful napkins, plastic cutlery and so forth in one cupboard to make them easy to locate.

3. Insulated lunch bags or boxes are difficult to clean after a day at school, so pack the lunch in a large resealable plastic bag placed inside the lunch container. The plastic bag becomes a lunch box "liner," and washing the lunch box is easier. When purchasing a new lunch container, consider a soft-sided, aluminum foil–lined one with a removable clear plastic liner held in with Velcro. An ice pack fits nicely between the bag and the clear liner to keep food cold.

4. Send lots of water, juice and milk — enough for both breaks and lunch.

5. Keep cold foods cold. Freeze a juice box to keep eggs, cheese, yogurt, pudding, sandwiches and poultry cold. It thaws by lunch.

6. Keep hot foods hot. Soups and casseroles can be sent in a wide-neck Thermos. Don't forget a spoon!

7. Prevent boredom by sending small treats. Having these prevents children from being tempted to share or trade, as they will be enticed by their own lunch. Remember, treats should be just a small part of the lunch.

8. Consider the nutritive value of the food you pack. Muffins made with carrots, bananas and raisins are better than those made with chocolate chips, and a container of GF trail mix is better than a candy bar.

Bread	Protein	Raw, Raw, Raw	To Quench	Treats
Banana Cranberry Muffins	Mediterranean Pizza Squares	baby carrots and celery sticks	white or chocolate milk	Carrot Apple Energy Bars
Crispy Multi-Seed Crackers	Macaroni and Cheese	red pepper strips and cucumber slices	100% fruit juice	Chocolate Orange Mini-Muffins
Focaccia	Incredibly Easy Pizza Soup	clementines or mandarins	fruit smoothie	Molasses Cookies
Cinnamon Raisin Bread	cream cheese or cheese cubes	apples, grapes or peaches	yogurt shakes	Caramel Apple Cake
Seedy Brown Bread	turkey, tuna, salmon or GF peanut butter	trail mix	water	Pumpkin Date Bars

Breakfast and Brunch

Linda's Granola

**Makes
16 cups (4 L)**

Every time you make this granola, challenge yourself to add variety coconut, soy nuts, walnuts, pistachios, pecans, buckwheat flakes, apricots, dates, dried apple slices, blueberries and pineapple. Serve for breakfast, as a snack or as a nibble on your next hike.

Tips

For the GF multigrain cereal, we used a purchased boxed cereal with a mixture of corn, flaxseeds, amaranth and quinoa.

For the mixed dried fruit, we used a mixture of banana slices, papaya, raisins and cranberries.

Nutritional value per 1 cup (250 mL) serving	
Calories	349
Fat, total	15 g
Fat, saturated	2 g
Cholesterol	0 mg
Sodium	167 mg
Carbohydrate	49 g
Fiber	15 g
Protein	6 g
Calcium	65 mg
Iron	2 mg

- **Preheat oven to 300°F (150°C)**
- **Two 15- by 10-inch (40 by 25 cm) jelly-roll pans, lightly greased**

½ cup	corn syrup or liquid honey	125 mL
1 tbsp	vegetable oil	15 mL
4 cups	GF multigrain cereal	1 L
2 cups	GF honeyed corn flakes cereal	500 mL
1 cup	mixed nuts	250 mL
1 cup	whole almonds	250 mL
½ cup	sunflower seeds	125 mL
½ cup	pumpkin seeds	125 mL
3 cups	mixed dried fruit	750 mL

1. In a glass measuring cup, combine corn syrup and oil. Microwave, uncovered, on High for 45 seconds, or until it can be easily poured.

2. In a very large bowl, combine multigrain cereal, corn flakes cereal, mixed nuts, almonds, sunflower seeds and pumpkin seeds. Pour in corn syrup mixture and stir to coat evenly. Spread in prepared pans.

3. Bake in preheated oven for 30 to 40 minutes, or until toasted, stirring every 10 minutes. Add dried fruit. Stir gently to combine. Bake for 10 minutes more. Let cool in oven for 1 hour, with the oven turned off. Let cool completely on pans on a cooling rack. Store at room temperature in airtight containers for up to 3 months.

Variations

Vary the mix of dried fruit and the kind of nuts; just keep the total volume at 4 cups (1 L).

For the GF multigrain cereal, substitute GF puffed rice.

Carrot Apple Energy Bars

Makes 18 bars

For a quick, easy, on-the-move breakfast or snack, choose these moist, nutritious bars. Lorraine Vinette, RD, a dietitian at Kingston General Hospital provided the nutritional analysis.

Tips

For the dried fruit mix, we used 1/4 cup (50 mL) dried cranberries, 1/4 cup (50 mL) raisins, 2 tbsp (25 mL) dried mangoes, 1 tbsp (15 mL) dried blueberries and 1 tbsp (15 mL) dried apricots.

Check for gluten if you purchase the fruit as a prepared mix.

For a lactose-free bar, omit the milk powder.

Nutritional value per serving (1 bar)	
Calories	145
Fat, total	4 g
Fat, saturated	4 g
Cholesterol	19 mg
Sodium	133 mg
Carbohydrate	24 g
Fiber	3 g
Protein	4 g
Calcium	92 mg
Iron	2 mg

- Preheat oven to 325°F (160°C)
- 13- by 9-inch (3 L) baking pan, lined with foil and lightly greased

1 1/4 cups	sorghum flour	300 mL
1/2 cup	amaranth flour	125 mL
1/3 cup	rice bran	75 mL
1/4 cup	ground flaxseed	50 mL
1/2 cup	nonfat (skim) milk powder	125 mL
1 1/2 tsp	xanthan gum	7 mL
1 tbsp	GF baking powder	15 mL
1/4 tsp	salt	1 mL
2 tsp	ground cinnamon	10 mL
2	eggs	2
1 cup	unsweetened applesauce	250 mL
1/3 cup	packed brown sugar	75 mL
1 1/2 cups	grated carrots	375 mL
3/4 cup	dried fruit mix	175 mL
1/2 cup	chopped walnuts	125 mL

1. In a large bowl or plastic bag, combine sorghum flour, amaranth flour, rice bran, ground flaxseed, milk powder, xanthan gum, baking powder, salt and cinnamon. Mix well and set aside.

2. In a separate bowl, using an electric mixer, beat eggs, applesauce and brown sugar until combined.

3. Add flour mixture and mix just until combined. Stir in carrots, dried fruit and nuts. Spoon into prepared pan, spread to edges with a moist rubber spatula and allow to stand for 30 minutes.

4. Bake in preheated oven for 30 to 35 minutes, or until a cake tester inserted in the center comes out clean. Let cool in pan on a cooling rack and cut into bars. Store in an airtight container at room temperature for up to 1 week or individually wrapped and frozen for up to 1 month.

Variations

Try substituting grated zucchini for all or half of the carrots.

Substitute cardamom for the cinnamon.

r-Own
Waffle Mix

or enoug
four batches, or
enough for about
forty 4-inch (10 cm)
pancakes or about
twenty-four 4½-inch
(11 cm) waffles

It's great to have this mix on hand when the grandkids come for the weekend. Share some with the adults too! Ron Pyatt emailed a request for a pancake mix recipe, as did the Kingston Chapter of the Canadian Celiac Association for their children's summer camp.

1 cup	almond flour	250 mL
1 cup	brown rice flour	250 mL
1 cup	sorghum flour	250 mL
1 cup	soy flour	250 mL
½ cup	potato starch	125 mL
½ cup	tapioca starch	125 mL
1 cup	buttermilk powder	250 mL
⅓ cup	granulated sugar	75 mL
2 tsp	xanthan gum	10 mL
3 tbsp	GF baking powder	45 mL
1 tbsp	baking soda	15 mL
½ tsp	salt	2 mL

1. In a very large bowl or a very large plastic bag, combine almond flour, brown rice flour, sorghum flour, soy flour, potato starch, tapioca starch, buttermilk powder, sugar, xanthan gum, baking powder, baking soda and salt. Mix well.

2. Store dry mix in an airtight container in the freezer for up to 6 months. (For added convenience, divide the mix into four portions of 1⅔ cups (400 mL) each and store in resealable plastic bags. Label and date before storing. We add the page number of the recipe to the label as a quick reference.) Warm to room temperature before using. Mix well before measuring.

Variation

Try substituting ¼ cup (50 mL) flaxseed meal for ¼ cup (50 mL) of the almond flour.

Nutritional value	per pancake	per waffle
Calories	83	138
Fat, total	2 g	3 g
Fat, saturated	0 g	0 g
Cholesterol	2 mg	3 mg
Sodium	232 mg	386 mg
Carbohydrate	13 g	22 g
Fiber	1 g	2 g
Protein	4 g	6 g
Calcium	106 mg	176 mg
Iron	1 mg	1 mg

"Small-Batch" Make-Your-Own Pancake/Waffle Mix

**Makes
1²⁄₃ cups (400 mL),**

or enough for
about ten 4-inch
(10 cm) pancakes or
about six 4¹⁄₂-inch
(11 cm) waffles

Craving pancakes but
don't want to make too
large a quantity? Use this
recipe to make just ten.
Great for seniors, singles
or hungry teens!

Tips

*Recipe can be doubled or
tripled.*

*Use "Small-Batch"
in place of ¹⁄₄ batch
Make-Your-Own Pancake/
Waffle Mix in the recipes
on pages 30 to 34.*

¹⁄₄ cup	almond flour	50 mL
¹⁄₄ cup	brown rice flour	50 mL
¹⁄₄ cup	sorghum flour	50 mL
¹⁄₄ cup	soy flour	50 mL
2 tbsp	potato starch	25 mL
2 tbsp	tapioca starch	25 mL
¹⁄₄ cup	buttermilk powder	50 mL
2 tbsp	granulated sugar	25 mL
¹⁄₂ tsp	xanthan gum	2 mL
2¹⁄₄ tsp	GF baking powder	11 mL
³⁄₄ tsp	baking soda	4 mL
Pinch	salt	Pinch

1. In a large bowl or plastic bag, combine almond flour, brown rice flour, sorghum flour, soy flour, potato starch, tapioca starch, buttermilk powder, sugar, xanthan gum, baking powder, baking soda and salt. Mix well.

2. Store dry mix in an airtight container in the freezer for up to 6 months. Warm to room temperature before using. Mix well before using.

Nutritional value	per pancake	per waffle
Calories	86	144
Fat, total	2 g	3 g
Fat, saturated	0 g	0 g
Cholesterol	2 mg	3 mg
Sodium	232 mg	386 mg
Carbohydrate	14 g	23 g
Fiber	1 g	2 g
Protein	4 g	6 g
Calcium	106 mg	176 mg
Iron	1 mg	1 mg

Plain Jane Pancakes

Makes about ten 4-inch (10 cm) pancakes

Early spring, and the sap is running. Get ready to make these pancakes. Serve smothered with fresh maple syrup.

Tips

See page 32 for some tips before making pancakes.

Make mini-pancakes for the kids. Be creative and try making panda bear, bunny and happy face shapes.

● **Griddle or nonstick skillet, lightly greased**

2	eggs	2
1	egg white	1
¾ cup	water	175 mL
2 tbsp	vegetable oil	25 mL
¼ batch	Make-Your-Own Pancake/Waffle Mix (see recipe, page 28)	¼ batch

1. In a bowl, using an electric mixer, beat eggs, egg white, water and oil until combined. Add pancake mix and beat until almost smooth.

2. Heat prepared griddle or skillet over medium-high heat. For each pancake, pour ¼ cup (50 mL) batter onto prepared griddle and cook until the bottom is deep golden and the top surface wrinkles around the edges (1 to 3 minutes). Turn and cook for 30 to 60 seconds longer, or until bottom is golden. Serve immediately. Repeat with remaining batter.

Nutritional value per serving (1 pancake)	
Calories	60
Fat, total	4 g
Fat, saturated	1 g
Cholesterol	33 mg
Sodium	76 mg
Carbohydrate	4 g
Fiber	0 g
Protein	2 g
Calcium	32 mg
Iron	0 mg

Plain Jane Waffles

. . . .

**Makes six
4½-inch (11 cm)
waffles**

The classic breakfast treat for lazy weekend mornings, these waffles can also be made ahead and enjoyed throughout the week. (See "Pancake/Waffle Know-How," page 32, for storage tips and reheating instructions.)

Tips

See page 32 for some tips before making waffles.

For a lighter waffle, warm the egg whites before beating (see Techniques Glossary, page 369).

• **Waffle maker, lightly greased, then preheated**

2	eggs, separated	2
¾ cup	water	175 mL
2 tbsp	vegetable oil	25 mL
¼ batch	Make-Your-Own Pancake/Waffle Mix (see recipe, page 28)	¼ batch

1. In a small bowl, using an electric mixer, beat egg whites until stiff but not dry.

2. In a separate bowl, using an electric mixer, beat egg yolks, water and oil until combined. Add waffle mix and beat until smooth. Fold in egg whites.

3. Pour in enough batter to fill preheated waffle maker two-thirds full. Close lid and cook for 6 to 8 minutes, or until no longer steaming. Repeat with remaining batter.

Variation

Add blueberries, chopped apple or nuts to the batter.

Nutritional value per serving (1 waffle)	
Calories	100
Fat, total	7 g
Fat, saturated	1 g
Cholesterol	55 mg
Sodium	126 mg
Carbohydrate	6 g
Fiber	1 g
Protein	4 g
Calcium	53 mg
Iron	1 mg

Pancake/Waffle Know-How

Preparing gluten-free pancakes differs in several ways from making wheat-based pancakes. Here are some tips from our test kitchen:

- Lightly coat the griddle or nonstick skillet with vegetable oil or cooking spray. Wipe off excess with a paper towel. Dark and light rings on the bottom of pancakes are the result of too much oil on the griddle or skillet.
- To test a nonstick griddle or skillet for the correct temperature (375°F/190°C), sprinkle a few drops of cold water on the hot surface. If the water bounces and dances across the pan, it is ready to use. If the water sizzles and evaporates, it is too hot. Adjust the heat if necessary to accomodate differences among cooking utensils and appliances.
- Resist the temptation to add extra liquid — the batter should be thick.
- Beat the batter until almost smooth — no need to leave it lumpy.
- Turn pancakes only once. During development, we kept watching for the bubbles to break before we turned the pancakes. They never did; the top just got wrinkled on the edges. The bottom became deep golden brown, and we were afraid they might burn if cooked any longer before turning. The tops still looked undercooked.
- If pancakes stick to the griddle or skillet, leave them for a few more seconds and try again — they often loosen themselves from the griddle or skillet when it's time to turn them.
- Pancake batter can be refrigerated, covered, for 2 to 3 days. No need to return to room temperature before using.
- Wrap pancakes or waffles well and freeze the extras for up to 1 month. Separate each with a layer of waxed or parchment paper. Reheat frozen pancakes or waffles, straight from the freezer, in either a toaster or a toaster oven.

Apple Pancakes

A perennial favorite, apple in the form of applesauce and chopped apples contributes the flavor for these pancakes.

Tips

Leave the peel on the apples; the skins soften as they cook.

See page 32 for some tips before making pancakes.

- **Griddle or nonstick skillet, lightly greased**

2	eggs	2
1	egg white	1
¾ cup	unsweetened applesauce	175 mL
¼ cup	water	50 mL
2 tbsp	vegetable oil	25 mL
¼ batch	Make-Your-Own Pancake/Waffle Mix (see recipe, page 28)	¼ batch
1 cup	diced apple	250 mL
1 tsp	ground cinnamon	5 mL

1. In a bowl, using an electric mixer, beat eggs, egg white, applesauce, water and oil until combined. Add the pancake mix, apple and cinnamon and beat until almost smooth.

2. Heat griddle or skillet over medium-high heat. For each pancake, pour ¼ cup (50 mL) batter onto prepared griddle and cook until the bottom is deep golden and the top surface wrinkles around the edges (1 to 3 minutes). Turn and cook for 30 to 60 seconds longer, or until bottom is golden. Serve immediately. Repeat with remaining batter.

Variation

Diced peach, plum or pear or chopped pecans can replace the apple.

Nutritional value per serving (1 pancake)

Calories	75
Fat, total	4 g
Fat, saturated	1 g
Cholesterol	33 mg
Sodium	76 mg
Carbohydrate	8 g
Fiber	1 g
Protein	2 g
Calcium	36 mg
Iron	0 mg

Blueberry Banana Pancakes

Makes about ten 4-inch (10 cm) pancakes

Bananas and blueberries are Donna's grandson Josh's favorite flavor combination — and these pancakes are even better when served with warm Blueberry Dessert Sauce (see recipe, page 320).

Tips

Drain thawed frozen blueberries well to prevent bleeding into the batter.

See page 32 for some tips before making pancakes.

For an all-banana version, omit the blueberries and add extra diced banana.

● **Griddle or nonstick skillet, lightly greased**

2	eggs	2
1	egg white	1
½ cup	mashed banana	125 mL
¼ cup	water	50 mL
2 tbsp	vegetable oil	25 mL
¼ batch	Make-Your-Own Pancake/Waffle Mix (see recipe, page 28)	¼ batch
⅔ cup	thawed and drained frozen blueberries	150 mL

1. In a bowl, using an electric mixer, beat eggs, egg white, banana, water and oil until combined. Add pancake mix and beat until almost smooth.

2. Heat prepared griddle or skillet over medium-high heat. For each pancake, pour ¼ cup (50 mL) batter onto prepared griddle. Sprinkle each with 1 to 2 tbsp (15 to 25 mL) blueberries and cook until the bottom is deep golden and the top surface wrinkles around the edges (1 to 3 minutes). Turn and cook for 30 to 60 seconds longer, or until bottom is golden. Serve immediately. Repeat with remaining batter.

Nutritional value per serving (1 pancake)	
Calories	75
Fat, total	4 g
Fat, saturated	1 g
Cholesterol	33 mg
Sodium	76 mg
Carbohydrate	7 g
Fiber	1 g
Protein	3 g
Calcium	32 mg
Iron	0 mg

Orange Marmalade

Looking for a change of spreads for your morning toast? You'll want to make extra so you can take a jar of this delicious marmalade with you the next time you visit friends.

Tips

Handle the marmalade carefully — it is still extremely hot after cooling for 30 minutes in the bread machine.

2 to 3 medium carrots yield 1¹/₂ cups (375 mL) grated.

If you don't have a Jam Cycle on your bread machine, try mixing ingredients for 5 to 6 minutes on the Basic Cycle. Turn off the bread machine, then restart it and select the Bake Cycle.

Nutritional value per 2 tbsp (25 mL) serving	
Calories	56
Fat, total	0 g
Fat, saturated	0 g
Cholesterol	0 mg
Sodium	3 mg
Carbohydrate	14 g
Fiber	1 g
Protein	0 g
Calcium	8 mg
Iron	0 mg

2	oranges	2
1	lemon	1
¹/₂ cup	water	125 mL
2¹/₂ cups	granulated sugar	625 mL
1¹/₂ cups	grated carrots	375 mL

1. Wash and scrub the peels of oranges and lemon. Cut each into eight pieces and remove tough center membranes and seeds.
2. In a food processor fitted with a metal blade, pulse oranges and lemon until coarsely chopped.
3. Pour water into bread machine baking pan. Add sugar, carrots, oranges and lemon. Insert pan into oven chamber and select the Jam Cycle.
4. At the end of the cycle, carefully open the lid of the bread machine and let baking pan remain in the machine for 30 minutes.
5. Remove baking pan carefully and ladle marmalade into sterilized jars, leaving ¹/₄-inch (0.5 cm) headspace. Store in the refrigerator for up to 4 weeks, freeze for up to 4 months or process in a water bath (see Techniques Glossary, page 371) for 5 minutes to preserve jam so it is shelf stable.

Variations

For thicker marmalade, add 2 to 3 tsp (10 to 15 mL) "light" pectin crystals with the fruit.

You can use Valencia oranges, but for a stronger flavor wait for the Seville orange harvest.

Asparagus- and Ham-Filled Crêpes

Invite your favorite friends for lunch and serve these savory crêpes, hot or cold, topped with corn relish. They'll be a sure hit!

Tips

The crêpes can be made ahead and frozen for up to 1 month. Thaw before filling.

15 to 20 spears of asparagus weigh approximately 1 lb (500 g).

Substitute GF fruit chutney, GF salsa or Black Bean Salsa (see recipe, page 103) for the corn relish.

Nutritional value per serving (1 crêpe)	
Calories	116
Fat, total	3 g
Fat, saturated	1 g
Cholesterol	55 mg
Sodium	956 mg
Carbohydrate	12 g
Fiber	2 g
Protein	10 g
Calcium	50 mg
Iron	1 mg

- 6-inch (15 cm) crêpe pan or nonstick skillet, lightly greased

Crepes

¼ cup	amaranth flour	50 mL
¼ cup	chickpea (garbanzo bean) flour	50 mL
2 tbsp	potato starch	25 mL
1 tsp	granulated sugar	5 mL
½ tsp	xanthan gum	2 mL
½ tsp	salt	2 mL
½ tsp	dried thyme	2 mL
2	eggs	2
⅔ cup	milk	150 mL
⅓ cup	water	75 mL
1 tbsp	melted butter	15 mL

Asparagus-Ham Filling

9	slices (each 1 oz/30 g) GF Black Forest ham	9
27	asparagus spears, steamed until just tender-crisp	27
1 cup	corn relish	250 mL

1. *Prepare the crêpes:* In a large bowl, mix together amaranth flour, chickpea flour, potato starch, sugar, xanthan gum, salt and thyme. Set aside.

2. In a small bowl, whisk together eggs, milk, water and melted butter. Pour over dry ingredients all at once and whisk until smooth. Cover and refrigerate for at least 1 hour or for up to 2 days. Bring batter back to room temperature before using.

3. Heat prepared pan over medium heat. Add 3 to 4 tbsp (45 to 50 mL) batter for each crêpe, tilting and rotating pan to ensure that batter covers the entire bottom of pan. Cook for 1 to 1½ minutes, or until edges begin to brown. Using a non-metal spatula, carefully turn and cook for another 30 to 45 seconds, or until bottom is dotted with brown spots. Remove to a plate and repeat with remaining batter.

Tip

For more information about making crêpes, see below.

4. *Fill the crêpes:* Place a slice of ham and 3 asparagus spears down the center of each warm crêpe, roll and place seam side down on an individual serving plate.
5. Warm in microwave, if desired. Top with corn relish.

Cooking Classic Crêpes

The secret to making perfect crêpes is simple: practice, practice, practice! In fact, the first crêpe of every batch is just that — a practice one!

- A well-seasoned crêpe pan should be oiled very lightly. Wipe out any excess with a paper towel.
- To test a nonstick crêpe pan or skillet for the correct temperature (375°F/190°C), sprinkle a few drops of cold water on the hot surface. If the water bounces and dances across the pan, it is ready to use. If the water sizzles and evaporates, it is too hot. Adjust the heat if necessary to accomodate differences among cooking utensils and appliances.
- The batter should be smooth and lump-free.
- Set the bowl of batter from the refrigerator directly into a sink of warm water to bring it quickly to room temperature.
- If crêpes stick to pan, cool pan slightly and re-oil. Wipe out any excess with a paper towel — too much oil on pan results in greasy crêpes. Reheat pan before making another crêpe.
- Stack between sheets of parchment or waxed paper as each crêpe is cooked.
- Keep crêpes separated with parchment or waxed paper and store wrapped air-tight in the refrigerator for several days or in the freezer for several weeks.
- To prevent tearing, thaw in the refrigerator before separating into individual crêpes.

Garden-Fresh Frittata

Makes 6 servings as a main course or 8 as appetizers

A frittata can be described as a Spanish-Italian omelet or a crustless quiche. We cleaned out the refrigerator to prepare this quick and easy any-time-of-day meal.

Tips

See Techniques Glossary, page 370, for information about cleaning leeks, and page 368 for instructions on cleaning a cast-iron skillet.

To ovenproof a nonstick skillet with a non-metal handle, wrap handle in a double layer of foil, shiny side out.

Nutritional value per main-course serving	
Calories	239
Fat, total	13 g
Fat, saturated	6 g
Cholesterol	134 mg
Sodium	744 mg
Carbohydrate	12 g
Fiber	3 g
Protein	19 g
Calcium	273 mg
Iron	2 mg

- **Preheat broiler**
- **9- to 10-inch (23 to 25 cm) ovenproof nonstick or cast-iron skillet**

1 tbsp	extra-virgin olive oil	15 mL
2	leeks, coarsely chopped, white and light green parts only	2
2	cloves garlic, minced	2
½	red bell pepper, cut into ½-inch (1 cm) cubes	½
2 cups	thickly sliced mushrooms	500 mL
1	small zucchini, cut into ¼-inch (0.5 cm) slices	1
8	egg whites (1 cup/250 mL)	8
4	eggs	4
1 tsp	Dijon mustard	5 mL
¼ cup	snipped fresh chives	50 mL
2 tbsp	snipped fresh parsley	25 mL
2 tsp	dried tarragon	10 mL
½ tsp	salt	2 mL
Pinch	freshly ground white pepper	Pinch
1 cup	broccoli florets, cooked	500 mL
1½ cups	shredded Swiss cheese	375 mL

1. In skillet, heat olive oil over medium heat. Add leeks, garlic, red pepper and mushrooms. Cook, stirring frequently, for 5 minutes, or until tender. Add zucchini and cook, stirring, for 2 to 3 minutes, or until vegetables are softened. Remove skillet from heat and reduce heat to medium-low.

2. In a large bowl, whisk together egg whites, eggs, Dijon mustard, chives, parsley, tarragon, salt and pepper. Add broccoli and Swiss cheese, stirring to combine.

3. Pour into skillet over vegetables. Cook, without stirring, for 9 to 11 minutes, or until bottom and sides are firm yet top is still slightly runny.

Tip

To prevent your cast-iron skillet from rusting, set it on a warm stove element to completely dry before storing. Be careful: the handle gets hot.

4. Place under preheated broiler, 3 inches (7.5 cm) from the element, until golden brown and set, 2 to 5 minutes.

5. Cut into wedges and serve hot from the oven or at room temperature. Refrigerate, covered, for up to 2 days. Reheat individual wedges, uncovered, in microwave on Medium (50%) for $1^1/_2$ to 2 minutes, just until hot, if desired.

Variations

For a change from a vegetarian frittata, add cooked chicken, smoked salmon or crisp bacon and use only 1 cup (250 mL) of mushrooms and 1 leek.

Use different varieties of mushrooms for a more intense flavor.

Busy Day Casserole

Makes 8 servings

Barbara Wahn, a local celiac, shared this recipe with us. We modified it for you. Corn, tomato and cheese are a favorite flavor combination from the 50s, still popular today.

Tips

Chili powder may contain gluten; check the label.

Freeze in portion-size pieces to defrost and warm for quick lunches.

When Barbara makes this casserole, she layers half the cornmeal mixture on the bottom, tops with meat and then finishes with the remaining cornmeal mixture. She also likes to double the recipe so she has lots in the freezer for a busy day.

Nutritional value per serving	
Calories	478
Fat, total	21 g
Fat, saturated	6 g
Cholesterol	133 mg
Sodium	553 mg
Carbohydrate	42 g
Fiber	5 g
Protein	32 g
Calcium	238 mg
Iron	3 mg

- **Preheat oven to 375°F (190°C)**
- **13- by 9-inch (3 L) baking pan, lightly greased**

¾ cup	cornmeal	175 mL
½ cup	milk	125 mL
½ cup	amaranth flour	125 mL
¼ cup	potato starch	50 mL
1 tsp	GF baking powder	5 mL
2 lbs	ground turkey or extra-lean ground beef	1 kg
2	cloves garlic, minced	2
1	onion, chopped	1
1	can (28 oz/796 mL) diced tomatoes	1
⅓	jalapeño pepper, chopped, or 1 tsp (5 mL) dried jalapeño pepper	⅓
2 tbsp	GF chili powder	25 mL
2 tbsp	cornstarch	25 mL
2	eggs, beaten	2
1	can (14 oz/398 mL) GF cream-style corn	1
3 tbsp	vegetable oil	45 mL
1 cup	shredded old Cheddar, Monterey Jack or Swiss cheese	250 mL
	Black Bean Salsa (see recipe, page 103)	

1. In a small bowl, combine cornmeal and milk. Soak for 20 minutes.

2. In another small bowl, combine the amaranth flour, potato starch and baking powder. Set aside.

3. In a frying pan, over medium heat, brown ground turkey until no pink remains. Add garlic and onion. Cook, stirring, over medium heat until onions are translucent. Drain off fat, if necessary. Add tomatoes, jalapeño pepper, chili powder and cornstarch. Heat until bubbly. Spoon into prepared baking pan.

4. In a large bowl, combine eggs, cream-style corn and oil. Add cornmeal mixture and dry ingredients; stir just until combined. Stir in cheese. Pour over turkey mixture, spreading evenly.

5. Bake in preheated oven for about 35 to 50 minutes, or until a toothpick comes out clean from the cornmeal portion. Serve immediately with Black Bean Salsa.

Crispy Pecan Chicken Fingers

Makes 4 servings

Slender strips of succulent chicken inside a crunchy pecan coating — what a modern, healthier way to eat "fried" chicken! Serve with Honey Mustard Dipping Sauce and Plum Dipping Sauce (see recipes, page 57 and 58).

Tips

Shake off excess egg and crumbs before baking.

Chicken is cooked when a digital instant-read thermometer (see Techniques Glossary, page 369) registers 170°F (78°C) and chicken is no longer pink inside.

Discard both leftover crumb mixture and the plastic bag — it is not safe to re-use either when raw chicken is involved.

Nutritional value per serving

Calories	502
Fat, total	22 g
Fat, saturated	3 g
Cholesterol	162 mg
Sodium	646 mg
Carbohydrate	41 g
Fiber	4 g
Protein	34 g
Calcium	104 mg
Iron	3 mg

- **Preheat oven to 425°F (220°C)**
- **Baking sheet, lightly greased**

4	boneless skinless chicken breasts (about 1 lb/500 g)	4
⅓ cup	brown rice flour	75 mL
2	eggs, beaten	2
1 tbsp	water	15 mL
1 tbsp	Dijon mustard	15 mL
1 cup	fresh GF bread crumbs (see page 368)	250 mL
⅔ cup	pecans, coarsely chopped	150 mL
½ cup	cornmeal	125 mL
¼ tsp	salt	1 mL
¼ tsp	freshly ground black pepper	1 mL

1. Cut each breast into strips ³/₄-inch (2 cm) wide. Pat dry.
2. Place the rice flour in a shallow dish or pie plate. In a second shallow dish or pie plate, whisk together eggs, water and Dijon mustard.
3. In a large plastic bag, combine bread crumbs, pecans, cornmeal, salt and pepper.
4. Coat chicken strips, a few at a time, first in rice flour, then in egg mixture. Shake in pecan–bread crumb mixture. Place in a single layer 1 inch (2.5 cm) apart on prepared baking sheet.
5. Bake in preheated oven for 20 to 25 minutes, or until coating is golden brown and crispy and chicken is cooked (see tip, at left).

Variations

Florentine Chicken Fingers: Top baked chicken fingers with grated Asiago cheese, 1 leaf of arugula and a strip of roasted red pepper and broil just until cheese is melted.

Pizza Chicken Fingers: Top baked chicken fingers with GF pizza sauce, grated mozzarella and, if desired, crumbled cooked bacon. Broil just until cheese melts.

Macaroni and Cheese

We received several emails requesting this recipe. We've updated this comfort food from our childhood using 2% evaporated milk and a mixture of cheeses. Martin, Donna's Texas grandson, the family connoisseur of mac and cheese, gives this recipe a "thumbs up."

Tips

Rinsing the cooked pasta well prevents the macaroni and cheese from becoming too thick.

Be sure to use orange-colored Cheddar cheese for a more attractive dish.

We prefer to use wild rice elbow pasta for this recipe.

1 cup	shredded old Cheddar cheese	250 mL
½ cup	shredded Swiss cheese	125 mL
¼ cup	freshly grated Parmesan cheese	50 mL
1 tbsp	sorghum flour	15 mL
½ tsp	dry mustard	2 mL
½ tsp	salt	2 mL
¼ tsp	freshly ground white pepper	1 mL
Pinch	cayenne pepper	Pinch
2 cups	GF elbow pasta	500 mL
1	can (14 oz/385 mL) 2% evaporated milk	1
¼ tsp	GF Worcestershire sauce	1 mL

1. In a small bowl, combine Cheddar, Swiss, Parmesan, sorghum flour, dry mustard, salt, white pepper and cayenne pepper. Set aside.

2. In a large saucepan, cook pasta in boiling water according to package instructions, until just tender. Rinse well under cold running water and drain well.

3. Return the pasta to the saucepan. Stir in milk, Worcestershire sauce and cheese mixture. Simmer, stirring gently, over low heat until mixture boils and thickens.

Variation

To turn this into a casserole, add canned tuna, peas and chopped onion or celery, transfer to a greased baking dish and bake in preheated 350°F (180°C) oven until hot.

Nutritional value per serving	
Calories	210
Fat, total	9 g
Fat, saturated	5 g
Cholesterol	31 mg
Sodium	374 mg
Carbohydrate	20 g
Fiber	1 g
Protein	12 g
Calcium	342 mg
Iron	374 mg

Appetizers

Dips and Sauces

Baked Mozzarella Sticks

Makes 12

Crave mozzarella sticks but don't want to deep-fry? These crispy baked sticks are worth the extra care.

Tips

To prevent melted cheese from leaking out, be sure each piece is completely coated with yogurt mixture and crumbs.

Serve with salsa, Broccoli Cilantro Pesto (page 83) or GF sour cream.

To freeze: Double or triple the recipe and freeze coated unbaked cheese sticks in a single layer in a jelly-roll pan. Once frozen, remove cheese sticks from pan and place in a heavy-duty freezer bag. Remove only the number you need — they won't stick together. Bake according to recipe.

- Preheat oven to 450°F (230°C)
- Baking sheet, lightly greased

8 oz	mozzarella cheese	250 g
2	egg yolks	2
1 cup	plain yogurt	250 mL
2 cups	extra-fine dry GF bread crumbs (see page 368 and Tips, page 49)	500 mL
2/3 cup	freshly grated Parmesan cheese	150 mL
1 tbsp	dried basil or dillweed	15 mL
Pinch	cayenne pepper	Pinch

1. Cut mozzarella cheese into sticks 3 by $1/2$ by $1/2$ inch (7.5 by 1 by 1 cm).
2. In a small bowl, combine egg yolks and yogurt.
3. In a shallow dish or pie plate, combine bread crumbs, Parmesan, basil and cayenne pepper.
4. Dip cheese into yogurt-mixture to generously coat, leaving as much mixture on the cheese as possible. Then dip into crumb mixture, pressing to coat ends and sides well.
5. Place the coated sticks in a single layer on prepared baking sheet and freeze for 2 to 4 hours, or until completely frozen. Bake in preheated oven for 5 to 8 minutes, or until coating is golden.
6. Transfer to a serving plate and serve immediately.

Nutritional value per serving (1 stick)	
Calories	169
Fat, total	9 g
Fat, saturated	5 g
Cholesterol	50 mg
Sodium	278 mg
Carbohydrate	12 g
Fiber	1 g
Protein	10 g
Calcium	282 mg
Iron	0 mg

Broccoli-Cheddar Cornbread

This tasty cornbread is ideal for entertaining. Cut into bite-size pieces, it can be served hot or cold as an hors d'oeuvre. It's also great for family meals.

Tip

Bake in a 2-quart (2 L) ovenproof casserole dish. Reduce baking temperature to 325°F (160°C). Serve hot, directly from the oven.

Nutritional value per serving (1 square)

Calories	275
Fat, total	6 g
Fat, saturated	3 g
Cholesterol	65 mg
Sodium	281 mg
Carbohydrate	48 g
Fiber	3 g
Protein	9 g
Calcium	190 mg
Iron	2 mg

- Preheat oven to 350°F (180°C)
- 9-inch (2.5 L) square baking pan, lightly greased

1 cup	cornmeal	250 mL
1 cup	brown rice flour	250 mL
¼ cup	potato starch	50 mL
¼ cup	tapioca starch	50 mL
1½ tsp	xanthan gum	7 mL
1 tbsp	GF baking powder	15 mL
1 tsp	baking soda	5 mL
½ tsp	salt	2 mL
1 cup	chopped onions	250 mL
¾ cup	shredded old Cheddar cheese	175 mL
¼ cup	freshly grated Parmesan cheese	50 mL
1 cup	broccoli florets	250 mL
1 tsp	cider vinegar	5 mL
3	eggs	3
2 tbsp	honey	25 mL
1	can (14 oz/398 mL) cream-style corn	1

1. In a large bowl, stir together cornmeal, rice flour, potato starch, tapioca starch, xanthan gum, baking powder, baking soda and salt. Stir in onions, Cheddar, Parmesan and broccoli. Set aside.
2. In a separate bowl, using an electric mixer, beat vinegar, eggs and honey until combined. Stir in corn.
3. Pour corn mixture over dry ingredients and stir just until combined. Spoon into prepared pan. Allow to stand for 30 minutes.
4. Bake in preheated oven for 35 to 45 minutes or until a cake tester inserted in the center comes out clean. Serve hot.

Variation
Substitute chopped red bell pepper for half the onions.

Cheddar Dill Shortbread

Makes 3 dozen cookies

A new twist on an old familiar favorite — turn a traditional sweet, rich cookie into a savory melt-in-your-mouth hors d'oeuvre.

Tips

If you want to make cookies another day, store the dough logs in the refrigerator for up to 1 week. Let stand at room temperature for 45 minutes to 1 hour before slicing and baking.

For longer storage of the dough logs, freeze for up to 2 months. Defrost in the refrigerator overnight and then let stand at room temperature for 45 minutes to 1 hour before slicing and baking.

Nutritional value per serving (1 cookie)	
Calories	71
Fat, total	5 g
Fat, saturated	3 g
Cholesterol	9 mg
Sodium	68 mg
Carbohydrate	5 g
Fiber	0 g
Protein	1 g
Calcium	33 mg
Iron	0 mg

- Preheat oven to 350°F (180°C)
- Baking sheet, ungreased

1 cup	shredded old Cheddar cheese	250 mL
¾ cup	butter, softened	175 mL
½ cup	brown rice flour	125 mL
⅓ cup	cornstarch	75 mL
¼ cup	potato starch	50 mL
2 tbsp	tapioca starch	25 mL
⅓ cup	sifted confectioner's (icing) sugar	75 mL
¼ cup	freshly grated Parmesan cheese	50 mL
1 to 2 tbsp	finely chopped fresh dill	15 to 25 mL

1. In a food processor fitted with a metal blade, pulse Cheddar, butter, rice flour, cornstarch, potato starch, tapioca starch, confectioner's sugar, Parmesan and dillweed to taste until mixed. Process until dough forms a ball.

2. Place dough on waxed paper, form into logs $1\frac{1}{2}$ inches (4 cm) in diameter, and wrap tightly. Refrigerate for at least 2 hours, or until firm. Cut into slices $\frac{1}{4}$ inch (0.5 cm) thick. Place 1 inch (2.5 cm) apart on baking sheet. Bake in preheated oven for 8 to 12 minutes, or until set but not browned. Remove immediately from baking sheet to cooling rack. Serve warm or at room temperature.

Variations

Select white Cheddar for a more traditional shortbread appearance.

Omit the dillweed and add a pinch of cayenne pepper or 1 to 2 tbsp (15 to 25 mL) GF curry powder.

Crispy Cheese Crackers

Makes 10 dozen crackers

Try to eat just one of these delicious morsels! If you make a double batch, you'll be able to hide some in the freezer. Use them as a base for hors d'oeuvres as a well as a cracker to serve with a soup or salad.

Tips

To prevent crackers from softening, store in an airtight container for up to 2 months.

You can also freeze the logs for 1 month. Thaw in refrigerator before slicing.

Nutritional value per serving (1 cracker)	
Calories	18
Fat, total	1 g
Fat, saturated	0 g
Cholesterol	2 mg
Sodium	17 mg
Carbohydrate	2 g
Fiber	0 g
Protein	1 g
Calcium	12 mg
Iron	0 mg

● Baking sheet, greased or lined with parchment

1 cup	brown rice flour	250 mL
¾ cup	sorghum flour	175 mL
¼ cup	cornstarch	50 mL
1 tsp	xanthan gum	5 mL
Pinch	cayenne pepper	Pinch
½ tsp	paprika	2 mL
½ cup	shredded old Cheddar cheese	125 mL
½ cup	freshly grated Parmesan cheese	125 mL
⅓ cup	butter, softened	75 mL
⅔ cup	GF sour cream	150 mL

1. In a large bowl, combine brown rice flour, sorghum flour, cornstarch, xanthan gum, cayenne pepper, paprika, Cheddar and Parmesan. Mix well and set aside.

2. In another bowl, using an electric mixer, cream butter and sour cream. Gradually beat in dry ingredients, mixing until blended. Squeeze handfuls of mixture to form into 6 logs, each 1½ inches (4 cm) in diameter. Wrap in plastic wrap and refrigerate overnight. Allow to stand at room temperature for 15 to 20 minutes.

3. Cut logs into ⅛-inch (3 mm) thick slices. Place on prepared baking sheet. Place at least 1 inch (2.5 cm) apart on baking sheet. Bake in 375°F (190°C) preheated oven for 6 to 8 minutes or until golden brown. One extra minute of baking can burn these thin crackers. Remove immediately. Serve warm or transfer onto racks to cool completely.

Variation

Purchase a shredded Tex-Mex mix of Mozzarella, Cheddar and Monterey Jack with jalapeños and substitute it for the Cheddar. Check for gluten before you purchase a packaged shredded cheese mix.

Crispy Multi-Seed Crackers

Makes about 40 crackers

Whether being dipped in salsa or served with a bowl of hot soup, these crisp, Lavosh-style crackers will add heart-healthy omega-3 fatty acids and fiber to your diet.

Tips

For a thin crisp cracker, roll dough to an even thickness as thinly as possible. Don't worry if it breaks into pieces.

If crackers become soft, re-crisp in a toaster oven or conventional oven at 350°F (180°C).

Just before baking, sprinkle with 1 tsp (5 mL) coarse salt or sesame seeds.

Nutritional value per serving (1 cracker)

Calories	39
Fat, total	2 g
Fat, saturated	0 g
Cholesterol	1 mg
Sodium	73 mg
Carbohydrate	4 g
Fiber	1 g
Protein	1 g
Calcium	25 mg
Iron	0 mg

- Preheat oven to 375°F (190°C)
- Baking sheets, ungreased

1/2 cup	water	125 mL
2 tbsp	extra-virgin olive oil	25 mL
1 tsp	cider vinegar	5 mL
1/2 cup	brown rice flour	125 mL
1/2 cup	sorghum flour	125 mL
1/4 cup	cornstarch	50 mL
1/3 cup	ground flaxseed	75 mL
1 1/2 tsp	xanthan gum	7 mL
1/2 tsp	GF baking powder	2 mL
1 tsp	salt	5 mL
1/4 cup	freshly grated Parmesan cheese	50 mL
1/4 cup	sesame seeds	50 mL
3 tbsp	dried oregano	45 mL
2 tbsp	poppy seeds	25 mL

1. In a small bowl, combine water, olive oil and vinegar. Mix well and set aside.

2. In a food processor fitted with a metal blade, pulse brown rice flour, sorghum flour, cornstarch, ground flaxseed, xanthan gum, baking powder, salt, Parmesan, sesame seeds, oregano and poppy seeds until mixed. With machine running, add liquid mixture through feed tube in a slow steady stream. Process until dough forms a ball.

3. Divide dough into four pieces. Place each on plastic wrap and flatten into a disk and wrap well. Let dough rest in refrigerator for 10 minutes. Place one disk between two sheets of waxed or parchment paper. To prevent the paper from moving while you're rolling out the dough, place it on a lint-free towel. Using a heavy stroke with a rolling pin, roll out the dough as thinly as possible. Carefully remove the top sheet of paper. Invert the dough onto the baking sheet. Remove remaining sheet of paper. Repeat with remaining dough.

4. Bake in preheated oven for 18 to 25 minutes, or until browned and crisp. (Pay close attention as crackers can burn easily.) Remove to a cooling rack and cool completely. Break into pieces. Store at room temperature in an airtight container for up to 2 weeks or freeze for up to 3 months.

Crispy-Coated Veggie Snacks

Makes 3 dozen

These healthier crispy baked tidbits are an appealing alternative to deep-fried fare.

Tips

For information on making dry bread crumbs, see page 368.

Serve with salsa, Broccoli Cilantro Pesto (page 83), GF sour cream or your favorite dipping sauce.

Use other vegetables, such as cauliflower, broccoli or white turnip.

Use any leftover savory bread, such as Italian Herb Bread (pages 214 and 244) or Southern Cornbread (see recipe, page 189) to make the bread crumbs.

- **Preheat oven to 375°F (190°C)**
- **Baking sheet, lightly greased**

1	small zucchini	1
1	small sweet potato	1
12	small mushrooms	12
3 cups	dry GF bread crumbs	750 mL
1 cup	freshly grated Parmesan cheese	250 mL
1 tbsp	dried rosemary or thyme	15 mL
Pinch	cayenne pepper	Pinch
2 cups	plain yogurt	500 mL
	Honey Mustard Dipping Sauce or Plum Dipping Sauce (see recipes, pages 57 and 58)	

1. Peel zucchini, cut in half crosswise and cut each half lengthwise into quarters.
2. Peel sweet potato, cut in half lengthwise and cut into slices $1/4$ inch (0.5 cm) thick.
3. Remove stems from mushrooms.
4. In a shallow dish or pie plate, combine bread crumbs, Parmesan cheese, rosemary and cayenne pepper.
5. Working with a few pieces at a time, dip zucchini, sweet potato and mushroom caps into yogurt to generously coat. Then dip into crumb mixture, pressing to coat well.
6. Arrange on prepared baking sheet in a single layer. Bake in preheated oven for 20 to 25 minutes, or until vegetables are tender and coating is golden.
7. Transfer to a serving plate and serve immediately with Honey Mustard Dipping Sauce or Plum Dipping Sauce.

Nutritional value per serving (1 crisp)*	
Calories	55
Fat, total	2 g
Fat, saturated	1 g
Cholesterol	4 mg
Sodium	67 mg
Carbohydrate	6 g
Fiber	0 g
Protein	3 g
Calcium	71 mg
Iron	0 mg

* does not include dipping sauce

Lavosh

Makes 1 flatbread or 8 servings

Keep this thin, low-fat, crisp Armenian flatbread on hand to serve as a snack with fresh vegetables, for dipping in salsa or with soups and salads.

Tips

The thinner the dough is spread, the more authentic the cracker will be.

Store crackers in an airtight container for up to 2 months. If necessary, crisp the Lavosh in the oven, before serving.

Nutritional value per serving	
Calories	118
Fat, total	4 g
Fat, saturated	0 g
Cholesterol	0 mg
Sodium	157 mg
Carbohydrate	19 g
Fiber	2 g
Protein	2 g
Calcium	15 mg
Iron	1 mg

- **Large baking sheet, lightly greased**

¾ cup	brown rice flour	175 mL
⅓ cup	tapioca starch	75 mL
1 tsp	granulated sugar	5 mL
1½ tsp	xanthan gum	7 mL
1½ tsp	bread machine or instant yeast	7 mL
½ tsp	salt	2 mL
¾ cup	water	175 mL
1 tsp	cider vinegar	5 mL
1 tbsp	vegetable oil	15 mL
¼ cup	sesame seeds	50 mL
1 to 2 tbsp	sweet rice flour	15 to 25 mL

Bread Machine Method

1. In a large bowl or plastic bag, combine brown rice flour, tapioca starch, sugar, xanthan gum, yeast and salt. Mix well and set aside.

2. Pour water, vinegar and oil into the bread machine baking pan. Select the Dough Cycle. Allow the liquids to mix until combined.

3. Gradually, add the dry ingredients as the bread machine is mixing, scraping with a rubber spatula while adding. Try to incorporate all the dry ingredients within 1 to 2 minutes. Allow the bread machine to complete the cycle.

Mixer Method

1. In a large bowl or plastic bag, combine brown rice flour, tapioca starch, sugar, xanthan gum, yeast and salt. Mix well and set aside.

2. Pour water, vinegar and oil into the large bowl of a heavy-duty mixer.

3. Using paddle attachment with the mixer on the lowest speed, slowly add the dry ingredients until combined. With a rubber spatula, scrape the bottom and sides of the bowl. With the mixer on medium speed, beat for 4 minutes.

For Both Methods

4. Sprinkle prepared baking sheet with half the sesame seeds. Remove dough to prepared sheet. Sprinkle generously with 1 tbsp (15 mL) sweet rice flour. Place waxed paper, generously dusted with sweet rice flour, on top of the dough. Gently pat the waxed paper to spread the dough, lifting and re-dusting frequently to check the dough thickness. Carefully remove the waxed paper. Sprinkle with remaining sesame seeds. Press lightly into dough. Bake in 375°F (190°C) preheated oven for 20 to 25 minutes or until lightly browned. Remove from oven. Allow to cool, then break into large pieces.

Variation

Try adding dried herbs to the soft dough and then sprinkling with freshly grated Parmesan cheese.

Mediterranean Pizza Squares

Makes 4 servings

Try our twist on a traditional pizza crust. This vegetarian pizza, with an easy-to-prepare crust, is delicious served hot or at room temperature for a snack, lunch or brunch.

Tips

See Techniques Glossary, page 369 for instructions on roasting garlic.

This is a very thin crust. There is enough dough to cover the bottom of the pan evenly with a thin layer. Take your time.

For fast, easy cutting, use a pizza wheel.

Cut into 48 bite-size appetizers for your next party.

Nutritional value per serving

Calories	605
Fat, total	33 g
Fat, saturated	17 g
Cholesterol	56 mg
Sodium	1223 mg
Carbohydrate	57 g
Fiber	9 g
Protein	20 g
Calcium	400 mg
Iron	5 mg

- Preheat oven to 425°F (220°C)
- 15- by 10-inch (40 by 25 cm) jelly-roll pan, lightly greased and sprinkled with cornmeal

1 cup	amaranth flour	250 mL
½ cup	quinoa flour	125 mL
¼ cup	cornstarch	50 mL
¼ cup	cornmeal	50 mL
1 tsp	xanthan gum	5 mL
1 tbsp	GF baking powder	15 mL
1 tsp	salt	5 mL
⅓ cup	shortening	75 mL
¾ cup	milk	175 mL
	Sweet rice flour	
3	plum tomatoes, thinly sliced	3
4	cloves garlic, roasted and chopped	4
⅔ cup	sliced black olives	150 mL
¼ cup	snipped fresh basil	50 mL
¼ tsp	freshly ground black pepper	1 mL
1 cup	shredded Monterey Jack cheese	250 mL
1 cup	crumbled feta cheese	250 mL

Traditional Method

1. In a large bowl, stir together amaranth flour, quinoa flour, cornstarch, cornmeal, xanthan gum, baking powder and salt. Using a pastry blender or two knives, cut in shortening until mixture resembles coarse crumbs. Add milk, all at once, stirring with a fork to make a soft dough.

Food Processor Method

1. In a food processor fitted with a metal blade, pulse amaranth flour, quinoa flour, cornstarch, cornmeal, xanthan gum, baking powder and salt. Add shortening and pulse until mixture resembles small peas, about 5 to 10 seconds. With the machine running, pour milk through feed tube and process until dough just holds together.

Tips

Substitute mozzarella, fontina or provolone cheese for the Monterey Jack.

Substitute an equal amount of chopped fresh rosemary for the basil.

To make the pizza kid-friendly, top with their favorite fixings. Keep one in the freezer for when they are invited to a pizza party.

For Both Methods

2. Transfer dough to prepared pan. Either cover with waxed paper and roll out with a rolling pin or gently pat out dough with fingers dusted with sweet rice flour to fill the pan evenly. Bake in the bottom third of preheated oven for 10 minutes or until slightly firm.

3. Arrange tomato slices over crust. Sprinkle with garlic, olives, basil and pepper. Sprinkle with Monterey Jack and feta.

4. Bake in preheated oven for 20 to 25 minutes, or until cheese is bubbly and crust is golden. Remove to a cutting board and cut into squares. Serve immediately. Transfer any extra squares to a cooling rack to prevent the crust from getting soggy.

Holiday Cheese Balls

The red, green and orange flecks of the bell peppers make this an ideal appetizer to serve at a holiday open house.

Tip

If the mixture is too soft to form into balls, refrigerate for 10 minutes before shaping. Use the cheese balls right away or freeze for up to 4 weeks to serve at a later time. They keep in the refrigerator for up to 1 week.

8 oz	cream cheese, softened	250 g
4 oz	blue cheese, crumbled	125 g
2 tsp	prepared horseradish	10 mL
3 to 4	drops hot pepper sauce	3 to 4
1	clove garlic, minced	1
3	green onions, finely chopped	3
½ cup	chopped red, orange and/or yellow bell pepper	125 mL
2 cups	shredded old Cheddar cheese	500 mL
2 to 3 cups	finely chopped pecans	500 to 750 mL

1. In a large bowl, combine cream cheese, blue cheese, horseradish, hot pepper sauce to taste and garlic. Set aside.
2. In a microwave-safe bowl, combine green onions and bell peppers. Microwave, covered, on High for 1 minute. (Or steam in a covered saucepan over low heat for 2 to 3 minutes or until tender-crisp.)
3. Combine onion-pepper mixture with Cheddar cheese. Fold into cream cheese mixture. Divide in half and form into 2 balls. Wrap in plastic wrap and chill for 30 minutes. Roll in pecans. Serve on a platter with crackers.

Variations

Make one large ball, if preferred.

Roll in snipped fresh parsley or decorate with whole unblanched almonds, instead of the pecans.

Nutritional value per 1 oz (30 g) serving	
Calories	115
Fat, total	10 g
Fat, saturated	3 g
Cholesterol	17 mg
Sodium	132 mg
Carbohydrate	2 g
Fiber	1 g
Protein	5 g
Calcium	97 mg
Iron	0 mg

Just for Kids

- It is important that young people who suffer from celiac disease feel part of the group and not different. All decisions should be made keeping this in mind, while ensuring the diet is strictly followed.
- Teach! Teach! Teach! Don't make decisions for even the youngest child. Every time a new food is selected or served, casually explain why it can or cannot be tolerated. Stress the positive. Soon the questions will come from the child. It is important for children with celiac disease to know that the parent will not always be with them. "When I was too young to read," says 11-year-old Deanna Jennett, "I wore a MedicAlert bracelet. Whenever adults offered me food, I could ask them if I should have it because of what my bracelet said." Teach them that "if in doubt, do without."
- When a school-aged child is invited to sleep over or to attend a birthday party, call ahead to ask about the menu and to explain to the parents the child's dietary restrictions. It's important to send something similar. You may also want to send along gluten-free treats such as Chocolate Chip Cookies (see recipe, page 331) that all children can enjoy. When sending individual pizzas or individual foods, wrap them in foil so they can be reheated without cross-contamination.
- Speak to your child's class and explain why your child cannot eat what the others do and why they cannot share. Take along a few gluten-free treats to share with the class. You will find others in the class with special dietary needs and soon the youngsters' natural curiosity will speed along the discussion. We really liked the way Deanna educated her peers about her intolerance to gluten. "I made a model of the surface of the intestine for a science project. I used clay and stuck small pieces of wool in it like hair. I demonstrated in front of my class how the 'hairs' were destroyed by gluten and since the 'hairs' absorbed the nutrition from the food, they realized how serious it was for me to not have any gluten."
- Grocery shop with the young celiac child. Show the importance of reading every label every time. It takes longer, but is certainly worth the effort and even a young pre-teen can recognize ingredients to avoid. "One of the ways I learned to read was by reading labels," states Deanna, diagnosed when she was five years old. "Sometimes, Mum would take something off the shelf and ask me if it was safe. It was a bit of a game."
- When it is a communal dish, such as salsa and chips or vegetables and dip, make sure celiac children take their food first. They know they can't share food with others.

Garlic Bean Dip

Makes 1½ cups (375 mL)

Cannellini beans are popular in Italy. Their creamy color, fluffy texture and mild, nutty taste blends well in this garlic-flavored bean dip.

Tips

Serve at either room temperature or straight from the refrigerator with Crispy Multi-Seed Crackers (see recipe, page 48).

Rinse and drain beans well to ensure a consistent thickness of dip each time you make it.

Substitute chickpeas for cannellini beans or one 19-oz (540 mL) can of Bean Medley or one 19-oz (540 mL) can of 6-Bean Blend.

Nutritional value per 2 tbsp (25 mL) serving

Calories	50
Fat, total	2 g
Fat, saturated	0 g
Cholesterol	2 mg
Sodium	133 mg
Carbohydrate	6 g
Fiber	2 g
Protein	2 g
Calcium	14 mg
Iron	1 mg

2	cloves garlic, minced	2
1	can (19 oz/540 mL) cannellini or white kidney beans, rinsed and drained	1
1 tbsp	cider vinegar	15 mL
½ tsp	salt	2 mL
½ tsp	ground cumin	2 mL
⅓ cup	GF light mayonnaise	75 mL
2 tbsp	fresh parsley	25 mL

1. In a food processor fitted with a metal blade, pulse garlic, beans, vinegar, salt and cumin until mixed. Add mayonnaise and parsley and process until smooth. Transfer to a bowl, cover and refrigerate for at least 6 hours or overnight to allow flavors to mix and mingle. Refrigerate for up to 1 week.

Variation

For a tangier flavor, substitute plain yogurt or GF sour cream for the mayonnaise.

Honey Mustard Dipping Sauce

**Makes
½ cup (125 mL)**

"Grandma, you make the best sauce in the whole wide world — please make more," declares Donna's grandson Andrew, holding up the last two Crispy Pecan Chicken Fingers (see recipe, page 41).

| ¼ cup | Dijon mustard | 50 mL |
| ¼ cup | liquid honey | 50 mL |

1. In a small bowl, combine Dijon mustard and honey. Serve at room temperature. (If the honey becomes too thick to pour, microwave, uncovered, on Medium (50%) for a few seconds until it pours easily.)

Variation
Substitute prepared or grainy mustard for the Dijon.

Nutritional value per 2 tbsp (25 mL) serving	
Calories	66
Fat, total	0 g
Fat, saturated	0 g
Cholesterol	0 mg
Sodium	288 mg
Carbohydrate	16 g
Fiber	0 g
Protein	0 g
Calcium	0 mg
Iron	0 g

Plum Dipping Sauce

Try this quick and easy, rich plum-colored sauce with Crispy Pecan Chicken Fingers (see recipe, page 41) for your next kids' party. Save some for the adults too!

Tips

Sauce can be stored, covered, in the refrigerator for up to 2 weeks.

To prevent cross-contamination, set out individual bowls for dipping sauces for each person.

Serve sauce warm or cold — it's delicious either way!

1	can (14 oz/398 mL) prune plums	1
⅓ cup	granulated sugar	75 mL
3 tbsp	vinegar	45 mL

1. Drain plums, reserving 2 tbsp (25 mL) liquid. Remove pits from plums. In a blender, purée plums and reserved liquid.
2. In a small saucepan, combine plum purée, sugar and vinegar. Heat over medium heat until mixture comes to a gentle boil. Remove from heat and let cool before serving.

Variations

In season, 8 fresh plums can be substituted for the canned plums. For an even quicker sauce, substitute one 7.5-oz (213 mL) jar of GF baby food strained plums.

To add tomato flavor, add 1 tbsp (15 mL) GF ketchup or GF barbecue sauce to the dipping sauce.

Nutritional value per 2 tbsp (25 mL) serving	
Calories	43
Fat, total	0 g
Fat, saturated	0 g
Cholesterol	0 mg
Sodium	1 mg
Carbohydrate	11 g
Fiber	0 g
Protein	0 g
Calcium	3 mg
Iron	1 mg

Soups, Salads and Dressings

Broccoli-Cheddar Soup

Makes 6 servings

The tiny crisp broccoli florets add a slight crunch to this creamy soup. It's perfect to serve on a cold winter day.

Tips

Select broccoli with thin, slender stalks. Two medium bunches yield 6 cups (1.5 L) chopped. Peel the stalks, if they are woody.

For a chunky soup, do not purée.

Use either a homemade gluten-free chicken stock or a commercial gluten-free chicken stock powder.

You can use a gluten-free vegetable stock for a vegetarian version.

2 tsp	vegetable oil	10 mL
1½ cups	chopped leeks, white and light green parts only	375 mL
1 cup	diced potato	250 mL
2	cloves garlic, minced	2
4 cups	diced broccoli stalks and florets	1 L
4 cups	GF chicken stock	1 L
1 tbsp	chopped fresh basil	15 mL
2 cups	chopped broccoli florets	500 mL
	Salt and freshly ground black pepper	
1 cup	shredded old Cheddar cheese	250 mL

1. In a large saucepan, heat oil over medium heat. Add leeks, potato and garlic. Cook, stirring frequently, until leeks are tender. Add diced broccoli and stock. Simmer, covered, for 15 minutes or until vegetables are tender.

2. In a food processor or blender, purée in batches. Return to saucepan. Add basil and chopped broccoli florets. Simmer until broccoli is tender. Season with salt and pepper to taste. Stir in cheese just before serving.

Variations

Substitute cauliflower for all or part of the broccoli.

Try thyme, marjoram or tarragon instead of the basil.

Nutritional value per serving	
Calories	203
Fat, total	10 g
Fat, saturated	5 g
Cholesterol	22 mg
Sodium	432 mg
Carbohydrate	19 g
Fiber	3 g
Protein	11 g
Calcium	195 mg
Iron	2 mg

Cheddar Corn Chowder

Enjoy this delicious chowder by itself for lunch, or add GF ham chunks for a hearty stew.

Tips

Use either a homemade GF chicken stock or reconstitute a commercial GF chicken stock powder.

2 stalks of celery yields 1/2 cup (125 mL) when sliced.

See Techniques Glossary, page 370, for information about working with fresh herbs.

For a vegetarian version, use GF vegetable stock.

Substitute snipped fresh basil or thyme for the cilantro.

2 tsp	olive oil	10 mL
2	large potatoes, diced	2
2	stalks celery, thinly sliced	2
1/2	medium onion, diced	1/2
1/2	orange bell pepper, diced	1/2
1 cup	GF chicken stock	250 mL
1	can (14 oz/398 mL) GF cream-style corn	1
1 cup	milk	250 mL
1/2 cup	frozen corn kernels	125 mL
1/4 tsp	dry mustard	1 mL
Pinch	hot pepper flakes	Pinch
3/4 cup	shredded old Cheddar cheese, preferably orange-colored	175 mL
2 tbsp to 1/4 cup	snipped fresh cilantro	25 to 50 mL
2 tbsp to 1/4 cup	snipped fresh parsley	25 to 50 mL
	Salt and freshly ground black pepper	

1. In a large saucepan, heat olive oil over medium heat. Add potatoes, celery, onion and bell pepper and cook, stirring often, for 5 minutes. Add stock and bring to a boil. Reduce heat to medium-low and simmer until potatoes are tender, about 15 to 20 minutes.

2. Stir in cream-style corn, milk, frozen corn, dry mustard and hot pepper flakes. Heat gently over medium-low until steaming; do not let boil. Add cheese, cilantro and parsley. Season with salt and pepper to taste. Serve immediately.

Nutritional value per serving	
Calories	268
Fat, total	8 g
Fat, saturated	4 g
Cholesterol	16 mg
Sodium	211 mg
Carbohydrate	41 g
Fiber	4 g
Protein	10 g
Calcium	179 mg
Iron	2 mg

Incredibly Easy Pizza Soup

Makes 4 servings

Don't want all the carbs but crave pizza? Try this version. It will satisfy your cravings.

Tips

Use either a homemade GF beef stock or reconstitute a commercial GF beef stock powder.

2 oz (60 g) fresh mushrooms yield ¹/₂ cup (125 mL) sliced.

For 1 cup (250 mL) shredded mozzarella cheese, purchase 4 oz (125 g).

Substitute cooked hot or mild GF Italian sausage or Italian Sausage Patties (see recipe, page 106) for the pepperoni.

2 tsp	vegetable oil	10 mL
1	small onion, chopped	1
1	clove garlic, minced	1
¹/₂ cup	sliced mushrooms	125 mL
¹/₄ cup	slivered yellow bell pepper	50 mL
1	can (28 oz/796 mL) diced tomatoes, with juice	1
5 oz	GF pepperoni, thinly sliced (about 1 cup/250 mL)	150 g
¹/₂ cup	GF beef stock	125 mL
1¹/₂ tsp	dried basil or 2 tbsp (25 mL) chopped fresh basil	7 mL
	Salt and freshly ground black pepper	
³/₄ cup	shredded mozzarella cheese	175 mL
¹/₄ cup	freshly grated Parmesan cheese	50 mL

1. In a large saucepan, heat oil over medium-high heat. Add onion, garlic, mushrooms and yellow pepper. Cook, stirring constantly, until tender, about 5 minutes. Stir in tomatoes, pepperoni, beef stock and basil and bring to a boil. Lower heat to medium-low and simmer for 10 minutes. Season with salt and pepper to taste.

2. Ladle into ovenproof or microwave-safe bowls. Sprinkle each with mozzarella and Parmesan. Broil or microwave on High for 45 to 60 seconds, or until cheese melts.

Nutritional value per serving	
Calories	213
Fat, total	9 g
Fat, saturated	4 g
Cholesterol	22 mg
Sodium	1081 mg
Carbohydrate	20 g
Fiber	5 g
Protein	14 g
Calcium	494 mg
Iron	1 mg

Mushroom Wild Rice Chowder

Select shiitake, oyster or button mushrooms to give this thick soup a new twist each time.

Tips

About 2 stalks of celery make ¹/₂ cup (125 mL) when chopped.

The half-and-half cream separates and curdles if the soup is allowed to boil.

1 cup	wild rice, uncooked	250 mL
2 tbsp	butter	25 mL
4 cups	sliced fresh mushrooms	1 L
¹/₂ cup	chopped celery	125 mL
1 cup	chopped leeks, white and light green parts only	250 mL
3	shallots, finely chopped	3
2	cloves garlic, minced	2
4 cups	GF chicken stock	1 L
1 tsp	dried marjoram	5 mL
¹/₄ tsp	freshly ground black pepper	1 mL
1 cup	half-and-half (10%) cream	250 mL

1. Rinse wild rice under cold, running water. Drain and set aside.
2. In a large saucepan, melt butter over medium heat. Add mushrooms, celery, leeks, shallots and garlic. Cook, stirring frequently, until vegetables are tender. Add stock, rice, marjoram and pepper. Simmer, covered, for 45 to 60 minutes or until rice is tender. Slowly stir in cream. Heat through but do not boil.

Variations

Use gluten-free vegetable stock for the gluten-free chicken stock.

Substitute milk for the half-and-half cream.

Nutritional value per serving	
Calories	303
Fat, total	9 g
Fat, saturated	5 g
Cholesterol	22 mg
Sodium	117 mg
Carbohydrate	45 g
Fiber	5 g
Protein	15 g
Calcium	108 mg
Iron	3 mg

Portobello Mushroom Soup

Makes 4 servings

Be sure to try this intensely flavored modern version of mushroom soup.

Tips

Mushrooms can be stored in a paper bag for up to 3 to 4 days in the refrigerator.

There are 4 portobello mushroom caps in 1 lb (500 g).

The longer and more slowly the mushrooms cook, the fuller the mushroom flavor.

Freeze soup for up to 6 weeks.

1 tbsp	vegetable oil	15 mL
8 oz	portobello mushrooms (caps sliced, stems whole)	250 g
1	onion, coarsely chopped	1
2	cloves garlic, finely chopped	2
1 tbsp	snipped fresh rosemary (or 1 tsp/5 mL dried)	15 mL
¼ tsp	salt	1 mL
¼ tsp	freshly ground white pepper	1 mL
2 tbsp	cornstarch	25 mL
1	can (14 oz/385 mL) 2% evaporated milk	1
1 cup	GF chicken or vegetable stock	250 mL

1. In a large saucepan, heat oil over medium-low heat. Cook mushrooms, onion, garlic, rosemary, salt and pepper, stirring occasionally, for 6 to 8 minutes, or until vegetables are tender but not browned.

2. In a bowl, combine cornstarch, evaporated milk and chicken broth. Add to saucepan and bring to a boil, stirring occasionally. Reduce heat to medium-low and simmer for 3 to 4 minutes, or until slightly thickened.

3. Discard mushroom stems. Serve hot.

Variations

Use a variety of mushrooms. Plan to include shiitake, cremini (firmer and with a stronger flavor than a regular white button) and portobellini, as well as portobello (mature cremini with a strong, concentrated flavor).

For a creamy soup, use a food processor to pulse to desired consistency.

For a richer, thicker soup, substitute an equal amount of cream for the evaporated milk.

Nutritional value per serving	
Calories	165
Fat, total	6 g
Fat, saturated	0 g
Cholesterol	16 mg
Sodium	285 mg
Carbohydrate	20 g
Fiber	2 g
Protein	9 g
Calcium	279 mg
Iron	285 mg

Sweet Potato Soup

This thick soup evokes the vibrant colors of autumn. Serve it along with the Ciabatta (see recipe, page 90).

Tip

If you prefer a thinner soup, add extra vegetable stock just before serving.

2 tsp	vegetable oil	10 mL
1½ cups	chopped onions, about 2 medium	375 mL
1 cup	diced potato	250 mL
2	cloves garlic, minced	2
4 cups	diced sweet potato, about 1¼ lbs (625 g)	1 L
4 cups	GF vegetable stock	1 L
1½ tsp	ground ginger	7 mL
	Salt and freshly ground black pepper	

1. In a large saucepan, heat oil over medium heat. Add onions, potato and garlic. Cook, stirring frequently, until onions are tender.

2. Add sweet potato and vegetable stock. Simmer, covered, for 20 minutes or until vegetables are tender. Add ginger.

3. In a food processor or blender, purée soup in batches. Heat to just below boiling. Season to taste with salt and pepper.

Variations

Use basil or nutmeg instead of ginger. Add a small amount at a time, simmer for a couple of minutes and taste.

Substitute winter squash or carrots for all or part of the sweet potato.

Add 2 large peeled and diced apples with the sweet potatoes.

Nutritional value per serving	
Calories	202
Fat, total	3 g
Fat, saturated	0 g
Cholesterol	0 mg
Sodium	295 mg
Carbohydrate	43 g
Fiber	8 g
Protein	3 g
Calcium	87 mg
Iron	2 mg

Broccoli Salad Toss

This versatile all-season salad can be made the day ahead. Be sure to try some of the variations for a different salad every time you make this recipe. Triple this recipe to take to a pot luck, family reunion or company picnic.

Tips

Salad can be made and refrigerated 2 to 3 days in advance. Reserve $1/3$ cup (75 mL) of the dressing and add it just before the salad is served.

You can vary the amounts of GF mayo, GF sour cream and yogurt, but keep the total amount at 1 cup (250 mL).

Dressing

$1/3$ cup	GF mayonnaise	75 mL
$1/3$ cup	GF sour cream	75 mL
$1/3$ cup	plain yogurt	75 mL
2 tbsp	freshly squeezed lemon juice	25 mL

Salad

1	bunch broccoli, cut into florets (about $6^{1}/2$ cups/1.6 L)	1
8 oz	GF bacon, cooked crisp and crumbled	250 g
$1/2$ cup	raw unsalted sunflower seeds	125 mL
$1/2$ cup	raisins	125 mL
2	green onions, sliced	2

1. *Prepare the dressing:* In a small bowl, combine mayonnaise, sour cream, yogurt and lemon juice. Set aside.
2. *Prepare the salad:* In a large bowl, combine broccoli, bacon, sunflower seeds, raisins and green onions. Add dressing and mix well.

Variations

To the basic salad, try adding cauliflower florets, cherry or grape tomatoes, mandarin oranges, feta cheese, red or yellow bell pepper, toasted sesame seeds, toasted slivered almonds, celery or red onions.

Steam broccoli for 1 to 2 minutes; plunge quickly into ice water to stop the cooking.

Nutritional value per serving	
Calories	315
Fat, total	21 g
Fat, saturated	5 g
Cholesterol	40 mg
Sodium	836 mg
Carbohydrate	17 g
Fiber	3 g
Protein	16 g
Calcium	82 mg
Iron	2 mg

Greek Pasta Salad

Enjoy this colorful salad mid-summer with garden-fresh cucumbers and tomatoes.

Tips

An 8-oz (227 g) package contains 4 cups (1 L) gluten-free pasta.

We tried several types of gluten-free pastas and preferred a rice fusilli with rice bran. Experiment to find what you like the best.

Dressing

½ cup	extra virgin olive oil	125 mL
3 tbsp	freshly squeezed lemon juice	45 mL
¼ cup	fresh oregano leaves, snipped	50 mL
4	cloves garlic, minced	4
¼ tsp	salt	1 mL
Pinch	freshly ground black pepper	Pinch

Salad

1 cup	GF pasta, macaroni, rotini or fusilli	250 mL
4	plum tomatoes, cut in wedges	4
1	seedless cucumber, cut in half lengthwise, then sliced	1
1	yellow or orange bell pepper, cut into ¼-inch (0.5 cm) strips	1
½	small red onion, cut in rings	½
½ cup	sliced Kalamata olives	125 mL
4 oz	feta cheese, broken into chunks	125 g

1. *Dressing:* In a small bowl, whisk together olive oil, lemon juice, oregano, garlic, salt and pepper until mixed.

2. *Salad:* In a large saucepan, cook pasta in boiling water according to package instructions or until just firm to the bite. Rinse in cold water and drain. Place in a large bowl.

3. Add tomatoes, cucumber, bell pepper, onion and olives. Pour dressing over pasta and vegetables. Toss lightly to coat. Chill several hours or overnight. Place in serving bowl then add feta and toss.

Variation

Substitute small zucchini for the cucumber — no need to peel.

Nutritional value per serving

Calories	293
Fat, total	24 g
Fat, saturated	5 g
Cholesterol	11 mg
Sodium	384 mg
Carbohydrate	15 g
Fiber	4 g
Protein	6 g
Calcium	120 mg
Iron	1 mg

Grilled Chicken Mandarin Salad with Sweet-and-Sour Dressing

This traditional salad has become popular at quick-service restaurants. Enjoy it at home. Try the variations for a different salad every time.

Tip

The small delicate spinach leaves are milder than the mature ones. Also referred to as young spinach.

To make this a warm salad, heat the dressing to just below boiling before pouring it over that salad topped with freshly grilled chicken. Perfect during cool weather.

Nutritional value per serving	
Calories	435
Fat, total	24 g
Fat, saturated	2 g
Cholesterol	73 mg
Sodium	315 mg
Carbohydrate	27 g
Fiber	5 g
Protein	31 g
Calcium	102 mg
Iron	3 mg

Sweet-and-Sour Dressing

¼ cup	vegetable oil	50 mL
2 tbsp	granulated sugar	25 mL
2 tbsp	white vinegar	25 mL
2 tbsp	snipped fresh parsley	25 mL
¼ tsp	salt	1 mL
Pinch	freshly ground black pepper	Pinch
2 to 3 drops	hot pepper sauce	2 to 3 drops

Salad

6 oz	baby spinach	175 g
1 cup	sliced celery	250 mL
¼ cup	thinly sliced green onions	50 mL
1	can (10 oz/284 mL) mandarin orange segments, drained	1
4	chicken breasts, grilled, cut into ¼-inch (0.5 cm) strips	4
	Caramelized Almonds (see recipe, opposite)	

1. *Sweet-and-Sour Dressing:* In a small bowl, whisk together oil, sugar, vinegar, parsley, salt, pepper and hot pepper sauce. Set aside for at least 1 hour. Refrigerate for up to 3 weeks.

2. *Salad:* In a salad bowl, toss together spinach, celery, green onions and mandarin orange segments.

3. Pour dressing over the salad and toss lightly. Top with grilled chicken strips and sprinkle with Caramelized Almonds.

Variation

Double the dressing recipe and use half to marinate the raw chicken for at least 30 minutes in the refrigerator before grilling. Be sure to drain the chicken and discard the marinade.

Caramelized Almonds

½ cup	slivered almonds	125 mL
2 tbsp	granulated sugar	25 mL

Makes
½ cup (125 mL)

For those who like an added crunch on their salad, make these nuts ahead of time to sprinkle on Grilled Chicken Mandarin Salad (see recipe, opposite) or another one of your favorite salads.

Tips

Remember, melted sugar is hotter than deep fat. Remove the pan from the heat just as the sugar melts and begins to darken, as it burns very easily.

Double the recipe so there is lots to nibble on while enjoying a glass of wine or to serve with Beef and Pepper Stir-Fry (see recipe, page 82.

1. In a small frying pan, cook almonds and sugar over medium heat, stirring constantly, until sugar is melted and almonds are coated and lightly browned. Set aside to cool then separate. Store in an airtight container for up to 3 months.

Variation

Substitute pecan halves, pine nuts or a mixture of nuts for the almonds.

Nutritional value per 2 tbsp (25 mL) serving

Calories	102
Fat, total	7 g
Fat, saturated	1 g
Cholesterol	0 mg
Sodium	0 mg
Carbohydrate	9 g
Fiber	2 g
Protein	3 g
Calcium	36 mg
Iron	1 mg

Shrimp Caesar Salad with Garlic Croutons

Restaurant sales of Caesar salads increase daily. Carry your own Dijon dressing and gluten-free croutons or make them to serve at home.

Tips

Extra salad dressing can be stored in the refrigerator for up to 3 weeks.

For a milder mustard flavor, reduce the Dijon mustard to 1 tbsp (15 mL).

Dijon Dressing

¾ cup	extra virgin olive oil	175 mL
⅓ cup	freshly squeezed lemon juice	75 mL
2 to 3 tbsp	Dijon mustard	25 to 45 mL

Salad

1	head romaine lettuce, torn into bite-size pieces	1
8 oz	large shrimp, cooked, peeled and deveined	250 g
	Garlic Croutons (see recipe, opposite)	

1. *Dijon Dressing:* In a small bowl, whisk together olive oil, lemon juice and Dijon mustard to taste. Set aside for at least 1 hour before serving to allow flavors to develop and blend.

2. *Salad:* In a large bowl, combine lettuce, shrimp and just enough dressing to moisten. Top with gluten-free garlic croutons.

Nutritional value per serving	
Calories	527
Fat, total	45 g
Fat, saturated	6 g
Cholesterol	132 mg
Sodium	815 mg
Carbohydrate	14 g
Fiber	4 g
Protein	17 g
Calcium	110 mg
Iron	2 mg

Garlic Croutons

This is a good way to use up gluten-free bread that you found in the freezer!

● **Preheat oven to 375°F (190°C)**

4	slices day-old GF bread, cut into 1-inch (2.5 cm) cubes	4
1 tbsp	extra virgin olive oil	15 mL
2	cloves garlic, minced	2

1. In a bowl, toss bread cubes with oil and garlic. Spread in a single layer on a baking sheet. Bake in preheated oven for 10 to 15 minutes or until crisp and golden, turning frequently. Cool completely then store in an airtight container.

Variation

Either add dried herbs or make croutons from any of the bread recipes on pages 200 to 252.

Nutritional value per serving (12 croutons)	
Calories	144
Fat, total	6 g
Fat, saturated	1 g
Cholesterol	0 mg
Sodium	120 mg
Carbohydrate	22 g
Fiber	2 g
Protein	2 g
Calcium	3 mg
Iron	1 mg

Baby Spinach Salad with Hot Lemon Dressing

Choose a young, nutritious green leaf to add variety to side salads year round. Increase the number of eggs to 8 to turn this recipe into 4 main-course lunch salads.

Tips

When preparing leafy greens in advance, wash, dry and then refrigerate, covered with a damp, lint-free tea towel.

Throw out any leftover dressing that was at room temperature for more than 30 minutes.

All prepackaged greens should be washed again before serving.

Nutritional value per serving

Calories	210
Fat, total	15 g
Fat, saturated	5 g
Cholesterol	199 mg
Sodium	397 mg
Carbohydrate	11 g
Fiber	3 g
Protein	11 g
Calcium	40 mg
Iron	2 mg

Salad

1	package (10 oz/ 300 g) baby spinach	1
6	slices GF bacon, cooked crisp and crumbled	6
4 oz	sliced mushrooms	125 g
4	hard-cooked eggs, sliced	4
3	thin slices red onion, separated into rings	3

Hot Lemon Dressing

1/4 cup	butter	50 mL
1	green onion, sliced	1
1 cup	water	250 mL
2 tbsp	sorghum flour	25 mL
2 tbsp	freshly squeezed lemon juice	25 mL
1 tbsp	prepared horseradish	15 mL
1/2 tsp	GF Worcestershire sauce	2 mL
2	hard-cooked eggs, chopped	2

1. *Prepare the salad:* Wash and trim spinach. In a large salad bowl, combine spinach, bacon and sliced mushrooms. Arrange egg slices and onion rings on top.

2. *Prepare the dressing:* In a small saucepan, melt butter over medium heat. Add green onion and cook, stirring, for 1 minute, or until tender. Stir in water, sorghum flour, lemon juice, horseradish and Worcestershire sauce. Bring to a boil, reduce heat to medium-low and simmer for 2 minutes, or until thickened. Stir in eggs. Serve immediately in a small heatproof pitcher alongside spinach salad.

Variation

Serve the dressing over broiled or grilled salmon or Pacific halibut (see recipes, pages 100 and 102).

Is Your Diet High in Fiber?

Most GF flours, starches and purchased, prepared products are low in fiber, yet studies have proven fiber's importance and that most of us don't get enough fiber in our diets. Here are some ways to increase fiber while enhancing flavor:

1. Choose flours that are higher in fiber than white rice flour, including amaranth, brown rice, buckwheat, quinoa, whole bean and chickpea (garbanzo bean).
2. Purchase brown rice in place of white rice and brown rice flour in place of white rice flour.
3. Enjoy high-fiber fruits, including berries, figs, pears and apples. Try Figgy Apple Muffins or Loaf (page 166), Blueberry Almond Dessert (page 258) and Pecan Pear Muffins or Loaf (page 172). When possible, leave the skin on apples, pears, and peaches. Choose raw fruit over juice.
4. Leave the peel on vegetables such as zucchini and cucumber when eating raw or cooked, chopping for a salad or baking in quick breads, muffins or cakes.
5. Add nuts, dried fruit and seeds to salads, breads, cakes and pies. Try Carrot Apple Energy Bars (page 27) and Henk's Flax Bread (pages 212 and 243). Remember to crack or grind flaxseed to enable the body to absorb the nutrients.
6. Purchase high-fiber GF cereals for breakfast, crumb crusts and toppings.
7. Plan to use peas, beans, quinoa and lentils for dips, salads and pilafs. Serve Halibut Steaks with Black Bean Salsa (page 102) with a generous serving of Savory Vegetarian Quinoa Pilaf (page 122).
8. Snack on roasted pumpkin seeds, sunflower seeds and toasted almonds. Make your own granola (Linda's Granola, page 26).

Cranberry Orange Vinaigrette

1¼ cups	unsweetened cranberry juice	300 mL
¾ cup	freshly squeezed orange juice	175 mL
⅔ cup	dried cranberries	150 mL
2 tbsp	red wine vinegar	25 mL
1 tsp	salt	5 mL
1 tsp	liquid honey	5 mL
1 tsp	Dijon mustard	5 mL
¼ tsp	freshly ground black pepper	1 mL
1 cup	vegetable oil	250 mL

Makes
2½ cups (625 mL)

The plumped dried cranberries add not only a delightful burst of flavor but also color. Spoon over a mixed green salad topped with a grilled chicken breast.

Tips

Cover and refrigerate for at least 2 hours to allow the flavors to blend and develop. Shake before serving to blend in the oil.

For a better cranberry flavor, choose unsweetened cranberry juice. Avoid drinks, punches or cocktails.

This thick vinaigrette coats the salad; before serving, thin with more orange juice if desired.

1. In a small saucepan, combine cranberry juice, orange juice, dried cranberries and vinegar. Bring to a boil over medium-high heat. Boil until reduced to 1½ cups (375 mL), about 15 to 20 minutes.

2. Remove from heat and whisk in salt, honey, mustard and pepper. Gradually whisk in oil until blended. Store in a covered jar in the refrigerator for up to 2 weeks.

Variation

For a tangier dressing, double the Dijon mustard and add a clove or two of minced garlic.

Nutritional value per 2 tbsp (25 mL) serving	
Calories	97
Fat, total	9 g
Fat, saturated	1 g
Cholesterol	0 mg
Sodium	98 mg
Carbohydrate	5 g
Fiber	0 g
Protein	0 g
Calcium	2 mg
Iron	0 mg

Green Goddess Salad Dressing

**Makes
1 cup (250 mL)**

Attractive, colorful, contrasting flecks of green — this is the dressing everyone requests. Use as a dip on a tray with your favorite crudités. Serve as a dressing over potato, pasta or carrot coleslaw salads.

Tips

This recipe can be halved or doubled, depending on the amount you require.

For the best color, be sure to purchase fresh parsley.

1	small clove garlic	1
1	green onion	1
¼ cup	fresh parsley	50 mL
1½ tsp	dried tarragon or 1 to 2 tbsp (15 to 25 mL) snipped fresh	7 mL
½ cup	GF sour cream	125 mL
½ cup	plain yogurt	125 mL
1 tbsp	freshly squeezed lemon juice	15 mL

1. In a food processor, combine garlic, green onion, parsley, tarragon, sour cream, yogurt and lemon juice. Process until smooth. Cover and refrigerate for a minimum of 2 hours to allow flavors to develop and blend. Refrigerate for up to 2 weeks.

Nutritional value per 2 tbsp (25 mL) serving	
Calories	33
Fat, total	2 g
Fat, saturated	2 g
Cholesterol	9 mg
Sodium	15 mg
Carbohydrate	2 g
Fiber	0 g
Protein	1 g
Calcium	32 mg
Iron	0 mg

Roasted Garlic with Sun-Dried Tomato Dressing

Makes
1½ cups (375 mL)

The colors of this dressing are reminiscent of the Mediterranean. Besides using it to dress a fresh green salad, enjoy it spread on a roast beef sandwich.

1	head garlic	1
1 cup	plain yogurt	250 mL
½ cup	GF sour cream	125 mL
½ cup	snipped sun-dried tomatoes	125 mL
¼ cup	snipped fresh parsley	50 mL

1. *To roast garlic:* Cut off top of head to expose clove tips. Drizzle with ¼ tsp (1 mL) olive oil and microwave on High for 70 seconds or until fork-tender. Or bake in a pie plate or baking dish at 375°F (190°C) for 15 to 20 minutes.

2. In a small bowl, stir together yogurt, sour cream, garlic, sun-dried tomatoes and parsley. Cover and refrigerate for a minimum of 2 hours to allow flavors to develop and blend. Refrigerate for up to 2 weeks. The longer the dressing is refrigerated, the stronger the flavor and the deeper the color becomes.

Variations

Substitute gluten-free mayonnaise for the gluten-free sour cream to turn this dressing into a dip.

For a dill-flavored dressing, substitute ¼ cup (50 mL) snipped fresh dill for fresh parsley.

Nutritional value per 2 tbsp (25 mL) serving	
Calories	28
Fat, total	1 g
Fat, saturated	1 g
Cholesterol	4 mg
Sodium	55 mg
Carbohydrate	3 g
Fiber	0 g
Protein	2 g
Calcium	52 mg
Iron	0 mg

The Main Event

continued on next page

Batter-Fried Fish

The crisp, light batter satisfies the craving for fish and chips. Treat yourself.

Tip

Don't omit the paprika — it helps the batter to lightly brown.

● **Preheat oil in deep fryer or wok to 350°F (180°C)**

2	egg whites	2
1/3 cup	cornstarch	75 mL
1/2 tsp	paprika	2 mL
1 lb	fish fillets, such as sole, haddock or tilapia	500 g
1/4 cup	sweet rice flour	50 mL
	Vegetable oil for frying	

1. In a small bowl, using an electric mixer, beat egg whites until stiff but not dry. Sift cornstarch and paprika over beaten egg whites. With a rubber spatula, fold in. Set aside.

2. Rinse fillets under cold running water and pat dry. Dredge in sweet rice flour. Dip into prepared batter to generously coat, leaving as much batter on the fish as possible.

3. Deep-fry fish for 2 to 4 minutes on each side or until coating is crisp and the fish is fork-tender. Drain on paper towels.

Variation

For a spicier coating, substitute a pinch of cayenne pepper for the paprika.

Nutritional value per serving	
Calories	165
Fat, total	3 g
Fat, saturated	1 g
Cholesterol	56 mg
Sodium	399 mg
Carbohydrate	16 g
Fiber	1 g
Protein	18 g
Calcium	28 mg
Iron	0 mg

Barbecued Pork Sandwiches

What is better than
a sloppy barbecued
sandwich served outside
on a hot summer day?

Tip

*For faster sauce
preparation, substitute
3 cups (750 mL)
commercial gluten-free
barbecue sauce. E-mail
the manufacturer of the
barbecue sauce to ask
whether it is gluten-free.
Many companies are
pleased to send a list of
gluten-free products.*

Sauce

1½ cups	GF ketchup	375 mL
1½ cups	GF chili sauce	375 mL
1 cup	water	250 mL
¼ cup	Dijon mustard	50 mL
⅓ cup	packed brown sugar	75 mL
2 tbsp	cider vinegar	25 mL
2 tsp	chili powder	10 mL
6	drops hot pepper sauce	6
6	cloves garlic, minced	6
2	large onions, diced	2

Pork

3 lbs	boneless pork shoulder or butt roast	1.5 kg
8	mini-sub buns or 6 hamburger buns (see recipe, page 104)	8

1. *Sauce:* In a saucepan, combine ketchup, chili sauce, water, Dijon mustard, brown sugar, vinegar, chili powder, hot pepper sauce, garlic and onions. Bring to a boil and simmer for 10 to 15 minutes, stirring occasionally, until thickened. Set aside to cool.

2. *Pork:* In a large glass or stainless steel bowl, pour sauce over pork roast and marinate overnight, covered, in the refrigerator.

3. Preheat barbecue to medium. Place the pork roast on a double layer of heavy-duty foil, reserving sauce. Add ½ cup (125 mL) of the sauce. Refrigerate remaining sauce. Fold foil using an envelope fold (see page 369).

4. Place pork roast on preheated barbecue, with lid closed, over medium coals or using indirect heat method for 1½ to 2 hours or until meat thermometer registers 160°F to 170°F (70°C to 75°C) (see Thermometers, page 361). Let roast stand for 10 to 15 minutes. Carve roast in thin slices, across the grain.

Nutritional value per serving (1 sandwich)	
Calories	702
Fat, total	20 g
Fat, saturated	5 g
Cholesterol	163 mg
Sodium	2092 mg
Carbohydrate	87 g
Fiber	3 g
Protein	43 g
Calcium	64 mg
Iron	3 mg

5. Meanwhile, in a saucepan, simmer remaining barbecue sauce until thickened, for at least 5 minutes. Pour sauce over sliced meat, cover and refrigerate at least 1 hour or until ready to serve. Make ahead, if you like. Then reheat in a saucepan or microwave until hot and bubbly.

6. To serve, slice each hamburger or mini-sub bun in half horizontally. On the bottom half, arrange meat slices and top with extra sauce. Top with other half of bun and press together. Serve with more sauce, if desired.

Variations

Add extra diced onions, if desired.

Use a less tender cut of beef to marinate. Ask your butcher for suggestions.

Instead of barbecuing, place foil-wrapped pork in a roasting pan. Roast at 350°F (180°C) for approximately 2 hours or until meat thermometer registers 160°F (70°C). Remove cover and roast for an extra 30 minutes.

Beef and Pepper Stir-Fry

Is your family asking for Chinese food tonight? Serve this quick stir-fry over rice or gluten-free noodles.

Tips

One 10-oz (284 mL) can of gluten-free stock can be substituted for 1¼ cups (300 mL) reconstituted gluten-free broth powder.

For more tender beef, slice in thin strips across the grain. Slice while the beef is partially frozen. It's easier!

1¼ lbs	boneless sirloin steak, sliced into ¼-inch (0.5 cm) strips	625 g
⅓ cup	GF soy sauce	75 mL
1 tbsp	vegetable oil	15 mL
1	each red and yellow bell pepper, cut into ¾-inch (2 cm) cubes	1
1	medium onion, halved lengthwise, then thickly sliced	1
3	cloves garlic, minced	3
1½ tsp	minced fresh gingerroot	7 mL
3 tbsp	cornstarch	45 mL
3 tbsp	granulated sugar	45 mL
1¼ cups	GF beef stock	300 mL
3	tomatoes, cut into wedges	3
	Salt and freshly ground black pepper	
	Rice or GF pasta	

1. Place beef, in a single layer, in a shallow baking dish. Pour soy sauce over and let marinate, covered, at room temperature for 30 minutes or in the refrigerator for at least 1 hour.

2. Drain beef and discard the marinade. In a large nonstick skillet, heat oil over high heat. Stir-fry beef in two batches, for 3 minutes each time. Transfer to a plate and keep warm.

3. Reduce heat to medium. Add bell peppers, onion, garlic and gingerroot. Cook, stirring frequently, for 5 to 8 minutes or until tender-crisp.

4. In a small bowl, combine cornstarch and sugar. Whisk in beef stock. Add to skillet and cook, stirring, for 2 to 3 minutes or until thickened. Add beef and tomatoes and heat through. Season with salt and pepper to taste.

5. Spoon the stir-fry over hot rice noodles, gluten-free pasta or rice.

Variation

Steam 2 cups (500 mL) small broccoli florets to add with tomatoes.

Substitute chicken or pork for the beef and gluten-free chicken stock or gluten-free vegetable stock for the gluten-free beef stock.

Nutritional value per serving	
Calories	208
Fat, total	6 g
Fat, saturated	1 g
Cholesterol	42 mg
Sodium	619 mg
Carbohydrate	20 g
Fiber	2 g
Protein	19 g
Calcium	40 mg
Iron	2 mg

Broccoli Cilantro Pesto with Pasta

Make good use of homegrown produce when it's at its best. Turn it into a meal by serving it with Italian Sausage Patties (see recipe, page 106) and fresh grape tomatoes.

Tips

4 cups (1 L) of broccoli florets weigh 1 pound (500 g).

Add more GF chicken stock if the pesto seems too thick.

Make lots of pesto during the summer, when herbs are plentiful, and freeze in small quantities.

Vary the herbs and the amounts used.

4 cups	broccoli florets	1 L
1	clove garlic, minced	1
$\frac{1}{2}$ cup	snipped fresh cilantro	125 mL
$\frac{1}{4}$ cup	snipped fresh basil	50 mL
$\frac{1}{4}$ cup	freshly grated Parmesan cheese	50 mL
$\frac{1}{4}$ cup	extra-virgin olive oil	50 mL
$\frac{1}{4}$ cup	GF chicken stock	50 mL
$\frac{1}{4}$ tsp	salt	1 mL
	Cooked GF pasta	

1. In a glass bowl, microwave broccoli florets, covered, on High (100%) for 3 to 5 minutes, or until tender-crisp, or steam in a vegetable steamer until tender-crisp.
2. In a food processor fitted with a metal blade, combine broccoli, garlic, cilantro, basil, Parmesan, olive oil, stock and salt. Process until coarsely chopped.
3. Toss pesto with hot cooked GF pasta.

Nutritional value per serving	
Calories	180
Fat, total	17 g
Fat, saturated	4 g
Cholesterol	8 mg
Sodium	297 mg
Carbohydrate	4 g
Fiber	2 g
Protein	6 g
Calcium	131 mg
Iron	1 mg

Chicken Cacciatore

Italian for "hunter-style," this dish is perfect to put in the slow cooker for weeknights when family members must eat at different times. It's even tastier the next day!

Tip

Boneless chicken breasts make this special when serving guests.

- **4-quart (4 L) slow cooker**

4	large bell peppers, assorted colors, cut into ½-inch (1 cm) strips	4
2	medium onions, thickly sliced	2
8 oz	large mushrooms, thickly sliced	250 g
8	skinless, bone-in chicken breasts	8
2 cups	GF pasta sauce	500 mL
¼ cup	dry red wine (optional)	50 mL
	Rice or GF pasta	

1. Place peppers, onions, mushrooms, chicken and pasta sauce in the slow cooker stoneware. Cook on High for 4 hours or on Low for 6 hours or until chicken is tender. If desired, add red wine during the last 30 minutes. Serve over rice or gluten-free pasta.

Variations

Use a whole chicken, skinned and cut into pieces, in place of the breasts.

Add raw shrimp in addition to or instead of the chicken. Add shrimp during the last 30 minutes of cooking.

Nutritional value per serving	
Calories	217
Fat, total	4 g
Fat, saturated	1 g
Cholesterol	76 mg
Sodium	316 mg
Carbohydrate	17 g
Fiber	3 g
Protein	28 g
Calcium	42 mg
Iron	2 mg

Crunchy Almond Chicken

Need a quick main dish for dinner? Sprinkle extra almonds on the pan to toast as the chicken bakes.

Tip

The chicken is cooked when an instant read thermometer registers 170°F (75°C).

- Preheat oven to 350°F (180°C)
- 15- by 10-inch (40 by 25 cm) jelly roll pan, lightly greased

⅓ cup	plain yogurt	75 mL
¼ cup	Dijon mustard	50 mL
½ cup	soft GF bread crumbs (see Techniques Glossary, page 368)	125 mL
⅓ cup	sliced almonds	75 mL
1 tsp	dried rosemary	5 mL
½ tsp	salt	2 mL
¼ tsp	freshly ground black pepper	1 mL
6	skinless, boneless chicken breasts	6

1. On a pie plate, combine yogurt and Dijon mustard. Set aside. On a second pie plate, combine bread crumbs, almonds, rosemary, salt and pepper.
2. Roll chicken first in yogurt-mustard mixture and then in the seasoned bread crumbs.
3. Place in a single layer on prepared pan. Bake in a preheated oven for 30 to 35 minutes or until golden brown and chicken juice runs clear.

Variations

Use commercial gluten-free rice crackers to make crumbs or substitute for gluten-free bread crumbs.

Substitute basil, marjoram or thyme for the rosemary.

Substitute boneless fish fillets for the chicken.

Nutritional value per serving	
Calories	214
Fat, total	27 g
Fat, saturated	1 g
Cholesterol	77 mg
Sodium	580 mg
Carbohydrate	9 g
Fiber	1 g
Protein	27 g
Calcium	51 mg
Iron	1 mg

Chicken Pot Pie

Makes 6 servings

Crave Grandma's country cooking? Take pleasure in the aroma of the chicken simmering when you're home during the weekend.

Tips

For a more flavorful stock, use bone-in chicken. If available, add a couple of backs and necks.

If only boneless chicken pieces are available, purchase 2 lbs (1 kg) and add at least 2 to 3 tsp (10 to 15 mL) gluten-free chicken stock powder.

Freeze any leftover stock to use in other recipes.

Nutritional value per serving

Calories	849
Fat, total	38 g
Fat, saturated	16 g
Cholesterol	202 mg
Sodium	580 mg
Carbohydrate	80 g
Fiber	5 g
Protein	46 g
Calcium	109 mg
Iron	3 mg

• **8-cup (2 L) shallow casserole**

Stock

2½ lbs	whole chicken or bone-in chicken pieces	1.25 kg
1	carrot, coarsely chopped	1
1	medium onion, thickly sliced	1
8	peppercorns	8
1	bay leaf	1
3 cups	water	750 mL

Stew

1 cup	green beans, cut into 1-inch (2.5 cm) pieces	250 mL
1 cup	baby carrots, cut in half	250 mL
2	medium potatoes, cut into ½-inch (1 cm) cubes	2
1	stalk celery, sliced	1
⅓ cup	cornstarch	75 mL
1 cup	milk	250 mL
2 tsp	dried thyme leaves	10 mL
4 cups	reserved stock from chicken	1 L
	Salt and freshly ground black pepper to taste	
½	Pie Pastry (see recipe, page 284)	½

1. *Stock:* In a large saucepan, combine chicken, carrot, onion, peppercorns, bay leaf and water. Bring to a boil. Then skim off froth. Reduce heat, cover, and simmer for 60 minutes or until chicken is tender.

2. Strain, reserving stock. Discard carrot, onion, peppercorns and bay leaf. Cut chicken into large chunks. Skim fat off stock.

3. *Stew:* In a steamer or microwave, steam green beans, carrots, potatoes and celery just until tender. Set aside.

Tip

Make stock in the slow cooker — just leave it on all day. Refrigerating the stock overnight makes it easier to remove any fat that has risen to the surface.

4. In a large saucepan, combine cornstarch, milk, thyme and 4 cups (1 L) reserved stock. Cook, stirring constantly, until mixture boils and thickens. Add chicken and vegetables. Spoon stew into the casserole.

5. Roll out pastry. Place on stew and cut steam vents. Bake in a 400°F (200°C) preheated oven for 25 to 35 minutes or until hot and bubbly.

Variation

Make 4 to 6 individual pot pies, then freeze them. To serve, bake from frozen until hot and bubbly or a meat thermometer registers 175°F (80°C).

Chicken Vegetable Bundles with Mushroom Sauce

Makes 4 servings

This dish is tasty enough to serve to company, but simple enough to make for your family any weeknight.

Tips

If you don't have a deep skillet, use an electric frying pan, a Dutch oven or a large covered saucepan.

Using evaporated milk instead of regular milk doubles the calcium.

See Techniques Glossary, page 369, for information on testing doneness with a digital instant-read thermometer.

Nutritional value per serving

Calories	326
Fat, total	9 g
Fat, saturated	1 g
Cholesterol	92 mg
Sodium	406 mg
Carbohydrate	28 g
Fiber	3 g
Protein	34 g
Calcium	292 mg
Iron	2 mg

- **9- to 10-inch (23 to 25 cm) skillet, 2 inches (5 cm) deep**

4	skinless boneless chicken breasts	4
16	snow peas	16
1	small zucchini, cut into ½-inch (1 cm) strips	1
1	small sweet potato, cut into ½-inch (1 cm) strips	1
1 tbsp	vegetable oil	15 mL
2	cloves garlic, finely chopped	2
1	medium onion, halved lengthwise and thickly sliced	1
8 oz	mushrooms, sliced	250 g
1 tsp	dried sage	5 mL
¼ tsp	salt	1 mL
	Freshly ground white pepper	
1	can (14 oz/385 mL) 2% evaporated milk	1
3 tbsp	cornstarch	45 mL
2 tbsp	water	25 mL
1 tsp	freshly squeezed lemon juice	5 mL
	Cooked rice noodles, GF pasta or rice	

1. With a sharp knife, cut chicken breasts lengthwise almost in half, being careful not to cut all the way through. Open and flatten. Place one quarter of the snow peas, zucchini strips and sweet potato strips on half of each chicken breast. Fold the remaining half of the chicken breast over the vegetables.

2. In a large nonstick skillet, heat oil over medium-low heat. Cook garlic, onion, mushrooms, sage, salt and pepper to taste, stirring occasionally, until vegetables are tender. Whisk in evaporated milk.

Tips

For a richer flavor, use a variety of mushrooms. You can include shiitake, cremini (firmer and with a stronger flavor than a regular white button), portobellini or portobello (mature cremini with a strong, concentrated flavor). There are two portobello mushroom caps in 8 oz (250 g).

Mushrooms can be stored in the refrigerator in a paper bag for up to 3 to 4 days.

3. Add chicken, seam side down, and bring to a boil. Cover, reduce heat and simmer gently for approximately 25 to 30 minutes, or until digital instant-read thermometer registers 170°F (78°C) and chicken is no longer pink inside. Remove chicken to a serving platter and keep warm.

4. In a small bowl, combine cornstarch and water. Add to skillet and cook, stirring, for 2 to 3 minutes, or until thickened. Stir in lemon juice.

5. Serve the chicken and mushroom sauce over hot rice noodles, gluten-free pasta or rice.

Variation

Substitute fresh asparagus, green beans, red pepper, winter squash or turnip for any of the vegetables.

Ciabatta

From the Italian for "old slipper," ciabattas are flat, chewy loaves that are fun to make. Poke them full of dimples before rising. The flour-coated crust provides an interesting, open texture. Our round version is easily cut in wedges.

Tips

When dusting with rice flour, use a flour sifter for a light, even sprinkle.

This bread freezes well. Cut into wedges and freeze individually for sandwiches.

Nutritional value per serving

Calories	212
Fat, total	7 g
Fat, saturated	1 g
Cholesterol	55 mg
Sodium	221 mg
Carbohydrate	33 g
Fiber	3 g
Protein	6 g
Calcium	23 mg
Iron	1 mg

• **8-inch (20 cm) round baking pan, lightly floured**

½ cup	whole bean flour	125 mL
½ cup	brown rice flour	125 mL
½ cup	tapioca starch	125 mL
2 tbsp	granulated sugar	25 mL
2 tsp	xanthan gum	10 mL
1 tbsp	bread machine or instant yeast	15 mL
½ tsp	salt	2 mL
¾ cup	water	175 mL
1 tsp	cider vinegar	5 mL
2 tbsp	extra virgin olive oil	25 mL
2	eggs	2
2 to 3 tbsp	sweet rice flour	25 to 45 mL

Bread Machine Method

1. In a large bowl or plastic bag, combine whole bean flour, brown rice flour, tapioca starch, sugar, xanthan gum, yeast and salt. Mix well and set aside.

2. Pour water, vinegar and oil into the bread machine baking pan. Add eggs. Select the Dough Cycle. Allow the liquids to mix until combined.

3. Gradually add the dry ingredients as the bread machine is mixing, scraping with a rubber spatula while adding. Try to incorporate all the dry ingredients within 1 to 2 minutes. Allow the bread machine to complete the cycle.

Mixer Method

1. In a large bowl or plastic bag, combine the whole bean flour, brown rice flour, tapioca starch, sugar, xanthan gum, yeast and salt. Mix well and set aside.

2. In a separate bowl, using a heavy-duty electric mixer with paddle attachment, combine water, vinegar, oil and eggs until well blended.

3. With the mixer on the lowest speed, slowly add the dry ingredients until combined. With a rubber spatula, scrape the bottom and sides of the bowl. With the mixer on medium speed, beat for 4 minutes.

Tip

Use English muffin rings, two-thirds full, to make individual ciabattas.

For Both Methods

4. Immediately, with a water-moistened rubber spatula, remove the sticky dough onto prepared pan. Spread evenly. Generously dust top with sweet rice flour. With well-floured fingers, make deep indents all over the dough, making sure to press all the way down to the pan. Allow to rise in a warm, draft-free place for 40 to 50 minutes or until almost double in volume. Bake in 425°F (220°C) preheated oven for 15 to 20 minutes. Remove immediately from pan to a cooling rack.

Variation

For a creamier-colored ciabatta, use 1 cup (250 mL) brown rice flour in place of the whole bean and brown rice flours.

Ciabatta Sandwich Filling

· ·

Makes 6 wedges

Here's a quick lunch for six adults or two teenage sons with large appetites. Our two boys devoured the whole thing between them.

Nutritional value per serving (1 wedge)	
Calories	527
Fat, total	29 g
Fat, saturated	13 g
Cholesterol	141 mg
Sodium	1098 mg
Carbohydrate	38 g
Fiber	4 g
Protein	35 g
Calcium	640 mg
Iron	3 mg

1	Ciabatta (see recipe, opposite)	1
1 to 2 tbsp	Dijon mustard	15 to 25 mL
12 oz	turkey, thinly sliced	375 g
12 oz	Swiss cheese, thinly sliced	375 g
2	large tomatoes, sliced	2
	Bean sprouts	
	Mesclun salad mix	

1. Slice baked ciabatta in half horizontally. On the bottom half, spread Dijon mustard. Arrange turkey, Swiss cheese, tomatoes, bean sprouts and mesclun greens. Top with other half of ciabatta. Cut into 6 wedges.

2. *To grill:* Brush both sides of the sandwich with a thin layer of extra virgin olive oil. Place on a hot barbecue or grill. Cook, turning once, until the sandwich is brown, crisp and the cheese is melted. Cut into wedges and serve hot. Omit Mesclun for hot sandwich.

Sun-Dried Tomato Ciabatta

Makes 1 ciabatta
or 6 servings

A traditional ciabatta with a modern twist. Sun-dried tomatoes, Parmesan cheese and fresh rosemary take this Italian flatbread a step above the ordinary.

Tips

To ensure success, see pages 199 and 228 for extra information on baking yeast bread in a bread machine or using the mixer method.

We like this ciabatta best served hot out of the oven.

Nutritional value per serving

Calories	338
Fat, total	18 g
Fat, saturated	6 g
Cholesterol	75 mg
Sodium	592 mg
Carbohydrate	33 g
Fiber	5 g
Protein	15 g
Calcium	277 mg
Iron	2 mg

- **9-inch (23 cm) round baking pan, lightly floured with sweet rice flour**

½ cup	brown rice flour	125 mL
½ cup	whole bean flour	125 mL
⅓ cup	tapioca starch	75 mL
2 tbsp	granulated sugar	25 mL
2 tsp	xanthan gum	10 mL
2 tbsp	bread machine or instant yeast	25 mL
¼ tsp	salt	1 mL
1 cup	freshly grated Parmesan cheese	250 mL
¼ cup	chopped fresh rosemary	50 mL
¾ cup	water	175 mL
¼ cup	extra-virgin olive oil	50 mL
1 tsp	cider vinegar	5 mL
2	eggs	2
2	cloves garlic, minced	2
⅔ cup	snipped sun-dried tomatoes	150 mL
	Sweet rice flour	

Bread Machine Method

1. In a large bowl or plastic bag, combine brown rice flour, whole bean flour, tapioca starch, sugar, xanthan gum, yeast, salt, Parmesan cheese and rosemary. Mix well and set aside.

2. Pour water, olive oil and vinegar into the bread machine baking pan. Add eggs, garlic and sun-dried tomatoes. Select the Dough Cycle. Allow the liquids to mix until combined. As the bread machine is mixing, gradually add the dry ingredients, scraping bottom and sides of pan with a rubber spatula. Try to incorporate all the dry ingredients within 1 to 2 minutes. Allow the bread machine to complete the cycle.

Tip

Break this bread into pieces to serve with soups or salads.

Mixer Method

1. In a large bowl or plastic bag, combine brown rice flour, whole bean flour, tapioca starch, sugar, xanthan gum, yeast, salt, Parmesan cheese and rosemary. Mix well and set aside.

2. In a separate bowl, using a heavy-duty electric mixer with paddle attachment, combine water, olive oil, vinegar, eggs, garlic and sun-dried tomatoes until well blended. With the mixer on its lowest speed, slowly add the dry ingredients until combined. Stop the machine and scrape the bottom and sides of the bowl with a rubber spatula. With the mixer on medium speed, beat for 4 minutes.

For Both Methods

3. Immediately transfer dough to prepared pan and spread evenly. Generously dust top with sweet rice flour. With well-floured fingers, make deep indents all over the dough, making sure to press all the way down to the pan. Let rise, uncovered, in a warm, draft-free place for 60 minutes, or until almost double in volume. Meanwhile, preheat oven to 425°F (220°C).

4. Bake in preheated oven for 20 to 25 minutes, or until bread is golden and sounds hollow when top is tapped. Remove from pan immediately and serve.

Variation

Substitute 2 to 3 tbsp (25 to 45 mL) dried basil or oregano for the fresh rosemary and sprinkle the risen dough with 2 tbsp (25 mL) freshly grated Parmesan cheese.

Focaccia

Makes 2 focaccia
or 6 servings

Plan to serve this chewy flatbread hot from the oven along with soup or salad lunches, or cut into small pieces and serve as hors d'oeuvres.

Tips

To ensure success, see pages 199 and 228 for extra information on baking yeast bread in a bread machine or using the mixer method.

Reheat under the broiler to enjoy crisp focaccia.

Can't decide which topping to make? Make a different topping for each pan.

Substitute any type of bean flour for the pea flour.

Nutritional value per serving	
Calories	176
Fat, total	3 g
Fat, saturated	1 g
Cholesterol	0 mg
Sodium	298 mg
Carbohydrate	32 g
Fiber	6 g
Protein	6 g
Calcium	19 mg
Iron	2 mg

● **Two 9-inch (2.5 L) square baking pans, lightly greased**

⅔ cup	amaranth flour	150 mL
½ cup	pea flour	125 mL
⅓ cup	potato starch	75 mL
¼ cup	tapioca starch	50 mL
1 tsp	granulated sugar	5 mL
2 tsp	xanthan gum	10 mL
1 tbsp	bread machine or instant yeast	15 mL
¾ tsp	salt	4 mL
1½ cups	water	375 mL
1 tbsp	extra-virgin olive oil	15 mL
1 tsp	cider vinegar	5 mL
	Topping mixture (see recipes, pages 95 to 97)	

Bread Machine Method

1. In a large bowl or plastic bag, combine amaranth flour, pea flour, potato starch, tapioca starch, sugar, xanthan gum, yeast and salt. Mix well and set aside.

2. Pour water, olive oil and vinegar into the bread machine baking pan. Select the Dough Cycle. Allow the liquids to mix until combined. As the bread machine is mixing, gradually add the dry ingredients, scraping bottom and sides of pan with a rubber spatula. Try to incorporate all the dry ingredients within 1 to 2 minutes. Stop bread machine as soon as the kneading portion of the cycle is complete. Do not let bread machine finish the cycle.

Mixer Method

1. In a large bowl or plastic bag, combine amaranth flour, pea flour, potato starch, tapioca starch, sugar, xanthan gum, yeast and salt. Mix well and set aside.

2. In a separate bowl, using a heavy-duty electric mixer with paddle attachment, combine water, olive oil and vinegar. With the mixer on its lowest speed, slowly add the dry ingredients until combined. Stop the machine and scrape the bottom and sides of the bowl with a rubber spatula. With the mixer on medium speed, beat for 4 minutes.

Tip

Focaccia can be reheated in a few minutes in a toaster oven at 375°F (190°C).

For Both Methods

3. Gently transfer the dough to prepared pans, leaving the tops rough and uneven. Do not smooth. Let rise, uncovered, in a warm, draft-free place for 30 minutes. Meanwhile, preheat oven to 400°F (200°C)

4. Bake in preheated oven for 10 minutes, or until bottom is golden.

5. Cover with preferred topping mixture. Bake for another 20 to 25 minutes, or until top is golden. Remove from pans immediately. Serve hot.

Parmesan Walnut Focaccia Topping

. . . .

Makes enough topping for one 9-inch (2.5 L) square baking pan or 6 servings

Walnuts with Parmesan is a combo of pleasing flavors.

Tip

Store walnuts in the refrigerator and taste for freshness before using.

2	cloves garlic, minced	2
1 to 2 tbsp	extra-virgin olive oil	15 to 25 mL
½ cup	finely chopped walnuts	125 mL
3 tbsp	freshly grated Parmesan cheese	45 mL

1. In a small bowl, combine garlic and olive oil. Let stand while focaccia rises. Drizzle over the partially cooked focaccia.

2. Sprinkle with walnuts and Parmesan.

Variation

Pine nuts can be substituted for walnuts and Romano or Asiago cheese for the Parmesan.

Nutritional value per serving	
Calories	102
Fat, total	10 g
Fat, saturated	1 g
Cholesterol	4 mg
Sodium	64 mg
Carbohydrate	1 g
Fiber	1 g
Protein	4 g
Calcium	53 mg
Iron	0 mg

Mediterranean Focaccia Topping

Top focaccia with sweet onions, slowly caramelized in a very small amount of olive oil until golden.

Tip

No need for extra oil: add 1 tbsp (15 mL) white wine or water to keep onions from sticking.

1 tbsp	extra-virgin olive oil	15 mL
2 cups	sliced Vidalia or other sweet onions	500 mL
2 tbsp	snipped fresh thyme	25 mL
1 tbsp	balsamic vinegar	15 mL
12	kalamata olives, pitted and sliced	12
$\frac{1}{2}$ cup	crumbled feta cheese	125 mL

1. In a skillet, heat olive oil over medium-low heat. Add onions, stirring frequently, until tender and deep golden brown, about 20 minutes. Remove from heat. Stir in thyme and vinegar. Cool slightly. Spoon over the partially cooked focaccia. Sprinkle with olives and feta.

Variation

Add $\frac{1}{2}$ cup (125 mL) snipped sun-dried tomatoes.

Nutritional value per serving

Calories	86
Fat, total	5 g
Fat, saturated	1 g
Cholesterol	5 mg
Sodium	183 mg
Carbohydrate	7 g
Fiber	1 g
Protein	2 g
Calcium	50 mg
Iron	0 mg

Triple-Cheese Focaccia Topping

Makes enough topping for one 9-inch (2.5 L) square baking pan or 6 servings

A trio of cheeses sprinkled over focaccia dough creates the perfect bread to accompany gazpacho on a hot summer's day.

Tip

Use the amount of cheese stated in the recipe: too much results in a greasy focaccia.

2	cloves garlic, minced	2
1 tbsp	extra-virgin olive oil	15 mL
1 tbsp	dried basil	15 mL
½ cup	shredded Asiago cheese	125 mL
½ cup	shredded mozzarella cheese	125 mL
¼ cup	freshly grated Parmesan cheese	50 mL
¾ cup	GF salsa	175 mL

1. In a small bowl, combine garlic, olive oil and basil. Let stand while focaccia rises.
2. In another small bowl, combine Asiago, mozzarella and Parmesan. Set aside.
3. Drizzle garlic-oil mixture over the partially cooked focaccia. Top with salsa and cheese mixture.

Variations

Substitute your favorite lower-fat varieties for the cheeses.

Substitute Black Bean Salsa (see recipe, page 103) for the prepared salsa.

Nutritional value per 2 tbsp (25 mL) serving	
Calories	122
Fat, total	9 g
Fat, saturated	4 g
Cholesterol	18 mg
Sodium	482 mg
Carbohydrate	3 g
Fiber	1 g
Protein	7 g
Calcium	203 mg
Iron	0 mg

Fresh Tomato-Leek Sauce with Sea Scallops

Makes 3 servings

Succulent tender sea scallops, nestled in a bed of gluten-free pasta and accented with a colorful Fresh Tomato-Leek Sauce.

Tips

1 cup (250 mL) snow peas or tender pea pods weighs about 4 oz (125 g).

See Techniques Glossary, page 370, for information about cleaning leeks.

There are approximately 12 sea scallops in 8 oz (250 g).

Vary the herb according to your preference. Try basil or dill.

Substitute GF chicken stock for the white wine.

1 cup	snow peas	250 mL
2 tbsp	extra-virgin olive oil	25 mL
2	leeks, white and light green parts only, cut into 1-inch (2.5 cm) slices	2
2	cloves garlic, minced	2
2	tomatoes, seeded and chopped	2
8 oz	scallops	250 g
1/4 cup	snipped fresh cilantro	50 mL
1/4 cup	dry white wine	50 mL
	Salt and freshly ground black pepper	
	Cooked rice or GF pasta	

1. Trim tops and remove strings from snow peas. Set aside.
2. In a large saucepan, heat olive oil over medium heat. Add snow peas, leeks and garlic and cook, stirring, for 5 minutes, or until tender-crisp. Add tomatoes, scallops, cilantro and wine. Reduce heat to medium-low and simmer for 3 to 5 minutes, or until scallops are opaque. Season with salt and pepper to taste.
3. Serve over hot rice or gluten-free pasta.

Variation

Shrimp, whitefish, clams or mussels, or a combination, can be substituted for the scallops.

Nutritional value per serving

Calories	244
Fat, total	11 g
Fat, saturated	1 g
Cholesterol	29 mg
Sodium	373 mg
Carbohydrate	17 g
Fiber	2 g
Protein	17 g
Calcium	78 mg
Iron	2 mg

Lemon Dill Sauce

**Makes
¾ cup (175 mL)**

This creamy sauce is delicious served with grilled salmon, steamed asparagus or roasted baby carrots.

Tip

Use any type of milk: skim (nonfat), 1%, 2%, or homogenized (whole) milk.

2 tbsp	butter	25 mL
3 tbsp	amaranth flour	45 mL
1 cup	milk	250 mL
1 tbsp	freshly squeezed lemon juice	15 mL
½ tsp	dried dillweed	2 mL
	Salt and freshly ground white pepper	

1. In a saucepan, melt butter over medium heat. Stir in amaranth flour and mix just until blended. Gradually add milk, stirring constantly. Bring to a boil and cook, stirring constantly, for 5 to 7 minutes, or until thickened. Stir in lemon juice and dillweed and season to taste with salt and pepper.

Variations

For a brown sauce, brown the amaranth flour and butter mixture for 3 to 5 minutes and substitute GF beef stock for the milk. Omit the lemon and dillweed.

Substitute whole bean flour for the amaranth flour.

Nutritional value per 2 tbsp (25 mL) serving	
Calories	57
Fat, total	4 g
Fat, saturated	2 g
Cholesterol	6 mg
Sodium	90 mg
Carbohydrate	4 g
Fiber	0 g
Protein	2 g
Calcium	49 mg
Iron	0 mg

Grilled Salmon and Roasted Peppers with Fusilli

Makes 4 servings

What an delicious way to increase your omega-3 fatty acids.

Tips

Roast peppers on the barbecue the next time you have it fired up. To heighten the flavor of the roasted peppers, be sure to cook them long enough for the skins to appear burnt and begin to flake off.

In the fall, when peppers are plentiful, roast extra and freeze them, so you'll have them available all winter long.

Nutritional value per serving

Calories	659
Fat, total	21 g
Fat, saturated	4 g
Cholesterol	107 mg
Sodium	773 mg
Carbohydrate	61 g
Fiber	6 g
Protein	56 g
Calcium	448 mg
Iron	5 mg

● **Barbeque, grill or broiler, preheated**

2	large red bell peppers	2
1	large orange bell pepper	1
1	large yellow bell pepper	1
4	salmon fillets, with skin, 1 inch (2.5 cm) thick (each 6 oz/175 g)	4
2 tsp	extra-virgin olive oil	10 mL
3	cloves garlic, thickly sliced	3
6 oz	GF fusilli noodles	175 g
¼ cup	toasted pine nuts	50 mL
	Lemon wedges	

Sauce

1	can (14 oz/385 mL) 2% evaporated milk	1
⅓ cup	freshly grated Parmesan cheese	75 mL
2 tbsp	cornstarch	25 mL
5 oz	baby spinach	150 g
½ tsp	salt	2 mL
¼ tsp	freshly ground black pepper	1 mL
½ tsp	freshly squeezed lemon juice	2 mL

1. Cut peppers in half and remove the stems, seeds and white membrane. Place peppers on preheated barbecue or on a baking sheet under broiler, cut side down, and grill or broil for 15 to 20 minutes, or until skin blisters, becomes scorched and blackens. Place peppers in a small glass bowl, cover tightly with plastic wrap and let stand for 15 minutes. When peppers have cooled slightly, peel off blackened skin. Cut each half into six strips.

2. Brush both sides of each salmon fillet with olive oil. Grill or broil on a broiler pan, turning once, for about 10 minutes per inch (2.5 cm) of thickness, or until fish is opaque and flakes easily when tested with a fork.

Tips

Salmon can be grilled directly from the freezer. Increase the cooking time to 20 minutes per inch (2.5 cm) of thickness. Turn only once.

If you use an indoor contact grill, there's no need to turn the fish, as both sides cook at once. Cooking time for both peppers and fish may be shorter; check the manufacturer's instructions.

See Techniques Glossary, page 370, under Nuts, for tips on toasting pine nuts.

3. Meanwhile, in a large saucepan of gently boiling water, cook garlic and fusilli according to pasta package directions. Drain and discard garlic.

4. *Prepare the sauce:* In a large saucepan, over medium heat, whisk together evaporated milk, Parmesan and cornstarch. Bring to a simmer; add spinach, salt and pepper. Simmer until spinach is wilted, about 3 minutes. Stir in pepper strips, cooked pasta and lemon juice. Heat thoroughly.

5. Spoon onto a large serving platter and top with salmon and toasted pine nuts. Garnish with wedges of lemon.

Variations

Substitute any firm fish fillet for the salmon.

Substitute an equal quantity of soy nuts for the pine nuts.

We used wild rice fusilli, but you can use GF pasta of any shape or flavor in this recipe.

Halibut Steaks with Black Bean Salsa

Makes 4 servings

Looking for a quick, nutritious supper for a busy weeknight? Nothing cooks faster than fish.

Tip

Grill halibut directly from the freezer. Increase cooking time to 20 minutes per inch (2.5 cm) of thickness. Turn only once.

- **Barbecue, grill or broiler, preheated**

2 tbsp	freshly squeezed lemon juice	25 mL
1 tbsp	extra-virgin olive oil	15 mL
4	Pacific halibut steaks (each 6 oz/175 g)	4
	Black Bean Salsa (see recipe, opposite)	

1. In a shallow glass dish, whisk together lemon juice and olive oil. Add fish and turn to coat.
2. Place fish on preheated barbecue, close lid and grill (or broil on a broiler pan) for about 10 minutes per inch (2.5 cm) of thickness, turning once, until fish is opaque and flakes easily when tested with a fork.
3. Spoon Black Bean Salsa over the halibut and serve.

Nutritional value per serving

Calories	559
Fat, total	36 g
Fat, saturated	6 g
Cholesterol	81 mg
Sodium	763 mg
Carbohydrate	25 g
Fiber	8 g
Protein	33 g
Calcium	75 mg
Iron	4 mg

Black Bean Salsa

1	can (19 oz/540 mL) black beans, rinsed and drained	1
2	green onions, thinly sliced	2
1	large red bell pepper, finely chopped	1
1	large tomato, seeded and finely chopped	1
¼ cup	snipped fresh cilantro	50 mL
2 tbsp	extra-virgin olive oil	25 mL
2 tbsp	red wine vinegar	25 mL
1 tbsp	chili powder	15 mL
	Salt and freshly ground black pepper	

1. In a large bowl, combine black beans, green onions, bell pepper, tomato, cilantro, olive oil, vinegar and chili powder. Season to taste with salt and pepper.

2. Cover and refrigerate for a minimum of 6 hours or overnight to allow flavors to develop and blend. Refrigerate for up to 2 weeks.

**Makes
3 cups (750 mL)
or 4 servings**

This salsa is perfect on Halibut Steaks (see recipe, opposite) but also good on Busy Day Casserole (page 40), Triple-Cheese Focaccia Topping (page 97) or in place of the corn relish in Asparagus- and Ham-Filled Crêpes (page 36).

Tips

If canned black beans are not available, cook 1 cup (250 mL) dried black beans. For instructions, see Techniques Glossary, page 368.

Substitute a canned bean salad mix for the black beans.

Add 1 cup (250 mL) well-drained whole corn kernels, either canned or frozen.

Nutritional value per serving

Calories	200
Fat, total	8 g
Fat, saturated	1 g
Cholesterol	0 mg
Sodium	623 mg
Carbohydrate	24 g
Fiber	8 g
Protein	8 g
Calcium	69 mg
Iron	3 mg

Hamburger/Mini-Sub Buns

Though formed into
the traditional shape for
hamburger or mini-subs,
these white bread rolls
make both great dinner
accompaniments and
sandwiches.

Tip

*If you don't have these
particular shaped pans, try
cast-iron corncob-shaped
bread pans, English muffin
rings or make free-form
buns on a lightly greased
baking sheet. Decrease the
water by 2 tbsp (25 mL) for
free-form buns.*

• **Hamburger or mini-sub pans, lightly greased
(see Tips, left and Equipment Glossary, page 360)**

1¾ cups	brown rice flour	425 mL
⅔ cup	potato starch	150 mL
⅓ cup	tapioca starch	75 mL
¼ cup	non-fat dry milk or skim milk powder	50 mL
¼ cup	granulated sugar	50 mL
2½ tsp	xanthan gum	12 mL
1 tbsp	bread machine or instant yeast	15 mL
1½ tsp	salt	7 mL
1¼ cups	water	300 mL
1 tsp	cider vinegar	5 mL
¼ cup	vegetable oil	50 mL
2	eggs	2
2	egg whites	2

Bread Machine Method

1. In a large bowl or plastic bag, combine rice flour, potato starch, tapioca starch, milk powder, sugar, xanthan gum, yeast and salt. Mix well and set aside.
2. Pour water, vinegar and oil into the bread machine baking pan. Add eggs and egg whites. Select the Dough Cycle. Allow the liquids to mix until combined.

Nutritional value	per hamburger bun	per mini-sub bun
Calories	378	284
Fat, total	11 g	9 g
Fat, saturated	1 g	1 g
Cholesterol	55 mg	41 mg
Sodium	640 mg	480 mg
Carbohydrate	63 g	48 g
Fiber	3 g	2 g
Protein	7 g	5 g
Calcium	46 mg	35 mg
Iron	1 mg	0 mg

Tips

For hamburger buns, use approximately $2/3$ cup (150 mL) dough and for mini-sub buns $1/2$ cup (125 mL) dough.

Smooth the tops with a water-moistened rubber spatula.

3. Gradually add the dry ingredients as the bread machine is mixing, scraping with a rubber spatula while adding. Try to incorporate all the dry ingredients within 1 to 2 minutes. Allow the bread machine to complete the cycle.

Mixer Method

1. In a large bowl or plastic bag, combine rice flour, potato starch, tapioca starch, milk powder, sugar, xanthan gum, yeast and salt. Mix well and set aside.

2. In a separate bowl, using a heavy-duty electric mixer with paddle attachment, combine water, vinegar, oil, eggs and egg whites until well blended.

3. With the mixer on lowest speed, slowly add the dry ingredients until combined. With a rubber spatula, scrape the bottom and sides of the bowl. With the mixer on medium speed, beat for 4 minutes.

For Both Methods

4. Spoon into prepared pan, mounding toward the center of each individual bun (see Tips, left). Let rise in a warm, draft-free place for 30 to 45 minutes or until the dough has almost doubled in volume. Do not allow dough to over-rise. Bake in 350°F (180°C) preheated oven for 15 to 20 minutes. Remove immediately from pan to a cooling rack.

Variation

Sprinkle the tops with sesame seeds before the dough rises.

Italian Sausage Patties

Serve these spicy meat patties over pasta, in a pesto sauce or with a mild tomato sauce. Make ahead and freeze for up to 3 months for a last-minute supper or snack.

Tips

If you use an indoor contact grill, there is no need to turn the patties. Cooking time will be much shorter; check the manufacturer's instructions.

See Equipment Glossary, page 361, for more information on meat thermometers.

For a stronger flavor, substitute caraway or anise seed for the fennel.

- **Barbecue, grill or broiler, preheated**

1 lb	lean ground beef	500 g
3	cloves garlic, minced	3
2 tsp	fennel seeds	10 mL
1 tsp	hot pepper flakes	5 mL
¾ tsp	salt	4 mL
½ tsp	freshly ground black pepper	2 mL
¼ tsp	cayenne pepper (optional)	1 mL

1. In a medium bowl, using a fork, gently combine beef, garlic, fennel seeds, hot pepper flakes, salt, pepper and cayenne pepper, if using. Form into 12 patties, 2 inches (5 cm) in diameter.

2. On preheated barbecue, grill patties for 2 to 3 minutes, turning only once, until meat thermometer registers 160°F (70°C) and patties are no longer pink inside.

Variations

Substitute ground veal, pork, chicken or turkey for the ground beef.

Make into meatballs. Bake on a baking sheet at 400°F (200°C) for 15 to 20 minutes, or until no longer pink in the center.

Nutritional value per serving (1 patty)	
Calories	50
Fat, total	2 g
Fat, saturated	1 g
Cholesterol	22 mg
Sodium	172 mg
Carbohydrate	1 g
Fiber	0 g
Protein	8 g
Calcium	6 mg
Iron	1 mg

Parsley Pesto Sauce

2	large cloves garlic	2
1 cup	fresh parsley leaves, tightly packed	250 mL
⅓ cup	fresh basil leaves, tightly packed	75 mL
1 tbsp	extra virgin olive oil	15 mL
¼ cup	freshly grated Parmesan cheese	50 mL
¼ cup	GF vegetable stock	50 mL

**Makes
⅔ cup (150 mL)**

When fresh basil is plentiful, make lots of sauce and freeze to use in the winter.

1. In a food processor, with processor on, drop garlic through the tube and process until chopped. Add basil, parsley, oil and Parmesan cheese. Process until well mixed. With a rubber spatula, scrape the sides once or twice. Add stock, process until well blended.

Nutritional value per 2 tbsp (25 mL) serving

Calories	47
Fat, total	4 g
Fat, saturated	1 g
Cholesterol	5 mg
Sodium	97 mg
Carbohydrate	1 g
Fiber	0 g
Protein	2 g
Calcium	81 mg
Iron	1 mg

Plain Pizza Crust

For a traditional pizza crust, try this recipe.

Tips

This recipe can be easily doubled to make two pizza crusts. Partially bake both, top one to bake and eat. Freeze the other to use later.

Warming the finished pizza for 5 minutes in the oven results in a very crisp crust.

● **One 12-inch (30 cm) pizza pan, generously greased**

¾ cup	brown rice flour	175 mL
⅓ cup	potato starch	75 mL
1 tsp	granulated sugar	5 mL
1½ tsp	xanthan gum	7 mL
1½ tsp	bread machine or instant yeast	7 mL
½ tsp	salt	2 mL
1 tsp	dried oregano leaves	5 mL
¾ cup	water	175 mL
1 tsp	cider vinegar	5 mL
1 tbsp	vegetable oil	15 mL
2 to 3 tbsp	sweet rice flour	25 to 45 mL

Bread Machine Method

1. In a large bowl or plastic bag, combine brown rice flour, potato starch, sugar, xanthan gum, yeast, salt and oregano. Mix well and set aside.

2. Pour water, vinegar and oil into the bread machine baking pan. Select the Dough Cycle. Allow the liquids to mix until combined.

3. Gradually add the dry ingredients as the bread machine is mixing, scraping with a rubber spatula while adding. Try to incorporate all the dry ingredients within 1 to 2 minutes. Allow the bread machine to complete the cycle.

Mixer Method

1. In a large bowl or plastic bag, combine brown rice flour, potato starch, sugar, xanthan gum, yeast, salt and oregano. Mix well and set aside.

2. In a separate bowl, using a heavy-duty electric mixer with paddle attachment, combine water, vinegar and oil until well blended.

3. With the mixer on the lowest speed, slowly add the dry ingredients until combined. With a rubber spatula, scrape the bottom and sides of the bowl. With the mixer on medium speed, beat for 4 minutes.

Nutritional value per serving	
Calories	142
Fat, total	3 g
Fat, saturated	0 g
Cholesterol	0 mg
Sodium	198 mg
Carbohydrate	28 g
Fiber	2 g
Protein	2 g
Calcium	4 mg
Iron	1 mg

Tip

Use as much sweet rice flour as you need to handle the dough. It is tasteless in the baked crust. You need less and less, the more you perfect this technique.

For Both Methods

4. With a wet rubber spatula, remove the very sticky dough to prepared pan, spreading out as much as possible. Generously sprinkle with sweet rice flour. With floured fingers, gently pat out dough to fill the pan evenly. Continue to sprinkle with sweet rice flour as required. Form a rim at the edge of pan. Allow to rise in a warm, draft-free place for 15 minutes. Bake in 400°F (200°C) preheated oven for 12 to 15 minutes or until firm. Spread with your choice of toppings (see recipes, pages 111 to 113). Return to oven and bake according to recipe topping directions.

Variation

Substitute your favorite herb for the oregano — try basil, marjoram or thyme.

Thin Pizza Crust

Makes 2 crusts		
or 12 servings		

Try our version of right-to-the-edge thin crust pizza.

Tip

This dough is thin enough to pour onto the pizza pans. It can be quickly spread to the edges with a moist rubber spatula.

Don't worry about the cracks on the surface of this crust after 10 minutes of baking. Expect slight shrinkage from the edges.

● **Two 12-inch (30 cm) pizza pans, lightly greased**

1 cup	whole bean flour	250 mL
1 cup	sorghum flour	250 mL
1/3 cup	tapioca starch	75 mL
1 tsp	granulated sugar	5 mL
1/2 tsp	xanthan gum	2 mL
1 1/2 tsp	bread machine or instant yeast	7 mL
1 tsp	salt	5 mL
1 tsp	dried oregano leaves	5 mL
1 3/4 cups	water	425 mL
1 tsp	cider vinegar	5 mL
2 tbsp	vegetable oil	25 mL

Bread Machine Method

1. In a large bowl or plastic bag, combine whole bean flour, sorghum flour, tapioca starch, sugar, xanthan gum, yeast, salt and oregano. Mix well and set aside.

2. Pour water, vinegar and oil into the bread machine baking pan. Select the Dough Cycle.

3. Gradually add the dry ingredients as the bread machine is mixing, scraping with a rubber spatula while adding. Try to incorporate all the dry ingredients within 1 to 2 minutes. Allow the bread machine to complete the cycle.

Mixer Method

1. In a large bowl or plastic bag, combine whole bean flour, sorghum flour, tapioca starch, sugar, xanthan gum, yeast, salt and oregano. Mix well and set aside.

2. In a separate bowl, using a heavy-duty electric mixer with paddle attachment, combine water, vinegar and oil until well blended.

3. With the mixer on the lowest speed, slowly add the dry ingredients until combined. With a rubber spatula, scrape the bottom and sides of the bowl. With the mixer on medium speed, beat for 4 minutes.

Nutritional value per serving	
Calories	124
Fat, total	4 g
Fat, saturated	0 g
Cholesterol	0 mg
Sodium	194 mg
Carbohydrate	20 g
Fiber	2 g
Protein	5 g
Calcium	10 mg
Iron	1 mg

Tip

This dough can be divided into equal portions to make eight 6-inch (15 cm) individual pizzas. Bake on greased baking sheets for 10 to 12 minutes.

For Both Methods

4. Immediately pour onto prepared pans. Spread evenly with a water-moistened rubber spatula. Allow to rise in a warm, draft-free place for 15 minutes. Bake in 400°F (200°C) preheated oven for 12 to 15 minutes or until firm. Spread with your choice of toppings (see recipes, below and pages 112 to 113). Return to oven and bake according to recipe topping directions.

Variations

Use 1 tbsp (15 mL) chopped fresh oregano for the dried herb.

Five-Cheese Pizza Topping

Makes topping for one 12-inch (30 cm) pizza or 6 servings

We love cheese and couldn't decide which we like the best on pizza — so we mixed five together. Check for gluten before you purchase a packaged shredded cheese mix.

Nutritional value per serving

Calories	260
Fat, total	11 g
Fat, saturated	5 g
Cholesterol	24 mg
Sodium	733 mg
Carbohydrate	32 g
Fiber	3 g
Protein	7 g
Calcium	165 mg
Iron	1 mg

● **Preheat oven to 400°F (200°C)**

1 to 2 oz	freshly grated Asiago cheese	30 to 60 g
1 to 2 oz	shredded old Cheddar cheese	30 to 60 g
1 to 2 oz	shredded Fontina cheese	30 to 60 g
1 to 2 oz	crumbled Gorgonzola cheese	30 to 60 g
1 to 2 oz	shredded Havarti cheese	30 to 60 g
1 cup	chunky salsa	250 ml
1	partially baked pizza crust (see recipes, page 108 and 110)	1

1. In a small bowl, mix together cheeses. Set aside.

2. Spread salsa over pizza crust, then top with cheese mixture.

3. Bake in preheated oven for 15 to 20 minutes or until cheese is lightly browned and heated through.

Variation

Use tomato or gluten-free pizza sauce for the salsa.

Leek-Mushroom Pizza Topping

Makes topping for one 12-inch (30 cm) pizza or 6 servings

Subtle leeks blend the flavors of mushrooms and pesto.

● **Preheat oven to 400°F (200°C)**

1 tbsp	extra virgin olive oil	15 mL
2	leeks, sliced in half lengthwise, then cut into 1/2-inch (1 cm) pieces, white and light green parts only	2
2 cups	cremini mushroom caps, halved then sliced into 1/2-inch (1 cm) pieces	500 mL
1/3 cup	Parsley Pesto Sauce (see recipe, page 107)	75 mL
2/3 cup	freshly grated Asiago cheese	150 mL
1/3 cup	freshly grated Parmesan cheese	75 mL
1	partially baked pizza crust (see recipes, pages 108 and 110)	1

1. In a frying pan, heat oil over medium-high heat. Add leeks and mushrooms and sauté, stirring constantly, until tender, about 3 to 5 minutes. Set aside.

2. Spread pesto over pizza crust. Top with leek-mushroom mixture, then Asiago and Parmesan cheese.

3. Bake the regular-size pizza in a preheated oven for 15 to 20 minutes or smaller pizzas for 10 to 12 minutes or until cheese is lightly browned and heated through.

Variations

Substitute extra Parmesan for the Asiago to make a totally Parmesan cheese topping.

Strips of cooked chicken can be added to the leek-mushroom mixture before adding the cheeses.

Substitute a commercial pesto sauce for the homemade.

Nutritional value per serving

Calories	312
Fat, total	15 g
Fat, saturated	5 g
Cholesterol	23 mg
Sodium	535 mg
Carbohydrate	36 g
Fiber	3 g
Protein	11 g
Calcium	271 mg
Iron	2 mg

Roasted Vegetable Pizza Topping

Makes topping for one 12-inch (30 cm) pizza or 6 servings

Like lots of topping with every bite of pizza? Try our simplified version — thin, edgeless and filled to the brim!

Tip

We like to sprinkle some of the cheese on the crust before topping as this helps the vegetables remain on the pizza.

- Preheat oven to 425°F (220°C)
- Roasting pan

1 tbsp	extra virgin olive oil	15 mL
2	small Italian eggplants, cut into ½-inch (1 cm) cubes	2
1	large red bell pepper, cut into ½-inch (1 cm) slices	1
1	large yellow bell pepper, cut into ½-inch (1 cm) slices	1
3 cups	portobello mushrooms, cut into ½-inch (1 cm) thick slices, about 10 oz (300 g)	750 mL
4	small zucchini, cut into ½-inch (1 cm) slices	4
6	cloves garlic, minced	6
⅔ cup	shredded mozzarella cheese	150 mL
½ cup	freshly grated Parmesan cheese	125 mL
1	partially baked pizza crust (see recipes, pages 108 and 110)	1

1. Measure oil into roasting pan. Add vegetables and garlic. Toss to coat. Roast in preheated oven, turning once, for 10 to 15 minutes or until tender. Do not overcook. Set aside to cool.

2. To assemble, sprinkle half the mozzarella cheese over the partially baked pizza crust. Top with roasted vegetables, remaining mozzarella and Parmesan. Reduce heat to 400°F (200°C) and bake for 12 to 15 minutes or until the topping is bubbly and cheese is melted, lightly browned and heated through. Serve immediately.

Variation

For a stronger cheese combination, try Asiago and Romano.

Nutritional value per serving	
Calories	308
Fat, total	11 g
Fat, saturated	4 g
Cholesterol	17 mg
Sodium	467 mg
Carbohydrate	45 g
Fiber	9 g
Protein	13 g
Calcium	331 mg
Iron	1 mg

Meatballs for Everyday

Whether you serve these meatballs with spaghetti, sweet-and-sour sauce or as hot hors d'oeuvres, they are sure to be a hit.

- Preheat oven to 400°F (200°C)
- 15- by 10-inch (40 by 25 cm) jelly roll pan, lightly greased

1 lb	extra lean ground beef	500 g
8 oz	ground pork	250 g
½ cup	finely chopped onion	125 mL
1	egg, lightly beaten	1
1 cup	soft GF bread crumbs (see Techniques Glossary, page 368)	250 mL
2 tbsp	snipped fresh parsley	25 mL
2 tbsp	snipped fresh basil leaves	25 mL
2 tbsp	snipped fresh oregano	25 mL
¼ tsp	freshly ground black pepper	1 mL

1. In a large bowl, gently mix together beef, pork, onion, egg, bread crumbs, parsley, basil, oregano and ground pepper. Shape into 1-inch (2.5 cm) balls. Place in a single layer on prepared pan.

2. Bake in a preheated oven for 20 minutes or until no longer pink in the center.

3. *To Freeze:* Cool slightly then freeze baked meatballs on the jelly roll pan. Once frozen, remove meatballs from pan and place in a heavy-duty freezer bag. Remove only the number you need — they won't stick together. Reheat meatballs from frozen directly in sauce or microwave just until thawed and then add to the sauce.

Variations

Use commercial gluten-free rice crackers to make crumbs and substitute for gluten-free bread crumbs. If using flavored crackers, such as barbecue or teriyaki, omit the basil and oregano.

Substitute ground turkey or chicken for all or part of the ground beef and pork.

Nutritional value per serving (1 meatball)

Calories	41
Fat, total	2 g
Fat, saturated	1 g
Cholesterol	15 mg
Sodium	12 mg
Carbohydrate	2 g
Fiber	0 g
Protein	4 g
Calcium	4 mg
Iron	0 mg

Sweet 'n' Sour Sauce

Try this familiar, not-too-sweet sauce next time you make Chinese food. Be sure to include it served over meatballs at your next party.

Tip

Serve this sauce over cooked meatballs, chicken or pork.

¼ cup	white vinegar	50 mL
¾ cup	water	175 mL
½ cup	packed brown sugar	125 mL
⅓ cup	granulated sugar	75 mL
2 tbsp	cornstarch	25 mL
2 tbsp	GF ketchup	25 mL
1	can (14 oz/398 mL) pineapple tidbits with juice	1

1. In a saucepan, bring vinegar, water, brown sugar and granulated sugar to a boil. Simmer gently for 2 to 3 minutes.
2. In a bowl, combine cornstarch and ketchup to form a paste. Add pineapple and juice.
3. Slowly stir pineapple mixture into the saucepan. Return to a gentle boil, stirring constantly. Simmer gently until thick and shiny.

Variation

For a more colorful sauce with a slight tomato flavor, increase the ketchup to ¼ cup (50 mL).

Nutritional value per 2 tbsp (25 mL) serving	
Calories	51
Fat, total	0 g
Fat, saturated	0 g
Cholesterol	0 mg
Sodium	21 mg
Carbohydrate	13 g
Fiber	0 g
Protein	0 g
Calcium	8 mg
Iron	0 mg

Quinoa-Stuffed Peppers

This entrée comes to mind in the late summer, when the vegetables are ripe in the garden. We often forget to make it in the winter.

Tips

Assemble early in the day, then refrigerate, covered, to serve for dinner. Allow double the cooking time if cold from the refrigerator.

Sprinkle any remaining stuffing in the bottom of the casserole.

See Techniques Glossary, page 371, for instructions on cooking quinoa.

Nutritional value per serving	
Calories	612
Fat, total	24 g
Fat, saturated	12 g
Cholesterol	116 mg
Sodium	691 mg
Carbohydrate	47 g
Fiber	8 g
Protein	47 g
Calcium	573 mg
Iron	6 mg

- Preheat oven to 400°F (200°C)
- 10-cup (2.5 L) covered casserole dish

1	large orange bell pepper	1
1	large yellow bell pepper	1
1	tomato, sliced into four thick slices	1
¼ cup	dry white wine	50 mL
1 cup	shredded Swiss cheese	250 mL

Stuffing

8 oz	extra-lean ground beef, turkey or chicken	250 g
½	small onion, chopped	½
½	red bell pepper, chopped	½
1 cup	sliced mushrooms	250 mL
1 tbsp	chopped fresh rosemary	15 mL
1 tbsp	chopped fresh thyme	15 mL
1	tomato, chopped	1
1	small zucchini, chopped	1
1 cup	cooked quinoa	250 mL
¼ tsp	salt	1 mL
¼ tsp	freshly ground black pepper	1 mL

1. Cut orange and yellow peppers in half lengthwise and remove core and seeds. Trim a thin slice off the bottom of each to allow them to lie flat. In the casserole dish, microwave peppers, covered, on High for 3 minutes, or until tender-crisp. Let cool to room temperature, covered. Drain and pat dry.

2. *Prepare the stuffing:* Meanwhile, in a large skillet, over medium heat, brown ground beef until no pink remains. Add onion, red pepper, mushrooms, rosemary and thyme. Cook, stirring, until onions are translucent, about 3 minutes. Drain off any fat. Add chopped tomato and zucchini and cook, stirring, for 5 minutes. Stir in quinoa, salt and pepper.

Tips

Vary the type of mushrooms — try portobello, cremini, oyster or shiitake.

Substitute 1 cup (250 mL) undrained chopped canned tomatoes for the fresh tomato slices and white wine.

3. In the casserole dish, arrange tomato slices and add wine. Set each pepper half, cut side up, on a tomato slice. Fill each pepper half with the beef mixture, mounding the stuffing.

4. Cover and bake in preheated oven for 15 minutes, or until bell peppers are fork-tender. Uncover, top with Swiss cheese and bake, uncovered, for 5 minutes more, or until cheese is melted.

Variations

Stuff zucchini in place of the bell peppers. Acorn squash or mini pumpkins can also be stuffed, but must be fully cooked first.

Substitute brown or wild rice for all or part of the quinoa.

Roast Stuffed Pork Tenderloin

No need to be concerned about entertaining those friends who are not celiacs — everyone enjoys these medallions of pork stuffed with broccoli.

Tips

To prevent the thin tip of pork tenderloin from drying, turn it under before adding the stuffing.

Bread crumbs can be prepared from any gluten-free bread you prefer. Do not let dry. (See Techniques Glossary, page 368).

- Preheat oven to 350°F (180°C)
- 9-inch (2.5 L) square baking pan, lightly greased

¾ cup	chopped cooked broccoli	175 mL
¾ cup	soft GF bread crumbs	175 mL
⅓ cup	chopped walnuts	75 mL
2 tbsp	GF chicken stock	25 mL
2 tbsp	tomato sauce	25 mL
2 tbsp	pure maple syrup	25 mL
2	pork tenderloins (each about 10 oz/300 g)	2
1 tbsp	crushed whole peppercorns	15 mL
¼ cup	tomato sauce	50 mL
¼ cup	GF chicken stock	50 mL

1. In a bowl, combine broccoli, bread crumbs, walnuts and chicken stock. Set aside.
2. In a small bowl, combine tomato sauce and maple syrup. Set aside.
3. With a sharp knife, cut tenderloins lengthwise almost in half, being careful not to cut all the way through. Open and flatten to butterfly. If still too thick, cut the thicker piece again, being careful to leave the tenderloin in one piece. Spoon half the broccoli stuffing over each of the tenderloins.
4. Starting at one long side, roll each tenderloin like a jelly roll and tie tightly with string. Roll in tomato-maple syrup mixture, then in crushed peppercorns. Place in prepared baking dish and bake in a preheated oven for 30 to 45 minutes or until meat thermometer registers 160°F (70°C) or a hint of pink remains in pork. Remove tenderloins and let stand for 5 minutes, covered lightly with foil to keep warm.
5. For sauce, add tomato sauce and stock to pan drippings. Stir and cook over medium heat until hot and bubbly. Pour sauce onto individual serving plates. Remove string. Slice tenderloins and place on top of sauce.

Variation

Short on time? No need to roll and tie the pork loin. After topping with stuffing, bake, stuffing-side up, in preheated oven for 20 to 30 minutes.

Nutritional value per serving

Calories	268
Fat, total	11 g
Fat, saturated	1 g
Cholesterol	49 mg
Sodium	164 mg
Carbohydrate	22 g
Fiber	2 g
Protein	20 g
Calcium	43 mg
Iron	2 mg

Santa Fe Chicken

Fire-roasted vegetables and strips of chicken breast over gluten-free pasta — no wonder it is a top seller in many restaurants.

Tips

Cook gluten-free pasta just until al dente.

This recipe can easily be halved to serve two.

Roast extra vegetables to serve another day.

For a spicier dish, substitute a hot pepper for one of the bell peppers.

To speed up the preparation, use a packaged mix of stir-fry vegetables instead of roasting the vegetables. Steam just until tender before adding.

Nutritional value per serving

Calories	548
Fat, total	20 g
Fat, saturated	9 g
Cholesterol	69 mg
Sodium	757 mg
Carbohydrate	60 g
Fiber	9 g
Protein	32 g
Calcium	351 mg
Iron	3 mg

- Preheat oven 425°F (220°C)
- Roasting pan

1 tbsp	extra virgin olive oil	15 mL
1	small Italian eggplant, cut into 1-inch (2.5 cm) cubes	1
1	large red or yellow bell pepper, cut into 1-inch (2.5 cm) strips	1
3 cups	portobello mushrooms, cut into 1/2-inch (1 cm) thick slices	750 mL
2	small zucchini, cut into 1/2-inch (1 cm) slices	2
6	cloves garlic, minced	6
8 to 12 oz	GF rice fettuccine or GF rotini pasta	250 to 375 g
1/4 cup	butter	50 mL
1	can (14 oz/385 mL) evaporated milk	1
1/2 cup	freshly grated Parmesan cheese	125 mL
1/3 cup	snipped fresh cilantro	75 mL
2	cooked skinless, boneless chicken breasts, cut into 1-inch (2.5 cm) strips	2
1	can (19 oz/540 mL) black beans, rinsed and drained	1
1 tbsp	freshly squeezed lime juice	15 mL
3/4 cup	shredded Monterey Jack cheese	175 mL

1. Measure oil into roasting pan. Add vegetables and garlic and toss to coat. Roast in preheated oven, turning once, for 10 to 15 minutes or until tender. Do not overcook. Set aside to cool.

2. In a large pot of boiling water, cook pasta according to package directions. Drain but do not rinse.

3. In a large saucepan, combine pasta, butter, evaporated milk, Parmesan cheese and cilantro. Cook over medium heat, stirring constantly, until hot and bubbly. Add roasted vegetables, chicken, black beans and lime juice. Heat until steaming.

4. Spoon into large serving bowl and top with cheese.

Variation

Substitute chunks of cooked pork or beef for the chicken.

Savory Stilton Cheesecake

Serve this make-ahead main dish and enjoy the delightful bursts of flavor — just imagine nippy Stilton combined with fresh herbs from your garden.

Tips

Cheesecake keeps for up to 2 days in the refrigerator. It can also be frozen in an airtight container for up to 2 weeks. We froze wedges individually for a quick dinner for two. Bring to room temperature before serving.

8 oz (250 g) of Stilton cheese yield 1$\frac{1}{2}$ cups (375 mL).

Use the hottest tap water available to fill the roasting pan in the oven to a depth of 1 inch (2.5 cm).

Nutritional value per serving

Calories	507
Fat, total	42 g
Fat, saturated	19 g
Cholesterol	159 mg
Sodium	665 mg
Carbohydrate	18 g
Fiber	1 g
Protein	17 g
Calcium	306 mg
Iron	1 mg

- **Preheat oven to 325°F (160°C)**
- **9-inch (23 cm) springform pan, lightly greased**

Base

1$\frac{1}{2}$ cups	fresh GF bread crumbs	375 mL
$\frac{2}{3}$ cup	chopped walnuts	150 mL
2 tbsp	melted butter	25 mL

Cheesecake

2	packages (each 8 oz/250 g) cream cheese, softened	2
1 tbsp	Dijon mustard	15 mL
3	eggs	3
1	clove garlic, minced	1
1 cup	plain yogurt	250 mL
$\frac{1}{4}$ cup	freshly grated Parmesan cheese	50 mL
2 tbsp	snipped fresh basil	25 mL
2 tbsp	snipped fresh sage	25 mL
1 tbsp	snipped fresh thyme	15 mL
$\frac{1}{4}$ tsp	freshly ground black pepper	1 mL
1$\frac{1}{2}$ cups	cubed Stilton cheese, ($\frac{1}{4}$-inch/0.5 cm cubes)	375 mL

1. *Prepare the base:* In a large bowl, combine bread crumbs, walnuts and butter. Mix well. Press into prepared pan and bake in preheated oven for 20 minutes to partially cook. Let cool to room temperature. Center springform pan on a large square of foil and press foil up sides of pan.

2. *Prepare the cheesecake:* In a large bowl, using an electric mixer, beat the cream cheese and Dijon mustard until smooth. Add eggs one at a time, beating well after each. Stir in garlic, yogurt, Parmesan, basil, sage, thyme and pepper until combined. Fold in Stilton cheese. Pour over base.

Tips

Leaving the cheesecake in the oven after turning it off helps prevent large cracks. Be sure to set a timer, as it is easy to forget.

After removing the baked cheesecake from the water bath, set the springform pan in an empty sink to carefully remove the foil. The water may leak out.

See Techniques Glossary, page 368, for information on making GF bread crumbs.

Substitute a lower-fat (but not whipped or spreadable) cream cheese.

Substitute GF Danish blue cheese for the Stilton.

3. Place the foil-wrapped springform pan in a larger roasting pan, and set on oven rack placed in the center of the preheated oven. Pour in enough hot water to fill the larger pan to a depth of 1 inch (2.5 cm). Bake for 70 to 80 minutes, or until center is just set and the blade of a knife comes out clean. Turn oven off and let cheesecake cool in oven for 1 hour (see Tip, left). Carefully remove springform pan from pan of water and remove the foil. Let cool in springform pan on a rack for 30 minutes. Refrigerate until chilled, about 3 hours. Bring to room temperature before serving.

Variation

For a stronger walnut flavor, toast the walnuts before chopping (see Techniques Glossary, page 370, under Nuts) and substitute walnut oil for the melted butter.

Savory Vegetarian Quinoa Pilaf

This delicious vegetarian dish is dotted with multicolored chunks of nutritious vegetables.

Tips

Quinoa is cooked when grains turn from white to transparent and the tiny spiral-like germ is separated.

For a richer, robust pilaf, substitute GF beef or GF chicken stock for the vegetable stock.

2 tsp	extra-virgin olive oil	10 mL
1	stalk celery, diced	1
1	medium carrot, coarsely chopped	1
½	small onion, coarsely chopped	½
1½ cups	GF vegetable stock	375 mL
½ cup	quinoa	125 mL
1 tsp	dried basil	5 mL
	Salt and freshly ground black pepper	
1	red bell pepper, cut into ½-inch (1 cm) cubes	1
1	orange bell pepper, cut into ½-inch (1 cm) cubes	1
2	green onions, green tops only, chopped	2

1. In a large saucepan, heat olive oil over medium-low heat. Add celery, carrot and onion and cook, stirring frequently, for about 8 to 10 minutes, or until tender. Add stock, quinoa and basil and bring to a boil.

2. Reduce heat to low. Cover and simmer for 18 to 20 minutes, or until water is absorbed and quinoa is tender. Season to taste with salt and pepper. Stir in red and orange peppers and green onion. Let stand, covered, for 2 to 3 minutes.

Variation

Add small broccoli florets with the bell peppers. They add a tender-crisp texture.

Nutritional value per serving	
Calories	93
Fat, total	3 g
Fat, saturated	0 g
Cholesterol	0 mg
Sodium	103 mg
Carbohydrate	15 g
Fiber	3 g
Protein	3 g
Calcium	29 mg
Iron	1 mg

Scalloped Potatoes with a New Twist

An old-fashioned comfort food updated for today. If you can't tolerate dairy products, it's a bonus.

Tips

Use the slicing blade of a food processor to slice potatoes thinly.

Dark green leaves of celery are most flavorful.

If the gluten-free chicken stock powder is unsalted, season with salt to taste.

- Preheat oven to 350°F (180°C)
- 10-cup (2.5 L) casserole

1	medium onion, diced	1
½ cup	celery leaves	125 mL
3 tbsp	butter or margarine	45 mL
2 tbsp	potato starch	25 mL
2 tbsp	GF chicken stock powder	25 mL
3 to 4 cups	water	750 mL to 1 L
¼ tsp	freshly ground black pepper	1 mL
2 lbs	potatoes, thinly sliced	1 kg

1. In a food processor, combine onion, celery leaves, butter, potato starch, chicken stock powder, 3 cups (750 mL) water and ground pepper until combined. Set aside.
2. In casserole, spread potatoes evenly. Pour sauce over top. If necessary, add extra water so potatoes are almost covered. The amount depends on the size and shape of the casserole.
3. Bake, uncovered, in preheated oven for 75 to 90 minutes or until potatoes are fork-tender.

Variation

For a potluck dish, double or triple the recipe and use a 20- to 30-cup (5 to 7.5 L) casserole and increase the baking time by 15 to 30 minutes or until fork-tender.

Nutritional value per serving	
Calories	190
Fat, total	6 g
Fat, saturated	3 g
Cholesterol	8 mg
Sodium	81 mg
Carbohydrate	32 g
Fiber	5 g
Protein	3 g
Calcium	28 mg
Iron	1 mg

Seafood Lasagna

Makes 8 servings

This is another example of a dish adopted by North Americans that has become a staple of our diet — enjoy our seafood version.

Tips

Use any combination of your favorite seafood — scallops, shrimp, whitefish, crab, lobster, clams or oysters.

A 6-oz (175 g) package of baby spinach contains approximately 3 cups (750 mL).

Purchase 7 oz (200 g) shredded mozzarella cheese.

Freeze leftover lasagna in individual amounts. Thaw and reheat in the microwave.

Nutritional value per serving	
Calories	447
Fat, total	12 g
Fat, saturated	7 g
Cholesterol	246 mg
Sodium	1616 mg
Carbohydrate	40 g
Fiber	3 g
Protein	40 g
Calcium	455 mg
Iron	3 mg

- **Preheat oven to 350°F (180°C)**
- **13- by 9-inch (3 L) baking pan**

9	GF rice lasagna noodles	9
2 tsp	extra virgin olive oil	10 mL
1	red or yellow bell pepper, diced	1
1	medium onion, diced	1
1	jar (25 oz/700 mL) GF pasta sauce	1
2 tbsp	dry white wine (optional)	25 mL
1½ lbs	cooked seafood	750 g
1 cup	cottage cheese	250 mL
1	egg, slightly beaten	1
6 oz	baby spinach, washed and dried	175 g
2 cups	shredded mozzarella cheese	500 mL
½ cup	freshly grated Parmesan cheese	125 mL

1. In a large pot of gently boiling water, cook lasagna noodles according to package directions. Drain, rinse well with cold water, then set aside.

2. In a saucepan, heat oil over medium-high heat. Add bell pepper and onion. Sauté until tender. Add pasta sauce and simmer for 5 to 10 minutes or until hot and bubbly. Add wine, if using, then set aside.

3. In a small bowl, combine cottage cheese and egg.

4. To assemble, spread a thin layer of pasta sauce mixture in baking pan. Top with 3 lasagna noodles. Cover with one-third of remaining pasta sauce, half the spinach, half the cottage cheese mixture, half the seafood and sprinkle with half the mozzarella cheese.

5. Cover with 3 lasagna noodles and repeat layering with half the remaining pasta sauce, the remaining spinach, cottage cheese mixture, seafood and mozzarella cheese. Cover with the remaining lasagna noodles, pasta sauce and Parmesan cheese.

6. Bake in preheated oven for 40 to 50 minutes or until bubbly and cheese is golden brown. Let stand 10 to 15 minutes before serving.

Variation

Use 1 lb (500 g) ground beef or chicken instead of the seafood. Cook the meat before sautéeing the vegetables.

Spinach Risotto

Packed with fresh vegetables, our variation of risotto — a northern Italian rice dish — is creamy, yet a light and easy-to-prepare side dish.

Tips

The large quantity of spinach might look like too much, but it wilts down to the correct amount for this recipe.

Serve immediately to keep the creamy texture.

For a creamier, more traditional risotto, increase the amount of liquid and add more as it becomes absorbed. Stir constantly while rice is cooking.

2 tsp	extra-virgin olive oil	10 mL
2	cloves garlic, minced	2
2	celery stalks, chopped	2
1	medium onion, chopped	1
1	carrot, diced	1
1 cup	Arborio rice	250 mL
1½ cups	GF chicken stock	375 mL
½ cup	dry white wine	125 mL
10 oz	baby spinach	300 g
1	small zucchini, chopped	1
¼ cup	freshly grated Parmesan cheese	50 mL
	Salt, pepper and dried dillweed or grated nutmeg	

1. In a large saucepan, heat olive oil over medium heat. Add garlic, celery, onion, carrot and rice. Cook, stirring, for 5 to 7 minutes, or until vegetables are softened. Stir in stock and wine and bring to a boil over high heat.

2. Reduce heat to medium-low and simmer, covered, for 20 minutes, or until all liquid is absorbed. Stir in spinach, zucchini and Parmesan. Season to taste with salt, pepper and dill or nutmeg. Heat, covered, for 2 minutes or until spinach is wilted.

Variations

Substitute milk for the GF chicken stock or for both the GF stock and wine.

Substitute a carnaroli or any short-grain rice for the Arborio rice.

Nutritional value per serving	
Calories	200
Fat, total	4 g
Fat, saturated	1 g
Cholesterol	5 mg
Sodium	385 mg
Carbohydrate	34 g
Fiber	4 g
Protein	7 g
Calcium	117 mg
Iron	2 mg

Sesame Thai Beef

Makes 4 servings

We first tasted this dish in a restaurant in Toronto. Joyce Parslow of the Canadian Beef Information Centre was kind enough to provide us with a recipe, which we have adapted for you. This is the perfect dish for a dinner party at which everyone contributes to the preparation of the meal.

Tip

You can use either a mandoline with the julienne $1/16$- to $1/4$-inch (2 to 5 mm) blade or a sharp knife to cut vegetables into matchstick-size pieces. This means sliced paper-thin, as the only cooking is from the hot stock in individual bowls.

Nutritional value per serving

Calories	643
Fat, total	28 g
Fat, saturated	4 g
Cholesterol	74 mg
Sodium	522 mg
Carbohydrate	52 g
Fiber	4 g
Protein	34 g
Calcium	99 mg
Iron	4 mg

Sesame Marinade

¼ cup	minced green onions	50 mL
¼ cup	vegetable oil	50 mL
¼ cup	dry sherry	50 mL
2 tbsp	toasted sesame seeds	25 mL
2 tbsp	sesame oil	25 mL
1 tbsp	minced gingerroot	15 mL
1 tbsp	GF soy sauce	15 mL
1 tbsp	minced garlic	15 mL
1½ tsp	sambal oelek	7 mL
1 lb	boneless beef strip loin (top loin) grilling steak, sliced into ⅛-inch (3 mm) strips	500 g

Noodle Bowl

5 cups	water	1.25 L
½ cup	sliced onions	125 mL
2 tbsp	GF chicken or vegetable stock powder	25 mL
2 tbsp	reserved sesame marinade	25 mL
1½ tsp	thinly sliced gingerroot	7 mL
1½ tsp	thinly sliced garlic	7 mL
7 oz	GF rice vermicelli or rice sticks, cooked	200 g
2 cups	shredded bok choy	500 mL
1½ cups	julienned red bell peppers	375 mL
1 cup	julienned carrots	250 mL
¾ cup	julienned green onions	175 mL
2 tbsp	snipped fresh cilantro	25 mL

1. *Prepare the sesame marinade:* In a resealable plastic freezer bag set in a bowl, combine green onions, vegetable oil, sherry, sesame seeds, sesame oil, gingerroot, soy sauce, garlic and sambal oelek. Set aside 2 tbsp (25 mL) of the marinade for the noodle bowl.

2. Add beef strips to remaining marinade, seal bag and refrigerate for at least 6 hours or overnight.

Tips

To make slicing easier, place the beef steak in the freezer until it's almost firm. For thin slices, be sure knife is sharp and slice across the grain.

Always discard leftover mixtures used for marinating raw meats, fish and poultry.

To learn more about sambal oelek, see Ingredient Glossary, page 366. It can be found in the Asian section of large chain grocery stores or at Asian grocers and Dutch delicatessens.

Use an equal amount of hot pepper flakes if sambal oelek is not available.

Try a flank steak instead of the strip loin steak.

Substitute unsweetened apple juice or water for the sherry.

Substitute 5 cups (1.25 L) homemade or commercial GF chicken or vegetable stock for the stock powder and water.

3. *Prepare the noodle bowl:* In a large saucepan, over high heat, combine water, onions, stock powder, reserved marinade, gingerroot and garlic and bring to a boil. Reduce heat and simmer for 5 minutes. Add noodles and boil for 1 minute, until hot. Drain, reserving stock mixture. Return stock to a boil and continue to gently simmer. Set noodles in a strainer over simmering stock to keep warm.

4. Heat a large nonstick skillet or wok over high heat until very hot. Drain beef strips from marinade, discarding marinade, and add to skillet. Cook, in batches, as necessary, for 1 minute on each side.

5. *To serve:* Divide bok choy, red peppers, carrots, green onions, noodles and beef among 4 large soup or pasta bowls. Pour 1 cup (250 mL) reserved boiling stock mixture over each. Garnish with cilantro.

Tempura

Today, we think of tempura to describe a light, crispy batter. Perfect for vegetables as well as seafood.

Tips

Don't omit the cayenne pepper — it helps the batter to brown.

If the cayenne is too hot for your taste buds, you can also use paprika (see Variations, below).

- **Preheat oil in deep fryer or wok to 350°F (180°C)**

1 cup	potato starch	250 mL
2 tsp	GF baking powder	10 mL
1/2 tsp	salt	2 mL
1/8 tsp	cayenne pepper	0.5 mL
3/4 cup	milk	175 mL
1 tbsp	vegetable oil	15 mL
1	egg	1
1/2 cup	sweet rice flour	125 mL
	Vegetable oil for frying	
1 lb	large shrimp, peeled and deveined	500 g
1 lb	large scallops	500 g
1	sweet potato, cut into 1/8-inch (0.25 cm) slices	1
2	small zucchini, cut into 1/4-inch (0.5 cm) slices	2
4 oz	button mushrooms	125 g
4	green onions, cut into 1-inch (2.5 cm) pieces	4

1. In a large bowl or plastic bag, combine potato starch, baking powder, salt and cayenne pepper. Mix well and set aside.

2. In a separate bowl, using an electric mixer, combine the milk, oil and egg. With the mixer on the lowest speed, slowly add the dry ingredients until combined. With a rubber spatula, scrape the bottom and sides of the bowl.

3. Dredge seafood and vegetables in sweet rice flour. Dip a few pieces at a time into prepared batter to generously coat.

4. Deep-fry until golden. Drain on paper towels. Serve immediately.

Variations

Substitute 1/4 tsp (1 mL) paprika for the cayenne pepper. Paprika also helps the batter to brown as it cooks.

Use whitefish fillets and any vegetable combination.

Nutritional value per serving	
Calories	331
Fat, total	5 g
Fat, saturated	1 g
Cholesterol	154 mg
Sodium	1034 mg
Carbohydrate	46 g
Fiber	1 g
Protein	25 g
Calcium	174 mg
Iron	1 mg

Ten-Minute Pasta Dinner

In a hurry again? Want to make dinner without stopping at a grocery store on the way home from work? Chances are you have every ingredient you need to make this in the cupboard and freezer.

Tips

Shrimp become rubbery when overcooked. They are cooked when they curl, turn pink and are firm to the touch.

Select from the many varieties of mixed frozen vegetables on the market today — Japanese Mix, California Combo, Asian or Thai Stir-Fry, Mexican- or Spanish-style or an Orleans mix.

Nutritional value per serving	
Calories	373
Fat, total	1 g
Fat, saturated	0 g
Cholesterol	107 mg
Sodium	932 mg
Carbohydrate	64 g
Fiber	5 g
Protein	20 g
Calcium	120 mg
Iron	3 mg

1½ cups	GF pasta	375 mL
4 cups	mixed frozen vegetables	1 L
12 oz	frozen raw extra-large or jumbo shrimp, thawed	340 g
1	can (28 oz/796 mL) GF diced tomatoes with herbs and spices	1
2 tsp	dried basil	10 mL
	Freshly grated Parmesan cheese	

1. In a large saucepan of boiling water, cook pasta according to package directions, or until just tender. Drain well and rinse in cold water. Set aside.

2. In a separate saucepan, cook frozen vegetables according to package directions. Add shrimp for the last 2 minutes, until shrimp turn pink.

3. Meanwhile, add tomatoes and basil to empty pasta saucepan and heat over medium-high heat until bubbling. Add cooked pasta and vegetable mixture and heat just until steaming.

4. Ladle into a serving bowl and sprinkle with Parmesan cheese.

Variations

Substitute 2 cups (500 mL) cooked chicken or ham, cut into cubes or strips, for the shrimp. Add during the last 2 minutes.

Substitute mussels for shrimp and steam until they open, about 5 to 8 minutes. Discard any mussels that do not open.

For a richer, thicker sauce, substitute a 23-oz (680 mL) can of GF Roasted Garlic and Herb Pasta Sauce for the tomatoes.

Turkey Meat Loaf

Makes 6 servings

Quick, easy and always popular, this meat loaf is great served with boiled new potatoes and fresh green beans.

Tip

For a conventional meat loaf, top with Mustard Sauce, then bake in an ungreased 9- by 5-inch (2 L) loaf pan in a 350°F (180°C) oven for 35 to 45 minutes.

- **Microwave-safe 9-inch (23 cm) ring mold, ungreased**

1½ lbs	extra lean ground turkey	750 g
½ cup	tomato sauce	125 mL
⅓ cup	soft GF bread crumbs (see Techniques Glossary, page 368)	75 mL
¼ cup	rice bran	50 mL
¼ cup	finely chopped onion	50 mL
1	egg, lightly beaten	1
½ tsp	salt	2 mL
¼ tsp	freshly ground black pepper	1 mL
	Mustard Sauce (see recipe, opposite)	

1. In a bowl, gently mix together turkey, tomato sauce, bread crumbs, rice bran, onion, egg, salt and pepper.
2. Spoon into mold and cover with waxed paper. Microwave on High for 10 minutes or until partially set. Drain.
3. Spoon Mustard Sauce over meat loaf. Microwave on High for 2 to 3 minutes or until meat thermometer registers 175°F (80°C).
4. Let stand covered with foil for 5 minutes before serving.

Variation

Substitute ground beef, veal, chicken or a combination for the ground turkey.

Nutritional value per serving	
Calories	223
Fat, total	4 g
Fat, saturated	1 g
Cholesterol	77 mg
Sodium	513 mg
Carbohydrate	15 g
Fiber	2 g
Protein	34 g
Calcium	14 mg
Iron	3 mg

Mustard Sauce

Cousin George loves to serve this slightly tangy sauce to complement meatballs, pork chops and veal.

½ cup	tomato sauce	125 mL
2 tbsp	packed brown sugar	25 mL
2 tbsp	freshly squeezed lemon juice	25 mL
1 tbsp	prepared mustard	15 mL

1. In a small bowl, combine tomato sauce, brown sugar, lemon juice and mustard.

Nutritional value per 2 tbsp (25 mL) serving	
Calories	29
Fat, total	0 g
Fat, saturated	0 g
Cholesterol	0 mg
Sodium	133 mg
Carbohydrate	7 g
Fiber	0 g
Protein	1 g
Calcium	6 mg
Iron	0 mg

Vegetable Cobbler

A recipe that originated in Romania inspired this drop biscuit-topped vegetable casserole. Although not a cobbler in the traditional sense, it is every bit as comforting.

Tips

To help preserve the vegetables' bright color, don't lift the lid while they are cooking.

Have the cobbler topping ready to drop on the vegetables as soon as they are cooked.

Be sure not to overcook the vegetables in Step 3. They will continue to cook as the biscuits bake.

Nutritional value per serving	
Calories	272
Fat, total	14 g
Fat, saturated	4 g
Cholesterol	9 mg
Sodium	673 mg
Carbohydrate	31 g
Fiber	6 g
Protein	7 g
Calcium	157 mg
Iron	2 mg

- **Preheat oven to 350°F (180°C)**
- **Deep 12-cup (3 L) covered casserole**

1½ cups	winter squash, peeled and cut into 1-inch (2.5 cm) cubes	375 mL
1 cup	green beans, cut into 1½-inch (4 cm) pieces	250 mL
2	medium carrots, cut into ½-inch (1 cm) thick slices	2
1	stalk celery, cut into ½-inch (1 cm) thick slices	1
½	large red bell pepper, cut into ¾-inch (2 cm) strips	½
1	medium zucchini, cut into ½-inch (1 cm) pieces	1
3	cloves garlic, minced	3
1	bay leaf	1
½ cup	GF chicken, beef or vegetable stock	125 mL
½ cup	water	125 mL
2 tbsp	extra virgin olive oil	25 mL
1 tsp	salt	5 mL
1 tsp	dried tarragon leaves	5 mL
2	medium tomatoes, quartered	2
	Cobbler Biscuit (see recipe, opposite)	

1. In casserole dish, mix together squash, beans, carrots, celery, bell pepper, zucchini, garlic and bay leaf. Set aside.
2. In a small bowl, combine stock, water, oil, salt and tarragon. Microwave on High for 2 to 4 minutes or heat in saucepan over medium heat until hot and bubbly. Pour stock mixture over vegetables.
3. Bake, covered, in preheated oven for 30 to 40 minutes or until vegetables are slightly crisp. Do not overcook. Meanwhile, prepare the Cobbler Biscuit.

Variations

Choose other vegetables you like such as parsnips, turnip, sweet potatoes, cauliflower, broccoli, eggplant and cabbage. Soft vegetables should be left in larger pieces so they cook in the same time as the harder vegetables.

Substitute fresh or dry herbs for the tarragon.

Tip

See Biscuits and Cobblers, page 157.

Cobbler Biscuit

1 cup	whole bean flour	250 mL
¼ cup	tapioca starch	50 mL
1 tbsp	granulated sugar	15 mL
1 tsp	xanthan gum	5 mL
1½ tsp	GF baking powder	7 mL
½ tsp	baking soda	2 mL
¼ tsp	salt	1 mL
¼ cup	shortening	50 mL
1 cup	buttermilk	250 mL

1. In a large bowl, stir together whole bean flour, tapioca starch, sugar, xanthan gum, baking powder, baking soda and salt.

2. Using a pastry blender or two knives, cut in shortening until mixture resembles coarse crumbs. Add buttermilk all at once, stirring with a fork to make very sticky dough. Let stand for up to 30 minutes.

3. Remove vegetables from oven. Quickly stir the tomatoes into the casserole. Drop prepared biscuit topping, by heaping tablespoonfuls (15 mL), onto hot bubbly vegetable mixture.

4. Increase oven temperature to 425°F (220°C). Bake for 15 to 20 minutes or until biscuits are browned. Serve immediately.

Nutritional value per serving

Calories	185
Fat, total	9 g
Fat, saturated	4 g
Cholesterol	9 mg
Sodium	252 mg
Carbohydrate	22 g
Fiber	4 g
Protein	6 g
Calcium	123 mg
Iron	1 mg

Eating Out
Restaurants, Weddings and Banquets

- When planning to dine out, call the restaurant ahead, if possible, to find out whether it offers gluten-free entrées. If the staff seem hesitant with their answers, choose a different restaurant.
- Choose restaurants that specialize in seafood, Mexican, Indian and Thai foods. These may be cooked to order — broiling, stir-frying or steaming individual portions.
- Establish a rapport with two or three local restaurants. It is great to know that your foods will be prepared safely, without you having to talk with the server and kitchen staff every time you want to eat out.
- Speak with the chef or person in charge of the food preparation. Most people pay attention to and understand the word "allergic" rather than "intolerance." Explain the consequences of eating just a small amount of gluten. A good example could be that even eating from a plate from which a bun that contained gluten was removed, may cause a reaction that lasts for weeks.
- Ask the server to check whether or not the fries are cooked in the same oil as the chicken fingers or other batter-fried foods.
- Carry a restaurant allergy identification card to present to the server and kitchen staff. You can make your own and laminate it. Make several, as they are easy to misplace or leave behind.
- Wear a MedicAlert bracelet at all times. It is often easier to point to the bracelet when asking for special consideration in a restaurant than to explain why you have brought some of your own food with you.
- For a special occasion celebration, call ahead to inquire about the menu and its suitability for your diet. Make suggestions of ways that they can accommodate you easily. It may mean something as simple as serving you the greens undressed and you bringing your own gluten-free salad dressing. Fresh fruit is always a good dessert.

Holiday Fare

Traveling with a Gluten Intolerance

- Take extra time to plan any trips, so that they will be more enjoyable and free from stress and worry. When making flight reservations, inform the travel agent of your gluten intolerance. If a meal is to be provided during the flight, advise the agent of your gluten-free dietary needs.
- Pack your own gluten-free bread, cookies or muffins when you travel. Take along your own condiments in your carry-on baggage so they arrive with you. There are lots of ways to do this conveniently. For instance, pack in hard-sided containers that won't be crushed in your luggage or carry-on baggage. Use stackable containers then, when empty, stack them inside each other for compact carrying on the trip home. Your onboard lunch can be packed in a small, collapsible insulated cooler tucked in a corner of your carry-on bag.
- Carry extra baked goods, wrapped in individual servings in airtight containers, in your suitcase.
- Take along fresh fruit and vegetables for snacks during the flight. Include cubes of cheese and gluten-free crackers as the protein and fat take longer to digest and help with hunger during short delays when no other food may be available.
- Before traveling, bake breads or quick breads in two smaller pans $4^1/_2$- by $2^1/_2$-inches (250 mL) or $5^3/_4$- by $3^1/_4$-inches (500 mL). Bake for 30 to 45 minutes or until done. The smaller-size loaves are more convenient to carry.
- A letter from your doctor explaining your special diet and your need to carry your own food may help avoid problems that stem from carrying food across international borders. Arrive early at the airport and be prepared for a long wait that your special diet may cause.
- Carry a restaurant allergy identification card to present to your server and kitchen staff. You can make your own and laminate it. It is a good idea to make several at the same time as they are easy to lose. When traveling to countries where English is not the first language, have the card translated before you go.
- Hotels may store foods in their freezer for you or you could request a room with a small refrigerator with freezer compartment. Call ahead to make arrangements.

Lemon Garlic Chicken

Plan a Greek menu for Easter or any other special occasion. Start with Lemon Garlic Chicken or Souvlaki (see recipe, page 139) with Tzatziki Sauce (see recipe, page 140) and serve with Lemon Jasmine Rice Pilaf (see recipe, page 138) and fresh steamed vegetables.

Tips

Chicken can be marinated at room temperature for up to 30 minutes if you are short of time. Any longer, make sure it is refrigerated. Throw out the plastic bag used for marinating.

Can't find the cover that fits your casserole? Cover it with aluminum foil, dull side out. Trace around the rim with your fingers to be sure foil forms a tight seal.

Nutritional value per serving

Calories	170
Fat, total	7 g
Fat, saturated	1 g
Cholesterol	76 mg
Sodium	283 mg
Carbohydrate	1 g
Fiber	0 g
Protein	25 g
Calcium	13 mg
Iron	1 mg

- **8-cup (2 L) covered casserole dish**

1	clove garlic, minced	1
2 tbsp	freshly squeezed lemon juice	25 mL
1 tbsp	extra-virgin olive oil	15 mL
1 tsp	dried thyme	5 mL
¼ tsp	salt	1 mL
Pinch	ground nutmeg	Pinch
Pinch	paprika	Pinch
Pinch	freshly ground white pepper	Pinch
4	skinless boneless chicken breasts	4

1. In a resealable plastic freezer bag set in a bowl, combine garlic, lemon juice, olive oil, thyme, salt, nutmeg, paprika and white pepper. Add chicken breasts to marinade, seal bag and refrigerate for 1 hour.

2. Preheat oven to 375°F (190°C). Place chicken breasts with marinade in the casserole dish, and cover tightly. Bake for 45 minutes, or until juices run clear and meat thermometer registers 170°F (78°C).

Variations

Rather than baking the chicken, barbecue or grill it for 5 to 8 minutes per side.

Substitute an equal amount of oregano for the thyme. Or use 1 tbsp (15 mL) snipped fresh thyme or oregano.

Lemon Jasmine Rice Pilaf

Makes 4 servings

We are always disappointed when we are served a rice pilaf with only an occasional fleck of vegetable. You don't have to dig for the vegetables in this one, which we like to serve with Lemon Garlic Chicken (see recipe, page 137).

Tips

A pilaf involves frying the rice (or any other grain) in seasonings and herbs to enhance the flavor before cooking liquid is added.

2 to 3 medium-size leeks yield 4 cups (1 L) sliced.

Substitute Vidalia onions for the leeks and GF vegetable stock powder for the chicken stock powder.

Nutritional value per serving	
Calories	270
Fat, total	4 g
Fat, saturated	1 g
Cholesterol	1 mg
Sodium	465 mg
Carbohydrate	54 g
Fiber	4 g
Protein	5 g
Calcium	96 mg
Iron	3 mg

1 tbsp	extra-virgin olive oil	15 mL
4 cups	sliced leeks, white and light green parts only	1 L
1 cup	diced carrots	250 mL
1 tsp	dried oregano	5 mL
1 cup	jasmine rice	250 mL
2 cups	water	500 mL
1 tbsp	GF chicken stock powder	15 mL
2 tbsp	grated lemon zest	25 mL
2 tbsp	freshly squeezed lemon juice	25 mL
	Salt and freshly ground white pepper	

1. In a heavy saucepan, heat oil over medium-high heat. Cook leeks, carrots and oregano, stirring occasionally, for 5 to 8 minutes, or until softened. Add rice and cook for 1 minute, stirring constantly.

Stove-Top Method

2. Add water and stock powder and bring to a boil. Reduce heat to low, cover and simmer for 15 minutes, or until rice is tender. Remove saucepan from heat and let stand, covered, for 3 to 5 minutes. Stir in lemon zest and juice and season to taste with salt and pepper. Fluff with a fork.

Microwave Method

2. Transfer rice mixture to a 2 to 3 quart (2 to 3 L) microwaveable casserole dish. Add water and stock powder. Cover and cook on High for 5 minutes, or until boiling. Cook, covered, on Medium (50%), for 15 minutes until liquid is absorbed and rice is tender. Let stand, covered, for 3 to 5 minutes. Stir in lemon zest and juice and season to taste with salt and pepper. Fluff with a fork.

Variation

Substitute brown, basmati or wild rice, or a combination, for the jasmine rice.

Souvlaki

Everybody loves this traditional Greek dish of marinated lamb chunks cooked on a skewer.

Tips

If desired, prepare the marinade, add the lamb and freeze for up to 1 month. Defrost in the refrigerator for at least 24 hours before cooking.

For faster, more even cooking, leave a space between the meat cubes when threading on the wooden skewers.

Serve over rice or wrapped in 10-inch (25 cm) GF corn tortillas.

- Barbecue, grill or broiler, preheated
- 12-inch (30 cm) wooden skewers

1	clove garlic, coarsely chopped	1
⅓ cup	freshly squeezed lemon juice	75 mL
2 tbsp	extra-virgin olive oil	25 mL
1 tbsp	dried oregano	15 mL
1 tbsp	chopped fresh rosemary	15 mL
¼ tsp	freshly ground black pepper	1 mL
1½ lb	boneless shoulder or leg of lamb, trimmed and cut into 1-inch (2.5 cm) cubes	750 g

1. In a resealable plastic freezer bag set in a bowl, combine garlic, lemon juice, olive oil, oregano, rosemary and pepper. Add lamb to marinade, seal bag and refrigerate for at least 4 hours or overnight.

2. Meanwhile, soak wooden skewers in water for 30 minutes. Thread lamb cubes evenly on skewers. Barbecue, turning frequently, for 8 to 10 minutes, or until medium-rare or desired doneness.

Variations

Substitute pork tenderloin or chicken breast for the lamb.

If you're in a hurry, drain marinade and place cubes in an 8-inch (2 L) square baking pan. Bake in a 350°F (180°C) oven for 30 minutes, or until meat is tender.

Alternate green pepper and onions with the meat on the skewer before grilling.

Nutritional value per serving	
Calories	450
Fat, total	33 g
Fat, saturated	12 g
Cholesterol	135 mg
Sodium	110 mg
Carbohydrate	2 g
Fiber	1 g
Protein	35 g
Calcium	42 mg
Iron	3 mg

Tzatziki Sauce

Serve this traditional sauce with souvlaki, or use as a dip with crudités or crackers.

Tips

No need to peel the English cucumber.

Drain the feta well before breaking it into chunks, or purchase crumbled feta.

Let yogurt drain overnight for a thicker sauce.

1½ cups	plain yogurt	375 mL
¼	English cucumber, grated	¼
3	cloves garlic, minced	3
4 oz	feta cheese, broken into chunks (about ¾ cup/175 mL)	125 g
2 tbsp	freshly squeezed lemon juice	25 mL

1. To a strainer lined with damp cheesecloth set inside a bowl, add yogurt. Refrigerate and let drain for 3 to 4 hours, or until reduced by half.

2. To a separate strainer lined with damp cheesecloth set inside a bowl, add grated cucumber. Refrigerate and let drain for 3 to 4 hours or overnight.

3. In a small bowl, combine drained yogurt, drained cucumber, garlic, feta cheese and lemon juice. Refrigerate, covered, for up to 3 days.

Variation

Have extra zucchini and dill in your garden? Substitute zucchini for the cucumber and add 1 tbsp (25 mL) chopped fresh dill.

Nutritional value per 2 tbsp (25 mL) serving	
Calories	38
Fat, total	2 g
Fat, saturated	1 g
Cholesterol	6 mg
Sodium	98 mg
Carbohydrate	3 g
Fiber	0 g
Protein	3 g
Calcium	77 mg
Iron	0 mg

Summery Yogurt Sauce

**Makes
1½ cups (375 mL)**

Here is a somewhat
different sauce to serve
with souvlaki. It can be
made in less time than it
takes the meat to cook.

Tip

*Use both the green and
the white parts of the
green onions.*

1½ cups	plain yogurt	375 mL
⅓ cup	diced green onions	75 mL
¼ cup	snipped fresh parsley	50 mL
1	tomato, seeded and diced	1

1. In a small bowl, combine yogurt, green onion, parsley
and tomato. Refrigerate, covered, for at least 30 minutes,
or until ready to serve. Store in the refrigerator for up to
1 week.

Variation

For a thicker sauce, put yogurt in a strainer lined with
damp cheesecloth set inside a bowl, and let it drain
overnight in the refrigerator.

Nutritional value per 2 tbsp (25 mL) serving	
Calories	19
Fat, total	0 g
Fat, saturated	0 g
Cholesterol	2 mg
Sodium	19 mg
Carbohydrate	2 g
Fiber	0 g
Protein	1 g
Calcium	49 mg
Iron	0 mg

Hot Cross Buns

Before its significance for Christians, the cross symbolized the four quarters of the lunar cycle. So ancient Aztecs, Egyptians and Saxons all enjoyed hot cross buns. They have been served on Easter since the early days of the Church.

Tips

In Canada, check for gluten-free confectioner's (icing) sugar. It may contain up to 5% starch, which could be from wheat.

Use a pastry bag and tip to pipe on the icing.

To ensure success, check out the extra information on baking yeast breads on pages 199 and 228.

Nutritional value per serving (1 bun)

Calories	241
Fat, total	5 g
Fat, saturated	1 g
Cholesterol	34 mg
Sodium	262 mg
Carbohydrate	45 g
Fiber	4 g
Protein	6 g
Calcium	49 mg
Iron	2 mg

● **Baking sheet, lightly greased**

¾ cup	sorghum flour	175 mL
½ cup	whole bean flour	125 mL
⅓ cup	potato starch	75 mL
¼ cup	tapioca starch	50 mL
1 tbsp	xanthan gum	15 mL
2 tsp	bread machine or instant yeast	10 mL
1 tsp	salt	5 mL
1¼ tsp	ground cinnamon	6 mL
¼ tsp	ground cloves	1 mL
¼ tsp	ground nutmeg	1 mL
¾ cup	milk	175 mL
⅓ cup	liquid honey	75 mL
2 tbsp	vegetable oil	25 mL
1 tbsp	fancy molasses	15 mL
1 tsp	cider vinegar	5 mL
2	eggs	2
1 cup	raisins	250 mL

Icing

¾ cup	GF sifted confectioner's (icing) sugar	175 mL
1 tbsp	milk	15 mL
¼ tsp	almond extract	1 mL

Bread Machine Method

1. In a large bowl or plastic bag, combine sorghum flour, whole bean flour, potato starch, tapioca starch, xanthan gum, yeast, salt, cinnamon, cloves and nutmeg. Mix well and set aside.

2. Pour milk, honey, oil, molasses and vinegar into the bread machine baking pan. Add eggs.

3. Select the Dough Cycle. Allow the liquids to mix until combined. Gradually add the dry ingredients as the bread machine is mixing, scraping sides with a rubber spatula. Incorporate all the dry ingredients within 1 to 2 minutes. Add raisins. Allow the bread machine to complete the cycle.

Tips

Replace the milk in the icing with thawed frozen orange juice concentrate.

To make these lactose-free, replace the milk with water in both the buns and the icing.

Mixer Method

1. In a large bowl or plastic bag, combine sorghum flour, whole bean flour, potato starch, tapioca starch, xanthan gum, yeast, salt, cinnamon, cloves and nutmeg. Mix well and set aside.

2. In a separate bowl, using a heavy-duty electric mixer with paddle attachment, combine milk, oil, vinegar and eggs until well blended. Add honey and molasses while mixing.

3. With the mixer on its lowest speed, slowly add the dry ingredients until combined. With a rubber spatula, scrape the bottom and sides of the bowl. With the mixer on medium speed, beat for 4 minutes. Stir in raisins.

For Both Methods

4. Drop batter by heaping spoonfuls onto prepared baking sheet. Using the handle of a wooden spoon or a rubber spatula, make two indents $1/8$ inch (3 cm) deep in the shape of a cross on the top of each bun. Let rise, uncovered, in a warm, draft-free place for 60 to 75 minutes, or until the buns have almost doubled in volume. Meanwhile, preheat oven to 350°F (180°C).

5. Bake for 20 to 25 minutes, or until buns are golden brown. Remove to a cooling rack immediately.

6. *Prepare the icing:* In a small bowl, combine confectioner's sugar, milk and almond extract. Drizzle the crosses of warm buns with icing.

Variation

To prepare California-style buns, add mixed candied peel and dates.

Cornish Game Hens with Cranberry and Wild Rice Stuffing

Susan Hodges, a listserv member, told us about her holiday tradition of serving a "personal turkey" (a.k.a. a Rock Cornish game hen) to her celiac daughter. Here is a stuffing you can use with either "personal" or "family" turkeys.

Tip

Use either a homemade GF chicken stock or a commercial GF chicken stock powder.

Nutritional value per serving*	
Calories	571
Fat, total	14 g
Fat, saturated	4 g
Cholesterol	220 mg
Sodium	357 mg
Carbohydrate	53 g
Fiber	4 g
Protein	56 g
Calcium	72 mg
Iron	3 mg

* does not include Plum Dipping Sauce

● **Roasting pan**

4 cups	GF chicken stock	1 L
¾ cup	brown rice	175 mL
½ cup	wild rice, rinsed	125 mL
1 tbsp	crumbled dried sage	15 mL
1 tbsp	crumbled dried thyme	15 mL
1 tbsp	butter	15 mL
1 tbsp	vegetable oil	15 mL
1	large onion, chopped	1
1 cup	sliced cremini mushroom caps (halved then sliced into ¼-inch/0.5 cm pieces)	250 mL
1 cup	diced celery	250 mL
1 cup	diced carrots	250 mL
¼ tsp	salt	1 mL
¼ tsp	freshly ground black pepper	1 mL
1 cup	dried cranberries	250 mL
2 tbsp	balsamic vinegar	25 mL
4 to 6	Cornish game hens (each about 1 to 1¼ lb/500 to 625 g)	4 to 6
	Plum Dipping Sauce (see recipe, page 58)	

1. In a large saucepan, over high heat, combine chicken stock, brown rice, wild rice, sage and thyme and bring to a boil. Reduce heat, cover and simmer gently for 45 to 55 minutes, or until rice is tender. Remove from heat and fluff with a fork. Set aside to cool completely.

Tips

When purchasing dried sage or thyme, use dried leaves and avoid the powdered variety.

This recipe makes enough stuffing for a 10-lb (4.5 kg) turkey or for 4 to 6 Cornish game hens.

To roast an unstuffed Cornish game hen: Roast uncovered, breast side up, in a preheated 425°F (220°C) oven for 45 minutes. Cut in half before serving.

To bake stuffing outside the hens: Place stuffing in a 3-quart (3 L) casserole dish and stir in ¹/₂ cup (125 mL) GF chicken stock. Cover and bake beside the hens.

2. In a skillet, heat butter and oil over medium-high heat. Add onion, mushrooms, celery, carrots, salt and pepper and cook, stirring constantly, until tender, about 8 to 10 minutes. Stir in dried cranberries and balsamic vinegar.

3. Add vegetable mixture to rice mixture and stir gently to combine. Loosely stuff into the game hens and place them breast side up in roasting pan.

4. Preheat oven to 350°F (180°C). Roast hens, uncovered, for 45 to 60 minutes, or until meat thermometer inserted in thigh registers 180°F (82°C). Remove the stuffing immediately.

5. Serve with Plum Dipping Sauce.

Poultry Stuffing Bread
(Bread Machine Method)

Makes 1 loaf
or 12 servings

The flavor of the herbs bakes right into each bite of this loaf. It's perfect to use in stuffing for Cornish game hens or turkey (see Poultry Stuffing, page 148).

Tips

If your machine doesn't have a Gluten-Free Cycle, see Dough Cycle and Bake Cycle, page 198.

To ensure success, see page 199 for extra information on baking yeast bread in a bread machine.

This is an excellent loaf for making croutons and bread crumbs (see page 368).

Nutritional value per serving

Calories	215
Fat, total	8 g
Fat, saturated	1 g
Cholesterol	27 mg
Sodium	306 mg
Carbohydrate	34 g
Fiber	3 g
Protein	4 g
Calcium	45 mg
Iron	2 mg

1½ cups	sorghum flour	375 mL
¾ cup	brown rice flour	175 mL
½ cup	potato starch	125 mL
¼ cup	tapioca starch	50 mL
2 tbsp	granulated sugar	25 mL
1 tbsp	xanthan gum	15 mL
2 tsp	bread machine or instant yeast	10 mL
1½ tsp	salt	7 mL
¼ cup	snipped fresh parsley	50 mL
3 tbsp	minced dried onion	45 mL
3 tbsp	each dried rubbed sage	45 mL
3 tbsp	dried savory	45 mL
1½ tsp	celery seeds	7 mL
1¼ cups	water	300 mL
⅓ cup	vegetable oil	75 mL
1 tsp	cider vinegar	5 mL
2	eggs	2

1. In a large bowl or plastic bag, combine flours, potato and tapioca starches, sugar, xanthan, yeast, salt, parsley, onion, sage, savory and celery seeds. Mix well and set aside.

2. Pour water, oil and vinegar into the bread machine baking pan. Add eggs.

3. Select the Gluten-Free Cycle. Allow the liquids to mix until combined. As the bread machine is mixing, gradually add the dry ingredients, scraping bottom and sides of pan with a rubber spatula. Try to incorporate all the dry ingredients within 1 to 2 minutes. When the mixing and kneading are complete, remove the kneading blade, leaving the bread pan in the bread machine. Quickly smooth the top of the loaf. Allow the cycle to finish.

4. At the end of the cycle, take the temperature of the loaf using an instant-read thermometer. It is baked at 200°F (100°C). If it's between 180°F (82°C) and 200°F (100°C), leave machine on the Keep Warm Cycle until baked. If it's below 180°F (82°C), turn on the Bake Cycle and check the internal temperature every 10 minutes. (Some bread machines are automatically set for 60 minutes; others need to be set by 10-minute intervals.)

Poultry Stuffing Bread
(Mixer Method)

**Makes 1 loaf
or 12 servings**

The flavor of the herbs bakes right into each bite of this loaf. It's perfect to use in stuffing for Cornish game hens or turkey (see Poultry Stuffing, page 148).

Tips

To ensure success, see page 228 for extra information on baking yeast bread using the mixer method.

This is an excellent loaf for making croutons and bread crumbs (see Techniques Glossary, page 368).

Substitute snipped fresh herbs for the dried — you'll need triple the amount.

Nutritional value per serving	
Calories	167
Fat, total	6 g
Fat, saturated	1 g
Cholesterol	27 mg
Sodium	256 mg
Carbohydrate	26 g
Fiber	3 g
Protein	4 g
Calcium	34 mg
Iron	2 mg

● **9- by 5-inch (2 L) loaf pan, lightly greased**

1 1/4 cups	sorghum flour	300 mL
1/2 cup	brown rice flour	125 mL
1/3 cup	potato starch	75 mL
1/3 cup	tapioca starch	75 mL
1 tbsp	granulated sugar	15 mL
2 1/2 tsp	xanthan gum	12 mL
2 tsp	bread machine or instant yeast	10 mL
1 1/4 tsp	salt	7 mL
1/4 cup	snipped fresh parsley	50 mL
2 tbsp	minced dried onion	25 mL
2 tbsp	dried rubbed sage	25 mL
2 tbsp	dried savory	25 mL
1 1/2 tsp	celery seeds	7 mL
2	eggs	2
1 1/4 cups	water	300 mL
1/4 cup	vegetable oil	50 mL
1 tsp	cider vinegar	5 mL

1. In a large bowl or plastic bag, combine sorghum flour, brown rice flour, potato starch, tapioca starch, sugar, xanthan gum, yeast, salt, parsley, dried onion, sage, savory and celery seeds. Mix well and set aside.

2. In a separate bowl, using a heavy-duty electric mixer with paddle attachment, combine eggs, water, oil and vinegar until well blended.

3. With the mixer on its lowest speed, slowly add the dry ingredients until combined. With a rubber spatula, scrape the bottom and sides of the bowl. With the mixer on medium speed, beat for 4 minutes.

4. Spoon into prepared pan, smoothing top. Let rise, uncovered, in a warm, draft-free place for 60 to 75 minutes, or until dough has risen to the top of the pan. Meanwhile, preheat oven to 350°F (180°C).

5. Bake for 30 to 40 minutes, or until loaf sounds hollow when tapped on the bottom. Remove from the pan immediately and let cool completely on a rack.

Poultry Stuffing

Traditional flavor with a modern twist! We introduced the idea of making stuffing that begins with poultry-seasoned bread crumbs when we first started developing bread machine recipes.

Tips

The United States Department of Agriculture (USDA) and Agriculture Canada both recommend baking stuffing separately, not inside the bird.

Allow 1 cup (250 mL) of stuffing for each 1 lb (500 g) raw poultry.

1	loaf Poultry Stuffing Bread (see recipes, pages 146 and 147), torn in chunks	1
2 cups	chopped celery	500 mL
1 cup	chopped onions	250 mL

1. In a food processor fitted with a metal blade, pulse bread into coarse crumbs.

2. In a large bowl, combine crumbs, celery and onions.

Baking Stuffing Outside the Bird

3. Place stuffing in a 4-quart (4 L) casserole dish and stir in $\frac{1}{2}$ cup (125 mL) pan juices or GF chicken stock. Cover and bake beside the bird for the last hour of roasting.

Baking Stuffing Inside the Bird

3. If you do stuff the bird, loosely fill the cavity and immediately put bird in the oven to roast. Remove the stuffing as soon as the bird is done. Refrigerate leftovers immediately.

Variation

If you want softer, moister stuffing, add $\frac{1}{2}$ cup (125 mL) water or GF chicken stock in Step 2.

Nutritional value per $\frac{1}{4}$ cup (50 mL) serving

Calories	60
Fat, total	2 g
Fat, saturated	0 g
Cholesterol	9 mg
Sodium	93 mg
Carbohydrate	10 g
Fiber	1 g
Protein	1 g
Calcium	15 mg
Iron	1 mg

Turkey Gravy

Makes 4 cups (1 L)

Crave a hot turkey sandwich? Be sure to make extra gravy for the next day!

Tips

4 cups (1 L) gravy is enough for a 15-lb (6.75 kg) turkey. Recipe can be doubled or tripled, but cooking time will need to be increased somewhat in each step.

Gravy thickens upon standing. When reheating, add extra liquid a little at a time until gravy reaches the desired consistency. Gravy can be reheated either on Medium (50%) in the microwave, or by simmering over medium-low heat on the stovetop.

½ cup	turkey pan drippings	125 mL
½ cup	sorghum flour	125 mL
3 to 4 cups	water, vegetable water or GF chicken stock	750 mL to 1 L
	Salt and freshly ground black pepper	

1. When turkey is removed from the roasting pan, skim fat from juices in pan. Place the pan on the stovetop burners over medium heat or transfer to a saucepan, making sure to scrape all the brown bits. Sprinkle sorghum flour over juices. Cook, stirring constantly, for 1 minute, or until gravy is the consistency of dry sand.

2. Pour in water. Bring to a boil, stirring and scraping up any brown bits from bottom of pan. Reduce heat and simmer, stirring frequently, for 3 to 5 minutes, or until thickened. Add more liquid if necessary. Season to taste with salt and pepper.

Variations

Follow the same method to make beef, pork or chicken gravy.

When making gravy and sauces, substitute an equal amount of amaranth flour for the sorghum flour. This substitution cannot be made when preparing cakes, cookies, breads or pastry.

Nutritional value per 2 tbsp (25 mL) serving	
Calories	33
Fat, total	3 g
Fat, saturated	1 g
Cholesterol	3 mg
Sodium	18 mg
Carbohydrate	2 g
Fiber	0 g
Protein	1 g
Calcium	1 mg
Iron	0 mg

Carol's Fruit Cake

Makes 12 pounds (5.5 kg) about 21 cups (5.25 L) or 72 servings

Don't halve Carol Coulter's fruitcake recipe — you can begin to enjoy this fruitcake the minute it cools. If you nibble daily, there won't be any left for Christmas. Carol fine-tuned and standardized her recipe in early June to meet our deadline. She measured pans, weighed and measured ingredients, raw batter and the baked cakes, and mailed us a sample. Thanks, Carol — we really appreciate it!

Tip

The recipe can be halved, if desired.

Nutritional value per serving

Calories	246
Fat, total	3 g
Fat, saturated	1 g
Cholesterol	26 mg
Sodium	74 mg
Carbohydrate	52 g
Fiber	3 g
Protein	3 g
Calcium	44 mg
Iron	7 mg

- **Preheat oven to 275°F (140°C)**
- **Two 9- by 5-inch (2 L) loaf pans**
- **Three 7½- by 3½-inch (1 L) loaf pans**

2 cups	soy flour	500 mL
1½ cups	tapioca starch	375 mL
½ cup	cornstarch	125 mL
1½ tsp	xanthan gum	7 mL
½ tsp	baking soda	2 mL
½ tsp	salt	2 mL
2 tsp	ground cinnamon	10 mL
1½ tsp	ground nutmeg	7 mL
1 tsp	ground cloves	5 mL
2 lbs	flat seeded raisins (Lexia or Muscat)	1 kg
1 lb	dark seeded raisins (Thompson)	500 g
1 lb	seedless golden raisins	500 g
1 lb	green and red glacé cherries, halved	500 g
1 lb	mixed candied peel	500 g
½ lb	dried currants	250 g
1 cup	butter, softened	250 mL
2 cups	granulated sugar	500 mL
2 cups	packed brown sugar	500 mL
10	eggs	10
1	can (19 oz/540 mL) crushed pineapple, including juice	1
1 tsp	vanilla	5 mL

1. Prepare loaf pans by greasing and completely lining bottoms and sides with a double thickness of heavy brown paper or parchment paper.

2. In a large bowl or plastic bag, mix together soy flour, tapioca starch, cornstarch, xanthan gum, baking soda, salt, cinnamon, nutmeg and cloves. Set aside.

3. In a very large bowl or plastic bag, mix together flat, dark and golden raisins, cherries, peel and currants. Set aside.

Tips

If you don't have a bowl or pot large enough for the whole recipe, use your roasting pan or divide the batter in half before stirring in dried fruit.

Each 9- by 5-inch (2 L) loaf pan holds 5 cups (1.25 L) batter. Each $7^1/_2$- by $3^1/_2$-inch (1 L) loaf pan holds $3^1/_2$ cups (875 mL) batter.

Purchase Muscat or Lexia flat seeded raisins — they are the only varieties with the deep, moist flavor characteristic of a dark fruitcake.

Purchasing Tips

2 cups (500 mL) glacé cherries, citron or mixed peel weigh about 1 lb (500 g).

3 cups (750 mL) seedless golden raisins or Thompson raisins weigh about 1 lb (500 g).

2 cups (500 mL) flat seeded raisins (Muscat, Lexia) weigh about 1 lb (500 g).

2 cups (500 mL) currants weigh about 8 oz (250 g).

4. In another very large bowl, using an electric mixer, cream butter, sugar and brown sugar until light and fluffy. Add eggs, one at a time, beating well after each addition; stir in crushed pineapple and vanilla. Gradually beat in dry ingredients, mixing just until smooth. Stir in dried fruit mixture.

5. Spoon into prepared loaf pans, filling only three quarters full; spread to edges and smooth tops with a moist rubber spatula.

6. Position the oven racks to divide the oven into thirds. Fill a large pan with 1 inch (2.5 cm) hot water and place on the bottom shelf.

7. Bake the cakes on the top shelf of preheated oven for about $2^1/_2$ hours for the smaller loaves and about $2^3/_4$ hours for the larger, or until cake tester inserted in the center right to the bottom of the pan comes out without any batter on it. There may be a little sticky raisin or cherry attached to it. Do not overbake.

8. Let cakes cool in the pan on a rack for 10 minutes. Remove cakes from pans to cooling rack. Let cool for 30 minutes before carefully peeling off the paper. Let cool completely before wrapping airtight.

9. Store in the refrigerator for up to 2 months and slice cold from the refrigerator. Or freeze for up to 1 year.

Variations

Add $1^3/_4$ cups (425 mL) whole blanched almonds (about 8 oz/250 g) and 1 cup (250 mL) slivered blanched almonds (about 4 oz/125 g), or $2^3/_4$ cups (675 mL) of chopped walnuts or pecans.

Top the cooled cakes with a thick layer of GF marzipan.

Cranberry Butter Tart Squares

Barbara Wahn, a local celiac, shared the base recipe with us. She was "determined to make a suitable base to have lots of squares for Christmas." This is the result of several attempts. See page 346 for Coconut Lemon Squares, another recipe that uses Barbara's base.

Tips

Double the recipe and bake in a 13- by 9-inch (3 L) baking pan for 30 to 35 minutes.

Make ahead and freeze in an airtight container for up to 1 month.

See Techniques Glossary, page 368, for information on melting chocolate.

Nutritional value per serving (1 square)	
Calories	117
Fat, total	5 g
Fat, saturated	2 g
Cholesterol	18 mg
Sodium	45 mg
Carbohydrate	18 g
Fiber	1 g
Protein	1 g
Calcium	14 mg
Iron	0 mg

- **Preheat oven to 350°F (180°C)**
- **9-inch (2.5 L) square baking pan, lightly greased**

Base

¼ cup	brown rice flour	50 mL
¾ cup	potato starch	175 mL
3 tbsp	tapioca starch	45 mL
¼ cup	packed brown sugar	50 mL
1 tsp	xanthan gum	5 mL
Pinch	salt	Pinch
½ cup	cold butter, cubed	125 mL
1	egg	1

Topping

¾ cup	packed brown sugar	175 mL
1 tbsp	sorghum flour or potato starch	15 mL
¼ tsp	GF baking powder	1 mL
2 tbsp	butter, softened	25 mL
2	eggs, beaten	2
1 tsp	vanilla	5 mL
1 cup	dried cranberries	250 mL
½ cup	raisins	125 mL
½ cup	chopped walnuts	125 mL
1 oz	white chocolate, melted	30 g

1. *Prepare the base:* In a food processor fitted with a metal blade, pulse rice flour, potato starch, tapioca starch, brown sugar, xanthan gum and salt. Add butter and pulse until mixture resembles small peas, about 5 to 10 seconds. With machine running, add egg through feed tube and process until dough just forms a ball. With a moistened rubber or metal spatula, spread evenly in bottom of prepared pan. Bake in preheated oven for 12 to 15 minutes, or until partially set.

Tip

No food processor? Use a pastry blender or two knives to cut the butter into the dry ingredients until mixture resembles small peas. Add the egg and mix until it forms a soft dough.

2. *Meanwhile, prepare the topping:* In a small bowl or plastic bag, combine brown sugar, sorghum flour and baking powder; set aside. In a medium bowl, using an electric mixer, cream butter, eggs and vanilla. Slowly beat in the dry ingredients until blended. Fold in cranberries, raisins and walnuts.

3. Pour topping over the hot base. Bake for 20 to 25 minutes, or until center is almost firm. Let cool completely in the pan on a cooling rack. Drizzle with melted chocolate and cut into squares.

Variation

Cranberry Pecan Butter Tart Squares: Use an additional 1 cup (250 mL) cranberries instead of the raisins and substitute pecans for the walnuts.

The Bird

Purchasing

- Allow 1 lb (500 g) raw turkey per person. Purchase extra to allow for leftovers.
- For boneless turkey, allow $1/4$ to $1/2$ lb (125 to 250 g) per person.
- Count on 1 cup (250 mL) stuffing for each 1 lb (500 g) of turkey.

Defrosting

- *Refrigerator method:* Allow $4^1/2$ hours per lb (10 hours per kg).
- *Cold water method:* Leaving turkey in its original wrapping, cover it with cold water. Change water every hour. Allow 1 hour per lb (2 hours per kg). Cook turkey as soon as it is defrosted.

Roasting

Place turkey, breast side up, on a rack in a large, shallow (no more than $2^1/2$ inches/ 6 cm deep) roasting pan. Insert a meat thermometer into the thickest part of the thigh, being careful it does not touch the bone. Roast turkey in a preheated 325°F (160°C) oven. See chart below for roasting times, or roast until the thermometer registers 180°F (82°C) in the thigh, 170°F (78°C) in the breast and 165°F (74°C) in the stuffing. (*Note:* The United States Department of Agriculture (USDA) and Agriculture Canada both recommend baking stuffing separately, not inside the bird.) Remove turkey from the oven and allow the bird to rest, tented loosely with foil, for 15 to 20 minutes before carving.

Roasting Times for Turkey*

Weight	Stuffed	Unstuffed
6 to 8 lbs (3 to 3.5 kg)	3 to $3^1/4$ hours	$2^1/2$ to $2^3/4$ hours
8 to 10 lbs (3.5 to 4.5 kg)	$3^1/4$ to $3^1/2$ hours	$2^3/4$ to 3 hours
10 to 12 lbs (4.5 to 5.5 kg)	$3^1/2$ to $3^3/4$ hours	3 to $3^1/4$ hours
12 to 16 lbs (5.5 to 7 kg)	$3^3/4$ to 4 hours	$3^1/4$ to $3^1/2$ hours
16 to 22 lbs (7 to 10 kg)	4 to $4^1/2$ hours	$3^1/2$ to 4 hours

* Canadian Turkey Marketing Agency

Leftovers

- Refrigerate or freeze leftover turkey within 1 hour of roasting.
- Take the meat off the bones to cool it more quickly. Store leftover turkey in the refrigerator for 4 to 6 days or in the freezer for 4 to 6 months. Label and date the containers.
- When packaging warm leftovers, use airtight containers no more than 2 to 3 inches (5 to 7.5 cm) deep.
- Place in the coldest part of the refrigerator or freezer with 1 to 2 inches (2 to 5 cm) of space around each container. This promotes quick, even cooling.
- When you reheat leftovers, make sure the internal temperature reaches 165°F (74°C).
- Sauces, soups and gravies should be brought to a rolling boil before serving.

Quick Breads

continued on next page

Quick Bread Mix Recipes

Quick Bread Baking Tips

- The batters should be the same consistency as wheat flour batters, but you can mix them more without producing tough products full of tunnels.
- Bake in muffin tins of a different size. Mini-muffins take 10 to 15 minutes to bake, while jumbo muffins bake in 20 to 40 minutes. Check jumbo muffins for doneness after 20 minutes, then again every 5 to 10 minutes. Keep in mind that the baking time will vary with the amount of batter in each muffin cup.
- Fill muffin tins to the top and loaf pans no more than three-quarters full. Let batter-filled pans stand for 30 minutes for a more tender product. It's worth the wait. We set a timer for 20 minutes, then preheat the oven so both are ready at the same time.
- If muffins stick to the lightly greased pan, let stand for a minute or two and try again. Loosen with a spatula or spoon if necessary.
- Muffins and biscuits can be reheated in the microwave, wrapped in a paper towel, for a few seconds on Medium (50%).

Biscuits and Cobblers

- Shortening or cold butter is cut into the dry ingredients with a pastry blender just until it resembles coarse cornmeal or pieces the size of small peas. Cold butter cuts in more quickly when pre-cut into 1-inch (2.5 cm) cubes.
- Fill lightly greased English muffin rings about two-thirds full. Smooth the top slightly for more traditional biscuits. The easiest way to grease English muffin rings (see Equipment Glossary, page 360) is to place them on a baking sheet then spray the sheet and the rings at the same time.
- Make only a few biscuits at a time. They are at their best served warm from the oven. Reheat for just a few seconds in the microwave.
- Cobbler toppings are a drop biscuit. The fruit or vegetable bases must be boiling and piping hot before the topping is spooned on. The bottom of the biscuit cooks from the heat of the bubbling liquid. If the base is cold, the center and bottom of the biscuit may be gummy when the top is browned and baked.
- Leave space between the biscuits for the hot liquid to bubble up, preventing them from boiling over.

Applesauce Raisin Muffins or Loaf

Makes 12 muffins or 1 loaf or 12 servings

Here's a truly "everything free" muffin — gluten-free, fat-free and yeast-free — everything except sweetness and flavor!

Tip

If sweetened applesauce is used, decrease the granulated sugar to $1/3$ cup (75 mL).

- Preheat oven to 350°F (180°C)
- 12-cup muffin tin or 9- by 5-inch (2 L) loaf pan, lightly greased
- Instant-read thermometer

1 $1/3$ cups	sorghum flour	325 mL
$1/3$ cup	whole bean flour	75 mL
$1/3$ cup	cornstarch	75 mL
$1/2$ cup	granulated sugar	125 mL
2 tsp	xanthan gum	10 mL
1 tsp	GF baking powder	5 mL
$1/2$ tsp	baking soda	2 mL
$1/4$ tsp	salt	1 mL
$1/2$ tsp	ground cinnamon	2 mL
1 cup	raisins	250 mL
1 $1/2$ cups	unsweetened applesauce or prune purée	375 mL
1 tsp	cider vinegar	5 mL
2	egg whites	2

1. In a large bowl or plastic bag, stir together sorghum flour, whole bean flour, cornstarch, sugar, xanthan gum, baking powder, baking soda, salt, cinnamon and raisins. Set aside.
2. In a separate bowl, using an electric mixer or whisk, beat applesauce, vinegar and egg whites until combined. Add dry ingredients and mix just until combined.

For Muffins

3. Spoon batter into each cup of prepared muffin tin. Let stand for 30 minutes. Bake in preheated oven for 20 to 25 minutes or until firm to the touch. Remove from the pan immediately and let cool completely on a rack.

For a Loaf

3. Spoon batter into a lightly greased 9- by 5-inch (2 L) loaf pan and bake for 65 to 75 minutes or until an instant-read thermometer registers 200°F (100°C). Let cool in the pan on a rack for 10 minutes. Remove from the pan and let cool completely on a rack.

Nutritional value per serving	
Calories	176
Fat, total	1 g
Fat, saturated	0 g
Cholesterol	0 g
Sodium	115 mg
Carbohydrate	40 g
Fiber	3 g
Protein	4 g
Calcium	31 mg
Iron	1 mg

Banana Cranberry Muffins or Loaf

Makes 12 muffins or 1 loaf

or 12 servings

Bake extras to store in the freezer for those mornings when you're running late. Everybody loves to grab a muffin, and add a chunk of cheese and an apple for a quick on-the-run breakfast.

Tips

If muffins stick to the pan, let stand for 2 to 3 minutes, then try again to remove them.

Use an ice cream scoop to portion an even amount of batter into each muffin cup.

For a tangier flavor, replace dried cranberries with fresh or frozen.

Nutritional value per serving

Calories	195
Fat, total	6 g
Fat, saturated	1 g
Cholesterol	27 mg
Sodium	166 mg
Carbohydrate	34 g
Fiber	3 g
Protein	3 g
Calcium	61 mg
Iron	1 mg

- Preheat oven to 350°F (180°C)
- 12-cup muffin tin or 9- by 5-inch (2 L) loaf pan, lightly greased
- Instant-read thermometer

1 cup	sorghum flour	250 mL
1/3 cup	quinoa or brown rice flour	75 mL
1/3 cup	tapioca starch	75 mL
1/2 cup	granulated sugar	125 mL
1 tsp	xanthan gum	5 mL
1 tbsp	GF baking powder	15 mL
1 tsp	baking soda	5 mL
1/4 tsp	salt	1 mL
2	eggs	2
1 1/4 cups	mashed banana (about 3)	300 mL
1/4 cup	vegetable oil	50 mL
1 tsp	cider vinegar	5 mL
3/4 cup	dried cranberries	175 mL

1. In a large bowl or plastic bag, combine sorghum flour, quinoa flour, tapioca starch, sugar, xanthan gum, baking powder, baking soda and salt. Mix well and set aside.

2. In a separate bowl, using an electric mixer, beat eggs, banana, oil and vinegar until combined. Add dry ingredients and mix just until combined. Stir in cranberries.

For Muffins

3. Spoon batter evenly into each cup of prepared muffin tin. Let stand for 30 minutes. Bake in preheated oven for 18 to 20 minutes, or until firm to the touch. Remove from the pan immediately and let cool completely on a rack.

For a Loaf

3. Spoon batter into prepared loaf pan. Let stand for 30 minutes. Bake in preheated oven for 55 to 65 minutes, or until an instant-read thermometer registers 200°F (100°C). Let cool in the pan on a rack for 10 minutes. Remove from the pan and let cool completely on a rack.

Banana Nut Muffins or Loaf

Makes 12 muffins or 1 loaf

or 12 servings

With all the same great moist banana flavor of traditional Banana Nut Bread, this gluten-free muffin is sure to please.

Tips

Stir the dry ingredients thoroughly before adding to the liquids. The rice flour and starches are so finely textured, they clump very easily.

If muffins stick to the pan, let stand for 2 to 3 minutes before trying again to remove them.

- Preheat oven to 350°F (180°C)
- 12-cup muffin tin or 9- by 5-inch (2 L) loaf pan, lightly greased
- Instant-read thermometer

1¼ cups	brown rice flour	300 mL
½ cup	potato starch	125 mL
¼ cup	tapioca starch	50 mL
½ tsp	xanthan gum	2 mL
1 tsp	GF baking powder	5 mL
1 tsp	baking soda	5 mL
¼ tsp	salt	1 mL
¾ cup	chopped walnuts or pecans	175 mL
1⅓ cups	mashed banana	325 mL
1 tsp	cider vinegar	5 mL
¼ cup	vegetable oil	50 mL
2	eggs	2
¼ cup	liquid honey	50 mL

1. In a large bowl or plastic bag, stir together rice flour, potato starch, tapioca starch, xanthan gum, baking powder, baking soda, salt and walnuts. Set aside.
2. In a separate bowl, using an electric mixer, beat banana, vinegar, oil and eggs until combined. Add honey while mixing. Add dry ingredients and mix just until combined.

For Muffins

3. Spoon batter into each cup of prepared muffin tin. Let stand for 30 minutes. Bake in preheated oven for 15 to 20 minutes or until firm to the touch. Remove from the pan immediately and let cool completely on a rack.

For a Loaf

3. For traditional Banana Bread, omit the walnuts and spoon the batter into a lightly greased 9- by 5-inch (2 L) loaf pan. Bake at 325°F (160°C) for 50 to 60 minutes or until an instant-read thermometer registers 200°F (100°C). Let cool in the pan on a rack for 10 minutes. Remove from the pan and let cool completely on a rack.

Nutritional value per serving

Calories	238
Fat, total	11 g
Fat, saturated	1 g
Cholesterol	27 mg
Sodium	167 mg
Carbohydrate	34 g
Fiber	2 g
Protein	4 g
Calcium	28 mg
Iron	1 mg

Apple Pancakes (page 33)

Crispy Pecan Chicken Fingers (page 41)

Grilled Chicken Mandarin Salad with
Sweet-and-Sour Dressing (page 68)

Batter-Fried Fish (page 79)

Mediterranean Focaccia (page 96)

Quinoa-Stuffed Peppers (page 116)

Poultry Stuffing (page 148)

Cranberry Orange Muffins (page 165)

Blueberry Orange Muffins or Loaf

If you enjoy blueberries, you'll love the intriguing flavor of this speckled orange treat.

Tips

Mix the dry ingredients thoroughly before adding to the liquids; the gluten-free flours and starch are so finely textured they clump very easily.

Using dried blueberries ensures that this breakfast bread or teatime snack doesn't have a bluish tinge, as it would with fresh or frozen blueberries.

Nutritional value per serving	
Calories	203
Fat, total	6 g
Fat, saturated	1 g
Cholesterol	28 mg
Sodium	114 mg
Carbohydrate	33 g
Fiber	3 g
Protein	4 g
Calcium	90 mg
Iron	2 mg

- **Preheat oven to 350°F (180°C)**
- **12-cup muffin tin or 9- by 5-inch (2 L) loaf pan, lightly greased**
- **Instant-read thermometer**

1¼ cups	amaranth flour	300 mL
½ cup	brown rice flour	125 mL
⅓ cup	tapioca starch	75 mL
½ cup	granulated sugar	125 mL
1½ tsp	xanthan gum	7 mL
1 tbsp	GF baking powder	15 mL
½ tsp	salt	2 mL
2	eggs	2
1 tbsp	grated orange zest	15 mL
1 cup	freshly squeezed orange juice	250 mL
2 tbsp	vegetable oil	25 mL
½ cup	slivered almonds	125 mL
½ cup	dried blueberries or cranberries	125 mL

1. In a large bowl or plastic bag, combine amaranth flour, brown rice flour, tapioca starch, sugar, xanthan gum, baking powder and salt. Mix well and set aside.
2. In a separate bowl, using an electric mixer, beat eggs, orange zest, orange juice and oil until combined. Add dry ingredients and mix just until combined. Fold in almonds and blueberries.

For Muffins

3. Spoon batter evenly into each cup of prepared muffin tin. Let stand for 30 minutes. Bake in preheated oven for 18 to 20 minutes, or until firm to the touch. Remove from the pan immediately and let cool completely on a rack.

For a Loaf

3. Spoon batter into prepared loaf pan. Let stand for 30 minutes. Bake in preheated oven for 55 to 65 minutes, or until an instant-read thermometer registers 200°F (100°C). Let cool in the pan on a rack for 10 minutes. Remove from the pan and let cool completely on a rack.

Blueberry Buckwheat Muffins or Loaf

Makes 12 muffins or 1 loaf

or 12 servings

If you enjoy blueberry buckwheat pancakes, you'll love the intriguing flavor of this speckled dark loaf.

Tip

If using frozen blueberries, leave them in the freezer until ready to use. This helps to prevent them from "bleeding" into the loaf.

- Preheat oven to 350°F (180°C)
- 12-cup muffin tin or 9- by 5-inch (2 L) loaf pan, lightly greased
- Instant-read thermometer

1¾ cup	brown rice flour	425 mL
¼ cup	buckwheat flour	50 mL
¼ cup	potato starch	50 mL
¼ cup	tapioca starch	50 mL
1½ tsp	xanthan gum	7 mL
2 tsp	GF baking powder	10 mL
1 tsp	baking soda	5 mL
½ tsp	salt	2 mL
1¼ cups	buttermilk	300 mL
1 tsp	cider vinegar	5 mL
¼ cup	vegetable oil	50 mL
2	eggs	2
½ cup	liquid honey	125 mL
1 cup	blueberries, fresh or frozen	250 mL

1. In a large bowl or plastic bag, stir together brown rice flour, buckwheat flour, potato starch, tapioca starch, xanthan gum, baking powder, baking soda and salt. Set aside.

2. In a separate bowl, using an electric mixer, beat buttermilk, vinegar, oil and eggs until combined. Add honey while mixing. Add dry ingredients and mix just until combined. Gently fold in blueberries.

For Muffins

3. Spoon batter into each cup of prepared muffin tin. Let stand for 30 minutes. Bake in preheated oven for 35 to 40 minutes or until firm to the touch. Remove from the pan immediately and let cool completely on a rack.

Nutritional value per serving	
Calories	181
Fat, total	6 g
Fat, saturated	1 g
Cholesterol	29 mg
Sodium	243 mg
Carbohydrate	30 g
Fiber	1 g
Protein	3 g
Calcium	68 mg
Iron	1 mg

Tip

Stir the dry ingredients thoroughly before liquids are added — the rice flour and starches are so finely textured, they clump very easily.

For a Loaf

3. Spoon batter into prepared loaf pan and bake for 70 to 80 minutes or until an instant-read thermometer registers 200°F (100°C). Let cool in the pan on a rack for 10 minutes. Remove from the pan and let cool completely on a rack.

Variations

Substitute chopped prunes, figs or plums for the blueberries.

If your diet does not permit buckwheat flour, you can replace it with soy or sorghum flour.

Country Harvest Muffins or Loaf

This is one of our favorite flavor combinations. The seeds add an interesting texture and crunch to the loaf.

Tips

Flaxseed needs to be slightly cracked or ground to be easily digested. Slightly crack the flaxseed in a blender, coffee mill or food processor.

To prevent seeds from becoming rancid, store in an airtight container in the refrigerator.

Nutritional value per serving

Calories	236
Fat, total	10 g
Fat, saturated	1 g
Cholesterol	29 mg
Sodium	172 mg
Carbohydrate	34 g
Fiber	2 g
Protein	4 g
Calcium	91 mg
Iron	1 mg

- Preheat oven to 350°F (180°C)
- 12-cup muffin tin or 9- by 5-inch (2 L) loaf pan, lightly greased
- Instant-read thermometer

1¼ cups	brown rice flour	300 mL
⅓ cup	cornstarch	75 mL
⅓ cup	tapioca starch	75 mL
1½ tsp	xanthan gum	7 mL
1 tbsp	GF baking powder	15 mL
¾ tsp	salt	4 mL
⅓ cup	cracked flaxseed	75 mL
⅓ cup	sunflower seeds	75 mL
2 tbsp	sesame seeds	25 mL
1 cup	milk	250 mL
1 tsp	cider vinegar	5 mL
⅓ cup	vegetable oil	75 mL
2	eggs	2
½ cup	liquid honey	125 mL

1. In a large bowl or plastic bag, stir together rice flour, cornstarch, tapioca starch, xanthan gum, baking powder, salt, flaxseed, sunflower seeds and sesame seeds. Set aside.

2. In a separate bowl, using an electric mixer, beat milk, vinegar, oil and eggs until combined. Add honey while mixing. Add dry ingredients and mix just until combined.

For Muffins

3. Spoon batter into each cup of prepared muffin tin. Let stand for 30 minutes. Bake in preheated oven for 35 to 40 minutes or until firm to the touch. Remove from the pan immediately and let cool completely on a rack.

For a Loaf

3. Spoon batter into prepared loaf pan and bake for 65 to 75 minutes or until an instant-read thermometer registers 200°F (100°C). Let cool in the pan on a rack for 10 minutes. Remove from the pan and let cool completely on a rack.

Cranberry Orange Muffins or Loaf

Each muffin is dotted with bright red cranberries and flavored with a hint of orange. The cake-like texture of this not-too-sweet muffin is perfect to serve warm for breakfast.

Tip

Leave cranberries in the freezer until just before using. This prevents them from "bleeding" into the bread. Sprinkle a little granulated sugar on top, just before baking, to help them brown.

Nutritional value per serving

Calories	202
Fat, total	6 g
Fat, saturated	1 g
Cholesterol	27 mg
Sodium	170 mg
Carbohydrate	37 g
Fiber	1 g
Protein	3 g
Calcium	66 mg
Iron	1 mg

- Preheat oven to 350°F (180°C)
- 12-cup muffin tin or 9- by 5-inch (2 L) loaf pan, lightly greased
- Instant-read thermometer

1½ cups	brown rice flour	375 mL
⅓ cup	each cornstarch and tapioca starch	75 mL
1½ tsp	xanthan gum	7 mL
1 tbsp	GF baking powder	15 mL
¾ tsp	salt	4 mL
⅔ cup	cranberry juice	150 mL
⅓ cup	water	75 mL
⅔ cup	Orange Marmalade (page 35) or store-bought	150 mL
1 tsp	cider vinegar	5 mL
¼ cup	vegetable oil	50 mL
2	eggs	2
1 cup	cranberries or blueberries, fresh or frozen	250 mL

1. In a large bowl or plastic bag, stir together rice flour, cornstarch, tapioca starch, xanthan gum, baking powder and salt. Set aside.

2. In a separate bowl, using an electric mixer, beat cranberry juice, water, marmalade, vinegar, oil and eggs until combined. Gently fold in cranberries.

For Muffins

3. Spoon batter into each cup of prepared muffin tin. Let stand for 30 minutes. Bake in preheated oven for 25 to 30 minutes or until firm to the touch and tops are golden. Remove from the pan immediately and let cool completely on a rack.

For a Loaf

3. Spoon batter into a lightly greased 9- by 5-inch (2 L) loaf pan and bake for 65 to 75 minutes or until an instant read thermometer registers 200°F (100°C). Let cool in the pan on a rack for 10 minutes. Remove from the pan and let cool completely on a rack.

Figgy Apple Muffins or Loaf

**Makes 12 muffins
or 1 loaf

or 12 servings**

Never baked with figs
before but always wanted
to try them? Bake these
moist, not-too-sweet
muffins that are sure to
please everyone.

Tips

*Make your own
applesauce: slice and core
apples, blend in blender
and sweeten to taste. No
need to peel or cook them.*

*This is a very dark loaf,
depending on the type of
pan used; you may want to
lower the oven temperature
by 25°F (20°C).*

*Substitute 3/4 cup (175 mL)
chopped apple for the
applesauce and 1/2 cup
(125 mL) fig spread for the
chopped dried figs.*

Nutritional value per serving	
Calories	204
Fat, total	7 g
Fat, saturated	1 g
Cholesterol	29 mg
Sodium	76 mg
Carbohydrate	33 g
Fiber	4 g
Protein	5 g
Calcium	115 mg
Iron	2 mg

- Preheat oven to 350°F (180°C)
- 12-cup muffin tin or 9- by 5-inch (2 L) loaf pan, lightly greased
- Instant-read thermometer

1 1/4 cups	sorghum flour	300 mL
1/3 cup	whole bean flour	75 mL
1/4 cup	cornstarch	50 mL
1/4 cup	rice bran	50 mL
1/3 cup	granulated sugar	75 mL
1 1/2 tsp	xanthan gum	7 mL
1 tbsp	GF baking powder	15 mL
1/4 tsp	salt	1 mL
1 tsp	ground cardamom	5 mL
2	eggs	2
1 cup	plain yogurt	250 mL
1/2 cup	sweetened applesauce	125 mL
1/4 cup	vegetable oil	50 mL
1 tsp	cider vinegar	5 mL
3/4 cup	chopped dried figs	175 mL

1. In a large bowl or plastic bag, combine sorghum flour, whole bean flour, cornstarch, rice bran, sugar, xanthan gum, baking powder, salt and cardamom. Mix well and set aside.

2. In a separate bowl, using an electric mixer, beat eggs, yogurt, applesauce, oil and vinegar until combined. Add dry ingredients and mix just until combined. Stir in figs.

For Muffins

3. Spoon batter evenly into each cup of prepared muffin tin. Let stand for 30 minutes. Bake in preheated oven for 18 to 23 minutes, or until firm to the touch. Remove from the pan immediately and let cool completely on a rack.

For a Loaf

3. Spoon batter into prepared loaf pan. Let stand for 30 minutes. Bake in preheated oven for 55 to 65 minutes, or until an instant-read thermometer registers 200°F (100°C). Let cool in the pan on a rack for 10 minutes. Remove from the pan and let cool completely on a rack.

Mock Date Bran Muffins or Loaf

Dark, moist and full of fruit! Serve these with a crisp apple and a wedge of five-year-old Cheddar.

Tips

These muffins remain moist longer than most. Carry them when you travel.

If you purchase chopped dates, check the packaging for hidden gluten in the coating.

- Preheat oven to 350°F (180°C)
- 12-cup muffin tin or 9- by 5-inch (2 L) loaf pan, lightly greased
- Instant-read thermometer

1 cup	sorghum flour	250 mL
½ cup	whole bean flour	125 mL
⅓ cup	tapioca starch	75 mL
⅓ cup	rice bran	75 mL
2 tsp	xanthan gum	10 mL
1 tsp	GF baking powder	5 mL
½ tsp	baking soda	2 mL
¼ tsp	salt	1 mL
1 cup	chopped dates	250 mL
1½ cups	buttermilk	375 mL
¼ cup	vegetable oil	50 mL
2	eggs	2
¼ cup	liquid honey	50 mL
2 tbsp	fancy molasses	25 mL

1. In a large bowl or plastic bag, stir together sorghum flour, whole bean flour, tapioca starch, rice bran, xanthan gum, baking powder, baking soda, salt and dates. Set aside.

2. In a separate bowl, using an electric mixer, beat buttermilk, oil and eggs until combined. Add honey and molasses while mixing. Add dry ingredients and mix just until combined.

For Muffins

3. Spoon batter into each cup of prepared muffin tin. Let stand for 30 minutes. Bake in preheated oven for 25 to 30 minutes or until firm to the touch. Remove from the pan immediately and let cool completely on a rack.

For a Loaf

3. Spoon batter into a lightly greased 9- by 5-inch (2 L) loaf pan and bake for 70 to 80 minutes or until an instant-read thermometer registers 200°F (100°C). Let cool in the pan on a rack for 10 minutes. Remove from the pan and let cool completely on a rack.

Glazed Lemon Coconut Muffins or Loaf

Brown rice flour gives this loaf — a delightfully sweet tea bread — a warm creamy color. Bake ahead and freeze it, so it's ready the next time a friend drops in.

Tip

Use either desiccated or shredded coconut in this recipe. If using a sweetened coconut, decrease the sugar by 1 or 2 tbsp (15 or 25 mL).

Nutritional value per serving	
Calories	271
Fat, total	9 g
Fat, saturated	4 g
Cholesterol	28 mg
Sodium	73 mg
Carbohydrate	48 g
Fiber	2 g
Protein	3 g
Calcium	81 mg
Iron	1 mg

- Preheat oven to 350°F (180°C)
- 12-cup muffin tin or 9- by 5-inch (2 L) loaf pan, lightly greased
- Instant-read thermometer

1 cup	brown rice flour	250 mL
1/3 cup	potato starch	75 mL
1/4 cup	tapioca starch	50 mL
1 cup	granulated sugar	250 mL
1 1/2 tsp	xanthan gum	7 mL
1 tbsp	GF baking powder	15 mL
1/4 tsp	salt	1 mL
2 tbsp	lemon zest	25 mL
3/4 cup	unsweetened coconut	175 mL
3/4 cup	milk	175 mL
1/4 cup	vegetable oil	50 mL
2	eggs	2
1/4 cup	freshly squeezed lemon juice	50 mL

Lemon Glaze

1 cup	GF sifted confectioner's (icing) sugar	250 mL
1/4 cup	freshly squeezed lemon juice	50 mL

1. In a large bowl or plastic bag, stir together brown rice flour, potato starch, tapioca starch, sugar, xanthan gum, baking powder, salt, zest and coconut. Set aside.

2. In a separate bowl, using an electric mixer or whisk, beat milk, oil and eggs until combined. Add lemon juice while mixing. Add dry ingredients and mix just until combined.

For Muffins

3. Spoon batter into each cup of prepared muffin tin. Let stand for 30 minutes. Bake in preheated oven for 35 to 40 minutes or until firm to the touch. Remove from the pan immediately and let cool completely on a rack.

For a Loaf

3. Spoon batter into prepared loaf pan and bake for 55 to 65 minutes or until an instant-read thermometer registers 200°F (100°C). Let cool in the pan on a rack for 10 minutes. Remove from the pan and let cool completely on a rack.

For Both Methods

4. *Meanwhile, prepare Lemon Glaze:* In a small bowl, stir together confectioner's sugar and lemon juice. With a wooden skewer, poke several holes through the hot muffins or loaf as soon as it is removed from the oven. Spoon the glaze over the hot muffins or loaf. Let the muffins or loaf cool in the pan on a rack for 30 minutes. Remove from the pan and let cool completely on a rack.

Variation

Orange zest and orange juice can replace the lemon for a slightly sweeter and more mild-flavored loaf.

Orange Pecan Streusel Muffins or Loaf

Makes 12 muffins or 1 loaf

or 12 servings

What an attractive, tasty treat! The golden crunchy streusel topping contrasts beautifully with the bright orange flecks of this muffin.

Tips

Remove the muffins carefully from the pan or the topping will shake off.

If muffins stick to the pan, let stand for 2 to 3 minutes, then try again. To provide space for the topping, fill each muffin cup only three-quarters full.

- Preheat oven to 350°F (180°C)
- 12-cup muffin tin or 9- by 5-inch (2 L) loaf pan, lightly greased
- Instant-read thermometer

Topping

¼ cup	packed brown sugar	50 mL
2 tbsp	pecan flour	25 mL
½ tsp	ground cinnamon	2 mL
1 tbsp	melted butter	15 mL

Muffin

1 cup	brown rice flour	250 mL
⅓ cup	pecan flour	75 mL
¼ cup	tapioca starch	50 mL
¼ cup	potato starch	50 mL
½ cup	granulated sugar	125 mL
1½ tsp	xanthan gum	7 mL
2 tsp	GF baking powder	10 mL
¼ tsp	baking soda	1 mL
½ tsp	salt	2 mL
2 tbsp	orange zest	25 mL
½ cup	chopped pecans	125 mL
¾ cup	orange juice	175 mL
¼ cup	vegetable oil	50 mL
2	eggs	2

1. In a small bowl, combine brown sugar, pecan flour and cinnamon. Add melted butter and mix until crumbly. Set aside streusel topping.

2. In a large bowl or plastic bag, stir together rice flour, pecan flour, tapioca starch, potato starch, sugar, xanthan gum, baking powder, baking soda, salt, orange zest and pecans. Set aside.

3. In a separate bowl, using an electric mixer or whisk, beat orange juice, oil and eggs until combined. Add dry ingredients and mix just until combined.

Nutritional value per serving	
Calories	197
Fat, total	12 g
Fat, saturated	2 g
Cholesterol	29 mg
Sodium	146 mg
Carbohydrate	23 g
Fiber	1 g
Protein	2 g
Calcium	59 mg
Iron	1 mg

Tip

If pecan flour is not readily available in your area, make your own (see Nut Flour, page 370).

For Muffins

4. Spoon batter into each cup of prepared muffin tin. Let stand for 30 minutes. Bake in preheated oven for 25 to 30 minutes or until firm to the touch. Remove from the pan immediately and let cool completely on a rack.

For a Loaf

4. Spoon batter into a lightly greased 9- by 5-inch (2 L) loaf pan and bake for 70 to 80 minutes or until an instant-read thermometer registers 200°F (100°C). Let cool in the pan on a rack for 10 minutes. Remove from the pan and let cool completely on a rack.

Variation

Substitute sunflower seeds for the pecans.

Pecan Pear Muffins or Loaf

Delicately flavored pears provide both moistness and fiber. Enjoy with dark grapes and a wedge of ripe Camembert, Boursin or Brie.

Tips

No need to peel the pears — the skins soften during baking.

For best results, fruit should be perfectly ripe. If necessary, ripen fruit in a paper bag on the counter until it is fragrant and yields to gentle thumb pressure near the base of the stem. Check daily — it may take anywhere from 1 to 8 days.

Nutritional value per serving

Calories	212
Fat, total	11 g
Fat, saturated	1 g
Cholesterol	28 mg
Sodium	121 mg
Carbohydrate	28 g
Fiber	3 g
Protein	4 g
Calcium	94 mg
Iron	1 mg

- Preheat oven to 350°F (180°C)
- 12-cup muffin tin or 9- by 5-inch (2 L) loaf pan, lightly greased
- Instant-read thermometer

1 cup	sorghum flour	250 mL
¼ cup	quinoa flour	50 mL
¼ cup	potato starch	50 mL
½ cup	granulated sugar	125 mL
1½ tsp	xanthan gum	7 mL
1 tbsp	GF baking powder	15 mL
½ tsp	salt	2 mL
1 tsp	ground ginger	5 mL
2	eggs	2
¾ cup	plain yogurt	175 mL
¼ cup	vegetable oil	50 mL
2 tsp	grated lemon zest	10 mL
2 tsp	freshly squeezed lemon juice	10 mL
1½ cups	coarsely chopped pears	375 mL
⅔ cup	coarsely chopped pecans	150 mL

1. In a large bowl or plastic bag, combine sorghum flour, quinoa flour, potato starch, sugar, xanthan gum, baking powder, salt and ginger. Mix well and set aside.

2. In a separate bowl, using an electric mixer, beat eggs, yogurt, oil, lemon zest and lemon juice until combined. Add dry ingredients and mix just until combined. Stir in pears and pecans.

For Muffins

3. Spoon batter evenly into each cup of prepared muffin tin. Let stand for 30 minutes. Bake in preheated oven for 18 to 20 minutes, or until firm to the touch. Remove from the pan immediately and let cool completely on a rack.

For a Loaf

3. Spoon batter into prepared loaf pan. Let stand for 30 minutes. Bake in preheated oven for 55 to 65 minutes, or until an instant-read thermometer registers 200°F (100°C). Let cool in the pan on a rack for 10 minutes. Remove from the pan and let cool completely on a rack.

Peppered Zucchini Muffins or Loaf

Makes 12 muffins or 1 loaf

or 12 servings

Confetti-like speckles of zucchini and bell pepper add to the moistness of this flavorful loaf. It's perfect for sandwiches or to serve along with a salad or stew.

Tips

Use red, orange or yellow bell peppers or a combination of colors.

To increase the fiber content, do not peel the zucchini.

For a little extra heat, substitute some chili or jalapeño pepper for a small amount of the bell pepper.

Nutritional value per serving

Calories	161
Fat, total	6 g
Fat, saturated	1 g
Cholesterol	28 mg
Sodium	128 mg
Carbohydrate	26 g
Fiber	1 g
Protein	3 g
Calcium	58 mg
Iron	1 mg

- Preheat oven to 350°F (180°C)
- 12-cup muffin tin or 9- by 5-inch (2 L) loaf pan, lightly greased
- Instant-read thermometer

1 cup	brown rice flour	250 mL
2/3 cup	tapioca starch	150 mL
1/3 cup	cornstarch	75 mL
1/4 cup	granulated sugar	50 mL
1 1/2 tsp	xanthan gum	7 mL
2 tsp	GF baking powder	10 mL
1/2 tsp	salt	2 mL
1/4 tsp	freshly ground black pepper	1 mL
3/4 cup	buttermilk	175 mL
1 tsp	cider vinegar	5 mL
1/4 cup	vegetable oil	50 mL
2	eggs	2
1 cup	unpeeled, shredded zucchini	250 mL
1/2 cup	finely chopped bell peppers	125 mL

1. In a large bowl or plastic bag, stir together rice flour, tapioca starch, cornstarch, sugar, xanthan gum, baking powder, salt and black pepper. Set aside.

2. In a separate bowl, using an electric mixer or whisk, beat buttermilk, vinegar, oil and eggs until combined. Add dry ingredients and mix just until combined. Fold in zucchini and bell peppers.

For Muffins

3. Spoon batter into each cup of prepared muffin tin. Let stand for 30 minutes. Bake in preheated oven for 35 to 40 minutes or until firm to the touch. Remove from the pan immediately and let cool completely on a rack.

For a Loaf

3. Spoon batter into prepared loaf pan and bake for 70 to 80 minutes or until an instant-read thermometer registers 200°F (100°C). Let cool in the pan on a rack for 10 minutes. Remove from the pan and let cool completely on a rack.

Pineapple Banana Muffins or Loaf

Makes 12 muffins or 1 loaf

or 12 servings

Here's a delightfully moist banana quick bread with bits of pineapple.

Tips

Include plenty of juice when spooning pineapple into the bowl.

If ground flaxseed is not available, purchase either golden or brown flaxseed and grind your own (see page 369). Whole flaxseed can be stored at room temperature for up to 1 year. Ground flaxseed can be stored in the refrigerator for up to 90 days, although for optimum freshness it is best to grind it as needed.

Nutritional value per serving	
Calories	186
Fat, total	5 g
Fat, saturated	0 g
Cholesterol	14 mg
Sodium	111 mg
Carbohydrate	36 g
Fiber	3 g
Protein	4 g
Calcium	65 mg
Iron	1 mg

- Preheat oven to 350°F (180°C)
- 12-cup muffin tin or 9 by 5-inch (2 L) loaf pan, lightly greased
- Instant-read thermometer

1 cup	brown rice flour	250 mL
¾ cup	sorghum flour	175 mL
¼ cup	tapioca starch	50 mL
⅓ cup	ground flaxseed or hemp seed flour	75 mL
½ cup	granulated sugar	125 mL
1½ tsp	xanthan gum	7 mL
1 tbsp	GF baking powder	15 mL
½ tsp	salt	2 mL
1	egg	1
1	egg white	1
1 cup	crushed pineapple, including juice	250 mL
¾ cup	mashed banana	175 mL
2 tbsp	vegetable oil	25 mL
1 tsp	cider vinegar	5 mL

1. In a large bowl or plastic bag, combine brown rice flour, sorghum flour, tapioca starch, ground flaxseed, sugar, xanthan gum, baking powder and salt. Mix well and set aside.

2. In another bowl, using an electric mixer, beat egg, egg white, pineapple, banana, oil and vinegar until combined. Add dry ingredients and mix just until combined.

For Muffins

3. Spoon batter evenly into each cup of prepared muffin tin. Let stand for 30 minutes. Bake in preheated oven for 18 to 20 minutes, or until firm to the touch. Remove from the pan immediately and let cool completely on a rack.

For a Loaf

3. Spoon batter into prepared loaf pan. Let stand for 30 minutes. Bake in preheated oven for 55 to 65 minutes, or until an instant-read thermometer registers 200°F (100°C). Let cool in the pan on a rack for 10 minutes. Remove from the pan and let cool completely on a rack.

Poppy Seed Cheddar Muffins or Loaf

On a cold winter's day, serve these scrumptious golden morsels warm with a piping hot bowl of chili.

Tips

If muffins stick to the pan, let stand for 2 to 3 minutes, then try again to remove.

For the amount of cheese to purchase, see the weight/ volume equivalents on page 363.

To heighten the cheese flavor, add a pinch of dry mustard.

Use two or three $5^1/_2$- by 3- by 2-inch (500 mL) pans and bake for 30 to 35 minutes.

Nutritional value per serving

Calories	161
Fat, total	8 g
Fat, saturated	3 g
Cholesterol	37 mg
Sodium	183 mg
Carbohydrate	17 g
Fiber	2 g
Protein	6 g
Calcium	187 mg
Iron	1 mg

- Preheat oven to 350°F (180°C)
- 12-cup muffin tin or 9- by 5-inch (2 L) loaf pan, lightly greased
- Instant-read thermometer

1 cup	amaranth flour	250 mL
$^1/_2$ cup	quinoa or brown rice flour	125 mL
$^1/_4$ cup	tapioca starch	50 mL
2 tbsp	granulated sugar	25 mL
$1^1/_2$ tsp	xanthan gum	7 mL
1 tbsp	GF baking powder	15 mL
$^1/_2$ tsp	salt	2 mL
1 cup	shredded old Cheddar cheese	250 mL
2 tbsp	poppy seeds	25 mL
2	eggs	2
1 cup	milk	250 mL
2 tbsp	vegetable oil	25 mL
1 tsp	cider vinegar	5 mL

1. In a large bowl or plastic bag, combine amaranth flour, quinoa flour, tapioca starch, sugar, xanthan gum, baking powder, salt, Cheddar and poppy seeds. Mix well and set aside.

2. In a separate bowl, using an electric mixer, beat eggs, milk, oil and vinegar until combined. Add dry ingredients and mix just until combined.

For Muffins

3. Spoon batter evenly into each cup of prepared muffin tin. Let stand for 30 minutes. Bake in preheated oven for 18 to 20 minutes, or until firm to the touch. Remove from the pan immediately and let cool completely on a rack.

For a Loaf

3. Spoon batter into prepared loaf pan. Let stand for 30 minutes. Bake in preheated oven for 55 to 65 minutes, or until an instant-read thermometer registers 200°F (100°C). Let cool in the pan on a rack for 10 minutes. Remove from the pan and let cool completely on a rack.

Pumpkin Muffins or Loaf

We love the colors of this quick bread. Bake as moist, spicy muffins or an easy-slicing, rich, dark loaf — or double the recipe and make both!

Tips

Be sure to buy pumpkin purée, not pumpkin pie filling, which is too sweet and contains too much moisture for this recipe.

Keep an eye on this one — it will become very dark as it bakes. You may need to tent the loaf with foil for the last 15 minutes. You will notice these are baked at a lower temperature than other muffins.

- Preheat oven to 350°F (180°C)
- 12-cup muffin tin or 9- by 5-inch (2 L) loaf pan, lightly greased
- Instant-read thermometer

½ cup	sorghum flour	125 mL
½ cup	whole bean flour	125 mL
¼ cup	tapioca starch	50 mL
1½ tsp	xanthan gum	7 mL
2 tsp	GF baking powder	10 mL
1 tsp	baking soda	5 mL
½ tsp	salt	2 mL
½ cup	chopped prunes	125 mL
½ cup	pumpkin seeds	125 mL
1 tsp	ground cinnamon	5 mL
½ tsp	ground nutmeg	2 mL
2	eggs	2
1 cup	canned pumpkin purée	250 mL
⅓ cup	vegetable oil	75 mL
1 tsp	cider vinegar	5 mL
½ cup	liquid honey	125 mL

1. In a large bowl or plastic bag, combine sorghum flour, whole bean flour, tapioca starch, xanthan gum, baking powder, baking soda, salt, prunes, pumpkin seeds, cinnamon and nutmeg. Mix well and set aside.

2. In a separate bowl, using an electric mixer, beat eggs, pumpkin purée, oil and vinegar until combined. Add honey while mixing. Add dry ingredients and mix just until combined.

For Muffins

3. Spoon batter evenly into each cup of prepared muffin tin. Let stand for 30 minutes. Bake in preheated oven for 18 to 20 minutes, or until firm to the touch. Remove from the pan immediately and let cool completely on a rack.

Nutritional value per serving

Calories	232
Fat, total	11 g
Fat, saturated	1 g
Cholesterol	27 mg
Sodium	216 mg
Carbohydrate	29 g
Fiber	3 g
Protein	5 g
Calcium	52 mg
Iron	2 mg

Tips

Toast pumpkin seeds for a nuttier flavor (see Techniques Glossary, page 371, under Sunflower seeds).

Vary the amount of cinnamon and nutmeg according to your tastes.

For a Loaf

3. Spoon batter into prepared loaf pan. Let stand for 30 minutes. Bake in preheated oven for 55 to 65 minutes, or until an instant-read thermometer registers 200°F (100°C). Let cool in the pan on a rack for 10 minutes. Remove from the pan and let cool completely on a rack.'

Variation

Substitute equal amounts of raisins and walnuts for the prunes and pumpkin seeds.

Pumpkin Seed Muffins or Loaf

Makes 12 muffins or 1 loaf

or 12 servings

Don't be put off by the long list of ingredients — nothing could be faster or easier than this comfort food.

Tip

For a nuttier flavor, toast the pumpkin and sunflower seeds (see Techniques Glossary, page 371, for instructions).

- Preheat oven to 350°F (180°C)
- 12-cup muffin tin or 9- by 5-inch (2 L) loaf pan, lightly greased
- Instant-read thermometer

¾ cup	sorghum flour	175 mL
¾ cup	whole bean flour	175 mL
¼ cup	cornstarch	50 mL
⅔ cup	packed brown sugar	150 mL
1½ tsp	xanthan gum	7 mL
2 tsp	GF baking powder	10 mL
2 tsp	baking soda	10 mL
½ tsp	salt	2 mL
1 tsp	ground ginger	5 mL
½ tsp	ground nutmeg	2 mL
¼ tsp	ground cloves	1 mL
⅓ cup	pumpkin seeds	75 mL
⅓ cup	sunflower seeds	75 mL
1 cup	canned pumpkin purée (not pie filling)	250 mL
1 tsp	cider vinegar	5 mL
⅓ cup	vegetable oil	75 mL
2	eggs	2

1. In a large bowl or plastic bag, stir together sorghum flour, whole bean flour, cornstarch, brown sugar, xanthan gum, baking powder, baking soda, salt, ginger, nutmeg, cloves, pumpkin seeds and sunflower seeds. Set aside.

2. In a separate bowl, using an electric mixer or whisk, beat pumpkin purée, vinegar, oil and eggs until combined. Add dry ingredients and mix just until combined.

For Muffins

3. Spoon batter into each cup of prepared muffin tin. Let stand for 30 minutes. Bake in preheated oven for 35 to 40 minutes or until firm to the touch. Remove from the pan immediately and let cool completely on a rack.

Nutritional value per serving	
Calories	243
Fat, total	12 g
Fat, saturated	1 g
Cholesterol	27 mg
Sodium	324 mg
Carbohydrate	31 g
Fiber	3 g
Protein	6 g
Calcium	66 mg
Iron	2 mg

Tip

Pumpkin pie spice may contain gluten fillers.

For a Loaf

3. Spoon batter into prepared loaf pan and bake for 70 to 80 minutes or until an instant-read thermometer registers 200°F (100°C). Let cool in the pan on a rack for 10 minutes. Remove from the pan and let cool completely on a rack.

Variation

Use your favorite combination of sweet spices instead of ginger, nutmeg and cloves.

Swedish Limpa Muffins or Loaf

Makes 12 muffins or 1 loaf

or 12 servings

The traditional Scandinavian flavor combination of anise, caraway and fennel seeds gives this orange-scented loaf a unique flavor.

Tip

For a smoother texture, use a food mill or a coffee mill to grind the seeds.

- Preheat oven to 350°F (180°C)
- 12-cup muffin tin or 9- by 5-inch (2 L) loaf pan, lightly greased
- Instant-read thermometer

²⁄₃ cup	whole bean flour	150 mL
½ cup	sorghum flour	125 mL
½ cup	potato starch	125 mL
½ cup	tapioca starch	125 mL
½ cup	packed brown sugar	125 mL
2 tsp	xanthan gum	10 mL
2 tsp	GF baking powder	10 mL
¾ tsp	salt	4 mL
1 tbsp	orange zest	15 mL
2 tsp	anise seeds	10 mL
2 tsp	caraway seeds	10 mL
2 tsp	fennel seeds	10 mL
1¼ cups	milk	300 mL
1 tsp	cider vinegar	5 mL
¼ cup	vegetable oil	50 mL
2	eggs	2

1. In a large bowl or plastic bag, stir together whole bean flour, sorghum flour, potato starch, tapioca starch, brown sugar, xanthan gum, baking powder, salt, orange zest, anise seeds, caraway seeds and fennel seeds. Set aside.

2. In a separate bowl, using an electric mixer or whisk, beat milk, vinegar, oil and eggs until combined. Add dry ingredients and mix just until combined.

For Muffins

3. Spoon batter into each cup of prepared muffin tin. Let stand for 30 minutes. Bake in preheated oven for 35 to 40 minutes or until firm to the touch. Remove from the pan immediately and let cool completely on a rack.

Nutritional value per serving	
Calories	199
Fat, total	7 g
Fat, saturated	1 g
Cholesterol	29 mg
Sodium	174 mg
Carbohydrate	32 g
Fiber	2 g
Protein	5 g
Calcium	94 mg
Iron	1 mg

For a Loaf

3. Spoon batter into prepared loaf pan and bake for 70 to 80 minutes or until an instant-read thermometer registers 200°F (100°C). Let cool in the pan on a rack for 10 minutes. Remove from the pan and let cool completely on a rack.

Variation

Vary the combination of seeds. Try poppy or sesame. For a milder-flavored version of the loaf, omit the seeds.

Zucchini Carrot Muffins or Loaf

Here's an exceptionally attractive muffin — confetti dots of bright orange carrot contrast with the brilliant green of zucchini.

Tips

For moister muffins, choose young carrots and zucchini fresh from the garden.

If muffins stick to the pan, let stand 2 to 3 minutes, then try again.

We found these muffins took a little longer to bake than others in this book.

Nutritional value per serving	
Calories	184
Fat, total	6 g
Fat, saturated	1 g
Cholesterol	29 mg
Sodium	127 mg
Carbohydrate	30 g
Fiber	3 g
Protein	4 g
Calcium	72 mg
Iron	1 mg

- Preheat oven to 350°F (180°C)
- 12-cup muffin tin or 9- by 5-inch (2 L) loaf pan, lightly greased
- Instant-read thermometer

1⅔ cups	sorghum flour	400 mL
⅓ cup	tapioca starch	75 mL
⅓ cup	potato starch	75 mL
⅓ cup	granulated sugar	75 mL
1½ tsp	xanthan gum	7 mL
2 tsp	GF baking powder	10 mL
½ tsp	salt	2 mL
¾ tsp	ground cinnamon	4 mL
¼ tsp	ground allspice	1 mL
¼ tsp	ground nutmeg	1 mL
1 cup	milk	250 mL
1 tsp	cider vinegar	5 mL
¼ cup	vegetable oil	50 mL
2	eggs	2
1 cup	unpeeled, grated zucchini	250 mL
1 cup	grated carrots	250 mL

1. In a large bowl or plastic bag, stir together sorghum flour, tapioca starch, potato starch, sugar, xanthan gum, baking powder, salt, cinnamon, allspice and nutmeg. Set aside.

2. In a separate bowl, using an electric mixer or whisk, beat milk, vinegar, oil and eggs until combined. Add dry ingredients and mix just until combined. Fold in zucchini and carrots.

For Muffins

3. Spoon batter into each cup of prepared muffin tin. Let stand for 30 minutes. Bake in preheated oven for 35 to 40 minutes or until firm to the touch. Remove from the pan immediately and let cool completely on a rack.

For a Loaf

3. Spoon batter into a lightly greased 9- by 5-inch (2 L) loaf pan and bake for 70 to 80 minutes or until an instant-read thermometer registers 200°F (100°C). Let cool in the pan on a rack for 10 minutes. Remove from the pan and let cool completely on a rack.

Variation

Add $3/4$ cup (175 mL) chopped walnuts, pecans or sunflower seeds with the dry ingredients.

Currant Drop Biscuits with Honey Butter

Makes 10 biscuits

Dried currants are a traditional ingredient in English tea biscuits. Here they're combined with a hint of orange. The honey butter makes a great accompaniment to these or any other biscuits.

Tips

Cold butter cuts more easily into dry ingredients than soft butter and produces flakier biscuits.

Honey butter can be stored, covered, in the refrigerator for up to 1 week. Bring to room temperature before serving.

Nutritional value per serving (1 biscuit)	
Calories	265
Fat, total	14 g
Fat, saturated	6 g
Cholesterol	19 mg
Sodium	195 mg
Carbohydrate	33 g
Fiber	2 g
Protein	3 g
Calcium	176 mg
Iron	1 mg

● **Baking sheet, lightly greased**

1 cup	boiling water	250 mL
1/3 cup	dried currants	75 mL
1 cup	amaranth flour	250 mL
1/2 cup	brown rice flour	125 mL
1/4 cup	granulated sugar	50 mL
1 1/2 tsp	xanthan gum	7 mL
2 tbsp	GF baking powder	25 mL
1/4 tsp	salt	1 mL
1 tbsp	grated orange zest	15 mL
1/4 cup	cold butter, cut into 1-inch (2.5 cm) cubes	50 mL
3/4 cup	milk	175 mL

Honey Butter

1/2 cup	butter, softened	125 mL
1/4 cup	creamed honey	50 mL
2 tsp	grated orange zest	10 mL

1. In a small bowl, pour boiling water over currants. Let stand for 5 minutes. Drain currants well and pat dry on paper towels. Set aside.

2. In a large bowl, combine amaranth flour, brown rice flour, sugar, xanthan gum, baking powder, salt and orange zest. Using a pastry blender or two knives, cut in butter until mixture resembles coarse crumbs. Stir in currants. Add milk all at once, stirring with a fork to make a soft, slightly sticky dough. Drop by heaping spoonfuls onto prepared baking sheet. Let stand for 30 minutes. Meanwhile, preheat oven to 425°F (220°C).

3. Bake in preheated oven for 10 to 13 minutes, or until tops are golden. Remove to a cooling rack.

4. *Prepare the honey butter:* In a small bowl, cream together butter, honey and orange zest. Serve with warm biscuits.

Variation

Substitute an equal amount of golden raisins for currants. Add raisins with dry ingredients. They do not require soaking, so omit water and skip Step 1.

Fresh Tomato Basil Drop Biscuits

These biscuits are packed with the flavor of late summer — juicy, sweet tomatoes and the pungent fragrance of fresh basil.

Tip

In season, use garden-fresh beefsteak tomatoes. Use an Italian plum or Roma tomato at other times of the year. Leave tomatoes in fairly large pieces.

- **Preheat oven to 425°F (220°C)**
- **Baking sheet, lightly greased**

¾ cup	brown rice flour	175 mL
¼ cup	tapioca starch	50 mL
¼ cup	potato starch	50 mL
2 tbsp	granulated sugar	25 mL
1 tsp	xanthan gum	5 mL
1 tbsp	GF baking powder	15 mL
¼ tsp	salt	2 mL
¼ cup	snipped fresh basil	50 mL
¼ cup	snipped fresh chives	50 mL
¼ cup	snipped fresh parsley	50 mL
¼ cup	shortening	50 mL
¾ cup	chopped fresh tomatoes	175 mL
½ cup	GF sour cream	125 mL

1. In a large bowl, stir together rice flour, tapioca starch, potato starch, sugar, xanthan gum, baking powder, salt, basil, chives and parsley.

2. Using a pastry blender or two knives, cut in shortening until mixture resembles coarse crumbs. Fold in tomatoes. Add sour cream all at once, stirring with a fork to make a soft, sticky dough. Drop by heaping tablespoonfuls (15 mL) onto prepared pan. Let stand for 30 minutes.

3. Bake in preheated oven for 12 to 15 minutes or until tops are golden. Remove to a cooling rack immediately. Serve warm.

Variation

Substitute an equal amount of plain yogurt for the gluten-free sour cream.

Nutritional value per serving (1 biscuit)	
Calories	99
Fat, total	4 g
Fat, saturated	2 g
Cholesterol	6 mg
Sodium	51 mg
Carbohydrate	15 g
Fiber	1 g
Protein	1 g
Calcium	68 mg
Iron	0 mg

Rosemary Scones Topped with Caramelized Vidalia Onions

Makes 6 wedges

What a lunch treat! Just cut into wedges and serve hot from the oven with a crisp salad.

Tips

For long, thin onion slices, cut the onion in half lengthwise before slicing.

For instructions on caramelizing onions, see Techniques Glossary, page 370.

- Preheat oven to 425°F (220°C)
- 8-inch (20 cm) round baking pan, lightly greased

Topping

1 tbsp	butter	15 mL
2 cups	sliced Vidalia onions	500 mL
1½ tsp	packed brown sugar	7 mL
2 tbsp	snipped fresh rosemary leaves	25 mL

Base

¾ cup	brown rice flour	175 mL
¼ cup	arrowroot starch	50 mL
¼ cup	potato starch	50 mL
1½ tsp	granulated sugar	7 mL
1 tsp	xanthan gum	5 mL
2 tsp	GF baking powder	10 mL
½ tsp	baking soda	2 mL
½ tsp	salt	2 mL
2 tbsp	snipped fresh rosemary leaves	25 mL
¼ cup	cold butter, cut into 1-inch (2.5 cm) cubes	50 mL
1	egg	1
⅔ cup	buttermilk	150 mL

1. *Topping:* In a large frying pan, melt butter over medium heat. Add onions, stirring frequently, until tender and a deep golden brown, about 20 minutes. Remove from heat. Stir in brown sugar and rosemary. Set aside to cool.

2. *Base:* In a large bowl, stir together brown rice flour, arrowroot starch, potato starch, sugar, xanthan gum, baking powder, baking soda, salt and rosemary.

3. Using a pastry blender or two knives, cut in butter until mixture resembles coarse crumbs.

Nutritional value per serving (1 wedge)	
Calories	255
Fat, total	11 g
Fat, saturated	5 g
Cholesterol	42 mg
Sodium	430 mg
Carbohydrate	37 g
Fiber	2 g
Protein	4 g
Calcium	122 mg
Iron	1 mg

4. In a small bowl, whisk together egg and buttermilk. Add to flour mixture all at once, stirring with a fork to make a soft, sticky dough. Spoon into prepared pan, spread evenly, leaving top rough. Let stand for 30 minutes. Spread with topping.

5. Bake in preheated oven for 20 to 25 minutes or until top is golden. Remove to a cooling rack immediately. Cut into 6 wedges. Serve warm.

Variations

Substitute fresh oregano or basil for the rosemary.

When Vidalia onions are out of season, try Spanish onions instead.

Spoon batter into 4 lightly greased English muffin rings placed on a baking sheet, three-quarters full. Do not press the dough down, spread with topping and bake for 12 to 15 minutes or until tops are golden.

Lemon Yogurt Scones

Tangy with yogurt and
lemon, these biscuits,
served warm from the
oven, quickly become
a favorite!

Tip

*Cold butter cuts more
easily into dry ingredients
than soft butter and it
produces flakier biscuits.
For easier handling, first
cut the butter into 1-inch
(2.5 cm) cubes.*

- Preheat oven to 425°F (220°C)
- English muffin rings placed on a baking sheet and lightly greased (see Equipment Glossary, page 360)

1 cup	brown rice flour	250 mL
1/3 cup	arrowroot starch	75 mL
1/3 cup	potato starch	75 mL
2 tbsp	granulated sugar	25 mL
1 tsp	xanthan gum	5 mL
1 tbsp	GF baking powder	15 mL
1/2 tsp	baking soda	2 mL
1 tbsp	lemon zest	15 mL
1/2 tsp	salt	2 mL
1/3 cup	cold butter, cut into 1-inch (2.5 cm) cubes	75 mL
1 cup	plain yogurt	250 mL

1. In a large bowl, stir together rice flour, arrowroot starch, potato starch, sugar, xanthan gum, baking powder, baking soda, lemon zest and salt.

2. Using a pastry blender or two knives, cut in butter until mixture resembles coarse crumbs. Add yogurt all at once, stirring with a fork to make a soft, sticky dough.

3. Spoon into rings, three-quarters full. If desired, smooth tops with wet fingers or a small spatula but do not press the dough down or drop by heaping tablespoonfuls (15 mL) onto greased baking sheet. Let stand for 30 minutes.

4. Bake in preheated oven for 12 to 15 minutes or until top is golden. Remove to a cooling rack immediately. Remove from rings and serve warm.

Variation

For a delicious shortcake biscuit, add an extra 1 tbsp (15 mL) granulated sugar to the dry ingredients. Top with sliced fresh strawberries, peaches or raspberries in season. Serve with whipped cream.

Nutritional value per serving (1 biscuit)	
Calories	221
Fat, total	8 g
Fat, saturated	4 g
Cholesterol	12 mg
Sodium	314 mg
Carbohydrate	34 g
Fiber	1 g
Protein	3 g
Calcium	138 mg
Iron	0 mg

Southern Cornbread

Here's a new twist on an old favorite — traditional cornbread nutritionally enhanced with amaranth flour, an excellent source of high-quality protein. Serve hot from the oven with soup, a salad or a casserole.

Tips

Amaranth flour provides iron, calcium and fiber as well as protein.

An equal amount of light or regular pancake syrup or liquid honey can be substituted for the maple syrup.

- 9-inch (2.5 L) square baking pan, lightly greased

1 cup	amaranth flour	250 mL
1 1/4 cups	cornmeal	300 mL
1 1/2 tsp	xanthan gum	7 mL
2 tsp	GF baking powder	10 mL
1 tsp	baking soda	5 mL
1/2 tsp	salt	2 mL
2	eggs	2
1 cup	buttermilk	250 mL
1/3 cup	vegetable oil	75 mL
1/3 cup	pure maple syrup	75 mL

1. In a large bowl or plastic bag, combine amaranth flour, cornmeal, xanthan gum, baking powder, baking soda and salt. Mix well and set aside.

2. In a separate bowl, using an electric mixer, beat eggs, buttermilk, oil and maple syrup until combined. Add dry ingredients and mix just until combined. Spoon into prepared pan. Let stand for 30 minutes. Meanwhile, preheat oven to 350°F (180°C).

3. Bake in preheated oven for 25 to 30 minutes, or until a cake tester inserted in the center comes out clean. Serve hot.

Variation

Jazz up this cornbread with 3 slices of cooked crisp crumbled bacon and hot pepper flakes to taste.

Nutritional value per serving (1 piece)	
Calories	259
Fat, total	11 g
Fat, saturated	1 g
Cholesterol	38 mg
Sodium	320 mg
Carbohydrate	37 g
Fiber	3 g
Protein	6 g
Calcium	112 mg
Iron	2 mg

Triple Cheese Scones

Makes 8 scones

You'll be easily tempted to go back for seconds of these cheesy biscuits. Serve hot with a steaming bowl of soup on a cold winter's day.

Tips

Warm in the microwave, wrapped in a paper towel, for 25 seconds on Medium (50%). Scones become rubbery when overheated.

Add 1/4 cup (50 mL) snipped fresh parsley and 1 1/2 tsp (7 mL) snipped fresh dill, rosemary, marjoram or savory to the dry ingredients to make a cheese-herb scone.

Add 6 slices of cooked crisp crumbled bacon to dry ingredients.

Nutritional value per serving (1 scone)

Calories	263
Fat, total	16 g
Fat, saturated	6 g
Cholesterol	22 mg
Sodium	372 mg
Carbohydrate	22 g
Fiber	2 g
Protein	9 g
Calcium	292 mg
Iron	1 mg

- **9-inch (2.5 L) round baking pan, ungreased**

3/4 cup	almond flour	175 mL
3/4 cup	brown rice flour	175 mL
3 tbsp	granulated sugar	45 mL
1 tsp	xanthan gum	5 mL
1 tbsp	GF baking powder	15 mL
1 tsp	baking soda	5 mL
1/4 tsp	salt	1 mL
3 tbsp	freshly grated Parmesan cheese	45 mL
Pinch	dry mustard	Pinch
1/4 cup	shortening or butter	50 mL
3/4 cup	shredded Swiss cheese	175 mL
1/4 cup	crumbled GF blue cheese	50 mL
3/4 cup	plain yogurt	175 mL

Traditional Method

1. In a large bowl, combine almond flour, brown rice flour, sugar, xanthan gum, baking powder, baking soda, salt, Parmesan and dry mustard. Using a pastry blender or two knives, cut in shortening until mixture resembles coarse crumbs. Stir in Swiss and blue cheese. Add yogurt all at once, stirring with a fork to make a soft, sticky dough.

Food Processor Method

1. In a food processor fitted with a metal blade, pulse almond flour, brown rice flour, sugar, xanthan gum, baking powder, baking soda, salt, Parmesan and dry mustard. Add shortening, Swiss and blue cheese and pulse until mixture resembles small peas, about 5 to 10 seconds. Add yogurt and pulse 3 or 4 times, until dough just holds together. Do not over-process.

For Both Methods

2. Spoon dough into pan, leaving top rough. Let stand for 30 minutes. Meanwhile, preheat oven to 425°F (220°C). Bake in preheated oven for 20 to 25 minutes, or until top is golden. Remove immediately to a cooling rack. Cut into 8 wedges and serve hot.

Make-Your-Own Quick Bread Mix

It's great to have this mix at the ready for those hectic days when your son reminds you It's his turn to provide a snack at school tomorrow or you remember you promised to bring the goodies for a Celiac Chapter meeting.

Tip

*Divide the mix into
5 portions, each about
2 1/2 cups (625 mL), and
store in resealable plastic
bags in the freezer for up to
6 months. Label and date
before freezing.*

3 1/2 cups	sorghum flour	825 mL
2 1/2 cups	amaranth flour	625 mL
2 cups	garbanzo-fava bean flour	500 mL
1 cup	quinoa flour	250 mL
1 cup	potato starch	250 mL
1/2 cup	tapioca starch	125 mL
1/2 cup	rice bran	125 mL
1 1/4 cups	packed brown sugar	300 mL
1 tbsp	xanthan gum	15 mL
1/4 cup	GF baking powder	50 mL
2 tbsp	baking soda	25 mL
1 tbsp	salt	15 mL

1. In a very large bowl, combine the sorghum flour, amaranth flour, garbanzo-fava bean flour, quinoa flour, potato starch, tapioca starch, rice bran, brown sugar, xanthan gum, baking powder, baking soda and salt. Mix well.
2. Store dry mix in an airtight container in the freezer for up to 6 months. Allow to warm to room temperature and mix well before using.

Variation

Substitute any type of bean or pea flour for the garbanzo-fava bean flour.

Nutritional value per serving (1 muffin)	
Calories	106
Fat, total	1 g
Fat, saturated	0 g
Cholesterol	0 mg
Sodium	247 mg
Carbohydrate	22 g
Fiber	3 g
Protein	3 g
Calcium	60 mg
Iron	1 mg

Apricot Date Muffins or Loaf

Makes 12 muffins or 1 loaf
or 12 servings

This tangy moist muffin that starts with our mix combines the complementary flavors of sweet dates, tart dried apricots and zesty orange. The perfect recipe for the time-pressured baker!

Tips

Use scissors to snip the apricots and dates. When scissors become sticky, dip them in hot water.

We prefer to snip apricots into large pieces ourselves. The tiny slivers you purchase are too small to give a burst of flavor.

When purchasing chopped dates, check for wheat starch in the coating.

Nutritional value per serving	
Calories	200
Fat, total	5 g
Fat, saturated	1 g
Cholesterol	29 mg
Sodium	280 mg
Carbohydrate	37 g
Fiber	4 g
Protein	6 g
Calcium	125 mg
Iron	2 mg

- **12-cup muffin tin or 9- by 5-inch (2 L) loaf pan, lightly greased**

⅕ batch	Make-Your-Own Quick Bread Mix (see recipe, page 191)	⅕ batch
⅔ cup	chopped apricots	150 mL
⅔ cup	chopped pitted dates	150 mL
3 tbsp	grated orange zest	45 mL
1 tsp	ground nutmeg	5 mL
2	eggs	2
1¼ cups	plain yogurt	300 mL
2 tbsp	vegetable oil	25 mL

1. In a large bowl or plastic bag, combine bread mix, apricots, dates, orange zest and nutmeg. Mix well and set aside.
2. In a separate bowl, using an electric mixer, beat eggs, yogurt and oil until combined. Add dry ingredients and stir just until combined.

For Muffins

3. Spoon batter evenly into each cup of prepared muffin tin. Let stand for 30 minutes. Bake in preheated oven for 18 to 20 minutes, or until firm to the touch. Remove from the pan immediately and let cool completely on a rack.

For a Loaf

3. Spoon batter into prepared loaf pan. Let stand for 30 minutes. Meanwhile, preheat oven to 350°F (180°C). Bake in preheated oven for 55 to 65 minutes, or until an instant read thermometer registers 200°F (100°C). Let cool in the pan on a rack for 10 minutes. Remove from the pan and let cool completely on a rack.

Variations

Add ⅓ cup (75 mL) chopped dried apple with the apricots and dates.

An equal amount of chopped pitted prunes can be substituted for either the apricots or the dates.

Cheddar Bacon Muffins or Loaf

Is there a cheese lover out there who doesn't enjoy Cheddar and bacon? Perfect with a salad for lunch.

Tip

Cook the bacon in the microwave for a crisper texture. Refer to your microwave manufacturer's "instructions for use" for power and time (it's usually about 1 minute per slice). Drain well on paper towels.

- 12-cup muffin tin or 9- by 5-inch (2 L) loaf pan, lightly greased

6	slices GF bacon, cooked crisp and crumbled	6
1/5 batch	Make-Your-Own Quick Bread Mix (see recipe, page 191)	1/5 batch
3/4 cup	shredded old Cheddar cheese	175 mL
2/3 cup	snipped chives or green onion tops	150 mL
1/4 cup	freshly grated Parmesan cheese	50 mL
1/4 tsp	dry mustard	1 mL
2	eggs	2
1 cup	buttermilk	250 mL
2 tbsp	vegetable oil	25 mL

1. In a large bowl or plastic bag, combine bacon, bread mix, Cheddar, chives, Parmesan and mustard. Mix well and set aside.
2. In a separate bowl, using an electric mixer, beat eggs, buttermilk and oil until combined. Add dry ingredients and stir just until combined.

For Muffins

3. Spoon batter evenly into each cup of prepared muffin tin. Let stand for 30 minutes. Bake in preheated oven for 18 to 20 minutes, or until firm to the touch. Remove from the pan immediately and let cool completely on a rack.

For a Loaf

3. Spoon batter into prepared loaf pan. Let stand for 30 minutes. Bake in preheated oven for 50 to 60 minutes, or until an instant read thermometer registers 200°F (100°C). Let cool in the pan on a rack for 10 minutes. Remove from the pan and let cool completely on a rack.

Variation

Substitute Swiss, GF Blue or GF Stilton cheese for the Cheddar.

Nutritional value per serving	
Calories	197
Fat, total	8 g
Fat, saturated	3 g
Cholesterol	41 mg
Sodium	416 mg
Carbohydrate	24 g
Fiber	3 g
Protein	8 g
Calcium	168 mg
Iron	2 mg

Chocolate Orange Muffins or Loaf

Makes 12 muffins or 1 loaf

or 12 servings

Who can resist the combination of chocolate and orange? The buttermilk brings out the chocolate flavor without adding a lot of calories. The recipe is super-fast, as it begins with our mix.

Tips

The chocolate pieces will partially melt or remain whole depending on whether you use mini-chips, regular-size chips or chocolate chunks.

Top a slice of loaf with a scoop of GF ice cream and Simple Hot Fudge Sauce (page 325) for a finale.

Nutritional value per serving	
Calories	247
Fat, total	10 g
Fat, saturated	3 g
Cholesterol	28 mg
Sodium	272 mg
Carbohydrate	35 g
Fiber	3 g
Protein	6 g
Calcium	81 mg
Iron	2 mg

• **12-cup muffin tin or 9- by 5-inch (2 L) loaf pan, lightly greased**

⅕ batch	Make-Your-Own Quick Bread Mix (see recipe, page 191)	⅕ batch
⅔ cup	semi-sweet chocolate chips	150 mL
¼ cup	unsweetened cocoa powder, sifted	50 mL
2 tbsp	grated orange zest	25 mL
2	eggs	2
⅔ cup	buttermilk	150 mL
⅔ cup	freshly squeezed orange juice	150 mL
¼ cup	vegetable oil	50 mL

1. In a large bowl or plastic bag, combine bread mix, chocolate chips, cocoa and orange zest. Mix well and se aside.

2. In a separate bowl, using an electric mixer, beat eggs, buttermilk, orange juice and oil until combined. Add dry ingredients and stir just until combined.

For Muffins

3. Spoon batter evenly into each cup of prepared muffin tin. Let stand for 30 minutes. Bake in preheated oven for 18 to 20 minutes, or until firm to the touch. Remove from the pan immediately and let cool completely on a rack.

For a Loaf

3. Spoon batter into prepared loaf pan. Let stand for 30 minutes. Bake in preheated oven for 55 to 65 minutes, or until an instant read thermometer registers 200°F (100°C). Let cool in the pan on a rack for 10 minutes. Remove from the pan and let cool completely on a rack.

Variations

To turn these muffins into sweeter cupcakes, add an extra 1 to 2 tbsp (15 to 25 mL) granulated sugar to the dry ingredients.

Instead of regular chocolate chips, try raspberry- or mint-flavored chocolate chips.

Morning Glory Muffins or Loaf

With so many wonderfully fresh ingredients in this recipe, starting with our mix, you may want to double it and give the extra to neighbors.

Tips

Don't drain the pineapple; just spoon both juice and pulp into your measuring cup.

Substitute an equal amount of shredded zucchini for the carrots.

- **12-cup muffin tin or 9- by 5-inch (2 L) loaf pan, lightly greased**

⅕ batch	Make-Your-Own Quick Bread Mix (see recipe, page 191)	⅕ batch
⅓ cup	unsweetened shredded coconut	75 mL
¼ cup	raisins	50 mL
1 tbsp	grated lemon zest	15 mL
1 tsp	ground cinnamon	5 mL
2	eggs	2
1 cup	unsweetened applesauce	250 mL
2 tbsp	vegetable oil	25 mL
1 cup	shredded carrots	250 mL
½ cup	crushed pineapple, including juice	125 mL

1. In a large bowl or plastic bag, combine bread mix, coconut, raisins, lemon zest and cinnamon. Mix well and set aside.

2. In a separate bowl, using an electric mixer, beat eggs, applesauce and oil until combined. Stir in carrots and pineapple. Add dry ingredients and stir just until combined.

For Muffins

3. Spoon batter evenly into each cup of prepared muffin tin. Let stand for 30 minutes. Bake in preheated oven for 18 to 20 minutes, or until firm to the touch. Remove from the pan immediately and let cool completely on a rack.

For a Loaf

3. Spoon batter into prepared loaf pan. Let stand for 30 minutes. Bake in preheated oven for 55 to 65 minutes, or until an instant read thermometer registers 200°F (100°C). Let cool in the pan on a rack for 10 minutes. Remove from the pan and let cool completely on a rack.

Nutritional value per serving	
Calories	184
Fat, total	6 g
Fat, saturated	2 g
Cholesterol	27 mg
Sodium	266 mg
Carbohydrate	30 g
Fiber	4 g
Protein	4 g
Calcium	74 mg
Iron	2 mg

Rhubarb Pistachio Muffins or Loaf

Nothing heralds the arrival of spring more than a neighbor knocking on your door with an armful of rosy rhubarb. Use it to prepare this recipe, which starts with our mix. Little bits of tanginess dot this soft, slightly sweet treat — it's perfect for breakfast.

Tips

For easy slicing of the loaf, the rhubarb must be finely chopped.

Warm muffins or loaf slices in the microwave, wrapped in a paper towel, for 25 seconds on Medium (50%) power.

Nutritional value per serving	
Calories	204
Fat, total	9 g
Fat, saturated	1 g
Cholesterol	27 mg
Sodium	258 mg
Carbohydrate	28 g
Fiber	4 g
Protein	5 g
Calcium	88 mg
Iron	2 mg

- **12-cup muffin tin or 9- by 5-inch (2 L) loaf pan, lightly greased**

⅕ batch	Make-Your-Own Quick Bread Mix (see recipe, page 191)	⅕ batch
½ cup	chopped pistachios	125 mL
2 tbsp	granulated sugar	25 mL
2 tbsp	grated orange zest	25 mL
1 tsp	ground ginger	5 mL
2	eggs	2
⅔ cup	freshly squeezed orange juice	150 mL
¼ cup	vegetable oil	50 mL
1¾ cups	finely chopped rhubarb	425 mL

1. In a large bowl or plastic bag, combine bread mix, pistachios, sugar, orange zest and ginger. Mix well and set aside.

2. In a separate bowl, using an electric mixer, beat eggs, orange juice and oil until combined. Stir in rhubarb. Add dry ingredients and stir just until combined.

For Muffins

3. Spoon batter evenly into each cup of prepared muffin tin. Let stand for 30 minutes. Bake in preheated oven for 18 to 20 minutes, or until firm to the touch. Remove from the pan immediately and let cool completely on a rack.

For a Loaf

3. Spoon batter into prepared loaf pan. Let stand for 30 minutes. Bake in preheated oven for 55 to 65 minutes, or until an instant read thermometer registers 200°F (100°C). Let cool in the pan on a rack for 10 minutes. Remove from the pan and let cool completely on a rack.

Variation

Substitute pecans or walnuts for the pistachios.

Bread Machine Recipes

Dough Cycle and Bake Cycle

1. In a large bowl or plastic bag, combine dry ingredients. Mix well and set aside.

2. Pour liquid ingredients into the bread machine baking pan. Add eggs and egg whites.

3. Select the Dough Cycle. As the bread machine is mixing, gradually add the dry ingredients, scraping bottom and sides of pan with a rubber spatula. Try to incorporate all the dry ingredients within 1 to 2 minutes. When the mixing and kneading are complete, remove the kneading blade, leaving the bread pan in the bread machine. Quickly smooth the top of the loaf. Allow the cycle to finish. Turn off the bread machine.

4. Select the Bake Cycle. Set time to 60 minutes and temperature to 350°F (180°C). Allow the cycle to finish. Do not turn machine off before taking the internal temperature of the loaf with an instant-read thermometer. It should be 200°F (100°C). If it's between 180°F (82°C) and 200°F (100°C), leave machine on the Keep Warm Cycle until baked. If it's below 180°F (82°C), turn on the Bake Cycle and check the internal temperature every 10 minutes. (Some bread machines are automatically set for 60 minutes; others need to be set by 10-minute intervals.)

5. Once the loaf has reached 200°F (100°C), remove it from the pan immediately and let cool completely on a rack.

Baking Bread Machine Yeast Breads

- The recipes were developed for 1.5 lb (750 g) and 2 lb (1 kg) bread machines with a Gluten-Free Cycle, a Dough then a Bake Cycle, or a programmable mode. A 58-Minute Rapid Cycle or 70-Minute Rapid Cycle are not long enough to rise and bake the loaves successfully.
- If your bread machine has a preheat, keep the top down until it starts so the heat doesn't escape. As soon as the liquids begin to mix, add the dry ingredients, scraping the sides and bottom of the baking pan with a rubber spatula. Watch that the spatula does not get caught under the blade. Quickly close the top.
- The dough should be the consistency of a thick batter. You can see the mixing pattern of the blade in the batter. Some doughs are thicker than others but do not adjust by adding more liquid ingredients.
- Some bread machines knead intermittently rather than continuously so the first few times you use a new machine listen carefully for the sounds of each cycle. Removing the blade as soon as the long knead is done prevents over-kneading and a collapsed loaf. Set a kitchen timer so you won't miss it. Dough is sticky so rinse a rubber spatula and your hand with cold water before removing the blade. Smooth the top quickly once the paddle is removed.
- At the end of the cycle, before turning off the bread machine, take the temperature of the loaf using an instant-read thermometer. It should read 200°F (100°C). If it hasn't reached the recommended temperature, leave the loaf in the machine for 10 to 15 minutes on the Keep Warm Cycle.

Banana Seed Bread

Makes 1 loaf
or 12 servings

The combination of sorghum and bean flour really enhances the banana flavor of this loaf. Serve it for dessert or with a slice of old Cheddar for lunch.

Tips

If your machine doesn't have a Gluten-Free Cycle, see Dough Cycle and Bake Cycle, page 198.

To ensure success, see page 199 for extra information on baking yeast bread in a bread machine.

Use raw, unroasted, unsalted sunflower seeds. For a nuttier flavor, toast the sunflower seeds (see Techniques Glossary, page 371, for instructions).

Nutritional value per serving

Calories	212
Fat, total	9 g
Fat, saturated	1 g
Cholesterol	27 mg
Sodium	256 mg
Carbohydrate	29 g
Fiber	4 g
Protein	7 g
Calcium	23 mg
Iron	2 mg

● **Instant-read thermometer**

1 cup	whole bean flour	250 mL
1 cup	sorghum flour	250 mL
¼ cup	tapioca starch	50 mL
¼ cup	packed brown sugar	50 mL
2 ½ tsp	xanthan gum	12 mL
1 tbsp	bread machine or instant yeast	15 mL
1¼ tsp	salt	6 mL
½ cup	sunflower or pumpkin seeds	125 mL
¾ cup	water	175 mL
1 cup	mashed banana	250 mL
1 tsp	cider vinegar	5 mL
¼ cup	vegetable oil	50 mL
2	eggs	2

1. In a large bowl or plastic bag, combine whole bean flour, sorghum flour, tapioca starch, brown sugar, xanthan gum, yeast, salt and sunflower seeds. Mix well and set aside.

2. Pour water, banana, vinegar and oil into the bread machine baking pan. Add eggs.

3. Select the Gluten-Free Cycle. Allow the liquids to mix until combined. As the bread machine is mixing, gradually add the dry ingredients, scraping bottom and sides of pan with a rubber spatula. Try to incorporate all the dry ingredients within 1 to 2 minutes. When the mixing and kneading are complete, remove the kneading blade, leaving the bread pan in the bread machine. Quickly smooth the top of the loaf. Allow the cycle to finish.

4. At the end of the cycle, take the temperature of the loaf using an instant-read thermometer. It is baked at 200°F (100°C). If it's between 180°F (82°C) and 200°F (100°C), leave machine on the Keep Warm Cycle until baked. If it's below 180°F (82°C), turn on the Bake Cycle and check the internal temperature every 10 minutes. (Some bread machines are automatically set for 60 minutes; others need to be set by 10-minute intervals.)

5. Once the loaf has reached 200°F (100°C), remove it from the pan immediately and let cool completely on a rack.

Brown Bread

· ·

Makes 1 loaf
or 12 servings

The perfect sandwich bread! Just add shaved roast beef, a leaf of romaine and a hint of mustard. It carries well for a tasty lunch.

Tips

If your machine doesn't have a Gluten-Free Cycle, see Dough Cycle and Bake Cycle, page 198.

To ensure success, see page 199 for extra information on baking yeast bread in a bread machine.

Slice this or any bread with an electric knife for thin, even sandwich slices.

For a mild-flavored bread, substitute 2 tbsp (25 mL) packed brown sugar for the molasses.

Nutritional value per serving	
Calories	191
Fat, total	5 g
Fat, saturated	1 g
Cholesterol	41 mg
Sodium	264 mg
Carbohydrate	34 g
Fiber	3 g
Protein	5 g
Calcium	14 mg
Iron	2 mg

• **Instant-read thermometer**

1½ cups	brown rice flour	375 mL
½ cup	sorghum flour	125 mL
½ cup	cornstarch	125 mL
½ cup	rice bran or brown rice flour	125 mL
1 tbsp	xanthan gum	15 mL
1 tbsp	bread machine or instant yeast	15 mL
1¼ tsp	salt	6 mL
1 cup	water	250 mL
1 tsp	cider vinegar	5 mL
2 tbsp	vegetable oil	25 mL
2 tbsp	liquid honey	25 mL
2 tbsp	fancy molasses	25 mL
3	eggs	3

1. In a large bowl or plastic bag, combine brown rice flour, sorghum flour, cornstarch, rice bran, xanthan gum, yeast and salt. Mix well and set aside.

2. Pour water, vinegar, oil, honey and molasses into the bread machine baking pan. Add eggs.

3. Select the Gluten-Free Cycle. Allow the liquids to mix until combined. As the bread machine is mixing, gradually add the dry ingredients, scraping bottom and sides of pan with a rubber spatula. Try to incorporate all the dry ingredients within 1 to 2 minutes. When the mixing and kneading are complete, remove the kneading blade, leaving the bread pan in the bread machine. Quickly smooth the top of the loaf. Allow the cycle to finish.

4. At the end of the cycle, take the temperature of the loaf using an instant-read thermometer. It is baked at 200°F (100°C). If it's between 180°F (82°C) and 200°F (100°C), leave machine on the Keep Warm Cycle until baked. If it's below 180°F (82°C), turn on the Bake Cycle and check the internal temperature every 10 minutes. (Some bread machines are automatically set for 60 minutes; others need to be set by 10-minute intervals.)

5. Once the loaf has reached 200°F (100°C), remove it from the pan immediately and let cool completely on a rack.

Cheese Onion Loaf

Makes 1 loaf
or 12 servings

This is a perfect accompaniment to homemade chili or beef stew. It slices well and stays moist for a second day.

Tips

If your machine doesn't have a Gluten-Free Cycle, see Dough Cycle and Bake Cycle, page 198.

To ensure success, see page 199 for extra information on baking yeast bread in a bread machine.

Do not substitute fresh onion for the dried flakes. The extra moisture results in a weak-flavored shorter loaf.

● **Instant-read thermometer**

1⅔ cups	brown rice flour	400 mL
⅔ cup	sorghum flour	150 mL
⅓ cup	arrowroot starch	75 mL
¼ cup	nonfat dry milk or skim milk powder	50 mL
2 tbsp	granulated sugar	25 mL
1 tbsp	xanthan gum	15 mL
1 tbsp	bread machine or instant yeast	15 mL
1¼ tsp	salt	6 mL
1 cup	shredded old Cheddar cheese	250 mL
2 tbsp	dried onion flakes	25 mL
¼ tsp	dry mustard	1 mL
1 cup	water	250 mL
2 tsp	cider vinegar	10 mL
2	eggs	2
2	egg whites	2

1. In a large bowl or plastic bag, combine rice flour, sorghum flour, arrowroot starch, milk powder, sugar, xanthan gum, yeast, salt, cheese, onion flakes and mustard. Mix well and set aside.

2. Pour water and vinegar into bread machine baking pan. Add eggs and egg whites.

3. Select the Gluten-Free Cycle. Allow the liquids to mix until combined. As the bread machine is mixing, gradually add the dry ingredients, scraping bottom and sides of pan with a rubber spatula. Try to incorporate all the dry ingredients within 1 to 2 minutes. When the mixing and kneading are complete, remove the kneading blade, leaving the bread pan in the bread machine. Quickly smooth the top of the loaf. Allow the cycle to finish.

Nutritional value per serving

Calories	187
Fat, total	5 g
Fat, saturated	2 g
Cholesterol	35 mg
Sodium	334 mg
Carbohydrate	31 g
Fiber	2 g
Protein	7 g
Calcium	92 mg
Iron	1 mg

Tip

For the amount of cheese to purchase, see the weight/ volume equivalents in the Ingredient Glossary, page 363.

4. At the end of the cycle, take the temperature of the loaf using an instant-read thermometer. It is baked at 200°F (100°C). If it's between 180°F (82°C) and 200°F (100°C), leave machine on the Keep Warm Cycle until baked. If it's below 180°F (82°C), turn on the Bake Cycle and check the internal temperature every 10 minutes. (Some bread machines are automatically set for 60 minutes; others need to be set by 10-minute intervals.)

5. Once the loaf has reached 200°F (100°C), remove it from the pan immediately and let cool completely on a rack.

Variation

Monterey Jack, Parmesan or Swiss cheese could be substituted for the Cheddar. Try a combination but do not exceed the total volume in the recipe or the loaf will be short and heavy.

Buckwheat Walnut

This is the bread for those who love to combine strong, robust flavors — buckwheat, whole bean flour and cardamom.

Tips

If your machine doesn't have a Gluten-Free Cycle, see Dough Cycle and Bake Cycle, page 198.

To ensure success, see page 199 for extra information on baking yeast bread in a bread machine.

Make sure buckwheat is on your list of allowable foods before you try this recipe.

- **Instant-read thermometer**

1¼ cups	whole bean flour	300 mL
½ cup	buckwheat or brown rice flour	125 mL
½ cup	potato starch	125 mL
¼ cup	tapioca starch	50 mL
⅓ cup	packed brown sugar	75 mL
1 tbsp	xanthan gum	15 mL
1 tbsp	bread machine or instant yeast	15 mL
1¼ tsp	salt	6 mL
1 tsp	ground cardamom or nutmeg	5 mL
1 cup	chopped walnuts	250 mL
1¾ cups	water	425 mL
1 tsp	cider vinegar	5 mL
¼ cup	vegetable oil	50 mL
2	eggs	2

1. In a large bowl or plastic bag, combine whole bean flour, buckwheat flour, potato starch, tapioca starch, brown sugar, xanthan gum, yeast, salt, cardamom and walnuts. Mix well and set aside.

2. Pour water, vinegar and oil into the bread machine baking pan. Add eggs.

3. Select the Gluten-Free Cycle. Allow the liquids to mix until combined. As the bread machine is mixing, gradually add the dry ingredients, scraping bottom and sides of pan with a rubber spatula. Try to incorporate all the dry ingredients within 1 to 2 minutes. When the mixing and kneading are complete, remove the kneading blade, leaving the bread pan in the bread machine. Quickly smooth the top of the loaf. Allow the cycle to finish.

4. At the end of the cycle, take the temperature of the loaf using an instant-read thermometer. It is baked at 200°F (100°C). If it's between 180°F (82°C) and 200°F (100°C), leave machine on the Keep Warm Cycle until baked. If it's below 180°F (82°C), turn on the Bake Cycle and check the internal temperature every 10 minutes. (Some bread machines are automatically set for 60 minutes; others need to be set by 10-minute intervals.)

5. Once the loaf has reached 200°F (100°C), remove it from the pan immediately and let cool completely on a rack.

Nutritional value per serving

Calories	257
Fat, total	13 g
Fat, saturated	1 g
Cholesterol	27 mg
Sodium	256 mg
Carbohydrate	30 g
Fiber	4 g
Protein	8 g
Calcium	29 mg
Iron	2 mg

Cinnamon Raisin Bread

Makes 1 loaf
or 12 servings

Enjoy a toasted slice or two of this deep golden loaf for breakfast — it's the perfect snack when served with a cup of hot cocoa.

Tips

If your machine doesn't have a Gluten-Free Cycle, see Dough Cycle and Bake Cycle, page 198.

To ensure success, see page 199 for extra information on baking yeast bread in a bread machine.

Thoroughly mix the dry ingredients before adding them to the liquids — they are powder-fine and can clump together.

Nutritional value per serving	
Calories	258
Fat, total	4 g
Fat, saturated	0 g
Cholesterol	28 mg
Sodium	280 mg
Carbohydrate	53 g
Fiber	3 g
Protein	5 g
Calcium	40 mg
Iron	1 mg

- Instant-read thermometer

1¾ cups	brown rice flour	425 mL
½ cup	potato starch	125 mL
¼ cup	tapioca starch	50 mL
½ cup	granulated sugar	125 mL
¼ cup	nonfat (skim) milk powder	50 mL
1 tbsp	xanthan gum	15 mL
1 tbsp	bread machine or instant yeast	15 mL
1¼ tsp	salt	6 mL
1 tbsp	ground cinnamon	15 mL
1 cup	water	250 mL
2 tbsp	vegetable oil	25 mL
2 tsp	cider vinegar	10 mL
2	eggs	2
2	egg whites	2
1½ cups	raisins	375 mL

1. In a large bowl or plastic bag, combine rice flour, potato starch, tapioca starch, sugar, milk powder, xanthan gum, yeast, salt and cinnamon. Mix well and set aside.

2. Pour water, oil and vinegar into the bread machine baking pan. Add eggs and egg whites.

3. Select the Gluten-Free Cycle. Allow the liquids to mix until combined. As the bread machine is mixing, gradually add the dry ingredients, scraping bottom and sides of pan with a rubber spatula. Try to incorporate all the dry ingredients within 1 to 2 minutes. When the mixing and kneading are complete, remove the kneading blade, leaving the bread pan in the bread machine. Quickly smooth the top of the loaf. Allow the cycle to finish.

4. At the end of the cycle, take the temperature of the loaf using an instant-read thermometer. It is baked at 200°F (100°C). If it's between 180°F (82°C) and 200°F (100°C), leave machine on the Keep Warm Cycle until baked. If it's below 180°F (82°C), turn on the Bake Cycle and check the internal temperature every 10 minutes. (Some bread machines are automatically set for 60 minutes; others need to be set by 10-minute intervals.)

5. Once the loaf has reached 200°F (100°C), remove it from the pan immediately and let cool completely on a rack.

Cornbread

**Makes 1 loaf
or 12 servings**

Tiny bits of moist kernel corn dot this warm-colored yellow loaf.

Tips

If your machine doesn't have a Gluten-Free Cycle, see Dough Cycle and Bake Cycle, page 198.

To ensure success, see page 199 for extra information on baking yeast bread in a bread machine.

Drain the canned corn before measuring. If using frozen corn, thaw and drain before measuring.

Nutritional value per serving	
Calories	228
Fat, total	7 g
Fat, saturated	1 g
Cholesterol	55 mg
Sodium	286 mg
Carbohydrate	38 g
Fiber	2 g
Protein	4 g
Calcium	10 mg
Iron	1 mg

● **Instant-read thermometer**

1 1/4 cups	brown rice flour	300 mL
1 cup	cornmeal	250 mL
1/2 cup	potato starch	125 mL
1/4 cup	tapioca starch	50 mL
3 tbsp	granulated sugar	45 mL
1 tbsp	xanthan gum	15 mL
1 tbsp	bread machine or instant yeast	15 mL
1 1/4 tsp	salt	6 mL
1 1/4 cups	water	300 mL
1 tsp	cider vinegar	5 mL
1/4 cup	vegetable oil	50 mL
1/2 cup	well-drained whole corn kernels	125 mL
4	eggs	4

1. In a large bowl or plastic bag, combine rice flour, cornmeal, potato starch, tapioca starch, sugar, xanthan gum, yeast and salt. Mix well and set aside.

2. Pour water, vinegar, oil and corn into bread machine baking pan. Add eggs.

3. Select the Gluten-Free Cycle. Allow the liquids to mix until combined. As the bread machine is mixing, gradually add the dry ingredients, scraping bottom and sides of pan with a rubber spatula. Try to incorporate all the dry ingredients within 1 to 2 minutes. When the mixing and kneading are complete, remove the kneading blade, leaving the bread pan in the bread machine. Quickly smooth the top of the loaf. Allow the cycle to finish.

4. At the end of the cycle, take the temperature of the loaf using an instant-read thermometer. It is baked at 200°F (100°C). If it's between 180°F (82°C) and 200°F (100°C), leave machine on the Keep Warm Cycle until baked. If it's below 180°F (82°C), turn on the Bake Cycle and check the internal temperature every 10 minutes. (Some bread machines are automatically set for 60 minutes; others need to be set by 10-minute intervals.)

5. Once the loaf has reached 200°F (100°C), remove it from the pan immediately and let cool completely on a rack.

Cottage Cheese Dill Loaf

Makes 1 loaf
or 12 servings

Try this twist on a traditional white bread to serve along with salmon or your favorite seafood entrée.

Tips

If your machine doesn't have a Gluten-Free Cycle, see Dough Cycle and Bake Cycle, page 198.

To ensure success, see page 199 for extra information on baking yeast bread in a bread machine.

Any type of cottage cheese — large or small curd, high or low fat — works well in this recipe.

Nutritional value per serving	
Calories	240
Fat, total	7 g
Fat, saturated	1 g
Cholesterol	55 mg
Sodium	351 mg
Carbohydrate	40 g
Fiber	1 g
Protein	5 g
Calcium	15 mg
Iron	0 mg

- **Instant-read thermometer**

2 cups	brown rice flour	500 mL
⅔ cup	potato starch	150 mL
⅓ cup	tapioca starch	75 mL
2½ tsp	xanthan gum	12 mL
2 tsp	bread machine or instant yeast	10 mL
1½ tsp	salt	7 mL
1 tbsp	snipped fresh dill	15 mL
1 cup	water	250 mL
1 tsp	cider vinegar	5 mL
½ cup	low-fat cottage cheese	125 mL
¼ cup	vegetable oil	50 mL
¼ cup	liquid honey	50 mL
4	eggs	4

1. In a large bowl or plastic bag, combine rice flour, potato starch, tapioca starch, xanthan gum, yeast, salt and dill. Mix well and set aside.

2. Pour water, vinegar, cottage cheese, oil and honey into bread machine baking pan. Add eggs.

3. Select the Gluten-Free Cycle. Allow the liquids to mix until combined. As the bread machine is mixing, gradually add the dry ingredients, scraping bottom and sides of pan with a rubber spatula. Try to incorporate all the dry ingredients within 1 to 2 minutes. When the mixing and kneading are complete, remove the kneading blade, leaving the bread pan in the bread machine. Quickly smooth the top of the loaf. Allow the cycle to finish.

4. At the end of the cycle, take the temperature of the loaf using an instant-read thermometer. It is baked at 200°F (100°C). If it's between 180°F (82°C) and 200°F (100°C), leave machine on the Keep Warm Cycle until baked. If it's below 180°F (82°C), turn on the Bake Cycle and check the internal temperature every 10 minutes. (Some bread machines are automatically set for 60 minutes; others need to be set by 10-minute intervals.)

5. Once the loaf has reached 200°F (100°C), remove it from the pan immediately and let cool completely on a rack.

Cranberry Wild Rice Loaf

This attractive loaf is sure to bring compliments from guests. The nutty taste with a hint of orange makes this a perfect accompaniment for duck or turkey.

Tips

If your machine doesn't have a Gluten-Free Cycle, see Dough Cycle and Bake Cycle, page 198.

To ensure success, see page 199 for extra information on baking yeast bread in a bread machine.

Nutritional value per serving

Calories	239
Fat, total	6 g
Fat, saturated	1 g
Cholesterol	27 mg
Sodium	315 mg
Carbohydrate	44 g
Fiber	2 g
Protein	4 g
Calcium	9 mg
Iron	1 mg

- **Instant-read thermometer**

1½ cups	brown rice flour	375 mL
⅔ cup	tapioca starch	150 mL
⅓ cup	potato starch	75 mL
¼ cup	granulated sugar	50 mL
2½ tsp	xanthan gum	12 mL
2 tsp	bread machine or instant yeast	10 mL
1½ tsp	salt	7 mL
2 tsp	orange zest	10 mL
¾ tsp	celery seeds	4 mL
⅛ tsp	freshly ground black pepper	0.5 mL
1 cup	cooked wild rice (see Techniques Glossary, page 371)	250 mL
¾ cup	dried cranberries	175 mL
1 cup	water	250 mL
¼ cup	frozen orange juice concentrate, thawed	50 mL
¼ cup	vegetable oil	50 mL
2	eggs	2
2	egg whites	2

1. In a large bowl or plastic bag, combine brown rice flour, tapioca starch, potato starch, sugar, xanthan gum, yeast, salt, zest, celery seeds, black pepper, wild rice and cranberries. Mix well and set aside.

2. Pour water, orange juice concentrate and oil into the bread machine baking pan. Add eggs and egg whites.

3. Select the Gluten-Free Cycle. Allow the liquids to mix until combined. As the bread machine is mixing, gradually add the dry ingredients, scraping bottom and sides of pan with a rubber spatula. Try to incorporate all the dry ingredients within 1 to 2 minutes. When the mixing and kneading are complete, remove the kneading blade, leaving the bread pan in the bread machine. Quickly smooth the top of the loaf. Allow the cycle to finish.

4. At the end of the cycle, take the temperature of the loaf using an instant-read thermometer. It is baked at 200°F (100°C). If it's between 180°F (82°C) and 200°F (100°C), leave machine on the Keep Warm Cycle until baked. If it's below 180°F (82°C), turn on the Bake Cycle and check the internal temperature every 10 minutes. (Some bread machines are automatically set for 60 minutes; others need to be set by 10-minute intervals.)

5. Once the loaf has reached 200°F (100°C), remove it from the pan immediately and let cool completely on a rack.

Variation

Substitute raspberry or orange-flavored dried cranberries.

Daffodil Loaf

Bring a little bit of springtime to your table! Enjoy this bread's light, cake-like texture, with its refreshing aroma and flavor of orange. Serve for a mid-morning coffee break.

Tips

If your machine doesn't have a Gluten-Free Cycle, see Dough Cycle and Bake Cycle, page 198.

To ensure success, see page 199 for extra information on baking yeast bread in a bread machine.

For thin, even slices, use an electric knife for this and all breads.

Nutritional value per serving

Calories	212
Fat, total	6 g
Fat, saturated	1 g
Cholesterol	27 mg
Sodium	260 mg
Carbohydrate	37 g
Fiber	3 g
Protein	4 g
Calcium	10 mg
Iron	1 mg

● **Instant-read thermometer**

1½ cups	brown rice flour	375 mL
¾ cup	quinoa flour	175 mL
½ cup	arrowroot starch	125 mL
¼ cup	tapioca starch	50 mL
1 tbsp	xanthan gum	15 mL
1 tbsp	bread machine or instant yeast	15 mL
1¼ tsp	salt	6 mL
1 cup	water	250 mL
¼ cup	vegetable oil	50 mL
3 tbsp	frozen orange juice concentrate, thawed	45 mL
2	eggs	2
½ cup	Orange Marmalade (see recipe, page 35)	125 mL

1. In a large bowl or plastic bag, combine brown rice flour, quinoa flour, arrowroot starch, tapioca starch, xanthan gum, yeast and salt. Mix well and set aside.

2. Pour water, oil and orange juice concentrate into the bread machine baking pan. Add eggs and marmalade.

3. Select the Gluten-Free Cycle. Allow the liquids to mix until combined. As the bread machine is mixing, gradually add the dry ingredients, scraping bottom and sides of pan with a rubber spatula. Try to incorporate all the dry ingredients within 1 to 2 minutes. When the mixing and kneading are complete, remove the kneading blade, leaving the bread pan in the bread machine. Quickly smooth the top of the loaf. Allow the cycle to finish.

4. At the end of the cycle, take the temperature of the loaf using an instant-read thermometer. It is baked at 200°F (100°C). If it's between 180°F (82°C) and 200°F (100°C), leave machine on the Keep Warm Cycle until baked. If it's below 180°F (82°C), turn on the Bake Cycle and check the internal temperature every 10 minutes. (Some bread machines are automatically set for 60 minutes; others need to be set by 10-minute intervals.)

5. Once the loaf has reached 200°F (100°C), remove it from the pan immediately and let cool completely on a rack.

Flaxseed with Banana Bread

Toasting a slice brings out the banana flavor. No need to butter this bread.

Tips

If your machine doesn't have a Gluten-Free Cycle, see Dough Cycle and Bake Cycle, page 198.

To ensure success, see page 199 for extra information on baking yeast bread in a bread machine.

Pancake syrup (light or regular) or packed brown sugar can be substituted for the pure maple syrup.

Nutritional value per serving	
Calories	229
Fat, total	8 g
Fat, saturated	1 g
Cholesterol	27 mg
Sodium	316 mg
Carbohydrate	39 g
Fiber	3 g
Protein	4 g
Calcium	22 mg
Iron	1 mg

- Instant-read thermometer

1½ cups	brown rice flour	375 mL
⅔ cup	potato starch	150 mL
⅓ cup	tapioca starch	75 mL
1 tbsp	xanthan gum	15 mL
2 tsp	bread machine or instant yeast	10 mL
1½ tsp	salt	7 mL
⅓ cup	cracked flaxseed (see Techniques Glossary, page 369)	75 mL
¾ cup	water	175 mL
1 cup	mashed banana	250 mL
2 tsp	cider vinegar	10 mL
¼ cup	vegetable oil	50 mL
¼ cup	pure maple syrup	50 mL
2	eggs	2
2	egg whites	2

1. In a large bowl or plastic bag, combine brown rice flour, potato starch, tapioca starch, xanthan gum, yeast, salt and flaxseed. Mix well and set aside.

2. Pour water, banana, vinegar, oil and maple syrup into the bread machine baking pan. Add eggs and egg whites.

3. Select the Gluten-Free Cycle. Allow the liquids to mix until combined. As the bread machine is mixing, gradually add the dry ingredients, scraping bottom and sides of pan with a rubber spatula. Try to incorporate all the dry ingredients within 1 to 2 minutes. When the mixing and kneading are complete, remove the kneading blade, leaving the bread pan in the bread machine. Quickly smooth the top of the loaf. Allow the cycle to finish.

4. At the end of the cycle, take the temperature of the loaf using an instant-read thermometer. It is baked at 200°F (100°C). If it's between 180°F (82°C) and 200°F (100°C), leave machine on the Keep Warm Cycle until baked. If it's below 180°F (82°C), turn on the Bake Cycle and check the internal temperature every 10 minutes. (Some bread machines are automatically set for 60 minutes; others need to be set by 10-minute intervals.)

5. Once the loaf has reached 200°F (100°C), remove it from the pan immediately and let cool completely on a rack.

Henk's Flax Bread

Henk Rietveld of Huntsville, Ontario, a recipe tester and member of the focus group for this book, suggested using the flax flour in this loaf.

Tips

If your machine doesn't have a Gluten-Free Cycle, see Dough Cycle and Bake Cycle, page 198.

To ensure success, see page 199 for extra information on baking yeast bread in a bread machine.

We tried this bread with sprouted flax powder, flax meal, ground flaxseed and flax flour, and there were really no differences.

Nutritional value per serving

Calories	233
Fat, total	8 g
Fat, saturated	1 g
Cholesterol	28 mg
Sodium	326 mg
Carbohydrate	36 g
Fiber	3 g
Protein	5 g
Calcium	42 mg
Iron	1 mg

- **Instant-read thermometer**

1⅓ cups	brown rice flour	325 mL
⅓ cup	flax flour	75 mL
⅔ cup	potato starch	150 mL
⅓ cup	cornstarch	75 mL
⅓ cup	cracked flaxseed (see Techniques Glossary, page 369)	75 mL
⅓ cup	nonfat (skim) milk powder	75 mL
2½ tsp	xanthan gum	12 mL
2¼ tsp	bread machine or instant yeast	11 mL
1½ tsp	salt	7 mL
1¼ cups	water	300 mL
¼ cup	vegetable oil	50 mL
¼ cup	liquid honey	50 mL
2 tsp	cider vinegar	10 mL
2	eggs	2
2	egg whites	2

1. In a large bowl or plastic bag, combine rice flour, flax flour, potato starch, cornstarch, flaxseed, milk powder, xanthan gum, yeast and salt. Mix well and set aside.

2. Pour water, oil, honey and vinegar into the bread machine baking pan. Add eggs and egg whites.

3. Select the Gluten-Free Cycle. Allow the liquids to mix until combined. As the bread machine is mixing, gradually add the dry ingredients, scraping bottom and sides of pan with a rubber spatula. Try to incorporate all the dry ingredients within 1 to 2 minutes. When the mixing and kneading are complete, remove the kneading blade, leaving the bread pan in the bread machine. Quickly smooth the top of the loaf. Allow the cycle to finish.

Tips

This bread is delicious thinly sliced and toasted.

Substitute raw hemp powder and hemp hearts® for flax, both flour and seeds.

Substitute an equal amount of packed brown sugar for the honey.

4. At the end of the cycle, take the temperature of the loaf using an instant-read thermometer. It is baked at 200°F (100°C). If it's between 180°F (82°C) and 200°F (100°C), leave machine on the Keep Warm Cycle until baked. If it's below 180°F (82°C), turn on the Bake Cycle and check the internal temperature every 10 minutes. (Some bread machines are automatically set for 60 minutes; others need to be set by 10-minute intervals.)

5. Once the loaf has reached 200°F (100°C), remove it from the pan immediately and let cool completely on a rack.

Italian Herb Bread

. . . .

Makes 1 loaf
or 12 servings

The fragrant aroma of this loaf makes waiting for it to bake extremely difficult. Serve this zesty herb bread with any course — soup, salad or entrée.

Tips

If your machine doesn't have a Gluten-Free Cycle, see Dough Cycle and Bake Cycle, page 198.

To ensure success, see page 199 for extra information on baking yeast bread in a bread machine.

Nutritional value per serving

Calories	223
Fat, total	8 g
Fat, saturated	1 g
Cholesterol	27 mg
Sodium	304 mg
Carbohydrate	34 g
Fiber	3 g
Protein	6 g
Calcium	21 mg
Iron	2 mg

● **Instant-read thermometer**

1½ cups	sorghum flour	375 mL
¾ cup	whole bean flour	175 mL
½ cup	potato starch	125 mL
¼ cup	tapioca starch	50 mL
⅓ cup	granulated sugar	75 mL
1 tbsp	xanthan gum	15 mL
2 tsp	bread machine or instant yeast	10 mL
1½ tsp	salt	7 mL
¼ cup	snipped fresh parsley	50 mL
1 tbsp	ground dried marjoram	15 mL
1 tbsp	ground dried thyme	15 mL
1¼ cups	water	300 mL
⅓ cup	vegetable oil	75 mL
1 tsp	cider vinegar	5 mL
2	eggs	2

1. In a large bowl or plastic bag, combine sorghum flour, whole bean flour, potato starch, tapioca starch, sugar, xanthan gum, yeast, salt, parsley, marjoram and thyme. Mix well and set aside.

2. Pour water, oil and vinegar into the bread machine baking pan. Add eggs.

3. Select the Gluten-Free Cycle. Allow the liquids to mix until combined. As the bread machine is mixing, gradually add the dry ingredients, scraping bottom and sides of pan with a rubber spatula. Try to incorporate all the dry ingredients within 1 to 2 minutes. When the mixing and kneading are complete, remove the kneading blade, leaving the bread pan in the bread machine. Quickly smooth the top of the loaf. Allow the cycle to finish.

Tips

This is an excellent loaf for making croutons and bread crumbs (see Techniques Glossary, page 368).

Substitute triple the amount of snipped fresh herbs for the dried. See Techniques Glossary, page 370, for information about working with fresh herbs.

4. At the end of the cycle, take the temperature of the loaf using an instant-read thermometer. It is baked at 200°F (100°C). If it's between 180°F (82°C) and 200°F (100°C), leave machine on the Keep Warm Cycle until baked. If it's below 180°F (82°C), turn on the Bake Cycle and check the internal temperature every 10 minutes. (Some bread machines are automatically set for 60 minutes; others need to be set by 10-minute intervals.)

5. Once the loaf has reached 200°F (100°C), remove it from the pan immediately and let cool completely on a rack.

Lemon Poppy Loaf

· ·

**Makes 1 loaf
or 12 servings**

A perennial favorite flavor combination — poppy seeds and lemon.

Tips

If your machine doesn't have a Gluten-Free Cycle, see Dough Cycle and Bake Cycle, page 198.

To ensure success, see page 199 for extra information on baking yeast bread in a bread machine.

Use a zester to make long thin strips of lemon zest. Be sure to remove only the colored outer skin, avoiding the bitter white pith beneath.

Nutritional value per serving

Calories	228
Fat, total	8 g
Fat, saturated	1 g
Cholesterol	27 mg
Sodium	264 mg
Carbohydrate	36 g
Fiber	2 g
Protein	4 g
Calcium	66 mg
Iron	1 mg

- **Instant-read thermometer**

1½ cups	brown rice flour	375 mL
⅔ cup	potato starch	150 mL
⅓ cup	arrowroot starch	75 mL
⅓ cup	granulated sugar	75 mL
1 tbsp	xanthan gum	15 mL
1 tbsp	bread machine or instant yeast	15 mL
1¼ tsp	salt	6 mL
2 tbsp	lemon zest	25 mL
⅓ cup	poppy seeds	75 mL
1¼ cups	water	300 mL
¼ cup	freshly squeezed lemon juice	50 mL
¼ cup	vegetable oil	50 mL
2	eggs	2
2	egg whites	2

1. In a large bowl or plastic bag, combine rice flour, potato starch, arrowroot starch, sugar, xanthan gum, yeast, salt, zest and poppy seeds. Mix well and set aside.

2. Pour water, lemon juice and oil into the bread machine baking pan. Add eggs and egg whites.

3. Select the Gluten-Free Cycle. Allow the liquids to mix until combined. As the bread machine is mixing, gradually add the dry ingredients, scraping bottom and sides of pan with a rubber spatula. Try to incorporate all the dry ingredients within 1 to 2 minutes. When the mixing and kneading are complete, remove the kneading blade, leaving the bread pan in the bread machine. Quickly smooth the top of the loaf. Allow the cycle to finish.

4. At the end of the cycle, take the temperature of the loaf using an instant-read thermometer. It is baked at 200°F (100°C). If it's between 180°F (82°C) and 200°F (100°C), leave machine on the Keep Warm Cycle until baked. If it's below 180°F (82°C), turn on the Bake Cycle and check the internal temperature every 10 minutes. (Some bread machines are automatically set for 60 minutes; others need to be set by 10-minute intervals.)

5. Once the loaf has reached 200°F (100°C), remove it from the pan immediately and let cool completely on a rack.

Nutmeg Loaf

Makes 1 loaf
or 12 servings

Flecks of brown nutmeg stand out against the white background in this tangy-sweet loaf. The aroma will have you slicing it hot.

Tips

If your machine doesn't have a Gluten-Free Cycle, see Dough Cycle and Bake Cycle, page 198.

To ensure success, see page 199 for extra information on baking yeast bread in a bread machine.

For the best flavor, use freshly grated whole nutmeg. Use approximately half as much fresh grated as ground.

Nutritional value per serving

Calories	179
Fat, total	6 g
Fat, saturated	1 g
Cholesterol	28 mg
Sodium	264 mg
Carbohydrate	29 g
Fiber	2 g
Protein	3 g
Calcium	25 mg
Iron	1 mg

• **Instant-read thermometer**

1 1/4 cups	brown rice flour	300 mL
1/2 cup	arrowroot starch	125 mL
1/4 cup	quinoa flour (see Tips, left)	50 mL
1/4 cup	tapioca starch	50 mL
1/3 cup	granulated sugar	75 mL
1 tbsp	xanthan gum	15 mL
1 tbsp	bread machine or instant yeast	15 mL
1 1/4 tsp	salt	6 mL
1 1/2 tsp	ground nutmeg	7 mL
1/3 cup	water	75 mL
1/2 cup	plain yogurt	125 mL
1/4 cup	vegetable oil	50 mL
2	eggs	2

1. In a large bowl or plastic bag, combine rice flour, arrowroot starch, quinoa flour, tapioca starch, sugar, xanthan gum, yeast, salt and nutmeg. Mix well and set aside.

2. Pour water, yogurt and oil into the bread machine baking pan. Add eggs.

3. Select the Gluten-Free Cycle. Allow the liquids to mix until combined. As the bread machine is mixing, gradually add the dry ingredients, scraping bottom and sides of pan with a rubber spatula. Try to incorporate all the dry ingredients within 1 to 2 minutes. When the mixing and kneading are complete, remove the kneading blade, leaving the bread pan in the bread machine. Quickly smooth the top of the loaf. Allow the cycle to finish.

4. At the end of the cycle, take the temperature of the loaf using an instant-read thermometer. It is baked at 200°F (100°C). If it's between 180°F (82°C) and 200°F (100°C), leave machine on the Keep Warm Cycle until baked. If it's below 180°F (82°C), turn on the Bake Cycle and check the internal temperature every 10 minutes. (Some bread machines are automatically set for 60 minutes; others need to be set by 10-minute intervals.)

5. Once the loaf has reached 200°F (100°C), remove it from the pan immediately and let cool completely on a rack.

Pumpernickel Loaf

Makes 1 loaf
or 12 servings

With all the hearty flavor of traditional pumpernickel, this version is great for sandwiches. Try it filled with sliced turkey, accompanied by a crisp, garlic dill pickle.

Tips

If your machine doesn't have a Gluten-Free Cycle, see Dough Cycle and Bake Cycle, page 198.

To ensure success, see page 199 for extra information on baking yeast bread in a bread machine.

- **Instant-read thermometer**

1 cup	whole bean flour	250 mL
1 cup	yellow pea flour	250 mL
⅔ cup	potato starch	150 mL
⅓ cup	tapioca starch	75 mL
3 tbsp	packed brown sugar	45 mL
2½ tsp	xanthan gum	12 mL
1 tbsp	bread machine or instant yeast	15 mL
1½ tsp	salt	7 mL
1 tbsp	instant coffee granules	15 mL
1 tbsp	unsweetened cocoa powder	15 mL
½ tsp	ground ginger	2 mL
1½ cups	water	375 mL
3 tbsp	fancy molasses	45 mL
1 tsp	cider vinegar	5 mL
2 tbsp	vegetable oil	25 mL
3	eggs	3

1. In a large bowl or plastic bag, combine whole bean flour, yellow pea flour, potato starch, tapioca starch, brown sugar, xanthan gum, yeast, salt, coffee granules, cocoa and ginger. Mix well and set aside.

2. Pour water, molasses, vinegar and oil into the bread machine baking pan. Add eggs.

3. Select the Gluten-Free Cycle. Allow the liquids to mix until combined. As the bread machine is mixing, gradually add the dry ingredients, scraping bottom and sides of pan with a rubber spatula. Try to incorporate all the dry ingredients within 1 to 2 minutes. When the mixing and kneading are complete, remove the kneading blade, leaving the bread pan in the bread machine. Quickly smooth the top of the loaf. Allow the cycle to finish.

4. At the end of the cycle, take the temperature of the loaf using an instant-read thermometer. It is baked at 200°F (100°C). If it's between 180°F (82°C) and 200°F (100°C), leave machine on the Keep Warm Cycle until baked. If it's below 180°F (82°C), turn on the Bake Cycle and check the internal temperature every 10 minutes. (Some bread machines are automatically set for 60 minutes; others need to be set by 10-minute intervals.)

Nutritional value per serving

Calories	211
Fat, total	4 g
Fat, saturated	1 g
Cholesterol	41 mg
Sodium	313 mg
Carbohydrate	36 g
Fiber	5 g
Protein	8 g
Calcium	29 mg
Iron	2 mg

Tip

Remember to thoroughly mix the dry ingredients before adding to the liquids because they are powder-fine and could clump together.

5. Once the loaf has reached 200°F (100°C), remove it from the pan immediately and let cool completely on a rack.

Variations

If yellow pea flour is unavailable, use chickpea or garbanzo bean flour. This recipe can either be made from any variety of bean flour or half pea and half bean flour.

For a milder flavor, omit the coffee and unsweetened cocoa powder.

Seedy Brown Bread

Makes 1 loaf
or 12 servings

A sandwich bread with a rich color and added crunch — what a treat!

Tips

If your machine doesn't have a Gluten-Free Cycle, see Dough Cycle and Bake Cycle, page 198.

To ensure success, see page 199 for extra information on baking yeast bread in a bread machine.

You can purchase buttermilk powder in bulk stores and health food stores. Store buttermilk powder in an airtight container to prevent lumping.

- **Instant-read thermometer**

1 cup	sorghum flour	250 mL
⅔ cup	whole bean flour	150 mL
⅓ cup	tapioca starch	75 mL
⅓ cup	rice bran	75 mL
⅓ cup	buttermilk powder	75 mL
1 tbsp	xanthan gum	15 mL
1 tbsp	bread machine or instant yeast	15 mL
1¼ tsp	salt	6 mL
⅓ cup	pumpkin seeds	75 mL
⅓ cup	raw unsalted sunflower seeds	75 mL
¼ cup	sesame seeds	50 mL
1 cup	water	250 mL
2 tbsp	vegetable oil	25 mL
2 tbsp	liquid honey	25 mL
2 tbsp	fancy molasses	25 mL
1 tsp	cider vinegar	5 mL
3	eggs	3

1. In a large bowl or plastic bag, combine sorghum flour, whole bean flour, tapioca starch, rice bran, buttermilk powder, xanthan gum, yeast, salt and pumpkin, sunflower and sesame seeds. Mix well and set aside.

2. Pour water, oil, honey, molasses and vinegar into the bread machine baking pan. Add eggs.

3. Select the Gluten-Free Cycle. Allow the liquids to mix until combined. As the bread machine is mixing, gradually add the dry ingredients, scraping bottom and sides of pan with a rubber spatula. Try to incorporate all the dry ingredients within 1 to 2 minutes. When the mixing and kneading are complete, remove the kneading blade, leaving the bread pan in the bread machine. Quickly smooth the top of the loaf. Allow the cycle to finish.

Nutritional value per serving	
Calories	224
Fat, total	10 g
Fat, saturated	1 g
Cholesterol	41 mg
Sodium	275 mg
Carbohydrate	27 g
Fiber	4 g
Protein	8 g
Calcium	39 mg
Iron	3 mg

Tips

For a nuttier flavor, toast the seeds (see Techniques Glossary, page 371).

Tent the loaf with foil partway through the baking time to prevent the top crust from becoming too dark.

4. At the end of the cycle, take the temperature of the loaf using an instant-read thermometer. It is baked at 200°F (100°C). If it's between 180°F (82°C) and 200°F (100°C), leave machine on the Keep Warm Cycle until baked. If it's below 180°F (82°C), turn on the Bake Cycle and check the internal temperature every 10 minutes. (Some bread machines are automatically set for 60 minutes; others need to be set by 10-minute intervals.)

5. Once the loaf has reached 200°F (100°C), remove it from the pan immediately and let cool completely on a rack.

Variations

Vary the seeds — choose either flax, hemp or poppy to substitute for the sesame. To crack flaxseeds, pulse in a coffee grinder to desired texture.

Substitute raw hemp powder or flaxseed meal for the rice bran.

For a milder-flavored bread, substitute packed brown sugar for the molasses.

Rice bran can be replaced by an equal amount of brown rice flour.

Sun-Dried Tomato Rice Loaf

Makes 1 loaf
or 12 servings

For those who prefer savory loaves to sweet, try this variation of the Cranberry Wild Rice Loaf suggested by Larry, a member of our focus group.

Tips

If your machine doesn't have a Gluten-Free Cycle, see Dough Cycle and Bake Cycle, page 198.

To ensure success, see page 199 for extra information on baking yeast bread in a bread machine.

Nutritional value per serving

Calories	214
Fat, total	6 g
Fat, saturated	1 g
Cholesterol	27 mg
Sodium	184 mg
Carbohydrate	38 g
Fiber	2 g
Protein	5 g
Calcium	12 mg
Iron	1 mg

• **Instant-read thermometer**

1½ cups	brown rice flour	375 mL
⅔ cup	tapioca starch	150 mL
⅓ cup	potato starch	75 mL
¼ cup	granulated sugar	50 mL
2½ tsp	xanthan gum	12 mL
2 tsp	bread machine or instant yeast	10 mL
½ tsp	salt	2 mL
¾ tsp	celery seeds	4 mL
¼ tsp	freshly ground black pepper	1 mL
1 cup	cooked wild rice (see Techniques Glossary, page 371)	250 mL
⅔ cup	sun-dried tomatoes	150 mL
1¼ cups	water	300 mL
¼ cup	vegetable oil	50 mL
2	eggs	2
2	egg whites	2

1. In a large bowl or plastic bag, combine brown rice flour, tapioca starch, potato starch, sugar, xanthan gum, yeast, salt, celery seeds, pepper, wild rice and sun-dried tomatoes. Mix well and set aside.

2. Pour water and oil into the bread machine baking pan. Add eggs and egg whites.

3. Select the Gluten-Free Cycle. Allow the liquids to mix until combined. As the bread machine is mixing, gradually add the dry ingredients, scraping bottom and sides of pan with a rubber spatula. Try to incorporate all the dry ingredients within 1 to 2 minutes. When the mixing and kneading are complete, remove the kneading blade, leaving the bread pan in the bread machine. Quickly smooth the top of the loaf. Allow the cycle to finish.

Tip

Select dry, not oil-packed, sun-dried tomatoes.

4. At the end of the cycle, take the temperature of the loaf using an instant-read thermometer. It is baked at 200°F (100°C). If it's between 180°F (82°C) and 200°F (100°C), leave machine on the Keep Warm Cycle until baked. If it's below 180°F (82°C), turn on the Bake Cycle and check the internal temperature every 10 minutes. (Some bread machines are automatically set for 60 minutes; others need to be set by 10-minute intervals.)

5. Once the loaf has reached 200°F (100°C), remove it from the pan immediately and let cool completely on a rack.

Variation

Substitute $1/4$ cup (50 mL) frozen orange juice concentrate, thawed, for the same amount of water.

Tomato Rosemary Bread

Makes 1 loaf	
or 12 servings	

A smaller loaf than some, this is just the size to accompany an Italian dinner!

Tips

If your machine doesn't have a Gluten-Free Cycle, see Dough Cycle and Bake Cycle, page 198.

To ensure success, see page 199 for extra information on baking yeast bread in a bread machine.

The tomato vegetable juice should be at room temperature. If using cold from the refrigerator, heat it on High in the microwave for 1 minute.

When substituting fresh herbs for the dried, triple the amount.

Nutritional value per serving

Calories	168
Fat, total	6 g
Fat, saturated	1 g
Cholesterol	27 mg
Sodium	175 mg
Carbohydrate	25 g
Fiber	3 g
Protein	5 g
Calcium	17 mg
Iron	1 mg

- **Instant-read thermometer**

1 cup	sorghum flour	250 mL
1/2 cup	whole bean flour	125 mL
1/2 cup	cornstarch	125 mL
1/4 cup	granulated sugar	50 mL
1 tbsp	xanthan gum	15 mL
1 tbsp	bread machine or instant yeast	15 mL
2 tsp	dried rosemary	10 mL
1/2 tsp	salt	2 mL
1/2 cup	snipped sun-dried tomatoes	125 mL
1 1/4 cups	tomato vegetable juice	300 mL
1/4 cup	vegetable oil	50 mL
2	eggs	2

1. In a large bowl or plastic bag, combine sorghum flour, whole bean flour, cornstarch, sugar, xanthan gum, yeast, rosemary, salt and tomatoes. Mix well and set aside.

2. Pour juice and oil into the bread machine baking pan. Add eggs.

3. Select the Gluten-Free Cycle. Allow the liquids to mix until combined. As the bread machine is mixing, gradually add the dry ingredients, scraping bottom and sides of pan with a rubber spatula. Try to incorporate all the dry ingredients within 1 to 2 minutes. When the mixing and kneading are complete, remove the kneading blade, leaving the bread pan in the bread machine. Quickly smooth the top of the loaf. Allow the cycle to finish.

4. At the end of the cycle, take the temperature of the loaf using an instant-read thermometer. It is baked at 200°F (100°C). If it's between 180°F (82°C) and 200°F (100°C), leave machine on the Keep Warm Cycle until baked. If it's below 180°F (82°C), turn on the Bake Cycle and check the internal temperature every 10 minutes. (Some bread machines are automatically set for 60 minutes; others need to be set by 10-minute intervals.)

5. Once the loaf has reached 200°F (100°C), remove it from the pan immediately and let cool completely on a rack.

Variation

Vary the herb — select oregano, basil or thyme.

Banana Seed Bread (page 200 or 229)

Baked Cheesecake (page 255) with
Fresh Peach Dessert Sauce (page 321)

Blueberry Peach Crisp (page 259)

Peachy Plum Hazelnut Galette (page 290)

Almond Sponge Cake (page 296)

Chocolate Fudge Cake (page 302)
with Orange Frosting (page 319)

Triple-Threat Mocha Chocolate Chip Cookies (page 332)

Fudgy Brownies (page 345)
and Nanaimo Bars (page 349)

White Bread

- -

We know you'll enjoy this moist all-purpose yeast bread, whether for sandwiches or to accompany your favorite salad.

Tips

If your machine doesn't have a Gluten-Free Cycle, see Dough Cycle and Bake Cycle, page 198.

To ensure success, see page 199 for extra information on baking yeast bread in a bread machine.

Remember to thoroughly mix the dry ingredients before adding to the liquids because they are powder-fine and could clump together.

Nutritional value per serving

Calories	224
Fat, total	6 g
Fat, saturated	1 g
Cholesterol	28 mg
Sodium	320 mg
Carbohydrate	39 g
Fiber	1 g
Protein	4 g
Calcium	23 mg
Iron	0 mg

- **Instant-read thermometer**

2 cups	brown rice flour	500 mL
⅔ cup	potato starch	150 mL
⅓ cup	tapioca starch	75 mL
¼ cup	nonfat dry milk or skim milk powder	50 mL
¼ cup	granulated sugar	50 mL
2½ tsp	xanthan gum	12 mL
2¼ tsp	bread machine or instant yeast	11 mL
1½ tsp	salt	7 mL
1¼ cups	water	300 mL
1 tsp	cider vinegar	5 mL
¼ cup	vegetable oil	50 mL
2	eggs	2
2	egg whites	2

1. In a large bowl or plastic bag, combine rice flour, potato starch, tapioca starch, milk powder, sugar, xanthan gum, yeast and salt. Mix well and set aside.
2. Pour water, vinegar and oil into the bread machine baking pan. Add eggs and egg whites.
3. Select the Gluten-Free Cycle. Allow the liquids to mix until combined. As the bread machine is mixing, gradually add the dry ingredients, scraping bottom and sides of pan with a rubber spatula. Try to incorporate all the dry ingredients within 1 to 2 minutes. When the mixing and kneading are complete, remove the kneading blade, leaving the bread pan in the bread machine. Quickly smooth the top of the loaf. Allow the cycle to finish.
4. At the end of the cycle, take the temperature of the loaf using an instant-read thermometer. It is baked at 200°F (100°C). If it's between 180°F (82°C) and 200°F (100°C), leave machine on the Keep Warm Cycle until baked. If it's below 180°F (82°C), turn on the Bake Cycle and check the internal temperature every 10 minutes. (Some bread machines are automatically set for 60 minutes; others need to be set by 10-minute intervals.)
5. Once the loaf has reached 200°F (100°C), remove it from the pan immediately and let cool completely on a rack.

Whole Grain Amaranth Bread

Makes 1 loaf
or 12 servings

This soft-textured, creamy, honey-colored bread is so delicious you won't even suspect how nutritious it is.

Tips

If your machine doesn't have a Gluten-Free Cycle, see Dough Cycle and Bake Cycle, page 198.

To ensure success, see page 199 for extra information on baking yeast bread in a bread machine.

Substitute ¹/₄ cup (50 mL) liquid egg whites for the 2 egg whites.

Amaranth is high in fiber, iron and calcium and lower in sodium than most grains.

Nutritional value per serving

Calories	203
Fat, total	7 g
Fat, saturated	1 g
Cholesterol	27 mg
Sodium	315 mg
Carbohydrate	33 g
Fiber	2 g
Protein	4 g
Calcium	20 mg
Iron	1 mg

- Instant-read thermometer

1 ¹/₄ cups	brown rice flour	300 mL
³/₄ cup	amaranth flour	175 mL
¹/₂ cup	potato starch	125 mL
¹/₃ cup	amaranth grain	75 mL
1 tbsp	xanthan gum	15 mL
2 tsp	bread machine or instant yeast	10 mL
1 ¹/₂ tsp	salt	7 mL
2 tbsp	grated orange zest	25 mL
1 cup	water	250 mL
¹/₄ cup	vegetable oil	50 mL
¹/₄ cup	liquid honey	50 mL
2 tsp	cider vinegar	10 mL
2	eggs	2
2	egg whites	2

1. In a large bowl or plastic bag, combine brown rice flour, amaranth flour, potato starch, amaranth grain, xanthan gum, yeast, salt and orange zest. Mix well and set aside.

2. Pour water, oil, honey and vinegar into the bread machine baking pan. Add eggs and egg whites.

3. Select the Gluten-Free Cycle. Allow the liquids to mix until combined. As the bread machine is mixing, gradually add the dry ingredients, scraping bottom and sides of pan with a rubber spatula. Try to incorporate all the dry ingredients within 1 to 2 minutes. When the mixing and kneading are complete, remove the kneading blade, leaving the bread pan in the bread machine. Quickly smooth the top of the loaf. Allow the cycle to finish.

4. At the end of the cycle, take the temperature of the loaf using an instant-read thermometer. It is baked at 200°F (100°C). If it's between 180°F (82°C) and 200°F (100°C), leave machine on the Keep Warm Cycle until baked. If it's below 180°F (82°C), turn on the Bake Cycle and check the internal temperature every 10 minutes. (Some bread machines are automatically set for 60 minutes; others need to be set by 10-minute intervals.)

5. Once the loaf has reached 200°F (100°C), remove it from the pan immediately and let cool completely on a rack.

Heavy-Duty Mixer Recipes

Baking Mixer-Method Yeast Breads

- Select a heavy-duty stand mixer to make gluten-free yeast breads. A lighter hand-held mixer may not be powerful enough to handle the thicker doughs.
- Use the paddle attachment. The dough is not thick enough to knead with the dough hook and yet too thick for the wire whip.
- If flours contain lumps, sift before measuring. Combine all the dry ingredients in a plastic bag or a large bowl before adding to the mixer bowl. Gluten-free flours and starches have a fine, powder-like consistency and lump easily unless mixed with other dry ingredients.
- Mix the eggs with the liquid ingredients on low speed for 1 to 2 minutes or until blended before adding the dry ingredients.
- Add the dry ingredients slowly as the machine is mixing. Stop the mixer and scrape the sides and bottom of the bowl and the blade with a rubber spatula.
- With the mixer set to medium speed, beat the dough for 4 minutes. Set a kitchen timer. You will be surprised how long 4 minutes actually seems as you wait.
- Scrape the dough into a lightly greased baking pan. It should fill the pan about two-thirds full. If too full, the loaf does not bake with a rounded top, similar to a wheat loaf, but overflows the sides, leaving a slightly flat top and mushroomed sides.
- Set aside to rise in a warm, draft-free place until the dough reaches the top of the pan. We leave them uncovered because the dough sticks if it touches any kind of cover. Do not let it over-rise — the loaf will mushroom slightly and collapse during baking, if over-risen.
- Test whether the bread is done with an instant-read metal stem thermometer inserted at least 2 inches (5 cm) into the loaf. The thermometer should register 190°F (90°C). A long wooden skewer, inserted in the center of the loaf, should come out clean. Tap on the bottom of the loaf and if the sound is hollow, the bread is baked.
- Remove from the pan to a wire rack immediately to prevent a soggy loaf. Cool completely on a wire rack.
- Slice and wrap while still warm in airtight individual sandwich bags, then place these in a larger freezer bag. Label and date, then freeze up to 6 weeks. For thin, even slices, use an electric knife or one with a serrated blade.

Banana Seed Bread

The combination of sorghum and bean flour really enhances the banana flavor of this loaf. Serve it for dessert or with a slice of old Cheddar for lunch.

Tip

Use raw, unroasted, unsalted sunflower seeds. For a nuttier flavor, toast the sunflower seeds (see Techniques Glossary, page 371, for instructions).

Nutritional value per serving

Calories	176
Fat, total	7 g
Fat, saturated	1 g
Cholesterol	27 mg
Sodium	207 mg
Carbohydrate	24 g
Fiber	3 g
Protein	6 g
Calcium	21 mg
Iron	1 mg

● **9- by 5-inch (2 L) loaf pan, lightly greased**

¾ cup	whole bean flour	175 mL
¾ cup	sorghum flour	175 mL
¼ cup	tapioca starch	50 mL
¼ cup	packed brown sugar	50 mL
2 tsp	xanthan gum	10 mL
1 tbsp	bread machine or instant yeast	15 mL
1 tsp	salt	5 mL
½ cup	sunflower seeds	125 mL
½ cup	water	125 mL
¾ cup	mashed banana	175 mL
1 tsp	cider vinegar	5 mL
3 tbsp	vegetable oil	45 mL
2	eggs	2

1. In a large bowl or plastic bag, combine whole bean flour, sorghum flour, tapioca starch, brown sugar, xanthan gum, yeast, salt and sunflower seeds. Mix well and set aside.

2. In a separate bowl, using a heavy-duty electric mixer with paddle attachment, combine water, banana, vinegar, oil and eggs until well blended.

3. With the mixer on lowest speed, slowly add the dry ingredients to the banana mixture until combined. With a rubber spatula, scrape the bottom and sides of the bowl. With the mixer on medium speed, beat for 4 minutes.

4. Spoon into prepared pan. Let rise, uncovered, in a warm, draft-free place for 60 to 75 minutes or until the dough has risen to the top of the pan. Meanwhile, preheat oven to 350°F (180°C). Tent with foil and bake for 20 to 25 minutes. Remove foil and continue baking for 15 to 20 minutes more or until the loaf sounds hollow when tapped on the bottom.

Variation

Pumpkin seeds or chopped pecans can replace the sunflower seeds.

Brown Bread

**Makes 1 loaf
or 12 servings**

The perfect sandwich bread! Just add shaved roast beef, a leaf of romaine and a hint of mustard. It carries well for a tasty lunch.

Tip

Slice this or any bread with an electric knife for thin, even sandwich slices.

- **9- by 5-inch (2 L) loaf pan, lightly greased**

1¼ cups	brown rice flour	300 mL
½ cup	sorghum flour	125 mL
½ cup	cornstarch	125 mL
½ cup	rice bran	125 mL
1 tbsp	xanthan gum	15 mL
1 tbsp	bread machine or instant yeast	15 mL
1¼ tsp	salt	6 mL
1 cup	water	250 mL
1 tsp	cider vinegar	5 mL
2 tbsp	vegetable oil	25 mL
2 tbsp	liquid honey	25 mL
2 tbsp	fancy molasses	25 mL
3	eggs	3

1. In a large bowl or plastic bag, combine brown rice flour, sorghum flour, cornstarch, rice bran, xanthan gum, yeast and salt. Mix well and set aside.

2. In a separate bowl, using a heavy-duty electric mixer with paddle attachment, combine water, vinegar, oil, honey, molasses and eggs until well blended.

3. With the mixer on lowest speed, slowly add the dry ingredients to the honey mixture until combined. With a rubber spatula, scrape the bottom and sides of the bowl. With the mixer on medium speed, beat for 4 minutes.

4. Spoon into prepared pan. Let rise, uncovered, in a warm, draft-free place for 60 to 75 minutes or until the dough has risen to the top of the pan. Meanwhile, preheat oven to 350°F (180°C). Bake for 35 to 45 minutes or until the loaf sounds hollow when tapped on the bottom.

Variations

For a mild-flavored bread, substitute 2 tbsp (25 mL) packed brown sugar for the molasses.

The rice bran can be replaced by an equal amount of brown rice flour.

Nutritional value per serving

Calories	179
Fat, total	5 g
Fat, saturated	1 g
Cholesterol	41 mg
Sodium	263 mg
Carbohydrate	31 g
Fiber	3 g
Protein	4 g
Calcium	14 mg
Iron	2 mg

Buckwheat Walnut

This is the bread for those who love to combine strong, robust flavors — buckwheat, whole bean flour and cardamom.

Tip

Make sure buckwheat is on your list of allowable foods before you try this recipe.

● **9- by 5-inch (2 L) loaf pan, lightly greased**

1 cup	whole bean flour	250 mL
1/3 cup	buckwheat flour	75 mL
1/2 cup	potato starch	125 mL
1/4 cup	tapioca starch	50 mL
1/4 cup	packed brown sugar	50 mL
2 tsp	xanthan gum	10 mL
1 tbsp	bread machine or instant yeast	15 mL
1 tsp	salt	5 mL
3/4 tsp	ground cardamom	4 mL
3/4 cup	chopped walnuts	175 mL
1 1/4 cups	water	300 mL
1 tsp	cider vinegar	5 mL
3 tbsp	vegetable oil	45 mL
2	eggs	2

1. In a large bowl or plastic bag, combine whole bean flour, buckwheat flour, potato starch, tapioca starch, brown sugar, xanthan gum, yeast, salt, cardamom and walnuts. Mix well and set aside.
2. In a separate bowl, using a heavy-duty electric mixer with paddle attachment, combine water, vinegar, oil and eggs until well blended.
3. With the mixer on lowest speed, slowly add the dry ingredients until combined. With a rubber spatula, scrape the bottom and sides of the bowl. With the mixer on medium speed, beat for 4 minutes.
4. Spoon into prepared pan. Let rise, uncovered, in a warm, draft-free place for 60 to 75 minutes or until the dough has risen to the top of the pan. Meanwhile, preheat oven to 350°F (180°C). Bake for 35 to 45 minutes or until the loaf sounds hollow when tapped on the bottom.

Variations

Substitute brown rice flour for the buckwheat flour.

Substitute fresh, dried or frozen blueberries for the walnuts. Fold the fruit in just before spooning into pan.

Substitute an equal amount of nutmeg for the cardamom.

Nutritional value per serving	
Calories	206
Fat, total	10 g
Fat, saturated	1 g
Cholesterol	27 mg
Sodium	207 mg
Carbohydrate	25 g
Fiber	3 g
Protein	7 g
Calcium	24 mg
Iron	1 mg

Cheese Onion Loaf

Makes 1 loaf
or 12 servings

This is a perfect accompaniment to homemade chili or beef stew. It slices well and stays moist for a second day.

Tips

Do not substitute fresh onion for the dried flakes. The extra moisture results in a weak-flavored shorter loaf.

For the amount of cheese to purchase, see the weight/ volume equivalents in the Ingredient Glossary, page 363.

See variations, page 203.

- 9- by 5-inch (2 L) loaf pan, lightly greased

1½ cups	brown rice flour	375 mL
½ cup	sorghum flour	125 mL
⅓ cup	arrowroot starch	75 mL
¼ cup	nonfat dry milk or skim milk powder	50 mL
2 tbsp	granulated sugar	25 mL
2½ tsp	xanthan gum	12 mL
2 tsp	bread machine or instant yeast	10 mL
1¼ tsp	salt	6 mL
¾ cup	shredded old Cheddar cheese	175 mL
2 tbsp	dried onion flakes	25 mL
¼ tsp	dry mustard	1 mL
1¼ cups	water	300 mL
2 tsp	cider vinegar	10 mL
2	eggs	2
2	egg whites	2

1. In a large bowl or plastic bag, combine rice flour, sorghum flour, arrowroot starch, milk powder, sugar, xanthan gum, yeast, salt, cheese, onion flakes and mustard. Mix well and set aside.

2. In a separate bowl, using a heavy-duty electric mixer with paddle attachment, combine water, vinegar, eggs and egg whites until well blended.

3. With the mixer on lowest speed, slowly add the dry ingredients until combined. With a rubber spatula, scrape the bottom and sides of the bowl. With the mixer on medium speed, beat for 4 minutes.

4. Spoon into prepared pan. Let rise, uncovered, in a warm, draft-free place for 60 to 75 minutes or until the dough has risen to the top of the pan. Meanwhile, preheat oven to 350°F (180°C). Bake for 35 to 45 minutes or until the loaf sounds hollow when tapped on the bottom.

Nutritional value per serving

Calories	167
Fat, total	3 g
Fat, saturated	2 g
Cholesterol	34 mg
Sodium	316 mg
Carbohydrate	28 g
Fiber	2 g
Protein	6 g
Calcium	75 mg
Iron	1 mg

Cinnamon Raisin Bread

Makes 1 loaf
or 12 servings

Enjoy a toasted slice or two of this deep golden loaf for breakfast — it's the perfect snack when served with a cup of hot cocoa.

Tips

To ensure success, see page 228 for extra information on baking yeast bread using the mixer method.

Thoroughly mix the dry ingredients before adding them to the liquids — they are powder-fine and can clump together.

Substitute other dried fruits for the raisins — try cranberries, currants, apricots or a mixture.

Nutritional value per serving

Calories	214
Fat, total	4 g
Fat, saturated	0 g
Cholesterol	28 mg
Sodium	274 mg
Carbohydrate	43 g
Fiber	3 g
Protein	4 g
Calcium	35 mg
Iron	1 mg

• 9- by 5-inch (2 L) loaf pan, lightly greased

1½ cups	brown rice flour	375 mL
⅓ cup	potato starch	75 mL
¼ cup	tapioca starch	50 mL
¼ cup	nonfat (skim) milk powder	50 mL
⅓ cup	granulated sugar	75 mL
1 tbsp	xanthan gum	15 mL
1 tbsp	bread machine or instant yeast	15 mL
1¼ tsp	salt	6 mL
2 tsp	cinnamon	10 mL
2	eggs	2
1	egg white	1
1 cup	water	250 ml
2 tbsp	vegetable oil	25 mL
1 tsp	cider vinegar	5 mL
1¼ cups	raisins	300 mL

1. In a large bowl or plastic bag, combine rice flour, potato starch, tapioca starch, milk powder, sugar, xanthan gum, yeast, salt and cinnamon. Mix well and set aside.

2. In a separate bowl, using a heavy-duty electric mixer with paddle attachment, combine eggs, egg white, water, oil and vinegar until well blended. With the mixer on its lowest speed, slowly add the dry ingredients until combined. Stop the machine and scrape the bottom and sides of the bowl with a rubber spatula. With the mixer on medium speed, beat for 4 minutes. Stir in raisins.

3. Spoon into prepared pan. Let rise, uncovered, in a warm, draft-free place for 75 to 90 minutes, or until dough has risen to the top of the pan. Meanwhile, preheat oven to 350°F (180°C).

4. Bake for 35 to 45 minutes, or until loaf sounds hollow when tapped on the bottom. Remove from the pan immediately and let cool completely on a rack.

Chocolate Fig Panettone

More like chocolate cake than bread, these mini-loaves are rich, sweet and brimming with fruit! Panettone originated in Milan, Italy, where it is served at Christmas and Easter, and for weddings and christenings. Break with tradition and try our modern flavor combination.

Tip

Thoroughly mix the dry ingredients before adding them to the liquids — they are powder-fine and can clump together.

Nutritional value per serving	
Calories	278
Fat, total	9 g
Fat, saturated	2 g
Cholesterol	31 mg
Sodium	283 mg
Carbohydrate	46 g
Fiber	3 g
Protein	5 g
Calcium	48 mg
Iron	2 mg

- **Three 5½- by 3-inch (500 mL) mini-loaf pans, lightly greased**

¾ cup	amaranth flour	175 mL
½ cup	brown rice flour	125 mL
½ cup	potato starch	125 mL
¼ cup	tapioca starch	50 mL
½ cup	granulated sugar	125 mL
¼ cup	nonfat (skim) milk powder	50 mL
¼ cup	unsweetened cocoa powder, sifted	50 mL
1 tbsp	xanthan gum	15 mL
1 tbsp	bread machine or instant yeast	15 mL
1¼ tsp	salt	6 mL
1 tsp	crushed anise seed	5 mL
2	eggs	2
2	egg whites	2
1 cup	water	250 mL
¼ cup	vegetable oil	50 mL
2 tsp	cider vinegar	10 mL
½ cup	chopped dried figs	125 mL
½ cup	chocolate chips	125 mL
½ cup	raisins	125 mL

1. In a large bowl or plastic bag, combine amaranth flour, brown rice flour, potato starch, tapioca starch, sugar, milk powder, cocoa powder, xanthan gum, yeast, salt and anise seed. Mix well and set aside.

2. In a separate bowl, using a heavy-duty electric mixer with paddle attachment, combine eggs, egg whites, water, oil and vinegar until well blended. With the mixer on its lowest speed, slowly add the dry ingredients until combined. Stop the machine and scrape the bottom and sides of the bowl with a rubber spatula. With the mixer on medium speed, beat for 4 minutes. Stir in figs, chocolate chips and raisins.

Tips

Purchase 4 to 5 medium-sized figs for the $^1/_2$ cup (125 mL) chopped figs.

Use a coffee grinder (reserved for spices) to crush the anise seed.

Bake in single-use mini-pans, wrap in festive cellophane and tie with a bow to give as gifts.

For a lactose-free loaf, omit the milk powder.

3. Spoon into prepared pans. Let rise, uncovered, in a warm, draft-free place for 60 to 75 minutes, or until dough has risen to the top of the pans. Meanwhile, preheat oven to 350°F (180°C).

4. Bake for 30 to 35 minutes, or until loaves sound hollow when tapped on the bottom. Remove from the pans immediately and let cool completely on a rack.

Variation

Substitute an equal amount of candied mixed peel and candied citron for the figs and chocolate chips.

Cornbread

Tiny bits of moist kernel corn dot this warm-colored yellow loaf.

Tip

Drain the canned corn before measuring. If using frozen corn, thaw and drain before measuring.

- **9- by 5-inch (2 L) loaf pan, lightly greased**

1 cup	brown rice flour	250 mL
¾ cup	cornmeal	175 mL
⅓ cup	potato starch	75 mL
¼ cup	tapioca starch	50 mL
2 tbsp	granulated sugar	25 mL
1 tbsp	xanthan gum	15 mL
1 tbsp	bread machine or instant yeast	15 mL
1 tsp	salt	5 mL
½ cup	well-drained whole corn kernels	125 mL
1 cup	water	250 mL
1 tsp	cider vinegar	5 mL
¼ cup	vegetable oil	50 mL
2	eggs	2

1. In a large bowl or plastic bag, combine rice flour, cornmeal, potato starch, tapioca starch, sugar, xanthan gum, yeast, salt and corn. Mix well and set aside.

2. In a separate bowl, using a heavy-duty electric mixer with paddle attachment, combine water, vinegar, oil and eggs until well blended.

3. With the mixer on lowest speed, slowly add the dry ingredients until combined. With a rubber spatula, scrape the bottom and sides of the bowl. With the mixer on medium speed, beat for 4 minutes.

4. Spoon into prepared pan. Let rise, uncovered, in a warm, draft-free place for 60 to 75 minutes or until the dough has risen to the top of the pan. Meanwhile, preheat oven to 350°F (180°C). Bake for 35 to 45 minutes or until the loaf sounds hollow when tapped on the bottom.

Variation

Add ¼ cup (50 mL) grated Parmesan cheese or ¼ cup (50 mL) finely chopped red and green bell peppers.

Nutritional value per serving

Calories	180
Fat, total	6 g
Fat, saturated	1 g
Cholesterol	27 mg
Sodium	227 mg
Carbohydrate	30 g
Fiber	2 g
Protein	3 g
Calcium	6 mg
Iron	1 mg

Cottage Cheese Dill Loaf

<table>
<tr><td colspan="2">Makes 1 loaf
or 12 servings</td></tr>
</table>

Try this twist on a traditional white bread to serve along with salmon or your favorite seafood entrée.

Tip

Any type of cottage cheese — large or small curd, high or low fat — works well in this recipe.

Nutritional value per serving

Calories	170
Fat, total	3 g
Fat, saturated	1 g
Cholesterol	28 mg
Sodium	350 mg
Carbohydrate	30 g
Fiber	1 g
Protein	4 g
Calcium	11 mg
Iron	0 mg

• **9- by 5-inch (2 L) loaf pan, lightly greased**

1½ cups	brown rice flour	375 mL
½ cup	potato starch	125 mL
¼ cup	tapioca starch	50 mL
2¼ tsp	xanthan gum	11 mL
2 tsp	bread machine or instant yeast	10 mL
1½ tsp	salt	7 mL
1 tbsp	snipped fresh dill	15 mL
¾ cup	water	175 mL
1 tsp	cider vinegar	5 mL
½ cup	low-fat cottage cheese	125 mL
2 tbsp	vegetable oil	25 mL
3 tbsp	liquid honey	45 mL
2	eggs	2
2	egg whites	2

1. In a large bowl or plastic bag, combine rice flour, potato starch, tapioca starch, xanthan gum, yeast, salt and dill. Mix well and set aside.

2. In a separate bowl, using a heavy-duty electric mixer with paddle attachment, combine water, vinegar, cottage cheese, oil, honey, eggs and egg whites until well blended.

3. With the mixer on lowest speed, slowly add the dry ingredients until combined. With a rubber spatula, scrape the bottom and sides of the bowl. With the mixer on medium speed, beat for 4 minutes.

4. Spoon into prepared pan. Let rise, uncovered, in a warm, draft-free place for 60 to 75 minutes or until the dough has risen to the top of the pan. Meanwhile, preheat oven to 350°F (180°C). Bake for 35 to 45 minutes or until the loaf sounds hollow when tapped on the bottom.

Variation

Omit the dill. Try rosemary, marjoram or savory.

Cranberry Wild Rice Loaf

Makes 1 loaf
or 12 servings

This attractive loaf is sure to bring compliments from guests. The nutty taste with a hint of orange makes this a perfect accompaniment for duck or turkey.

• 9- by 5-inch (2 L) loaf pan, lightly greased

1¼ cups	brown rice flour	300 mL
½ cup	tapioca starch	125 mL
¼ cup	potato starch	50 mL
3 tbsp	granulated sugar	45 mL
2½ tsp	xanthan gum	12 mL
2 tsp	bread machine or instant yeast	10 mL
1½ tsp	salt	7 mL
2 tsp	orange zest	10 mL
¾ tsp	celery seeds	4 mL
⅛ tsp	fleshly ground black pepper	0.5 mL
¾ cup	cooked wild rice (see Techniques Glossary, page 371)	175 mL
½ cup	dried cranberries	125 mL
¾ cup	water	175 mL
¼ cup	frozen orange juice concentrate, thawed	50 mL
¼ cup	vegetable oil	50 mL
2	eggs	2
1	egg white	1

1. In a large bowl or plastic bag, combine brown rice flour, tapioca starch, potato starch, sugar, xanthan gum, yeast, salt, zest, celery seeds, pepper, wild rice and cranberries. Mix well and set aside.

2. In a separate bowl, using a heavy-duty electric mixer with paddle attachment, combine water, orange juice concentrate, oil, eggs and egg white until well blended.

3. With the mixer on lowest speed, slowly add the dry ingredients until combined. With a rubber spatula, scrape the bottom and sides of the bowl. With the mixer on medium speed, beat for 4 minutes.

4. Spoon into prepared pan. Let rise, uncovered, in a warm, draft-free place for 60 to 75 minutes or until the dough has risen to the top of the pan. Meanwhile, preheat oven to 350°F (180°C). Bake for 35 to 45 minutes or until the loaf sounds hollow when tapped on the bottom.

Variation

Substitute raspberry or orange-flavored dried cranberries.

Nutritional value per serving

Calories	197
Fat, total	6 g
Fat, saturated	1 g
Cholesterol	27 mg
Sodium	310 mg
Carbohydrate	34 g
Fiber	2 g
Protein	4 g
Calcium	9 mg
Iron	1 mg

Daffodil Loaf

Bring a little bit of springtime to your table! Enjoy this bread's light, cake-like texture, with its refreshing aroma and flavor of orange. Serve for a mid-morning coffee break.

Tips

To ensure success, see page 228 for extra information on baking yeast bread using the mixer method.

For thin, even slices, use an electric knife for this and all breads.

Substitute lime or three-fruit marmalade for the orange marmalade.

Nutritional value per serving

Calories	156
Fat, total	6 g
Fat, saturated	1 g
Cholesterol	27 mg
Sodium	258 mg
Carbohydrate	24 g
Fiber	2 g
Protein	3 g
Calcium	7 mg
Iron	1 mg

• **9- by 5-inch (2 L) loaf pan, lightly greased**

1¼ cups	brown rice flour	300 mL
⅓ cup	quinoa flour	75 mL
⅓ cup	arrowroot starch	75 mL
¼ cup	tapioca starch	50 mL
1 tbsp	xanthan gum	15 mL
1 tbsp	bread machine or instant yeast	15 mL
1¼ tsp	salt	6 mL
2	eggs	2
¾ cup	water	175 mL
⅓ cup	Orange Marmalade (see recipe, page 35)	75 mL
¼ cup	vegetable oil	50 mL
3 tbsp	frozen orange juice concentrate, thawed	45 mL

1. In a large bowl or plastic bag, combine brown rice flour, quinoa flour, arrowroot starch, tapioca starch, xanthan gum, yeast and salt. Mix well and set aside.

2. In a separate bowl, using a heavy-duty electric mixer with paddle attachment, combine eggs, water, marmalade, oil and orange juice concentrate until well blended. With the mixer on its lowest speed, slowly add the dry ingredients until combined. Stop the machine and scrape the bottom and sides of the bowl with a rubber spatula. With the mixer on medium speed, beat for 4 minutes.

3. Spoon into prepared pan. Let rise, uncovered, in a warm, draft-free place for 60 to 75 minutes, or until dough has risen to the top of the pan. Meanwhile, preheat oven to 350°F (180°C).

4. Bake for 35 to 45 minutes, or until loaf sounds hollow when tapped on the bottom. Remove from the pan immediately and let cool completely on a rack.

Egg-Free, Corn-Free, Lactose-Free Brown Bread

<table>
<tr><td colspan="2">Makes 1 loaf
or 12 servings</td></tr>
</table>

The perfect sandwich bread! Just add shaved roast beef, a leaf of romaine and a hint of mustard. It carries well for a tasty lunch.

Tips

Slice this or any bread with an electric knife for thin, even sandwich slices.

For information about egg replacer, see page 364.

For a milder-flavored bread, substitute 2 tbsp (25 mL) packed brown sugar for the molasses.

The rice bran can be replaced by an equal amount of brown rice flour.

Nutritional value per serving

Calories	149
Fat, total	4 g
Fat, saturated	0 g
Cholesterol	0 mg
Sodium	248 mg
Carbohydrate	27 g
Fiber	3 g
Protein	3 g
Calcium	6 mg
Iron	2 mg

● **9- by 5-inch (2 L) loaf pan, lightly greased**

1¼ cups	brown rice flour	300 mL
½ cup	sorghum flour	125 mL
½ cup	rice bran	125 mL
¼ cup	tapioca starch	50 mL
1 tbsp	powdered egg replacer	15 mL
1 tbsp	xanthan gum	15 mL
1 tbsp	bread machine or instant yeast	15 mL
1¼ tsp	salt	6 mL
1⅓ cups	water	325 mL
2 tbsp	vegetable oil	25 mL
2 tbsp	liquid honey	25 mL
1 tbsp	fancy molasses	15 mL
1 tsp	cider vinegar	5 mL

1. In a large bowl or plastic bag, combine brown rice flour, sorghum flour, rice bran, tapioca starch, egg replacer, xanthan gum, yeast and salt. Mix well and set aside.

2. In a separate bowl, using a heavy-duty electric mixer with paddle attachment, combine water, oil, honey, molasses and vinegar until well blended. With the mixer on its lowest speed, slowly add the dry ingredients until combined. Stop the machine and scrape the bottom and sides of the bowl with a rubber spatula. With the mixer on medium speed, beat for 4 minutes.

3. Spoon into prepared pan. Let rise, uncovered, in a warm, draft-free place for 60 to 75 minutes, or until dough has risen to the top of the pan. Meanwhile, preheat oven to 350°F (180°C).

4. Bake for 35 to 45 minutes, or until loaf sounds hollow when tapped on the bottom. Remove from the pan immediately and let cool completely on a rack.

Egg-Free, Corn-Free, Lactose-Free White Bread

Makes 1 loaf
or 12 servings

We know you'll enjoy this moist, all-purpose yeast bread, whether for sandwiches or to accompany your favorite salad.

Tips

Thoroughly mix the dry ingredients before adding them to the liquids — they are powder-fine and can clump together.

Use any leftovers to make bread crumbs (see page 368).

To make your own almond flour, see page 370, under Nut flour.

For information about egg replacer, see page 364.

Nutritional value per serving	
Calories	163
Fat, total	4 g
Fat, saturated	0 g
Cholesterol	0 mg
Sodium	249 mg
Carbohydrate	31 g
Fiber	2 g
Protein	3 g
Calcium	7 mg
Iron	1 mg

- 9- by 5-inch (2 L) loaf pan, lightly greased

1¾ cups	brown rice flour	425 mL
¼ cup	almond flour	50 mL
½ cup	potato starch	125 mL
¼ cup	tapioca starch	50 mL
1 tbsp	powdered egg replacer	15 mL
2 tbsp	granulated sugar	25 mL
2½ tsp	xanthan gum	12 mL
2 tsp	bread machine or instant yeast	10 mL
1¼ tsp	salt	6 mL
1⅓ cups	water	325 mL
2 tbsp	vegetable oil	25 mL
2 tsp	cider vinegar	10 mL

1. In a large bowl or plastic bag, combine rice flour, almond flour, potato starch, tapioca starch, egg replacer, sugar, xanthan gum, yeast and salt. Mix well and set aside.

2. In a separate bowl, using a heavy-duty electric mixer with paddle attachment, combine water, oil and vinegar until well blended. With the mixer on its lowest speed, slowly add the dry ingredients until combined. Stop the machine and scrape the bottom and sides of the bowl with a rubber spatula. With the mixer on medium speed, beat for 4 minutes.

3. Spoon into prepared pan. Let rise, uncovered, in a warm, draft-free place for 60 to 75 minutes, or until dough has risen to the top of the pan. Meanwhile, preheat oven to 350°F (180°C).

4. Bake for 35 to 45 minutes, or until loaf sounds hollow when tapped on the bottom. Remove from the pan immediately and let cool completely on a rack.

Flaxseed with Banana Bread

Makes 1 loaf
or 12 servings

Toasting a slice brings out the banana flavor. No need to butter this bread.

● **9- by 5-inch (2 L) loaf pan, lightly greased**

1⅓ cups	brown rice flour	325 mL
⅓ cup	potato starch	75 mL
¼ cup	tapioca starch	50 mL
1 tbsp	xanthan gum	15 mL
2 tsp	bread machine or instant yeast	10 mL
1¼ tsp	salt	6 mL
¼ cup	cracked flaxseed (see page 369)	50 mL
⅔ cup	water	150 mL
¾ cup	mashed banana	175 mL
1 tsp	cider vinegar	5 mL
¼ cup	vegetable oil	50 mL
3 tbsp	pure maple syrup	45 mL
2	eggs	2

1. In a large bowl or plastic bag, combine brown rice flour, potato starch, tapioca starch, xanthan gum, yeast, salt and flaxseed. Mix well and set aside.

2. In a separate bowl, using a heavy-duty electric mixer with paddle attachment, combine water, banana, vinegar, oil, maple syrup and eggs until well blended.

3. With the mixer on lowest speed, slowly add the dry ingredients until combined. With a rubber spatula, scrape the bottom and sides of the bowl. With the mixer on medium speed, beat for 4 minutes.

4. Spoon into prepared pan. Let rise, uncovered, in a warm, draft-free place for 60 to 75 minutes or until the dough has risen to the top of the pan. Meanwhile, preheat oven to 350°F (180°C). Bake for 35 to 45 minutes or until the loaf sounds hollow when tapped on the bottom.

Variation

Liquid honey or packed brown sugar can be substituted for the maple syrup.

Nutritional value per serving

Calories	184
Fat, total	7 g
Fat, saturated	1 g
Cholesterol	27 mg
Sodium	258 mg
Carbohydrate	29 g
Fiber	3 g
Protein	3 g
Calcium	17 mg
Iron	1 mg

Henk's Flax Bread

Henk Rietveld of Huntsville, Ontario, a recipe tester and member of the focus group for this book, suggested using the flax flour in this loaf.

Tips

To ensure success, see page 228 for extra information on baking yeast bread using the mixer method.

We tried this bread with sprouted flax powder, flax meal, ground flaxseed and flax flour, and there were really no differences.

This bread is delicious thinly sliced and toasted.

Nutritional value per serving

Calories	174
Fat, total	5 g
Fat, saturated	1 g
Cholesterol	28 mg
Sodium	274 mg
Carbohydrate	28 g
Fiber	3 g
Protein	5 g
Calcium	33 mg
Iron	1 mg

- **9- by 5-inch (2 L) loaf pan, lightly greased**

1¼ cups	brown rice flour	300 mL
¼ cup	flax flour	50 mL
½ cup	potato starch	125 mL
¼ cup	cornstarch	50 mL
¼ cup	cracked flaxseed (see page 369)	50 mL
¼ cup	nonfat (skim) milk powder	50 mL
2½ tsp	xanthan gum	12 mL
2 tsp	bread machine or instant yeast	10 mL
1¼ tsp	salt	6 mL
2	eggs	2
2	egg whites	2
1 cup	water	250 mL
2 tbsp	vegetable oil	25 mL
2 tbsp	liquid honey	25 mL
2 tsp	cider vinegar	10 mL

1. In a large bowl or plastic bag, combine rice flour, flax flour, potato starch, cornstarch, flaxseed, milk powder, xanthan gum, yeast and salt. Mix well and set aside.

2. In a separate bowl, using a heavy-duty electric mixer with paddle attachment, combine eggs, egg whites, water, oil, honey and vinegar until well blended. With the mixer on its lowest speed, slowly add the dry ingredients until combined. Stop the machine and scrape the bottom and sides of the bowl with a rubber spatula. With the mixer on medium speed, beat for 4 minutes.

3. Spoon into prepared pan. Let rise, uncovered, in a warm, draft-free place for 60 to 75 minutes, or until dough has risen to the top of the pan. Meanwhile, preheat oven to 350°F (180°C).

4. Bake for 35 to 45 minutes, or until loaf sounds hollow when tapped on the bottom. Remove from the pan immediately and let cool completely on a rack.

Variations

Substitute raw hemp powder and hemp hearts® for flax, both flour and seeds.

Substitute an equal amount of packed brown sugar for the honey.

Italian Herb Bread

Makes 1 loaf
or 12 servings

The fragrant aroma of this loaf makes waiting for it to bake extremely difficult. Serve this zesty herb bread with any course — soup, salad or entrée.

Tips

To ensure success, see page 228 for extra information on baking yeast bread using the mixer method.

This is an excellent loaf for making croutons and bread crumbs (see page 368).

Substitute triple the amount of snipped fresh herbs for the dried. See Techniques Glossary, page 370, for information about working with fresh herbs.

Nutritional value per serving

Calories	175
Fat, total	6 g
Fat, saturated	1 g
Cholesterol	27 mg
Sodium	255 mg
Carbohydrate	27 g
Fiber	3 g
Protein	4 g
Calcium	16 mg
Iron	2 mg

• **9- by 5-inch (2 L) loaf pan, lightly greased**

1¼ cups	sorghum flour	300 mL
½ cup	whole bean flour	125 mL
⅓ cup	potato starch	75 mL
⅓ cup	tapioca starch	75 mL
¼ cup	granulated sugar	50 mL
2½ tsp	xanthan gum	12 mL
2 tsp	bread machine or instant yeast	10 mL
1¼ tsp	salt	7 mL
¼ cup	snipped fresh parsley	50 mL
2 tsp	ground dried marjoram	10 mL
2 tsp	ground dried thyme	10 mL
2	eggs	2
1¼ cups	water	300 mL
¼ cup	vegetable oil	50 mL
1 tsp	cider vinegar	5 mL

1. In a large bowl or plastic bag, combine sorghum flour, whole bean flour, potato starch, tapioca starch, sugar, xanthan gum, yeast, salt, parsley, marjoram and thyme. Mix well and set aside.

2. In a separate bowl, using a heavy-duty electric mixer with paddle attachment, combine eggs, water, oil and vinegar until well blended. With the mixer on its lowest speed, slowly add the dry ingredients until combined. Stop the machine and scrape the bottom and sides of the bowl with a rubber spatula. With the mixer on medium speed, beat for 4 minutes.

3. Spoon into prepared pan. Let rise, uncovered, in a warm, draft-free place for 60 to 75 minutes, or until dough has risen to the top of the pan. Meanwhile, preheat oven to 350°F (180°C).

4. Bake for 35 to 45 minutes, or until loaf sounds hollow when tapped on the bottom. Remove from the pan immediately and let cool completely on a rack.

Lemon Poppy Loaf

Makes 1 loaf
or 12 servings

A perennial favorite flavor combination — poppy seeds and lemon.

Tips

Use a zester to make long thin strips of lemon zest. Be sure to remove only the colored outer skin, avoiding the bitter white pith beneath.

Freshly squeezed lemon juice enhances the flavor. Roll the lemon on the counter or between your hands to loosen the juice.

Keep a lemon in the freezer. Zest while frozen, then juice after warming in the microwave.

Nutritional value per serving

Calories	181
Fat, total	6 g
Fat, saturated	1 g
Cholesterol	27 mg
Sodium	211 mg
Carbohydrate	29 g
Fiber	2 g
Protein	3 g
Calcium	51 mg
Iron	1 mg

- **9- by 5-inch (2 L) loaf pan, lightly greased**

1¼ cups	brown rice flour	300 mL
½ cup	potato starch	125 mL
¼ cup	arrowroot starch	50 mL
¼ cup	granulated sugar	50 mL
1 tbsp	xanthan gum	15 mL
1 tbsp	bread machine or instant yeast	15 mL
1 tsp	salt	5 mL
2 tbsp	lemon zest (see Tips, left)	25 mL
¼ cup	poppy seeds	50 mL
1 cup	water	250 mL
¼ cup	freshly squeezed lemon juice	50 mL
3 tbsp	vegetable oil	45 mL
2	eggs	2
1	egg white	1

1. In a large bowl or plastic bag, combine rice flour, potato starch, arrowroot starch, sugar, xanthan gum, yeast, salt, zest and poppy seeds. Mix well and set aside.

2. In a separate bowl, using a heavy-duty electric mixer with paddle attachment, combine water, lemon juice, oil, eggs and egg white until well blended.

3. With the mixer on lowest speed, slowly add the dry ingredients until combined. With a rubber spatula, scrape the bottom and sides of the bowl. With the mixer on medium speed, beat for 4 minutes.

4. Spoon into prepared pan. Let rise, uncovered, in a warm, draft-free place for 60 to 75 minutes or until the dough has risen to the top of the pan. Meanwhile, preheat oven to 350°F (180°C). Bake for 35 to 45 minutes or until the loaf sounds hollow when tapped on the bottom.

Variation

Substitute double the amount of orange zest for lemon and use orange juice instead of lemon juice.

Nutmeg Loaf

Makes 1 loaf
or 12 servings

Flecks of brown nutmeg stand out against the white background in this tangy-sweet loaf. The aroma will have you slicing it hot.

Tip

For the best flavor, use freshly grated whole nutmeg. Use approximately half as much freshly grated as ground.

- **9- by 5-inch (2 L) loaf pan, lightly greased**

1¼ cups	brown rice flour	300 mL
⅓ cup	arrowroot starch	75 mL
⅓ cup	quinoa flour	75 mL
¼ cup	tapioca starch	50 mL
2 tbsp	granulated sugar	25 mL
1 tbsp	xanthan gum	15 mL
1 tbsp	bread machine or instant yeast	15 mL
1¼ tsp	salt	6 mL
1¼ tsp	ground nutmeg	6 mL
⅔ cup	water	150 mL
⅔ cup	plain yogurt	150 mL
¼ cup	vegetable oil	50 mL
2	eggs	2

1. In a large bowl or plastic bag, combine rice flour, arrowroot starch, quinoa flour, tapioca starch, sugar, xanthan gum, yeast, salt and nutmeg. Mix well and set aside.

2. In a separate bowl, using a heavy-duty electric mixer with paddle attachment, combine water, yogurt, oil and eggs until well blended.

3. With the mixer on lowest speed, slowly add the dry ingredients until combined. With a rubber spatula, scrape the bottom and sides of the bowl. With the mixer on medium speed, beat for 4 minutes.

4. Spoon into prepared pan. Let rise, uncovered, in a warm, draft-free place for 60 to 75 minutes or until the dough has risen to the top of the pan. Meanwhile, preheat oven to 350°F (180°C). Bake for 35 to 45 minutes or until the loaf sounds hollow when tapped on the bottom.

Variations

If you cannot tolerate quinoa or it is unavailable, increase the rice flour by ⅓ cup (75 mL).

Vanilla yogurt or gluten-free sour cream can replace the plain yogurt. Read the label carefully because some contain wheat starch.

Nutritional value per serving	
Calories	164
Fat, total	6 g
Fat, saturated	1 g
Cholesterol	28 mg
Sodium	267 mg
Carbohydrate	25 g
Fiber	2 g
Protein	4 g
Calcium	31 mg
Iron	1 mg

Pumpernickel Loaf

Makes 1 loaf
or 12 servings

With all the hearty flavor of traditional pumpernickel, this version is great for sandwiches. Try it filled with sliced turkey, accompanied by a crisp, garlic dill pickle.

Tips

Remember to thoroughly mix the dry ingredients before adding to the liquids because they are powder-fine and could clump together.

For a milder flavor, omit the coffee and unsweetened cocoa powder.

Nutritional value per serving

Calories	160
Fat, total	4 g
Fat, saturated	0 g
Cholesterol	27 mg
Sodium	257 mg
Carbohydrate	26 g
Fiber	4 g
Protein	6 g
Calcium	20 mg
Iron	2 mg

- **9- by 5-inch (2 L) loaf pan, lightly greased**

¾ cup	whole bean flour	175 mL
¾ cup	yellow pea flour	175 mL
½ cup	potato starch	125 mL
¼ cup	tapioca starch	50 mL
2 tbsp	packed brown sugar	25 mL
2 tsp	xanthan gum	10 mL
1 tbsp	bread machine or instant yeast	15 mL
1¼ tsp	salt	6 mL
2 tsp	instant coffee granules	10 mL
2 tsp	unsweetened cocoa powder	10 mL
½ tsp	ground ginger	2 mL
1¼ cups	water	300 mL
2 tbsp	fancy molasses	25 mL
1 tsp	cider vinegar	5 mL
2 tbsp	vegetable oil	25 mL
2	eggs	2

1. In a large bowl or plastic bag, combine whole bean flour, yellow pea flour, potato starch, tapioca starch, brown sugar, xanthan gum, yeast, salt, coffee granules, cocoa and ginger. Mix well and set aside.

2. In a separate bowl, using a heavy-duty electric mixer with paddle attachment, combine water, molasses, vinegar, oil and eggs until well blended.

3. With the mixer on lowest speed, slowly add the dry ingredients until combined. With a rubber spatula, scrape the bottom and sides of the bowl. With the mixer on medium speed, beat for 4 minutes.

4. Spoon into prepared pan. Let rise, uncovered, in a warm, draft-free place for 60 to 75 minutes or until the dough has risen to the top of the pan. Meanwhile, preheat oven to 350°F (180°C). Bake for 35 to 45 minutes or until the loaf sounds hollow when tapped on the bottom.

Variation

If yellow pea flour is unavailable, use chickpea or garbanzo bean flour. This recipe can either be made from any variety of bean flour or half pea and half bean flour.

Seedy Brown Bread

Makes 1 loaf	
or 12 servings	

A sandwich bread with a rich color and added crunch — what a treat!

Tips

To ensure success, see page 228 for extra information on baking yeast bread using the mixer method.

Store buttermilk powder in an airtight container to prevent lumping.

Tent the loaf with foil partway through the baking time to prevent the top crust from becoming too dark.

See page 221 for more tips and variations.

Nutritional value per serving

Calories	191
Fat, total	8 g
Fat, saturated	1 g
Cholesterol	28 mg
Sodium	269 mg
Carbohydrate	23 g
Fiber	4 g
Protein	7 g
Calcium	32 mg
Iron	2 mg

- **9- by 5-inch (2 L) loaf pan, lightly greased**

1 cup	sorghum flour	250 mL
1/2 cup	whole bean flour	125 mL
1/3 cup	tapioca starch	75 mL
1/4 cup	rice bran	50 mL
1/3 cup	buttermilk powder	75 mL
1 tbsp	xanthan gum	15 mL
1 tbsp	bread machine or instant yeast	15 mL
1 1/4 tsp	salt	6 mL
1/4 cup	pumpkin seeds	50 mL
1/4 cup	raw unsalted sunflower seeds	50 mL
1/4 cup	sesame seeds	50 mL
2	eggs	2
1 cup	water	250 mL
2 tbsp	vegetable oil	25 mL
2 tbsp	liquid honey	25 mL
1 tbsp	fancy molasses	15 mL
1 tsp	cider vinegar	5 mL

1. In a large bowl or plastic bag, combine sorghum flour, whole bean flour, tapioca starch, rice bran, buttermilk powder, xanthan gum, yeast, salt and pumpkin, sunflower and sesame seeds. Mix well and set aside.

2. In a separate bowl, using a heavy-duty electric mixer with paddle attachment, combine eggs, water, oil, honey, molasses and vinegar until well blended. With the mixer on its lowest speed, slowly add the dry ingredients until combined. Stop the machine and scrape the bottom and sides of the bowl with a rubber spatula. With the mixer on medium speed, beat for 4 minutes.

3. Spoon into prepared pan. Let rise, uncovered, in a warm, draft-free place for 70 to 80 minutes, or until dough has risen to the top of the pan. Meanwhile, preheat oven to 350°F (180°C).

4. Bake for 35 to 45 minutes, or until loaf sounds hollow when tapped on the bottom. Remove from the pan immediately and let cool completely on a rack.

Sun-Dried Tomato Rice Loaf

Makes 1 loaf
or 12 servings

For those who prefer savory loaves to sweet, try this variation of the Cranberry Wild Rice Loaf suggested by Larry, a member of our focus group.

Tip

Select dry, not oil-packed, sun-dried tomatoes.

Nutritional value per serving

Calories	195
Fat, total	6 g
Fat, saturated	1 g
Cholesterol	27 mg
Sodium	148 mg
Carbohydrate	33 g
Fiber	2 g
Protein	4 g
Calcium	11 mg
Iron	1 mg

• 9- by 5-inch (2 L) loaf pan, lightly greased

1¼ cups	brown rice flour	300 mL
½ cup	tapioca starch	125 mL
¼ cup	potato starch	50 mL
3 tbsp	granulated sugar	45 mL
2½ tsp	xanthan gum	12 mL
2 tsp	bread machine or instant yeast	10 mL
½ tsp	salt	2 mL
¾ tsp	celery seeds	4 mL
⅛ tsp	freshly ground black pepper	0.5 mL
¾ cup	cooked wild rice (see page 371)	175 mL
⅓ cup	sun-dried tomatoes	75 mL
1 cup	water	250 mL
¼ cup	vegetable oil	50 mL
2	eggs	2
1	egg white	1

1. In a large bowl or plastic bag, combine brown rice flour, tapioca starch, potato starch, sugar, xanthan gum, yeast, salt, celery seeds, pepper, wild rice and sun-dried tomatoes. Mix well and set aside.

2. In a separate bowl, using a heavy-duty electric mixer with paddle attachment, combine water, oil, eggs and egg white until well combined.

3. With the mixer on lowest speed, slowly add the dry ingredients until combined. With a rubber spatula, scrape the bottom and sides of the bowl. With the mixer on medium speed, beat for 4 minutes.

4. Spoon into prepared pan. Let rise, uncovered, in a warm, draft-free place for 60 to 75 minutes or until the dough has risen to the top of the pan. Meanwhile, preheat oven to 350°F (180°C). Bake for 35 to 45 minutes or until the loaf sounds hollow when tapped on the bottom.

Variation

Substitute ¼ cup (50 mL) frozen orange juice concentrate, thawed, for the same amount of water.

Tomato Rosemary Bread

Makes 1 loaf
or 12 servings

A smaller loaf than some, this is just the size to accompany an Italian dinner!

Tips

The tomato vegetable juice should be at room temperature. If using cold from the refrigerator, heat it on High in the microwave for 1 minute.

When substituting fresh herbs for the dried, triple the amount.

Use dry (not oil-packed) sun-dried tomatoes.

Nutritional value per serving	
Calories	155
Fat, total	6 g
Fat, saturated	1 g
Cholesterol	27 mg
Sodium	159 mg
Carbohydrate	22 g
Fiber	3 g
Protein	5 g
Calcium	16 mg
Iron	1 mg

- **9- by 5-inch (2 L) loaf pan, lightly greased**

1 cup	sorghum flour	250 mL
½ cup	whole bean flour	125 mL
⅓ cup	cornstarch	75 mL
3 tbsp	granulated sugar	45 mL
1 tbsp	xanthan gum	15 mL
1 tbsp	bread machine or instant yeast	15 mL
½ tsp	salt	2 mL
1½ tsp	dried rosemary	7 mL
⅓ cup	snipped sun-dried tomatoes	75 mL
1¼ cups	tomato vegetable juice	300 mL
¼ cup	vegetable oil	50 mL
2	eggs	2

1. In a large bowl or plastic bag, combine sorghum flour, whole bean flour, cornstarch, sugar, xanthan gum, yeast, salt, rosemary and tomatoes. Mix well and set aside.

2. In a separate bowl, using a heavy-duty electric mixer with paddle attachment, combine juice, oil and eggs until well blended.

3. With the mixer on lowest speed, slowly add the dry ingredients until combined. With a rubber spatula, scrape the bottom and sides of the bowl. With the mixer on medium speed, beat for 4 minutes.

4. Spoon into prepared pan. Let rise, uncovered, in a warm, draft-free place for 60 to 75 minutes or until the dough has risen to the top of the pan. Meanwhile, preheat oven to 350°F (180°C). Bake for 35 to 45 minutes or until the loaf sounds hollow when tapped on the bottom.

Variation

Vary the herb — select oregano, basil or thyme.

White Bread

We know you'll enjoy this moist all-purpose yeast bread, whether for sandwiches or to accompany your favorite salad.

Tips

Remember to thoroughly mix the dry ingredients before adding to the liquids because they are powder-fine and could clump together.

Use any leftovers to make bread crumbs (see Techniques Glossary, page 368).

Nutritional value per serving

Calories	172
Fat, total	3 g
Fat, saturated	0 g
Cholesterol	28 mg
Sodium	271 mg
Carbohydrate	31 g
Fiber	1 g
Protein	3 g
Calcium	23 mg
Iron	0 mg

• **9- by 5-inch (2 L) loaf pan, lightly greased**

1¾ cups	brown rice flour	425 mL
½ cup	potato starch	125 mL
¼ cup	tapioca starch	50 mL
¼ cup	nonfat dry milk or skim milk powder	50 mL
2 tbsp	granulated sugar	25 mL
2½ tsp	xanthan gum	12 mL
2 tsp	bread machine or instant yeast	10 mL
1¼ tsp	salt	6 mL
1 cup	water	250 mL
2 tsp	cider vinegar	10 mL
2 tbsp	vegetable oil	25 mL
2	eggs	2
2	egg whites	2

1. In a large bowl or plastic bag, combine rice flour, potato starch, tapioca starch, milk powder, sugar, xanthan gum, yeast and salt. Mix well and set aside.

2. In a separate bowl, using a heavy-duty electric mixer with paddle attachment, combine water, vinegar, oil, eggs and egg whites until well blended.

3. With the mixer on lowest speed, slowly add the dry ingredients until combined. With a rubber spatula, scrape the bottom and sides of the bowl. With the mixer on medium speed, beat for 4 minutes.

4. Spoon into prepared pan. Let rise, uncovered, in a warm, draft-free place for 60 to 75 minutes or until the dough has risen to the top of the pan. Meanwhile, preheat oven to 350°F (180°C). Bake for 35 to 45 minutes or until the loaf sounds hollow when tapped on the bottom.

Whole Grain Amaranth Bread

Makes 1 loaf

or 12 servings

This soft-textured, creamy, honey-colored bread is so delicious you won't even suspect how nutritious it is.

Tips

To ensure success, see page 228 for extra information on baking yeast bread using the mixer method.

Substitute $1/4$ cup (50 mL) liquid egg whites for the 2 egg whites.

Store amaranth grain in an airtight container in the refrigerator for up to 6 months.

Amaranth is high in fiber, iron and calcium and lower in sodium than most grains.

Nutritional value per serving

Calories	170
Fat, total	5 g
Fat, saturated	1 g
Cholesterol	27 mg
Sodium	266 mg
Carbohydrate	28 g
Fiber	2 g
Protein	4 g
Calcium	18 mg
Iron	1 mg

- **9- by 5-inch (2 L) loaf pan, lightly greased**

1 cup	brown rice flour	250 mL
$2/3$ cup	amaranth flour	150 mL
$1/2$ cup	potato starch	125 mL
$1/4$ cup	amaranth grain	50 mL
1 tbsp	xanthan gum	15 mL
2 tsp	bread machine or instant yeast	10 mL
$1 1/4$ tsp	salt	6 mL
2 tbsp	grated orange zest	25 mL
2	eggs	2
2	egg whites	2
$3/4$ cup	water	175 mL
3 tbsp	vegetable oil	45 mL
3 tbsp	liquid honey	45 mL
2 tsp	cider vinegar	10 mL

1. In a large bowl or plastic bag, combine brown rice flour, amaranth flour, potato starch, amaranth grain, xanthan gum, yeast, salt and orange zest. Mix well and set aside.

2. In a separate bowl, using a heavy-duty electric mixer with paddle attachment, combine eggs, egg whites, water, oil, honey and vinegar until well blended. With the mixer on its lowest speed, slowly add the dry ingredients until combined. Stop the machine and scrape the bottom and sides of the bowl with a rubber spatula. With the mixer on medium speed, beat for 4 minutes.

3. Spoon into prepared pan. Let rise, uncovered, in a warm, draft-free place for 70 to 80 minutes, or until dough has risen to the top of the pan. Meanwhile, preheat oven to 350°F (180°C).

4. Bake for 35 to 45 minutes, or until loaf sounds hollow when tapped on the bottom. Remove from the pan immediately and let cool completely on a rack.

Delicious Desserts

continued on next page

Cakes

Glazes, Frostings and Sauces

Baked Cheesecake

Decadent, delicious and delightful — need we say more?

Tips

Leave the cheesecake in the oven for 30 minutes after turning the oven off. This helps prevent large cracks. Be sure to set the timer, as it is easy to forget.

Make ahead and cut into wedges and freeze. Wrap airtight for up to 4 weeks. Thaw overnight in the refrigerator.

- Preheat oven to 350°F (180°C)
- 10-inch (25 cm) springform pan, lightly greased

Base

¼ cup	melted butter	50 mL
¼ cup	packed brown sugar	50 mL
3 cups	White Cake crumbs (see recipe, page 315)	750 mL

Cheesecake

2	packages (each 8 oz/250 g) cream cheese, softened	2
1 cup	granulated sugar	250 mL
2 tbsp	cornstarch	25 mL
1 tsp	freshly squeezed lemon juice	5 mL
4	eggs	4
1 cup	milk	250 mL

1. *Base:* In a large bowl, combine butter, brown sugar and cake crumbs. Mix well. Press into prepared pan. Set aside.

2. *Cheesecake:* In a large bowl, using an electric mixer, beat the cream cheese until smooth. Slowly add sugar, cornstarch and lemon juice. Beat until light and fluffy. Add eggs, one at a time, beating well after each. Mix in milk. Pour over the base.

3. Bake in preheated oven for 45 to 55 minutes or until the center is just set. Let cool in oven for 30 minutes with the oven turned off (see Tip, left). Let cool in pan on rack for 30 minutes before refrigerating. Refrigerate until chilled, about 3 hours. Keeps for up to 2 days in the refrigerator.

Variations

Substitute an equal amount of shortbread cookie crumbs from Sue's Shortbread (see recipe, page 339) for the cake crumbs in the base.

Substitute a lower-fat but not whipped or spreadable cream cheese.

Cake crumbs easily if it is slightly frozen.

Nutritional value per serving

Calories	539
Fat, total	24 g
Fat, saturated	11 g
Cholesterol	164 mg
Sodium	454 mg
Carbohydrate	67 g
Fiber	2 g
Protein	13 g
Calcium	193 mg
Iron	1 mg

Banana-Pecan Sticky Buns

Makes 9 buns

Thought you'd never be able to enjoy sticky buns again? Well, think again. These are for you.

Tip

We baked this recipe using two types of baking pans. The heavy dark pan baked in the stated time, while the lightweight lighter-colored pan almost burned and the topping hardened on cooling. Adjust baking time according to your baking pan. (See Choosing Baking Pans, page 19.)

- **Preheat oven to 375°F (190°C)**
- **8-inch (2 L) square baking pan, ungreased**

⅔ cup	sorghum flour	150 mL
½ cup	brown rice flour	125 mL
⅓ cup	potato starch	75 mL
¼ cup	tapioca starch	50 mL
2 tsp	xanthan gum	10 mL
2 tsp	bread machine or instant yeast	10 mL
1¼ tsp	salt	6 mL
1 tsp	ground cinnamon	5 mL
¼ cup	water	50 mL
¾ cup	mashed banana	175 mL
¼ cup	liquid honey	50 mL
1 tsp	cider vinegar	5 mL
¼ cup	butter, softened	50 mL
2	eggs	2

Pan Glaze

⅓ cup	melted butter	75 mL
⅓ cup	packed brown sugar	75 mL
⅓ cup	corn syrup	75 mL
½ cup	pecan halves	125 mL
½ cup	raisins	125 mL

Bread Machine Method

1. In a large bowl or plastic bag, combine sorghum flour, rice flour, potato starch, tapioca starch, xanthan gum, yeast, salt and cinnamon. Mix well and set aside.

2. Pour water, banana, honey, vinegar, butter and eggs into the bread machine baking pan. Select the Dough Cycle. Allow the liquids to mix until combined.

3. Gradually add the dry ingredients as the bread machine is mixing, scraping with a rubber spatula while adding. Try to incorporate all the dry ingredients within 1 to 2 minutes. Allow the bread machine to complete the cycle.

Nutritional value per serving (1 bun)	
Calories	407
Fat, total	17 g
Fat, saturated	6 g
Cholesterol	52 mg
Sodium	455 mg
Carbohydrate	62 g
Fiber	4 g
Protein	4 g
Calcium	27 mg
Iron	1 mg

Mixer Method

1. In a large bowl or plastic bag, combine sorghum flour, rice flour, potato starch, tapioca starch, xanthan gum, yeast, salt and cinnamon. Mix well and set aside.

2. In a large bowl, using a heavy-duty mixer with paddle attachment, beat water, banana, honey, vinegar, butter and eggs until well blended.

3. With the mixer on lowest speed, slowly add the dry ingredients until combined. With a rubber spatula, scrape the bottom and sides of the bowl. With the mixer on medium speed, beat for 4 minutes.

For Both Methods

4. *Pan Glaze:* In baking pan, combine melted butter, brown sugar and corn syrup. Sprinkle with pecans and raisins. Drop the soft dough by nine heaping spoonfuls on top of the pan glaze. Do not smooth tops. Let rise in a warm, draft-free place for 40 to 50 minutes or until the dough has almost doubled in volume. Bake in preheated oven for 30 to 40 minutes or until sticky buns sound hollow when tapped on the top. Immediately invert pan over a serving platter. Allow to stand for 1 to 2 minutes before removing pan. Serve warm.

Variation

This recipe can be doubled and baked in two 8-inch (2 L) square baking pans or a single 13- by 9-inch (3 L) baking pan, increasing the baking time by 15 minutes for the large pan.

Blueberry Almond Dessert

Anne Lindsay, PHEc, a cookbook author known for her healthy-eating recipes, told us this is her most popular recipe. With Anne's permission, we have developed a gluten-free version for you. This soft, creamy dessert is delicious with its hint of almond flavor in the crust and topping.

Tips

This dessert can be made ahead, covered with plastic wrap and refrigerated for up to 2 days.

When using frozen blueberries, there is no need to defrost.

Substitute fresh or frozen cranberries, or a berry mix, for the blueberries.

Nutritional value per serving	
Calories	330
Fat, total	16 g
Fat, saturated	4 g
Cholesterol	37 mg
Sodium	152 mg
Carbohydrate	41 g
Fiber	4 g
Protein	9 g
Calcium	172 mg
Iron	2 mg

- Preheat oven to 325°F (160°C)
- Six ¾-cup (175 mL) ramekins or ceramic soufflé dishes, lightly buttered

Base

⅓ cup	almond flour	75 mL
⅓ cup	amaranth flour	75 mL
¼ cup	granulated sugar	50 mL
1 tsp	GF baking powder	5 mL
½ tsp	xanthan gum	2 mL
Pinch	salt	Pinch
1	egg white	1
3 tbsp	cold butter, cut into 1-inch (2.5 cm) cubes	45 mL
½ tsp	almond extract	2 mL
2 cups	fresh or frozen blueberries	500 mL

Topping

⅓ cup	granulated sugar	75 mL
2 tbsp	tapioca starch	25 mL
1	egg, lightly beaten	1
1 cup	plain yogurt	250 mL
1½ tsp	grated lemon zest	7 mL
¼ tsp	almond extract	1 mL
¾ cup	sliced almonds	175 mL

1. *Prepare the base:* In a food processor fitted with a metal blade, pulse the almond flour, amaranth flour, sugar, baking powder, xanthan gum and salt. Add egg white, butter and almond extract; pulse until dough forms a ball. Divide among prepared ramekins. Do not press down.

2. Bake in preheated oven for 10 to 12 minutes, just until light golden. Sprinkle blueberries over hot base.

3. *Prepare the topping:* In a small bowl, using an electric mixer, combine sugar and tapioca starch. Add egg, yogurt, lemon zest and almond extract and mix until smooth. Pour over blueberries. Sprinkle with almonds.

4. Bake in preheated oven for 20 minutes, or until top is set. Let cool to room temperature in ramekins on a rack before serving or refrigerating.

Blueberry Peach Crisp

Late summer means peaches are plentiful and evenings are cool — time to make this comfort food.

Tips

To increase the fiber, leave the peel on the peaches.

Check with the manufacturer to be sure buckwheat flakes are gluten-free.

If using frozen fruit, there is no need to defrost before using; just increase the baking time until fruit is fork-tender.

Instead of baking, microwave, uncovered, on High for 4 minutes. Turn dish one-quarter turn and microwave on High for 3 to 4 minutes longer, or until fruit is tender. Let stand for 5 minutes.

Nutritional value per serving

Calories	278
Fat, total	11 g
Fat, saturated	4 g
Cholesterol	10 mg
Sodium	69 mg
Carbohydrate	41 g
Fiber	5 g
Protein	6 g
Calcium	36 mg
Iron	2 mg

- Preheat oven to 375°F (190°C)
- 8-cup (2 L) casserole dish, lightly greased

Topping

1/3 cup	sorghum flour	75 mL
1/3 cup	whole bean flour	75 mL
1/4 cup	packed brown sugar	50 mL
1 tbsp	grated orange zest	15 mL
1/2 tsp	ground nutmeg	2 mL
1/3 cup	melted butter	75 mL
3/4 cup	GF buckwheat flakes	175 mL
1/2 cup	sliced almonds	125 mL

Base

4 cups	sliced fresh peaches, about 5 large	1 L
1 cup	fresh or frozen blueberries	250 mL
1/4 cup	cornstarch	50 mL
2 tbsp	granulated sugar	25 mL

1. *Prepare the topping:* In a medium bowl, combine sorghum flour, whole bean flour, brown sugar, orange zest and nutmeg. Drizzle with melted butter and mix until crumbly. Add buckwheat flakes and almonds. Set aside.
2. *Prepare the base:* In prepared casserole dish, combine peaches, blueberries, cornstarch and sugar.
3. Sprinkle topping over the fruit. Do not pack.
4. Bake in preheated oven for 20 to 25 minutes, or until fruit is bubbly and topping is browned. Serve warm.

Variations

For a crisper topping, cover with foil for the first half of the baking time.

Substitute nectarines for the peaches.

Recipe can be divided in half and baked in a lightly greased 9- by 5-inch (2 L) loaf pan.

Cherry Clafouti

Makes 6 servings

Friends drop in at dinnertime? Serve this easy-to-prepare custard pudding warm from the oven.

Tip

This is just as delicious served cold the next day.

- Preheat oven to 400°F (200°C)
- 8-cup (2 L) oval or square baking dish, lightly greased

3 cups	pitted sour cherries	750 mL
1/4 cup	granulated sugar	50 mL
1/3 cup	brown rice flour	75 mL
2 tbsp	tapioca starch	25 mL
1/2 tsp	xanthan gum	2 mL
Pinch	salt	Pinch
1 cup	milk	250 mL
1 tbsp	butter	15 mL
2	eggs	2
1/3 cup	granulated sugar	75 mL
1 tsp	vanilla extract	5 mL

1. Combine cherries and 1/4 cup (50 mL) sugar in the bottom of prepared baking dish. Set aside.

2. In a small bowl, combine rice flour, tapioca starch, xanthan gum and salt. Mix well and set aside.

3. In a small saucepan, heat milk and butter over medium heat until tiny bubbles form around the edge. Mix well and set aside.

4. In a large bowl, using an electric mixer, beat eggs and 1/3 cup (75 mL) sugar until light and fluffy. Gradually beat in dry ingredients until smooth. Blend in milk mixture and vanilla extract. Pour over cherries.

5. Bake in preheated oven for 30 to 35 minutes, until puffed and slightly golden. Serve hot.

Variation

Omit sugar, if you want to use sweet cherries instead of the sour. If you're using frozen cherries, thaw them first. If using sour cherries from a jar, drain off juices before measuring.

Nutritional value per serving	
Calories	215
Fat, total	4 g
Fat, saturated	2 g
Cholesterol	60 mg
Sodium	111 mg
Carbohydrate	41 g
Fiber	2 g
Protein	5 g
Calcium	71 mg
Iron	1 mg

Creamy Rice Pudding

As far as we're concerned, this is the ultimate in comfort foods.

Tip

For an extra-creamy pudding, choose short-grain rice.

2 cups	milk	500 mL
1/3 cup	short-grain rice	75 mL
3 tbsp	granulated sugar	45 mL
2 tsp	butter	10 mL
Pinch	salt	Pinch
1/2 tsp	vanilla extract	2 mL
1/4 tsp	ground nutmeg	1 mL
1/3 cup	raisins	75 mL

1. In a large saucepan over medium heat, combine milk, rice, sugar, butter and salt. Heat, stirring often, until tiny bubbles form around the edge. Reduce heat to low. Cover and simmer, stirring occasionally, for 1 hour or until rice is tender. Remove from heat. Stir in vanilla, nutmeg and raisins. Serve warm or chilled.

Variations

Substitute brown rice for the short-grain white and increase cooking time by 45 minutes. And increase milk to 2 1/2 cups (625 mL).

Substitute cinnamon for nutmeg and dates for raisins.

Nutritional value per serving	
Calories	214
Fat, total	3 g
Fat, saturated	2 g
Cholesterol	10 mg
Sodium	158 mg
Carbohydrate	40 g
Fiber	1 g
Protein	6 g
Calcium	158 mg
Iron	1 mg

Chocolate Lover's Hazelnut Surprise

Makes 6 servings

These individual decadent chocolate delights are a close relative of the molten lava cake, oozing with bittersweet chocolate and hazelnut liqueur. Serve garnished with fresh strawberries or raspberries in season.

Tips

One individually wrapped square of baking chocolate weighs 1 oz (30 g).

For instructions on warming eggs to room temperature, see Techniques Glossary, page 369.

Nutritional value per serving	
Calories	457
Fat, total	37 g
Fat, saturated	19 g
Cholesterol	131 mg
Sodium	188 mg
Carbohydrate	33 g
Fiber	4 g
Protein	7 g
Calcium	22 mg
Iron	2 mg

- **Preheat oven to 450°F (220°C)**
- **Six ¾-cup (175 mL) ramekins or ceramic soufflé dishes**

2 tsp	butter, softened	10 mL
2 tsp	unsweetened cocoa powder	10 mL
8 oz	bittersweet chocolate, chopped	250 g
½ cup	butter	125 mL
2 tbsp	hazelnut flour	25 mL
2 tbsp	sorghum flour	25 mL
½ tsp	xanthan gum	2 mL
4	eggs, at room temperature	4
½ cup	GF confectioner's (icing) sugar	125 mL
2 tbsp	hazelnut liqueur	25 mL

1. Using a scrunched-up piece of waxed paper, lightly butter the bottom and sides of ramekins. Coat bottom and sides with cocoa.

2. In a large microwave-safe bowl, microwave chocolate and butter, uncovered, on Medium (50%) for 3 minutes, or until partially melted. Stir until completely melted. Let cool to room temperature.

3. In a small bowl, combine hazelnut flour, sorghum flour and xanthan gum. Set aside.

4. In a large bowl, using an electric mixer, beat eggs, confectioner's sugar and liqueur until thick and lemon-colored, approximately 8 minutes. (Set a kitchen timer, as 8 minutes seems like forever.) With mixer on low, add cooled melted chocolate; continue beating until combined. Add dry ingredients and beat just until blended. Ladle into each ramekin and place on baking sheet.

Tips

Baking time is critical; even one extra minute will cause the center to become solid instead of molten and the top crust to burn.

We tried to make this dessert with ¹/₂-cup (125 mL) dishes without success. Your ramekins are the correct size if they hold ³/₄ cup (175 mL) water when full to the top.

Garnish with large white chocolate curls. To make curls, peel room-temperature chocolate firmly along its length with a sharp vegetable peeler.

For easier cleanup, allow ramekins to soak in hot soapy water.

Substitute an equal amount of coffee liqueur or cold double-strength coffee for the hazelnut liqueur.

You can also serve the "Surprise" right in the ramekins, topped with chopped toasted hazelnuts (see Techniques Glossary, page 370, for instructions on toasting nuts). Ramekins should still be hot from the oven when you serve.

5. Bake immediately or refrigerate for up to 4 hours. Remove from refrigerator to bring to room temperature (approximately 45 minutes) before baking. Bake in preheated oven for 11 minutes, or until "Surprise" is puffed and crusted, but center is still soft. Let cool on a rack for 3 minutes. Run a knife around the inside edge of each ramekin to loosen. Cover with individual dessert plates and invert. Remove hot ramekin. Serve immediately. (Ramekins can be left on for up to 20 minutes before removing for serving.)

Chocolate-Glazed Pavlova

Pavlova is an Australian dessert named for the Russian ballerina, Anna Pavlova. It consists of a crisp crunchy meringue exterior and a creamy marshmallow interior shell filled with whipped cream and mounded with fresh fruit. Try our alternative lighter filling.

Tips

This is an ideal time to use liquid egg whites, available in cartons. Use 1/2 cup (125 mL) for this recipe.

If berry (castor or fruit/instant dissolving) sugar is not available, use granulated sugar. Add very slowly.

- Preheat oven to 275°F (140°C)
- Baking sheet, lined with parchment paper

Meringue

4	egg whites, at room temperature	4
1/4 tsp	cream of tartar	1 mL
1 cup	berry (castor or fruit/instant dissolving) sugar	250 mL
1 tbsp	cornstarch	15 mL
1 tsp	white vinegar	5 mL

Filling

1 cup	whipping (35%) cream	250 mL
2 cups	sliced mixed fruit, such as peaches, kiwi and strawberries	500 mL

Glaze

1 oz	semi-sweet chocolate, chopped	30 g
1/2 tsp	vegetable oil	2 mL
3/4 cup	toasted slivered almonds	175 mL

Alternative Filling

4 oz	light cream cheese, softened	125 g
1/3 cup	GF confectioner's (icing) sugar	75 mL
Dash	almond extract	Dash
2 cups	sliced mixed fruit, such as peaches, kiwi and strawberries	500 mL

1. Using a pencil, draw an 8-inch (20 cm) circle in the center of the parchment (you can trace an 8-inch/20 cm cake pan or cardboard circle). Flip parchment over.

2. *Prepare the meringue:* In a large glass or metal bowl, using an electric mixer, beat egg whites and cream of tartar until soft peaks form. Gradually beat in berry sugar, a little at a time, until stiff, glossy peaks form. Fold in cornstarch and vinegar. Spoon the meringue to fill the circle on the parchment paper. Using the back of a large metal spoon, lightly smooth top.

Nutritional value per serving	
Calories	376
Fat, total	20 g
Fat, saturated	9 g
Cholesterol	50 mg
Sodium	97 mg
Carbohydrate	46 g
Fiber	4 g
Protein	8 g
Calcium	122 mg
Iron	1 mg

Tips

Make sure the mixer bowl and beaters are completely free of grease. Plastic tends to retain grease more readily than metal or glass.

For instructions on warming egg whites to room temperature, see Techniques Glossary, page 369.

For instructions on toasting nuts and whipping cream, see Techniques Glossary, pages 370 and 371.

Meringue shell can be kept at room temperature in a plastic bag for up to 3 days.

3. Bake in preheated oven for 60 to 75 minutes, or until crisp and lightly browned but still soft in the middle. Turn off oven; let stand in oven 1 hour to dry. Remove from oven and invert onto a large serving plate. Meringue will deflate in the center. Let cool completely.

4. *Prepare the filling:* In a small bowl, using an electric mixer, whip cream until soft peaks form. Spread over meringue shell to within 1 inch (2.5 cm) of the edge. Top with fresh fruit.

5. *Prepare the glaze:* In a small microwave-safe bowl, microwave chocolate and oil, uncovered, on Medium (50%) for 1 to 2 minutes, or until chocolate is partially melted. Stir until completely melted. Drizzle in ribbons over fruit and sprinkle with toasted almonds.

Alternative Filling

1. In a small bowl, using an electric mixer, beat cream cheese, confectioner's sugar and almond extract until light and fluffy. Spread over meringue shell to within 1 inch (2.5 cm) of the edge. Top with fresh fruit.

Variation

Make eight 4-inch (10 cm) individual meringues. Spoon mixture into mounds and spread each into a 4-inch (10 cm) circle or heart shape, heaping mixture at edges to form a nest. Bake for 45 minutes. Let stand in oven, with oven turned off, for 45 minutes.

Cranberry-Apple Küchen

Best served the day it is made! Start with a buttery-almond crust, then add tangy cranberries and a tart cooking apple.

Tips

For ease of spreading the dough in the pan, keep dipping the metal spoon in a glass of water.

Use the cranberries directly from the freezer — no need to thaw them.

- Preheat oven to 350°F (180°C)
- 10-inch (25 cm) springform pan, lightly greased

Crust

½ cup	sorghum flour	125 mL
¼ cup	cornstarch	50 mL
¼ cup	tapioca starch	50 mL
¼ cup	sweet rice flour	50 mL
¼ cup	almond flour	50 mL
1 tsp	xanthan gum	5 mL
½ tsp	baking soda	2 mL
¼ tsp	salt	1 mL
½ cup	butter, softened	125 mL
½ cup	granulated sugar	125 mL
¼ cup	plain yogurt	50 mL
1	egg yolk	1
½ cup	sliced almonds	125 mL

Filling

4 cups	sliced apples	1 L
2 cups	cranberries, fresh or frozen	500 mL
¼ cup	granulated sugar	50 mL
2 tbsp	arrowroot starch	25 mL
1 tsp	ground cinnamon	5 mL
¼ cup	sliced almonds	50 mL

Glaze

⅓ cup	crabapple jelly	75 mL
2 tbsp	water	25 mL

1. *Crust:* In a large bowl or plastic bag, combine sorghum flour, cornstarch, tapioca starch, sweet rice flour, almond flour, xanthan gum, baking soda and salt. Mix well and set aside.

2. In a large bowl, using an electric mixer, cream butter and sugar. Beat in yogurt and egg yolk. Stir in dry ingredients. Mix just until blended. Stir in almonds.

Nutritional value per serving	
Calories	411
Fat, total	18 g
Fat, saturated	6 g
Cholesterol	39 mg
Sodium	261 mg
Carbohydrate	60 g
Fiber	5 g
Protein	5 g
Calcium	54 mg
Iron	1 mg

If almond flour is not readily available, make your own (see Nut Flour, page 370).

3. Using the back of a moistened metal spoon, spread dough evenly on the bottom of and $3/4$ inches (2 cm) up the side of prepared pan. Let stand for 30 minutes before baking.

4. *Filling:* In a large bowl, toss apples, cranberries, sugar, arrowroot starch and cinnamon. Pour the fruit mixture into the crust, heaping the fruit in the center, leaving the rim of crust exposed. Sprinkle almonds on the rim of the crust.

5. Bake in preheated oven for 60 to 80 minutes or until the crust edge is golden brown and fruit is tender. Let cool in the pan on a rack.

6. *Glaze:* In a small saucepan, bring crabapple jelly and water to a boil, whisking constantly. Reduce heat and boil gently for 4 to 5 minutes or until thickened, whisking occasionally. Brush over fruit. Chill before serving. Keeps for up to 2 days in the refrigerator.

Variations

Substitute $1/2$ tsp (2 mL) of any sweet spice for the cinnamon. Try cloves, allspice or nutmeg.

Choose any fruit combination you like. Depending on the fruit, only 5 cups (1.25 L) may be needed to fill the crust. Try peaches and blueberries, strawberries and rhubarb or apples and raspberries.

Cornstarch can be substituted for arrowroot.

Crêpes Suzette

Makes nine 6-inch (15 cm) crêpes

Soaked in orange and brandy, then flambéed at the table, these crêpes are sure to impress your guests. Only you need to know that they are gluten-free.

Tip

Brandy flames easily when warmed to body temperature before lighting.

- 6-inch (15 cm) crêpe pan or nonstick skillet, lightly greased

Crêpes

¼ cup	amaranth flour	50 mL
¼ cup	chickpea (garbanzo bean) flour	50 mL
2 tbsp	potato starch	25 mL
2 tsp	granulated sugar	10 mL
½ tsp	xanthan gum	2 mL
½ tsp	salt	2 mL
2	eggs	2
⅔ cup	milk	150 mL
⅓ cup	water	75 mL
1 tbsp	melted butter	15 mL
1 tbsp	grated orange zest	15 mL

Orange Sauce

½ cup	butter	125 mL
½ cup	frozen orange juice concentrate, thawed	125 mL
½ cup	orange-flavored liqueur	125 mL
4 tsp	granulated sugar	20 mL
¼ cup	brandy	50 mL

1. *Prepare the crêpes:* In a large bowl or plastic bag, mix together amaranth flour, chickpea flour, potato starch, sugar, xanthan gum and salt.

2. In a small bowl, whisk together eggs, milk, water, melted butter and orange zest. Pour mixture over dry ingredients all at once, whisking until smooth. Cover and refrigerate for at least 1 hour or for up to 2 days. Bring batter back to room temperature before making crêpes.

Nutritional value per serving (1 crêpe)

Calories	243
Fat, total	13 g
Fat, saturated	5 g
Cholesterol	53 mg
Sodium	255 mg
Carbohydrate	21 g
Fiber	1 g
Protein	3 g
Calcium	38 mg
Iron	1 mg

Tips

For more information about making crêpes and storing crêpes made in advance, see page 37.

Any orange liqueur can be used in this recipe — Grand Marnier, Cointreau or Triple Sec.

3. Heat prepared pan over medium heat; add 3 to 4 tbsp (45 mL to 50 mL) batter for each crêpe, tilting and rotating pan to ensure batter covers entire bottom. Cook for 1 to 1½ minutes, or until edges begin to brown. Turn carefully with a non-metal spatula. Cook for another 30 to 45 seconds, or until bottom is dotted with brown spots. Remove to a plate and repeat with remaining batter.

4. *Prepare the orange sauce:* In a nonstick skillet or crêpe pan, melt butter over medium heat. Add orange juice, orange liqueur and sugar.

5. Add a crêpe and spoon sauce over crêpe until well saturated. Gently fold crêpe in half and then into quarters. Gently remove to a heatproof dish and keep warm. Repeat with remaining crêpes. Pour any remaining sauce over crêpes.

6. In a small saucepan, over medium-low heat, warm the brandy just until heated through but not boiling. Remove from heat. Using a long match, ignite brandy; immediately pour over crêpes in dish. Serve 2 to 3 crêpes per person.

Double Chocolate Cheesecake with Raspberry Coulis

Makes 10 servings

Chocolate and raspberry are two flavors that go together naturally. Who can resist a sliver of cheesecake served with extra fresh raspberries in season?

- Preheat oven to 350°F (180°C)
- 10-inch (25 cm) springform pan, lightly greased

Base

2 cups	Fudgy Brownie crumbs (see recipe, page 345)	500 mL

Cheesecake

2	packages (each 8 oz/250 g) cream cheese, softened	2
⅔ cup	granulated sugar	150 mL
2 tbsp	sorghum flour	25 mL
3	eggs	3
1 tsp	vanilla extract	5 mL
1 cup	plain yogurt	250 mL
8 oz	semi-sweet chocolate, melted (see Chocolate, page 368)	250 g

Raspberry Coulis

1	package (15 oz/425 g) frozen sweetened raspberries, thawed and juice reserved	1

1. *Base:* Press brownie crumbs onto the bottom of prepared pan. Bake in preheated oven for 10 minutes. Set aside to cool at room temperature.

2. *Cheesecake:* In a large bowl, using an electric mixer, beat the cream cheese until smooth. Slowly add the sugar and sorghum flour. Beat until light and fluffy. Add eggs, one at a time, beating well after each. Add vanilla extract. Fold in yogurt and melted chocolate. Pour over the cooled base.

3. Increase oven temperature to 450°F (230°C). Bake in preheated oven for 10 minutes. Then reduce oven temperature to 250°F (120°C) and continue baking for 35 to 40 minutes or until the center is just set. Let cool in oven for 30 minutes with oven off. Let cool in pan on rack for 30 minutes before refrigerating. Refrigerate until chilled, about 3 hours. Keeps for up to 2 days in the refrigerator.

Nutritional value per serving	
Calories	510
Fat, total	25 g
Fat, saturated	13 g
Cholesterol	100 mg
Sodium	210 mg
Carbohydrate	60 g
Fiber	6 g
Protein	15 g
Calcium	172 mg
Iron	2 mg

Tip

Cheesecake can be frozen for up to 6 weeks. Serve frozen or thaw it in the refrigerator overnight.

4. *Raspberry Coulis:* In a food processor or blender, purée thawed raspberries with juice. Press through a fine sieve. Spoon the purée onto individual serving plates. Top with a wedge of cheesecake.

Variations

Substitute an equal amount of Chocolate Fudge Cake (see recipe, page 302) for the Fudgy Brownie.

For a less tangy cheesecake, substitute whipping cream for the yogurt.

Gingerbread

. . . .

Makes 9 servings

A tangy lemon sauce is what turns this traditional gingerbread into something special. In fact, to make sure you don't run out, we suggest that you double the Lotsa Lemon Sauce (see recipe, page 322).

Tip

The batter thickens during the standing time before baking. Allowing the batter to stand results in a more tender cake.

Nutritional value per serving

Calories	333
Fat, total	12 g
Fat, saturated	5 g
Cholesterol	45 mg
Sodium	123 mg
Carbohydrate	52 g
Fiber	3 g
Protein	6 g
Calcium	77 mg
Iron	3 mg

- **Preheat oven to 350°F (180°C)**
- **8-inch (2 L) square baking pan, lightly greased**

1 cup	boiling water	250 mL
½ cup	shortening	125 mL
¾ cup	whole bean flour	175 mL
¾ cup	sorghum flour	175 mL
¼ cup	tapioca starch	50 mL
1 tsp	xanthan gum	5 mL
½ tsp	GF baking powder	2 mL
¼ tsp	baking soda	1 mL
¼ tsp	salt	1 mL
1½ tsp	ground ginger	7 mL
¾ tsp	ground cinnamon	4 mL
2	eggs	2
⅔ cup	fancy molasses	150 mL
⅔ cup	granulated sugar	150 mL
	Lotsa Lemon Sauce (see recipe, page 322)	

1. In a small bowl, pour boiling water over shortening. Set aside to melt and cool slightly.

2. In a large bowl, sift together whole bean flour, sorghum flour, tapioca starch, xanthan gum, baking powder, baking soda, salt, ginger and cinnamon. Resift and set aside.

3. In a separate bowl, using an electric mixer, beat eggs, molasses and sugar. Add shortening mixture and beat until smooth. Stir in dry ingredients. Mix just until blended. Pour into prepared pan. Let stand for 30 minutes before baking.

4. Bake in preheated oven for 45 to 55 minutes or until a cake tester inserted in the center comes out clean. Let cool in the pan on a rack for 10 minutes. Remove from the pan and serve warm with Lotsa Lemon Sauce.

Variations

Substitute potato starch for the tapioca.

Add ½ cup (125 mL) sunflower seeds to the batter.

Harvest Caramel

Pumpkin, maple syrup and spices add a delicious twist to a classic dessert.

Tip

Using a pastry brush dipped in water, occasionally brush down any sugar crystals that appear on the side of the pan while heating the sugar.

- Preheat oven to 350°F (180°C)
- Seven individual heatproof ramekins or custard cups

Caramel

1 cup	granulated sugar	250 mL
¼ cup	water	50 mL
⅛ tsp	freshly squeezed lemon juice	0.5 mL

Custard

8	egg yolks	8
½ cup	pure maple syrup	125 mL
1½ cups	pumpkin purée (not pie filling)	375 mL
½ tsp	ground cinnamon	2 mL
½ tsp	ground ginger	2 mL
Pinch	ground allspice	Pinch
Pinch	ground nutmeg	Pinch
2 cups	half-and-half (10%) cream	500 mL

1. *Caramel:* In a heavy saucepan over low heat, dissolve sugar in water. Add lemon juice. Without stirring, cook over medium heat until mixture begins to boil. Continue to cook until mixture turns a deep caramel brown. Remove from heat immediately, as mixture continues to cook. Pour into cups.

2. *Custard:* In a large bowl, using an electric mixer, beat egg yolks with maple syrup. Add pumpkin and spices and mix until blended.

3. Heat cream over medium heat until tiny bubbles form around the edge. Stirring constantly, gradually add cream to the pumpkin mixture. Divide evenly among custard cups.

4. Place custard cups in a larger pan. Pour boiling water into the larger pan to reach half way up the sides of the custard cups. Bake in preheated oven for 30 minutes or until knife blade inserted near the center comes out clean. Remove cups from hot water. Let stand for 30 minutes. Refrigerate until serving for up to one week. If desired, turn custards out onto individual serving plates.

Variation

Use cooked, puréed winter squash for the pumpkin.

Nutritional value per serving

Calories	345
Fat, total	12 g
Fat, saturated	7 g
Cholesterol	245 mg
Sodium	49 mg
Carbohydrate	52 g
Fiber	2 g
Protein	6 g
Calcium	156 mg
Iron	1 mg

Hot Apple Crêpes

This make-ahead dessert can be assembled at the last minute for your next dinner party.

Tips

For more information about making crêpes and storing crêpes made in advance, see page 37.

1¹/₂ lbs (750 g) of apples yield 6 cups (1.5 L) sliced.

Apple filling can be stored in the refrigerator in an airtight container for up to 4 days. To reheat, microwave on Medium (50%) for 2 to 4 minutes.

Nutritional value per serving (1 crêpe)	
Calories	238
Fat, total	9 g
Fat, saturated	4 g
Cholesterol	48 mg
Sodium	230 mg
Carbohydrate	37 g
Fiber	3 g
Protein	3 g
Calcium	61 mg
Iron	1 mg

- 6-inch (15 cm) crêpe pan or nonstick skillet, lightly greased

Crêpes

¼ cup	amaranth flour	50 mL
¼ cup	chickpea (garbanzo bean) flour	50 mL
2 tbsp	potato starch	25 mL
2 tsp	granulated sugar	10 mL
½ tsp	xanthan gum	2 mL
½ tsp	salt	2 mL
2	eggs	2
⅔ cup	milk	150 mL
⅓ cup	water	75 mL
1 tbsp	melted butter	15 mL

Apple Filling

⅓ cup	butter	75 mL
¾ cup	packed brown sugar	175 mL
6 cups	thickly sliced apples	1.5 L
1½ tsp	ground cinnamon	7 mL
	GF vanilla-flavored yogurt	

1. *Prepare the crêpes:* In a large bowl or plastic bag, mix together amaranth flour, chickpea flour, potato starch, sugar, xanthan gum and salt.

2. In a small bowl, whisk together eggs, milk, water and melted butter. Pour mixture over dry ingredients all at once, whisking until smooth. Cover and refrigerate for at least 1 hour or for up to 2 days. Bring batter back to room temperature before making crêpes.

3. Heat prepared pan over medium heat; add 3 to 4 tbsp (45 mL to 50 mL) batter for each crêpe, tilting and rotating pan to ensure batter covers entire bottom. Cook for 1 to 1½ minutes, or until edges begin to brown. Turn carefully with a non-metal spatula. Cook for another 30 to 45 seconds, or until bottom is dotted with brown spots. Remove to a plate and repeat with remaining batter.

Tips

You can also prepare the apple filling in the microwave: In a large microwave-safe bowl, microwave butter, uncovered, on High for 1 minute, or until melted. Add apples, brown sugar and cinnamon and microwave, uncovered, on High, for 2 to 4 minutes, stirring once or twice, or until apples are just tender.

Substitute 2 cups (500 mL) of your favorite prepared GF fruit pie filling for the apple filling.

Substitute whipped cream, GF frozen yogurt or GF ice cream for the GF yogurt.

4. *Prepare the apple filling:* In a saucepan, melt butter over medium heat. Add brown sugar, apples and cinnamon and simmer gently for 4 to 6 minutes, or until apples are just tender.

5. *Assemble the crêpes:* Spoon an equal portion of hot apple filling down the center of each crêpe. Roll and serve seam side down, topped with GF vanilla yogurt.

Lemon Sponge Pudding

Makes 6 servings

Whether you remember this as Lemon Cups, Lemon Pudding or Lemon Sponge Pudding, it's still a heavenly light soufflé-like pudding on top with a rich lemony custard sauce beneath.

Tip

It is worth the time to squeeze lemons for freshly squeezed lemon juice. Don't eliminate the zest.

- **Preheat oven to 325°F (160°C)**
- **8-cup (2 L) casserole, greased**

1 cup	granulated sugar	250 mL
¼ cup	sweet rice flour	50 mL
½ tsp	xanthan gum	2 mL
2 tbsp	vegetable oil	25 mL
Pinch	salt	Pinch
2 tsp	lemon zest	10 mL
⅓ cup	freshly squeezed lemon juice	75 mL
1½ cups	milk	375 mL
3	egg yolks	3
3	egg whites, stiffly beaten	3

1. In a bowl, combine sugar, sweet rice flour, xanthan gum, oil, salt, lemon zest and juice. Set aside.
2. In a small saucepan, heat milk over medium heat until tiny bubbles form around the edge. Set aside.
3. In a separate large bowl, using an electric mixer, beat egg yolks until light and fluffy. Blend in milk and lemon mixture. Fold in beaten egg whites. Pour into prepared casserole.
4. Place casserole in a larger pan. Pour boiling water into the larger pan to reach half way up the sides of the casserole. Bake in preheated oven for 40 minutes or until the top is set and cake is slightly golden. Serve warm or chilled.

Variation

Substitute orange or lime or a combination of both for the lemon.

Nutritional value per serving	
Calories	255
Fat, total	8 g
Fat, saturated	2 g
Cholesterol	96 mg
Sodium	113 mg
Carbohydrate	43 g
Fiber	1 g
Protein	6 g
Calcium	89 mg
Iron	0 mg

Praline Pumpkin Delight

Crave pumpkin pie? With a moist texture, subtle spiciness and the crunch of pecans, this is an excellent dessert to serve everyone.

Tips

If pan gets too full or too heavy to lift, pour in two-thirds of filling. After pan is set on rack, pour in remaining filling to within 1/2 inch (1 cm) of top.

If using a dark nonstick springform pan, reduce oven to 350°F (180°C) and decrease baking time to 50 to 60 minutes.

Don't add more caramel sauce than is called for; if you do, the base will become brittle and impossible to cut, and you may not be able to remove the side of the pan.

Nutritional value per serving

Calories	372
Fat, total	17 g
Fat, saturated	4 g
Cholesterol	87 mg
Sodium	445 mg
Carbohydrate	48 g
Fiber	4 g
Protein	8 g
Calcium	172 mg
Iron	2 mg

- Preheat oven to 375°F (190°C)
- 9-inch (23 cm) springform pan

Praline Base

1 1/4 cups	Gingerbread Crumbs (see recipe, page 283)	425 mL
2 tbsp	melted butter	25 mL
1 cup	pecan halves or pieces	250 mL
1/2 cup	GF caramel sauce (see Tip, left)	125 mL

Pumpkin Filling

4	eggs	4
1	can (14 oz/385 mL) 2% evaporated milk	1
2 cups	pumpkin purée (not pie filling)	500 mL
2/3 cup	packed brown sugar	150 mL
2 tsp	ground cinnamon	10 ml
1 tsp	ground allspice	5 mL
1 tsp	ground ginger	5 mL
1 tsp	salt	5 mL

1. *Prepare the praline base:* In a small bowl, combine Gingerbread Crumbs and butter; mix well. Press crumbs into bottom of pan. Sprinkle with pecans. Bake in preheated oven for 6 to 8 minutes, or until pecans are toasted. Immediately drizzle with caramel sauce, leaving a 1-inch (2.5 cm) circle around the edge. Let cool to room temperature.

2. *Prepare the pumpkin filling:* In a large bowl, using an electric mixer, combine eggs, evaporated milk, pumpkin purée, brown sugar, cinnamon, allspice, ginger and salt.

3. Holding a large spoon or spatula over the praline base, slowly pour the pumpkin filling over the spoon and let drizzle into pan (this prevents the filling from disturbing the base). (If there is too much filling for the springform pan, pour the excess into a lightly greased ovenproof casserole dish and bake for 15 to 20 minutes, until set.)

4. Bake in preheated oven for 60 to 70 minutes, or until filling is set and a knife inserted in the center comes out clean. Let cool to room temperature in pan on a rack before serving.

Rhubarb Crisp

. . . .

Makes 6 servings

Looking for a delicious way to celebrate the first fruit of the season? Here it is.

Tips

Recipe can be halved successfully.

Purchase either gluten-free rice flakes or rolled rice cereal.

For a crisper topping, cover with foil for the first half of the baking time.

- Preheat oven to 375°F (190°C)
- 8-cup (2 L) casserole, lightly greased

Topping

1/2 cup	packed brown sugar	125 mL
1/2 cup	sorghum flour	125 mL
1/2 cup	GF rice cereal	125 mL
2 tsp	orange zest	10 mL
1/2 tsp	ground ginger	2 mL
1/3 cup	cold butter, cut into 1-inch (2.5 cm) cubes	75 mL
1/2 cup	chopped walnuts	125 mL

Base

1/2 cup	corn syrup, warmed	125 mL
3 tbsp	cornstarch	45 mL
5 to 6 cups	chopped fresh rhubarb	1.25 to 1.5 L

1. *Topping:* In a bowl, combine brown sugar, sorghum flour, rice cereal, orange zest and ginger. With a pastry blender or two knives, cut in butter until crumbly. Add walnuts. Set aside.

2. *Base:* In prepared casserole, mix corn syrup and cornstarch to form a paste. Add rhubarb and stir until coated. Sprinkle crumb topping over the rhubarb. Do not pack.

3. Bake crisp in preheated oven for 50 minutes or until the rhubarb is tender. Serve warm.

Variations

Substitute thawed, frozen rhubarb for the fresh.

Replace half the rhubarb with the same quantity of sliced, fresh strawberries. Reduce corn syrup to 1/3 cup (75 mL).

Nutritional value per serving	
Calories	393
Fat, total	17 g
Fat, saturated	5 g
Cholesterol	13 mg
Sodium	130 mg
Carbohydrate	61 g
Fiber	4 g
Protein	5 g
Calcium	114 mg
Iron	1 mg

Sticky Date Pudding

We all know how the British love their puddings, often called "puds." Donna fell in love with this one on a recent holiday in the British Isles. The traditional way to serve it is warm with a warm toffee sauce. We've adapted it for you to enjoy. So will we!

Tips

When purchasing chopped dates, check for wheat starch in the coating.

Pudding can be wrapped airtight and frozen for up to 2 months, and individual pieces can be defrosted in the microwave on Medium (50%) for 2 to 4 minutes, or until warm.

Nutritional value per serving*	
Calories	192
Fat, total	5 g
Fat, saturated	2 g
Cholesterol	32 mg
Sodium	178 mg
Carbohydrate	35 g
Fiber	2 g
Protein	3 g
Calcium	54 mg
Iron	1 mg

* does not include Toffee Sauce

- **Preheat oven to 350°F (180°C)**
- **9-inch (2.5 L) square baking pan, lightly greased**

½ cup	sorghum flour	125 mL
½ cup	whole bean flour	125 mL
¼ cup	tapioca starch	50 mL
1½ tsp	GF baking powder	7 mL
1 tsp	xanthan gum	5 mL
Pinch	salt	Pinch
1 cup	coarsely chopped pitted dates	250 mL
1 cup	water	250 mL
1 tsp	baking soda	5 mL
¼ cup	butter, softened	50 mL
¾ cup	packed brown sugar	175 mL
1 tsp	vanilla	5 mL
2	eggs	2
	Toffee Sauce (see recipe, page 326)	

1. In a large bowl or plastic bag, mix together sorghum flour, whole bean flour, tapioca starch, baking powder, xanthan gum and salt. Set aside.

2. In a small saucepan, combine dates and water and bring to a boil over high heat. Reduce heat to medium-low and simmer until softened, about 5 minutes. Remove from heat and add baking soda; stir until foaming stops. Let cool to room temperature.

3. In a large bowl, using an electric mixer, cream butter. Gradually add brown sugar and beat for 2 minutes, until light and fluffy. Using a rubber spatula, scrape the bottom and sides of the bowl. Beat in vanilla; add eggs one at a time, beating for 2 minutes after each. Stir in date mixture and dry ingredients. Combine well. Spoon batter into prepared pan. Using a moistened rubber spatula, spread to edges and smooth top.

4. Bake in preheated oven for 25 to 35 minutes, or until cake tester inserted in the center comes out clean. Let pudding cool in the pan on a rack for 10 minutes. Remove from pan and serve warm with warm Toffee Sauce.

Variation

Use Nutmeg Rum Sauce (page 323) instead of Toffee Sauce.

Summertime Trifle

Trifle is a traditional English dessert that looks spectacular layered in a large glass bowl. It is a lifesaver when you have to feed a crowd, and everyone loves it. Our version features citrus to contrast with sweet, colorful fruit and the velvet creaminess of custard.

Tips

Choose pears and cranberries; blackberries, raspberries or a mixture of berries; or stewed rhubarb and strawberries.

If custard boils after the eggs are added, it curdles. Watch carefully!

Cover custard with waxed paper or plastic wrap directly on the surface and refrigerate for up to 1 day.

Nutritional value per serving	
Calories	290
Fat, total	10 g
Fat, saturated	3 g
Cholesterol	123 mg
Sodium	141 mg
Carbohydrate	45 g
Fiber	3 g
Protein	7 g
Calcium	154 mg
Iron	1 mg

- **6-cup (1.5 L) clear glass bowl or individual serving dishes**

3 tbsp	cornstarch	45 mL
1/3 cup	granulated sugar	75 mL
2 cups	milk	500 mL
3	egg yolks	3
1/2 tsp	almond extract	2 mL
1/4	White Cake, cut into 3/4-inch (2 cm) cubes, (see recipe, page 315)	1/4
2 to 3 tbsp	orange-flavored liqueur	25 to 45 mL
3 cups	fresh fruit (see Tips, left)	750 mL
1/4 cup	toasted sliced almonds (see Nuts, page 370)	50 mL

Microwave Method

1. In a large bowl, combine cornstarch and sugar. Add milk. Microwave on High for 5 to 6 minutes or until steaming, stirring every 2 minutes. Whisk about one-third of hot milk mixture into egg yolks. Gradually whisk yolk into remaining milk mixture and microwave on High for 1 to 2 minutes or until bubbly around the edge. Do not let boil. Stir in almond extract. Set aside to cool.

Stove-Top Method

1. In a saucepan, combine cornstarch and sugar. Add milk. Heat over medium for 5 to 6 minutes or until steaming, stirring constantly. Whisk about one-third of hot milk mixture into egg yolks. Gradually whisk yolk mixture into remaining milk mixture and return to heat for 3 to 5 minutes or until thick. Do not let boil. Stir in almond extract. Set aside to cool.

For Both Methods

2. In a large serving bowl, line the bottom and sides with cake cubes. Sprinkle with liqueur. Spread half of custard over the cake. Spread with fruit and top with remaining custard. Chill for at least 1 hour or up to 8 hours. Garnish with toasted almond slices.

Variation

Garnish with whipped cream, if desired.

Three-Fruit Cobbler

This cobbler is a variation of the famous Nova Scotia dessert, blueberry grunt, but without the blueberries. It brings together our favorite summertime fruits — peaches, plums and pears.

Tips

See tips for Biscuits and Cobblers, page 157.

We suggest a deep casserole dish so the cobbler doesn't boil over onto your clean oven.

No need to peel the tender fruit — the skins soften as the cobbler bakes.

For best results, fruit should be ripe. If necessary, ripen in a paper bag on the counter until fragrant and it yields to gentle pressure.

Nutritional value per serving

Calories	327
Fat, total	9 g
Fat, saturated	4 g
Cholesterol	11 mg
Sodium	244 mg
Carbohydrate	54 g
Fiber	6 g
Protein	9 g
Calcium	96 mg
Iron	2 mg

- Preheat oven to 400°F (200°C)
- Deep 8-cup (2 L) casserole dish

Cobbler Biscuit

1 cup	soy flour	250 mL
⅔ cup	brown rice flour	150 mL
¼ cup	tapioca starch	50 mL
¼ cup	granulated sugar	50 mL
1 tsp	xanthan gum	5 mL
1½ tsp	GF baking powder	7 mL
½ tsp	baking soda	2 mL
¼ tsp	salt	1 mL
⅓ cup	cold butter, cut into 1-inch (2.5 cm) cubes	75 mL
⅔ cup	buttermilk	150 mL

Base

⅓ cup	granulated sugar	75 ml
1 tbsp	cornstarch	15 mL
2 cups	coarsely chopped peaches or nectarines, about 3 medium	500 mL
2 cups	coarsely chopped pears, about 3 medium	500 mL
2 cups	coarsely chopped plums, about 4 large	500 mL
1 tbsp	freshly squeezed lemon juice	15 mL

1. *Cobbler Biscuit:* In a large bowl, sift together soy flour, brown rice flour, tapioca starch, sugar, xanthan gum, baking powder, baking soda and salt. Using a pastry blender or two knives, cut in butter until mixture resembles small peas. Add buttermilk all at once, stirring with a fork to make a sticky dough. Let stand for 30 minutes.

2. *Base:* In casserole dish, mix together sugar and cornstarch. Gently stir in peaches, pears, plums and lemon juice. Place in preheated oven for 15 minutes or until hot and bubbly.

3. Drop biscuit topping, by heaping tablespoonfuls (15 mL), onto hot bubbly fruit mixture. Bake in preheated oven for 20 to 25 minutes or until top is golden. Serve immediately.

Pastry Making Tips

- We provide directions for both the food processor and the traditional methods of making pastry. The food processor method is easier to mix without over-handling. Process the ingredients, by pulsing, until the dough begins to stick together. With your fingertips, gather the dough into a light ball and gently press together.

- In the traditional method, when using a pastry blender or two knives to cut in the shortening or butter, cut only until the pieces are the size of small peas. This results in a tender, flaky pastry. If too finely cut in or mashed, the pastry tends to be tough and heavy.

- Form enough dough to make one shell into a round, flattened disk. This shape is easier to roll out into the circle for a pie plate.

- Refrigerate the dough, tightly wrapped, for at least 1 hour before rolling out. It can be left in the refrigerator up to 3 days or in the freezer for 3 months.

- Roll out the dough between two sheets of waxed paper — it is easier to handle. Or, generously flour a wooden board and rolling pin with sweet rice flour. Re-flour the board and rolling pin occasionally to prevent sticking.

- Roll out the dough using light, long strokes from the center to the edges. Roll out to each side, then back to the center. Repeat until the dough is 1-inch (2.5 cm) larger than the pie plate. It should be about $1/4$ inch (0.5 cm) thick.

- Ease the pastry into the pie plate. Do not worry if it breaks where it touches the rim of the plate. Just patch the shell with pastry scraps.

Gingerbread Crumbs

Our crumb crust, made from these crumbs, is the perfect flavor partner for Peach Cheesecake (page 307) and Praline Pumpkin Delight (page 277).

Tips

Store crumbs in an airtight freezer bag at room temperature for up to 2 weeks or freeze for up to 3 months.

Spreading batter to an even thickness ensures the center is cooked before the edges become too dark.

Bake the two pans at the same time, in the top and bottom thirds of the oven; switch and rotate the pans halfway through.

Nutritional value per serving

Calories	290
Fat, total	13 g
Fat, saturated	5 g
Cholesterol	36 mg
Sodium	268 mg
Carbohydrate	42 g
Fiber	3 g
Protein	4 g
Calcium	57 mg
Iron	2 mg

- Preheat oven to 325°F (160°C)
- Two 15- by 10-inch (40 by 25 cm) jelly-roll pans, lightly greased

1⅔ cups	sorghum flour	400 mL
1 cup	chickpea (garbanzo bean) flour	250 mL
⅓ cup	tapioca starch	75 mL
1 tsp	xanthan gum	5 mL
1 tsp	baking soda	5 mL
½ tsp	salt	2 mL
2 tsp	ground ginger	10 mL
1 tsp	ground cinnamon	5 mL
½ tsp	ground cloves	2 mL
1 cup	shortening or butter, softened	250 mL
¾ cup	granulated sugar	175 mL
1 cup	fancy molasses	250 mL
2	eggs	2

1. In a large bowl or plastic bag, combine sorghum flour, chickpea flour, tapioca starch, xanthan gum, baking soda, salt, ginger, cinnamon and cloves; set aside.

2. In another large bowl, using an electric mixer, cream shortening, sugar, molasses and eggs. Slowly beat in dry ingredients until combined. Using a moistened rubber or metal spatula, spread half the dough in each prepared pan. Remoisten spatula when the batter begins to stick to it.

3. Bake in preheated oven for 20 minutes. Let cool completely in pans on a rack. Break into pieces, then pulse a few pieces at a time in a food processor until crumb consistency.

Variations

Recipe can be doubled to make 16 cups (4 L) so you'll always have crumbs at the ready.

Substitute garbanzo-fava (garfava) bean flour or whole bean flour for the chickpea flour.

Pie Pastry

Easy as pie — truer words were never spoken and making pie becomes easier each time you do it. We'd like to say that this is truly a no-fail pastry.

Tip

Recipe can be doubled or tripled but leave salt at 1/2 tsp (2 mL).

1/3 cup	ice water	75 mL
2 tsp	cider vinegar	10 mL
2	egg yolks	2
1 cup	brown rice flour	250 mL
1 cup	cornstarch	250 mL
1/2 cup	tapioca starch	125 mL
2 tsp	xanthan gum	10 mL
1/4 tsp	salt	1 mL
1 cup	shortening, softened	250 mL

Food Processor Method

1. In a small bowl, combine ice water, vinegar and egg yolks. Set aside.
2. In a food processor fitted with a metal blade, pulse rice flour, cornstarch, tapioca starch, xanthan gum and salt until mixed.
3. Add shortening and pulse until mixture resembles small peas, about 5 to 10 seconds. With machine running, add egg yolk mixture in a slow steady stream. Process until dough just holds together. Do not let it form a ball.

Traditional Method

1. In a small bowl, combine ice water, vinegar and egg yolks. Set aside.
2. In a large bowl, sift rice flour, cornstarch, tapioca starch, xanthan gum and salt. Resift.

Nutritional value	per single-crust pie	per double-crust pie
Calories	176	351
Fat, total	12 g	23 g
Fat, saturated	5 g	10 g
Cholesterol	33 mg	66 mg
Sodium	39 mg	77 mg
Carbohydrate	16 g	32 g
Fiber	1 g	1 g
Protein	1 g	2 g
Calcium	3 mg	6 mg
Iron	0 mg	0 mg

3. Using a pastry blender or two knives, cut in shortening until mixture resembles small peas. Stirring with a fork, sprinkle egg yolk mixture, a little at a time, over the flour-shortening mixture to make soft dough.

For Both Methods

4. Divide dough in half. Gently gather dough into a ball and place each half on plastic wrap and flatten into a disk and wrap well. Refrigerate for at least 1 hour. Let cold pastry stand for 10 minutes at room temperature before rolling out.

5. Place the pastry disk between two sheets of waxed paper. Gently, with quick, light strokes of the rolling pin, roll out the pastry dough into a circle 1 inch (2.5 cm) larger than the diameter of the pie plate. Carefully remove the top sheet of waxed paper. Invert the pastry over the pie plate, easing it in. Carefully remove the remaining sheet of waxed paper.

6. Trim excess pastry to edge of pie plate and patch any cracks with trimmings. Press edge with a fork. For a more attractive finish, using a sharp knife, trim the edge evenly, leaving a 1-inch (2.5 cm) overhang. Tuck pastry under to form a raised double rim. Flute or crimp the edges.

7. *To bake unfilled pastry shell:* To prevent pastry from shrinking or puffing up, prick bottom and sides with a fork. Bake at 425°F (220°C) for 18 to 20 minutes or until golden. Let cool completely before filling.

8. *To bake filled pastry shell:* Do not prick. Spoon the filling into unbaked pastry shell and bake according to individual recipe directions.

Variation

This can be made into tart shells to fill with custard and fresh fruit.

Hazelnut Pastry

Quick and easy, shortbread tender and simple to serve — no need to wait for the holidays or special occasions to enjoy the hazelnut flavor. We use Hazelnut Pastry for fruit, pumpkin and cream pies.

Tips

This recipe can be doubled or tripled but leave salt at 1/4 tsp (1 mL).

For a pre-baked pie shell, prick bottom and sides of shell with a fork before baking.

Work quickly to keep the pastry cold and to prevent the butter from softening.

3 tbsp	ice water	45 mL
1 tsp	cider vinegar	5 mL
1	egg yolk	1
1/2 cup	sorghum flour	125 mL
1/4 cup	cornstarch	50 mL
1/4 cup	tapioca starch	50 mL
1/4 cup	sweet rice flour	50 mL
1/4 cup	hazelnut flour	50 mL
1 tsp	xanthan gum	5 mL
1/4 tsp	salt	1 mL
1/2 cup	cold butter, cut into 1-inch (2.5 cm) cubes	125 mL

Food Processor Method

1. In a small bowl, combine ice water, vinegar and egg yolk. Set aside.

2. In a food processor fitted with a metal blade, pulse sorghum flour, cornstarch, tapioca starch, sweet rice flour, hazelnut flour, xanthan gum and salt until mixed.

3. Add butter. Pulse until mixture resembles small peas, about 5 to 10 seconds. With machine running, add egg yolk mixture in a slow steady stream. Process until dough just holds together. Do not let it form a ball.

Traditional Method

1. In a small bowl, combine ice water, vinegar and egg yolk. Set aside.

2. In a large bowl, sift sorghum flour, cornstarch, tapioca starch, sweet rice flour, hazelnut flour, xanthan gum and salt. Resift.

3. Using a pastry blender or two knives, cut in butter until mixture resembles small peas. Stirring with a fork, sprinkle egg yolk mixture, a little at a time, over the flour-butter mixture to make soft dough.

Nutritional value per serving	
Calories	201
Fat, total	14 g
Fat, saturated	5 g
Cholesterol	38 mg
Sodium	175 mg
Carbohydrate	17 g
Fiber	2 g
Protein	2 g
Calcium	8 mg
Iron	1 mg

Tip

If hazelnut flour is not readily available, make your own (see Nut Flour, page 370).

For Both Methods

4. Gently gather dough into a ball and place on plastic wrap and flatten into a disk. Wrap well. Refrigerate for at least 1 hour.

5. Place the pastry disk between two sheets of waxed paper. Gently, with quick, light strokes of the rolling pin, roll out the pastry dough into a circle 1 inch (2.5 cm) larger than the diameter of the pie plate. Carefully remove the top sheet of waxed paper. Invert the pastry over the pie plate, easing it in. Carefully remove the remaining sheet of waxed paper.

6. Trim excess pastry to edge of pie plate and patch any cracks with trimmings. Press edge with a fork. For a more attractive finish, using a sharp knife, trim the edge evenly, leaving a 1-inch (2.5 cm) overhang. Tuck pastry under to form a raised double rim. Flute or crimp the edges.

7. *To bake unfilled pastry shell:* To prevent pastry from shrinking or puffing up, prick bottom and sides with a fork. Bake at 425°F (220°C) for 18 to 20 minutes or until golden. Let cool completely before filling.

8. *To bake filled pastry shell:* Do not prick. Spoon the filling into unbaked pastry shell and bake according to individual recipe directions.

Variation

Substitute pecan flour or almond flour for hazelnut flour.

Trendy Pastry

People today are
concerned about what
type of fat they're eating.
This recipe is in answer to
a request for pastry made
with vegetable oil. Though
not quite as tender as that
made with shortening or
butter, this pastry is just as
easy to work with.

Tips

*If the pastry cracks while
you're handling it, don't
worry: just use the excess
to patch.*

1 1/2 cups	sorghum flour	375 mL
1 cup	cornstarch	250 mL
1/2 cup	tapioca starch	125 mL
1 tbsp	granulated sugar	15 mL
2 tsp	GF baking powder	10 mL
1 tsp	salt	5 mL
1	egg	1
1/2 cup	ice water	125 mL
1/3 cup	vegetable oil	75 mL
2 tbsp	cider vinegar	25 mL

Food Processor Method

1. In a food processor fitted with a metal blade, pulse
sorghum flour, cornstarch, tapioca starch, sugar, baking
powder and salt until mixed. Set aside.

2. In a small bowl, whisk together egg, ice water, oil and
vinegar.

3. With food processor running, add egg mixture through
feed tube in a slow, steady stream. Process until dough
just holds together. Do not let it form a ball.

Traditional Method

1. In a large bowl, sift sorghum flour, cornstarch, tapioca
starch, sugar, baking powder and salt. Set aside.

2. In a small bowl, whisk together egg, ice water, oil and
vinegar.

Nutritional value	per single-crust pie	per double-crust pie
Calories	136	272
Fat, total	5 g	11 g
Fat, saturated	0 g	1 g
Cholesterol	10 mg	21 mg
Sodium	151 mg	301 mg
Carbohydrate	21 g	42 g
Fiber	1 g	2 g
Protein	2 g	4 g
Calcium	29 mg	58 mg
Iron	1 mg	2 mg

Tips

This pastry can also be made into tart shells to fill with custard and fresh fruit or to make mini-quiches or hors d'oeuvre tartlets.

You can freeze the pastry for up to 3 months. Thaw in refrigerator. Bring to room temperature before rolling out.

While rolling out the first half of the dough, cover remaining half to prevent it from drying out.

3. Stirring with a fork, sprinkle egg mixture, a little at a time, over the flour mixture to make a soft dough.

For Both Methods

4. Divide dough in half. Gently gather each piece into a ball and flatten into a disc. Place the pastry disc between two sheets of parchment paper. Using quick, firm strokes of the rolling pin, roll out the dough into a circle about 1-inch (2.5 cm) larger than the diameter of the inverted pie plate. Carefully remove the top sheet of parchment paper and invert the pastry over the pie plate, easing it in. Carefully peel off the remaining sheet of parchment paper.

5. To prepare another single-crust pie, repeat Step 4 with the remaining dough. To prepare the top crust for a double crust pie, roll out the remaining dough as directed above, then set aside.

For a Single-Crust Pie

Trim excess pastry to edge of pie plate, patch any cracks with trimmings, and press edges with a fork. Or, for a more attractive finish, using a sharp knife, trim the pastry evenly, leaving a 1-inch (2.5 cm) overhang. Tuck pastry under to form a raised double rim. Flute or crimp the edges.

To Bake an Unfilled Pastry Shell

To prevent pastry from shrinking or puffing up, prick bottom and sides with a fork. Bake in oven preheated to 425°F (220°C) for 18 to 20 minutes, or until golden. Let cool completely before filling.

To Bake a Filled Pastry Shell

Do not prick the pastry. Spoon filling into unbaked pastry shell and bake according to individual recipe directions.

For a Double-Crust Pie

For instructions on finishing and baking, see recipe for Strawberry Rhubarb Pie, page 294.

Peachy Plum Hazelnut Galette

Makes 12 servings

Simpler than pie but with all the same homemade goodness, this galette makes excellent use of an abundance of summer fruits.

Tips

If hazelnut flour is not readily available in your area, make your own from hazelnuts (see Nut Flour, page 370).

The jelly spreads more evenly when microwaved on High for 20 seconds.

- **Preheat oven to 425°F (220°C)**
- **Large baking sheet, generously dusted with sweet rice flour**

1	Hazelnut Pastry (see recipe, page 286)	1
3 cups	peeled, sliced peaches, about 5 medium	750 mL
2 cups	sliced red or purple plums, about 4 large	500 mL
¼ cup	hazelnut flour	50 mL
¼ cup	granulated sugar	50 mL
2 tbsp	cornstarch	25 mL
1 tbsp	butter	15 mL
⅓ cup	chopped hazelnuts	75 mL
1 tbsp	granulated sugar	15 mL
2 tbsp	grape or red currant jelly	25 mL

1. Place the chilled Hazelnut Pastry disk in the center of prepared pan. Cover with waxed paper and roll out to a 12-inch (30 cm) circle.

2. In a large bowl, lightly toss together peaches, plums, hazelnut flour, ¼ cup (50 mL) sugar and cornstarch. Set aside.

3. Carefully remove the waxed paper. Place the fruit mixture on pastry to within 2 inches (5 cm) of the edge. Dot with butter and sprinkle with hazelnuts. Carefully fold the pastry up over the filling to form a ragged edge, leaving fruit exposed in the center. Sprinkle pastry with 1 tbsp (15 mL) sugar.

4. Bake in preheated oven for 15 minutes. Reduce heat to 375°F (190°C) and bake for 25 to 30 minutes longer or until fruit is tender and pastry is lightly browned. Brush with jelly.

Variation

Prepare the pastry with almond flour and sprinkle the prepared galette with sliced almonds. Almonds toast as the galette bakes.

Nutritional value per serving	
Calories	239
Fat, total	14 g
Fat, saturated	4 g
Cholesterol	27 mg
Sodium	125 mg
Carbohydrate	28 g
Fiber	3 g
Protein	3 g
Calcium	16 mg
Iron	1 mg

Strawberry Mousse Pie

Makes 8 servings

Strawberries, a crowd pleaser, give this a refreshing light taste on a hot summer day.

Tips

If the filling appears to be too thin, before folding into the beaten evaporated milk, chill in the refrigerator until it molds when dropped from a spoon. This may take up to 30 minutes.

To get maximum volume from the evaporated milk, chill milk, bowl and beaters for at least 30 minutes.

1	package (¼ oz/7 g) unflavored gelatin	1
¾ cup	orange juice	175 mL
1	package (14 oz/425 g) frozen sweetened strawberries, partially thawed	1
½ cup	chilled evaporated milk	125 mL
2 tbsp	granulated sugar	25 mL
1	baked 9-inch (23 cm) single-crust pie shell (see recipes, pages 284 to 288)	1

1. In a small saucepan, sprinkle gelatin over orange juice. Let stand for 1 minute to soften. Warm over medium heat, whisking constantly, for about 2 minutes or until dissolved.
2. Add partially frozen strawberries and stir until berries are thawed and mixture is consistency of egg whites. Chill if necessary (see Tips, left).
3. In a large bowl, using an electric mixer, beat evaporated milk until soft peaks form. Gradually add sugar, beating until stiff. Slowly add one-quarter of thickened strawberry mixture to beaten evaporated milk, beating constantly. Fold in remaining strawberry mixture. Spoon into baked pastry shell. Refrigerate for at least 3 hours or until set. Garnish with fresh strawberries.

Variations

Substitute raspberries for the strawberries.

If substituting unsweetened strawberries for the sweetened, increase granulated sugar to ¼ cup (50 mL).

In a hurry? Spoon the strawberry mousse into parfait glasses or a large glass serving bowl.

Nutritional value per serving	
Calories	256
Fat, total	14 g
Fat, saturated	5 g
Cholesterol	41 mg
Sodium	195 mg
Carbohydrate	29 g
Fiber	3 g
Protein	4 g
Calcium	86 mg
Iron	1 mg

Pear Almond Torte

Makes 8 servings

This is a thin torte that does not rise much. No fancy pastry-making techniques required here: it is prepared completely in the food processor. Serve warm from the oven or cold straight from the fridge.

Tips

To quickly peel pears, use a vegetable peeler.

Torte can be made up to 2 days ahead. Cover with plastic wrap and refrigerate.

● **9-inch (23 cm) springform pan, lightly greased and dusted with rice flour**

Topping

2 tsp	granulated sugar	10 mL
1 tsp	ground cinnamon	5 mL
½ tsp	ground nutmeg	2 mL
2	pears, peeled, cored and cut into eighths	2
⅓ cup	slivered almonds	75 mL

Base

½ cup	almond flour	125 mL
½ cup	brown rice flour	125 mL
1 tsp	xanthan gum	5 mL
2 tsp	GF baking powder	10 mL
¼ tsp	salt	1 mL
½ cup	butter, softened	125 mL
1 cup	granulated sugar	250 mL
1 tsp	almond extract	5 mL
2	eggs	2

1. *Prepare the topping:* In a medium bowl, stir together sugar, cinnamon and nutmeg; add pears and toss until evenly coated; set aside.

2. *Prepare the base:* In a small bowl, combine almond flour, rice flour, xanthan gum, baking powder and salt until mixed; set aside.

3. In the bowl of a food processor fitted with the metal blade, pulse the butter, sugar and almond extract until smooth and creamy; scrape down sides. Add eggs, one at a time, pulsing just until mixed. Add flour mixture; pulse until mixed. Scrape batter into prepared pan. Spread to edges and smooth top with a moist rubber spatula.

4. Arrange the coated pear wedges in a circle over the batter and sprinkle with almonds. Let stand for 30 minutes. Meanwhile, preheat oven to 325°F (160°C).

Nutritional value per serving

Calories	349
Fat, total	18 g
Fat, saturated	6 g
Cholesterol	56 mg
Sodium	194 mg
Carbohydrate	45 g
Fiber	4 g
Protein	5 g
Calcium	95 mg
Iron	1 mg

Tips

A ripe pear will yield slightly when you apply gentle thumb pressure near the base of the stem. Ripen pears in a paper bag on the counter. Check daily — ripening may take 1 to 6 days.

If desired, drizzle torte with Simple Hot Fudge Sauce (see recipe, page 325).

5. Bake in preheated oven for 50 to 55 minutes, or until top is a rich golden color and a cake tester inserted in the center comes out clean. Transfer to a rack. Run a knife around the inside edge of pan. Let stand 10 minutes, then remove ring. Serve warm or let cool completely on base on rack.

Variation

In season, substitute apples, plums, peaches or apricots for the pears. Use enough fruit to cover the base generously and finish a whole piece of fruit.

Strawberry Rhubarb Pie

We can hardly wait until fresh local rhubarb and strawberries are both at their prime, to enjoy our yearly feast of crisps, cobblers and pies.

Tips

For the best flavor and color, purchase fresh local berries while they're in season. Choose firm stalks of rhubarb that are fresh and crisp; slender stalks are more tender than thick ones.

To make a rhubarb pie, substitute rhubarb for the strawberries and increase the granulated sugar to $1^1/_4$ cups (300 mL).

Nutritional value per serving

Calories	411
Fat, total	11 g
Fat, saturated	1 g
Cholesterol	21 mg
Sodium	304 mg
Carbohydrate	77 g
Fiber	4 g
Protein	5 g
Calcium	117 mg
Iron	2 mg

* 9-inch (23 cm) deep-dish pie plate

4 cups	chopped (1-inch/2.5 cm) fresh rhubarb (or frozen rhubarb, thawed)	1 L
2 cups	quartered fresh strawberries	500 mL
1 cup	granulated sugar	250 mL
$^1/_3$ cup	tapioca starch	75 mL
2 tsp	freshly squeezed lemon juice	10 mL
	Trendy Pastry (see recipe, page 288)	

1. In a large bowl, toss together rhubarb, strawberries, sugar and tapioca starch. Add the lemon juice. Let stand for 15 minutes. Meanwhile, preheat oven to 425°F (220°C).

2. Roll out pastry for a double-crust pie and press the bottom pastry into pie plate as directed on pages 288 to 289. Spoon filling into the unbaked pie shell and moisten the edge. Carefully remove the top sheet of parchment paper from the top pastry, invert and cover the filling. Carefully peel off the remaining sheet of parchment paper. Trim pastry, leaving a $^3/_4$-inch (2 cm) overhang. Fold overhang under bottom pastry rim, seal and flute edge.

3. Make numerous $^1/_2$-inch (1 cm) slits near the center of the pie through the crust to the filling or cut out a 1-inch (2.5 cm) circle in the center of the crust.

4. Position the oven racks to divide the oven into thirds. Place a baking sheet on the bottom rack to catch the drips if pie boils over. Bake in preheated oven on the top rack for 20 minutes. Reduce heat to 350°F (180°C) and bake for 40 to 50 minutes, or until crust is golden and filling is bubbly. Shield edges with foil if they are browning too quickly. Let cool completely on a rack.

Variation

No time to roll out a top crust? Form the entire recipe of dough into one large disc. On a rimless baking sheet, roll out dough into a 17-inch (43 cm) circle, leaving edge uneven. Leaving a 4-inch (10 cm) border, spoon filling into the center. Fold pastry border over filling, leaving fruit exposed in the center. Bake in 425°F (220°C) oven for 10 minutes. Reduce heat to 375°F (190°C) and bake for 50 to 60 minutes more, or until crust is golden and filling is bubbly. Let cool on sheet on a rack.

Cake Baking Tips

- We recommend sifting then resifting the dry ingredients because the batter is mixed very little. If the gluten-free flours and starches lump or are not mixed well, the cake may bake with pockets of these dry ingredients.
- Cake recipes often require creaming the shortening or butter and sugar before adding the eggs. Creaming the butter first, then slowly beating in the sugar improves the texture. Adding the eggs, one at a time, beating after each, results in an even lighter cake.
- Adding the dry and liquid ingredients alternately, mixing just until blended after each, results in a more even-textured cake. This mixing may be done using low speed of the electric mixer or a rubber spatula.
- To lighten baked foods containing eggs, separate the eggs and beat the whites until stiff but not dry and fold them into the batter as the last step before putting the batter into the baking pan.
- Letting the batter stand for 30 minutes at room temperature before baking results in a lighter-textured, more-tender cake. However, if you are short of time, bake the cake immediately.
- There are three ways to tell whether a cake is done: if the top, when pressed lightly, springs back; when a wooden skewer inserted in the center comes out clean; and when the cake just begins to pull away from the pan.
- Unless the recipe recommends differently, let the cake cool for 10 minutes in the pan. Then, using a metal spatula or knife, trace around the edge between the pan and cake and turn it out onto a cooling rack to cool completely before frosting.
- To remove the cake from a springform pan, be sure to loosen the cake from edge of pan before removing the side by opening the clip on the side.

Almond Sponge Cake

Makes 16 servings

The perfect cake — light, airy, and not too sweet! Serve topped with fresh fruit and drizzled with Simple Hot Fudge Sauce (see recipe, page 325).

Tips

This is the ideal time to use liquid egg whites purchased in cartons. Substitute 1¼ cups (300 mL) liquid egg whites for the 10 egg whites.

Make sure the mixer bowl, wire whisk attachment, rubber spatula and tube pan are completely free of grease.

To slice without squishing cake, use dental floss or a knife with a serrated edge, such as an electric knife.

Nutritional value per serving	
Calories	85
Fat, total	3 g
Fat, saturated	1 g
Cholesterol	46 mg
Sodium	75 mg
Carbohydrate	11 g
Fiber	1 g
Protein	4 g
Calcium	15 mg
Iron	0 mg

- Preheat oven to 350°F (180°C)
- 10-inch (4 L) tube pan, ungreased, bottom lined with parchment paper

½ cup	almond or amaranth flour	125 mL
⅓ cup	cornstarch	75 mL
1 tsp	xanthan gum	5 mL
10	egg whites, at room temperature	10
1 tbsp	freshly squeezed lemon juice	15 mL
1½ tsp	cream of tartar	7 mL
1 tsp	almond extract	5 mL
¼ tsp	salt	1 mL
⅓ cup	granulated sugar	75 mL
4	egg yolks, at room temperature	4
¼ cup	granulated sugar	50 mL

1. In a small bowl or plastic bag, combine almond flour, cornstarch and xanthan gum. Set aside.

2. In a large bowl, using an electric mixer with wire whisk attachment, beat egg whites until foamy. While beating, add lemon juice, cream of tartar, almond extract and salt. Continue to beat until egg whites form stiff peaks. Gradually add the ⅓ cup (75 mL) sugar. Continue to beat until mixture is very stiff and glossy but not dry.

3. In a small deep bowl, using an electric mixer, beat egg yolks and the ¼ cup (50 mL) sugar until thick and pale-lemon in color, approximately 5 minutes. Fold egg yolks into beaten egg white mixture. Sift in dry ingredients, one-third at a time. Gently fold in each addition until well blended. Spoon into prepared pan.

4. Bake in preheated oven for 25 to 30 minutes, or until cake is golden and springs back when lightly touched. Invert pan over a funnel or bottle until completely cooled. Using a spatula, loosen the outside and inside edges of the pan and remove cake.

Variation

Turn this into a daffodil cake by folding in 2 tbsp (25 mL) grated lemon zest and 1 tbsp (15 mL) grated orange zest with the dry ingredients. Drizzle wedges of cake with lots of lemon sauce.

Angel Food Cake

Makes 16 servings

White as snow and light as a feather, this fat-free cake is delicious with fresh fruit or dressed up for any special occasion.

Tips

This is an ideal time to use liquid egg whites available in cartons. Store the cake at room temperature for up to 3 days or freeze, wrapped airtight, for up to 1 month.

Make sure the mixer bowl, beaters and the tube pan are completely free of grease.

It is easier to separate an egg when it is cold, right from the refrigerator, because the yolk is less apt to break.

Nutritional value per serving

Calories	90
Fat, total	0 g
Fat, saturated	0 g
Cholesterol	0 mg
Sodium	78 mg
Carbohydrate	19 g
Fiber	0 g
Protein	3 g
Calcium	2 mg
Iron	0 mg

- Preheat oven to 350°F (180°C)
- 10-inch (4 L) tube pan, completely free of grease

½ cup	brown rice flour	125 mL
⅓ cup	cornstarch	75 mL
⅓ cup	GF confectioner's (icing) sugar	75 mL
1 tsp	xanthan gum	5 mL
12	eggs whites, warmed to room temperature (see Techniques Glossary, page 369)	12
1 tbsp	freshly squeezed lemon juice	15 mL
1½ tsp	cream of tartar	7 mL
¼ tsp	salt	1 mL
¾ cup	granulated sugar	175 mL
1 tsp	almond extract	5 mL

1. In a small bowl, sift together rice flour, cornstarch, confectioner's sugar and xanthan gum. Resift and set aside.

2. In a separate large bowl, using an electric mixer, beat egg whites until foamy. While beating, add lemon juice, cream of tartar and salt. Continue to beat until egg whites are stiff. Gradually add sugar. Continue to beat until mixture is very stiff and glossy but not dry.

3. Sift dry ingredients, one-quarter at a time, over beaten egg whites. Gently fold in each addition until well blended. Fold in almond extract. Spoon into prepared pan. Run a knife through the batter to remove large air bubbles. Smooth top with a moist rubber spatula.

4. Bake immediately in preheated oven for 30 to 40 minutes or until the cake springs back when lightly touched. Invert pan over a funnel or bottle until completely cooled. Using a spatula, loosen the outside and inside edges of the pan. Remove from pan.

Variation

Add ¼ cup (50 mL) unsweetened cocoa powder to the dry ingredients to make a Chocolate Angel Food Cake. For a Mocha Angel Food Cake, add 1 tsp (5 mL) of instant coffee granules with the cocoa.

Applesauce-Date Snacking Cake

No need to feel guilty! You would never guess this deliciously moist cake is low in fat, too! Serve with clementines in season or add a sweet touch of Orange Glaze (see recipe, page 317).

Tips

When purchasing chopped dates, check for wheat starch in the coating.

For a more intense flavor, substitute brown rice flour for the sorghum.

- **Preheat oven to 350°F (180°C)**
- **8-inch (2 L) square pan, lightly greased**

⅔ cup	whole bean flour	150 mL
⅔ cup	sorghum flour	150 mL
¼ cup	tapioca starch	50 mL
1 tsp	xanthan gum	5 mL
½ tsp	GF baking powder	2 mL
½ tsp	baking soda	2 mL
⅛ tsp	salt	0.5 mL
1 tsp	unsweetened cocoa powder	5 mL
1 tsp	ground cinnamon	5 mL
¼ tsp	ground nutmeg	1 mL
⅛ tsp	ground cloves	0.5 mL
¼ cup	butter or shortening, softened	50 mL
½ cup	packed brown sugar	125 mL
1	egg	1
1 tsp	vanilla extract	5 mL
1 cup	unsweetened applesauce	250 mL
¾ cup	chopped dates	175 mL

1. In a large bowl, sift together whole bean flour, sorghum flour, tapioca starch, xanthan gum, baking powder, baking soda, salt, cocoa, cinnamon, nutmeg and cloves. Resift and set aside.

2. In a separate bowl, using an electric mixer, cream butter and brown sugar. Add egg and vanilla extract. Beat until light and fluffy.

3. Stir in dry ingredients, alternately with applesauce, to butter-sugar mixture, making three additions of dry ingredients and two of applesauce. Stir just until combined after each addition. Stir in dates. Spoon batter into prepared pan. Spread to edges and smooth top with a moist rubber spatula. Let stand for 30 minutes.

4. Bake in preheated oven for 25 to 30 minutes or until a cake tester inserted in the center comes out clean. Let cake cool in the pan on a rack for 10 minutes. Remove from pan and let cool completely on a rack.

Nutritional value per serving

Calories	275
Fat, total	7 g
Fat, saturated	3 g
Cholesterol	28 mg
Sodium	178 mg
Carbohydrate	49 g
Fiber	4 g
Protein	6 g
Calcium	275 mg
Iron	2 mg

Banana Poppy Seed Cake

Makes 12 servings

For those who love their bananas with poppy seeds. The best part is you can eat this delight when you're on the run — the slices are the perfect size to carry with you.

Tips

The batter should fill the pan half-full.

Instead of greasing, line the bottom of the tube pan with parchment or waxed paper. Remove the tube and trace the bottom. Invert and trace the center. Cut the center circle large enough so that the parchment paper slips over the tube.

Substitute any variety of bean flour for the yellow pea flour.

Nutritional value per serving	
Calories	220
Fat, total	7 g
Fat, saturated	1 g
Cholesterol	27 mg
Sodium	169 mg
Carbohydrate	37 g
Fiber	4 g
Protein	5 g
Calcium	101 mg
Iron	2 mg

- 10-inch (4 L) tube or 10-inch (3 L) Bundt pan, lightly greased

1 cup	sorghum flour	250 mL
1/2 cup	yellow pea flour	125 mL
1/4 cup	potato starch	50 mL
1/4 cup	tapioca starch	50 mL
1 1/2 tsp	xanthan gum	7 mL
1 tbsp	GF baking powder	15 mL
1 tsp	baking soda	5 mL
1/4 tsp	salt	1 mL
3 tbsp	poppy seeds	45 mL
1/2 tsp	ground nutmeg	2 mL
2	eggs	2
2 cups	mashed banana	500 mL
1/2 cup	packed brown sugar	125 mL
1/4 cup	vegetable oil	50 mL
1 tsp	cider vinegar	5 mL

1. In a large bowl or plastic bag, combine sorghum flour, pea flour, potato starch, tapioca starch, xanthan gum, baking powder, baking soda, salt, poppy seeds and nutmeg. Mix well and set aside.

2. In another large bowl, using an electric mixer, beat eggs, banana, brown sugar, oil and vinegar until combined. Add dry ingredients and mix just until combined. Spoon batter into prepared pan, Using a moistened rubber spatula, spread to edges and smooth top. Let stand for 30 minutes. Meanwhile, preheat oven to 325°F (160°C).

3. Bake in preheated oven for 40 to 45 minutes, or until a cake tester inserted in the center comes out clean. Let cake cool in the pan on a rack for 10 minutes. Remove from pan and let cool completely on a rack.

Variation

For crunch, add 3/4 cup (175 mL) chopped pecans, walnuts or hazelnuts.

Caramel Apple Cake

Just one small piece of this moist delight will have you craving more! No need for frosting — the topping bakes right on.

Tips

Wrap individual pieces and freeze, then grab a piece when you're packing your lunch. It will be perfectly thawed by noon.

We used Fuji apples, but you can choose any baking variety; there's no need to peel.

- 13- by 9-inch (3 L) baking pan, lightly greased and bottom lined with parchment paper

1¼ cups	sorghum flour	300 mL
½ cup	quinoa flour	125 mL
⅓ cup	tapioca starch	75 mL
2 tsp	xanthan gum	10 mL
1½ tsp	GF baking powder	7 mL
1 tsp	baking soda	5 mL
¼ tsp	salt	1 mL
1 tsp	ground cinnamon	5 mL
½ cup	butter, softened	125 mL
¾ cup	packed brown sugar	175 mL
2	eggs	2
1 cup	plain yogurt	250 mL
1 tsp	vanilla	5 mL
2 cups	diced apples	500 mL
¾ cup	toffee bits	175 mL

Topping

⅓ cup	sorghum flour	75 mL
2 tbsp	packed brown sugar	25 mL
¼ cup	cold butter, cubed	50 mL
¾ cup	toffee bits	175 mL
½ cup	white chocolate chips	125 mL

1. In a large bowl or plastic bag, combine the sorghum flour, quinoa flour, tapioca starch, xanthan gum, baking powder, baking soda, salt and cinnamon. Mix well and set aside.

2. In another large bowl, using an electric mixer, cream the butter and brown sugar until well combined. Add eggs and beat until light and fluffy. Beat in yogurt and vanilla until blended. Gradually mix in dry ingredients, mixing just until smooth, about 2 minutes. Stir in apples and toffee bits. Spoon into prepared pan. Using a moistened rubber spatula, spread to edges and smooth top. Let stand for 30 minutes. Meanwhile, preheat oven to 350°F (180°C).

Nutritional value per serving	
Calories	313
Fat, total	12 g
Fat, saturated	4 g
Cholesterol	42 mg
Sodium	225 mg
Carbohydrate	50 g
Fiber	3 g
Protein	4 g
Calcium	84 mg
Iron	1 mg

Tip

Half of an 8-oz (225 g) package of toffee bits yields 3/4 cup (175 mL). They are found in the baking aisle with chocolate chips and dried fruit at major grocery stores.

3. *Prepare the topping:* In a small bowl, stir together sorghum flour and brown sugar. Using a pastry blender or two knives, cut in butter until mixture resembles coarse crumbs. Stir in toffee bits and white chocolate chips. Sprinkle topping over the batter. Do not pack.

4. Bake in preheated oven for 30 to 35 minutes, or until a cake tester inserted in the center comes out clean. Let cool in the pan on a rack for 10 minutes. Remove from pan, quickly remove parchment and let cool completely, topping side up, on a rack.

Variation

Substitute an equal amount of chopped pecans for the toffee bits in both the cake and topping, and an equal amount of ground ginger for the cinnamon in the cake only. Your family will never recognize this as the same recipe.

Chocolate Fudge Cake

Susan, a celiac in our neighborhood, cuts our fudge cake into cubes and freezes them. Then when she has a chocolate attack, she can take a piece for a quick treat. The cake tastes just as delicious as it looks on the cover.

Tips

Sifting the dry ingredients twice helps distribute the cocoa evenly.

It is easier to spread the thick batter to the edges of the pan with a moist rubber spatula.

Refrigerate frosted cake for up to 3 days. Freeze individual layers, wrapped airtight, for up to 1 month.

Nutritional value per serving*

Calories	479
Fat, total	20 g
Fat, saturated	9 g
Cholesterol	83 mg
Sodium	486 mg
Carbohydrate	65 g
Fiber	3 g
Protein	10 g
Calcium	150 mg
Iron	2 mg

* does not include Orange Frosting

- **Preheat oven to 350°F (180°C)**
- **Two 8-inch (20 cm) round pans, lightly greased**

¾ cup	whole bean flour	175 mL
¾ cup	sorghum flour	175 mL
½ cup	potato starch	125 mL
¼ cup	tapioca starch	50 mL
1 tsp	xanthan gum	5 mL
½ tsp	GF baking powder	2 mL
1½ tsp	baking soda	7 mL
½ tsp	salt	2 mL
¾ cup	unsweetened cocoa powder	175 mL
¾ cup	shortening or butter, softened	175 mL
1½ cups	packed brown sugar	375 mL
3	eggs	3
2 tsp	vanilla extract	10 mL
2 cups	GF sour cream	500 mL
	Orange Frosting (see recipe, page 319)	

1. In a large bowl, sift together whole bean flour, sorghum flour, potato starch, tapioca starch, xanthan gum, baking powder, baking soda, salt and cocoa. Resift and set aside.

2. In a separate bowl, using an electric mixer, cream shortening and brown sugar until light and fluffy. Add eggs, one at a time, beating well after each addition. Stir in vanilla extract. Stir in dry ingredients alternately with sour cream to shortening-sugar mixture, making three additions of dry ingredients and two of sour cream. Stir just until combined after each addition. Spoon into prepared pans. Spread to edges and smooth tops with a moist rubber spatula. Let stand for 30 minutes.

3. Bake in preheated oven for 35 to 45 minutes or until a cake tester inserted in the center comes out clean. Let cakes cool in pans on racks for 10 minutes. Remove from pans and let cool completely on racks. Frost with Orange Frosting.

Variation

For a milk chocolate-flavored cake, decrease the unsweetened cocoa powder by ¼ cup (50 mL) and substitute granulated sugar for the packed brown sugar.

Cranberry-Banana Cupcakes

This easy-to-carry cupcake can be put in a lunch bag, still frozen. It will help keep your sandwich cold.

Tips

Mash and freeze ripe bananas so they are ready when you need them. Thaw and bring to room temperature before using.

Fill muffin cups almost level with the top.

- Preheat oven to 350°F (180°C)
- Muffin tins, lightly greased

¾ cup	sorghum flour	175 mL
¾ cup	soy flour	175 mL
¼ cup	potato starch	50 mL
¼ cup	tapioca starch	50 mL
2 tsp	xanthan gum	10 mL
1 tsp	GF baking powder	5 mL
¾ tsp	baking soda	4 mL
½ tsp	salt	2 mL
¼ cup	vegetable oil	50 mL
2	eggs	2
1 cup	packed brown sugar	250 mL
1 tsp	vanilla extract	5 mL
1 cup	mashed banana, about 2 to 3	250 mL
½ cup	plain yogurt	125 mL
1 cup	dried cranberries	250 mL

1. In a large bowl, sift together sorghum flour, soy flour, potato starch, tapioca starch, xanthan gum, baking powder, baking soda and salt. Resift and set aside.

2. In a separate bowl, using an electric mixer, beat together oil and eggs. While beating, add brown sugar, vanilla extract, bananas and yogurt. Beat until well blended. Gradually beat in dry ingredients, mixing just until smooth, about 2 minutes. Stir in cranberries. Spoon into each cup of prepared muffin tins. Let stand for 30 minutes.

3. Bake in preheated oven for 20 to 25 minutes or until a cake tester inserted in the center comes out clean. Let cool in the pan on a rack for 5 minutes. Remove from the pan and let cool completely on a rack.

Variations

Substitute fresh or dried blueberries, dried cherries or golden raisins for the cranberries.

For a traditional banana cake, spoon batter into a lightly greased 9-inch (2.5 L) square baking pan and bake for 35 minutes or until a cake tester inserted in the center comes out clean.

Nutritional value per serving (1 cupcake)	
Calories	257
Fat, total	6 g
Fat, saturated	1 g
Cholesterol	28 mg
Sodium	199 mg
Carbohydrate	46 g
Fiber	3 g
Protein	6 g
Calcium	71 mg
Iron	1 mg

Gingered Pumpkin Snacking Cake

It's perfect for a Halloween party — but serve this moist spice cake year round. It makes an excellent snack to carry in lunches or for a mid-morning break.

Tip

Fresh gingerroot has too strong a flavor to substitute for the candied or crystallized ginger.

- Preheat oven to 350°F (180°C)
- 13- by 9-inch (3 L) baking pan, lightly greased

1 cup	sorghum flour	250 mL
¾ cup	whole bean flour	175 mL
¼ cup	potato starch	50 mL
¼ cup	tapioca starch	50 mL
2 tsp	xanthan gum	10 mL
1½ tsp	GF baking powder	7 mL
¾ tsp	baking soda	4 mL
½ tsp	salt	2 mL
1 tsp	ground cinnamon	5 mL
½ tsp	ground allspice	2 mL
½ tsp	ground ginger	2 mL
½ tsp	ground nutmeg	2 mL
½ cup	butter or shortening, softened	125 mL
1 cup	packed brown sugar	250 mL
¼ cup	frozen orange juice concentrate, thawed	50 mL
2	eggs	2
1 tsp	vanilla extract	5 mL
1 cup	canned pumpkin purée (not pie filling)	250 mL
½ cup	chopped pecans	125 mL
⅓ cup	chopped candied or crystallized ginger	75 mL

Nutritional value per serving	
Calories	265
Fat, total	12 g
Fat, saturated	4 g
Cholesterol	30 mg
Sodium	209 mg
Carbohydrate	37 g
Fiber	3 g
Protein	5 g
Calcium	54 mg
Iron	2 mg

1. In a large bowl, sift together sorghum flour, whole bean flour, potato starch, tapioca starch, xanthan gum, baking powder, baking soda, salt, cinnamon, allspice, ginger and nutmeg. Resift and set aside.

2. In a separate bowl, using an electric mixer, cream butter and brown sugar. Add orange juice, eggs, vanilla extract and pumpkin purée and beat well. Gradually beat in dry ingredients, mixing just until smooth, about 2 minutes. Stir in pecans and candied ginger. Spoon into prepared pan. Spread to edges and smooth top with a moist rubber spatula. Let stand for 30 minutes.

Tip

Be sure to buy pumpkin purée, not pumpkin pie filling, which is too sweet and contains too much moisture for this snacking cake.

3. Bake in preheated oven for 25 to 35 minutes or until a cake tester inserted in the center comes out clean. Let cool in the pan on a rack for 10 minutes. Remove from the pan and let cool completely on a rack.

Variations

For a stronger pumpkin flavor, omit the candied or crystallized ginger.

To dress up this snacking cake, drizzle it with double the Orange Glaze (see recipe, page 317).

Orange Hazelnut Bundt Cake

Not too big, not too sweet, but just right to finish off a weekday meal — and perfect to take along to your next casual neighborhood get-together.

Tips

Set a kitchen timer for 3 minutes when beating. You will be surprised by how long 3 minutes seems.

It is worth the effort to zest the fresh orange and then juice it for the best orange flavor. First, zest the orange cold from the refrigerator, then warm orange in the microwave on High for 30 seconds and roll it on the counter to loosen the juice.

Nutritional value per serving

Calories	235
Fat, total	14 g
Fat, saturated	3 g
Cholesterol	38 mg
Sodium	137 mg
Carbohydrate	25 g
Fiber	3 g
Protein	4 g
Calcium	235 mg
Iron	2 mg

- **10-inch (3 L) Bundt pan, lightly greased**

¾ cup	amaranth flour	175 mL
⅔ cup	hazelnut flour	150 mL
⅔ cup	sorghum flour	150 mL
⅓ cup	potato starch	75 mL
1½ tsp	xanthan gum	7 mL
2 tsp	GF baking powder	10 mL
¾ tsp	baking soda	4 mL
½ tsp	salt	2 mL
½ cup	butter or shortening, softened	125 mL
¾ cup	granulated sugar	175 mL
3	eggs	3
2 tbsp	grated orange zest	25 mL
⅔ cup	freshly squeezed orange juice	150 mL
1 tsp	almond extract	5 mL
1 cup	coarsely chopped hazelnuts	250 mL
	Simple Hot Fudge Sauce (see recipe, page 325)	

1. In a large bowl or plastic bag, combine the amaranth flour, hazelnut flour, sorghum flour, potato starch, xanthan gum, baking powder, baking soda and salt. Mix well and set aside.

2. In another large bowl, using an electric mixer, cream butter and sugar until well combined. Add eggs, one at a time, and cream until light and fluffy. Stir in orange zest and juice and almond extract. Add dry ingredients and beat on medium for 3 minutes. Fold in hazelnuts. Spoon into prepared pan. Using a moistened rubber spatula, spread to edges and smooth top. Let stand for 30 minutes. Meanwhile, preheat oven to 350°F (180°C).

3. Bake in preheated oven for 40 to 50 minutes, or until a cake tester inserted in the center comes out clean. Let cake cool in the pan on a rack for 10 minutes. Remove from pan and let cool completely on a rack. Drizzle with Simple Hot Fudge Sauce.

Variation

Substitute almond or pecan flour for the hazelnut flour and almonds or pecans for the chopped hazelnuts.

Peach Cheesecake

- -

Makes 10 servings

Baskets of peaches ready at the market, family reunion coming soon — put these together for a memorable dessert.

Tips

Use enough fruit to cover the base generously and finish a whole piece of fruit.

Ultra low-fat cream cheese or fat-free cream cheese should not be substituted for regular in baked cheesecakes. However, light cream cheese can be used.

When using a dark-colored springform pan, decrease the oven temperature by 25°F (20°C).

Nutritional value per serving

Calories	355
Fat, total	18 g
Fat, saturated	8 g
Cholesterol	105 mg
Sodium	326 mg
Carbohydrate	35 g
Fiber	3 g
Protein	12 g
Calcium	179 mg
Iron	1 mg

- **Preheat oven to 325°F (160°C)**
- **8-inch (20 cm) springform pan**

Base and Topping

2¼ cups	Gingerbread Crumbs (see recipe, page 283)	550 mL
2 tbsp	melted butter	25 mL
3 to 4	peaches, peeled and thickly sliced	3 to 4

Cheesecake

2	packages (each 8 oz/250 g) light or regular cream cheese, softened	2
¼ cup	packed brown sugar	50 mL
1 tbsp	grated lemon zest	15 mL
2 tbsp	freshly squeezed lemon juice	25 mL
3	eggs	3
1 cup	GF sour cream	250 mL

1. Center springform pan on a large square of foil and press foil up the sides of the pan.
2. *Prepare the base:* In a bowl, combine Gingerbread Crumbs and butter; mix well. Set aside ½ cup (125 mL) to use for the topping. Press remainder of crumbs into bottom of prepared pan. Refrigerate until chilled, about 15 minutes. Arrange the peaches over the chilled base.
3. *Prepare the cheesecake:* In a large bowl, using an electric mixer, beat cream cheese until smooth. Slowly add brown sugar, lemon zest and juice. Beat until light and fluffy. Add eggs one at a time, beating well after each. Stir in sour cream. Pour over the peach-lined base.
4. *Add the topping:* Sprinkle reserved crumb mixture over filling.
5. Bake in preheated oven for 65 to 70 minutes, or until center is just set. Let cool to room temperature in pan on a rack. Cover and refrigerate overnight before serving.

Variation

When peaches are not in season, use about 2 cups (500 mL) well-drained canned peach slices.

Peach Upside-Down Cake

Makes 9 servings

Everyone is sure to request seconds of this quick-to-prepare dessert. Luscious, sweet peaches top a moist but not-too-sweet white cake.

Tips

Purchase sliced peaches packed in juice, not syrup.

The addition of dry ingredients and juice may be done either with the mixer on the lowest speed or with a rubber spatula or wooden spoon.

Sprinkle $1/3$ to $1/2$ cup (75 to 125 mL) fresh blueberries over the peaches before the batter is spooned on.

- Preheat oven to 350°F (180°C)
- 9-inch (2.5 L) square pan, lightly greased

Base

$1/2$ cup	apricot jam	125 mL
1	can (28 oz/796 mL) sliced peaches in pear juice, drained	1

Cake

$2/3$ cup	brown rice flour	150 mL
$1/2$ cup	tapioca starch	125 mL
$1/3$ cup	cornstarch	75 mL
$3/4$ tsp	xanthan gum	4 mL
$1 1/2$ tsp	GF baking powder	7 mL
$1/2$ tsp	salt	2 mL
$1/2$ cup	shortening or butter, softened	125 mL
$2/3$ cup	granulated sugar	150 mL
3	eggs	3
$1/4$ tsp	almond extract	1 mL

1. *Base:* Drain peaches, reserving $1/2$ cup (125 mL) of the juice. Set aside. Spread jam evenly in prepared pan. Arrange peach slices over top.

2. *Cake:* In a large bowl or plastic bag, combine rice flour, tapioca starch, cornstarch, xanthan gum, baking powder and salt. Mix well and set aside.

3. In a separate bowl, using an electric mixer, cream shortening and sugar until light and fluffy. Add eggs, one at a time, beating well after each addition. Stir in almond extract. Stir in dry ingredients alternately with reserved juice, making three additions of dry ingredients and two of juice. Stir just until combined after each addition. Spoon over peaches in prepared pan. Smooth top with a moist rubber spatula. Let stand for 30 minutes.

4. Bake in preheated oven for 45 to 50 minutes or until a cake tester inserted in the center comes out clean. Let cool in the pan on a rack for 5 minutes. Invert the pan over a serving plate. Remove pan and serve warm.

Variation

Substitute 4 or 5 medium, fresh peeled peaches for the canned peaches and milk for the juice.

Nutritional value per serving	
Calories	342
Fat, total	11 g
Fat, saturated	5 g
Cholesterol	68 mg
Sodium	255 mg
Carbohydrate	58 g
Fiber	1 g
Protein	3 g
Calcium	48 mg
Iron	1 mg

Pineapple-Carrot Cake

Makes 16 servings

This cake is so well loved by everyone that many brides choose it for their wedding cake. The pineapple adds a moist sweetness. Perfect topped with Cream Cheese Frosting (see recipe, page 318).

Tip

Watch for the deep, rich golden color of the soy flour; you may want to tent this cake with foil partway through the baking to slow down the browning. Line the bottom of baking pan with waxed paper to prevent sticking.

Nutritional value per serving

Calories	227
Fat, total	6 g
Fat, saturated	1 g
Cholesterol	34 mg
Sodium	261 mg
Carbohydrate	37 g
Fiber	3 g
Protein	8 g
Calcium	67 mg
Iron	1 mg

- Preheat oven to 350°F (180°C)
- 10-inch (3 L) Bundt pan, lightly greased

1¼ cups	brown rice flour	300 mL
1 cup	soy flour	250 mL
¼ cup	potato starch	50 mL
¼ cup	tapioca starch	50 mL
1 tsp	xanthan gum	5 mL
1 tsp	GF baking powder	5 mL
2 tsp	baking soda	10 mL
½ tsp	salt	2 mL
1½ tsp	ground cinnamon	7 mL
½ tsp	ground nutmeg	2 mL
3	eggs	3
1¼ cups	granulated sugar	300 mL
¾ cup	GF sour cream	175 mL
1 cup	crushed pineapple, including juice	250 mL
2 cups	shredded carrots	500 mL
¾ cup	chopped walnuts	175 mL

1. In a large bowl, sift together brown rice flour, soy flour, potato starch, tapioca starch, xanthan gum, baking powder, baking soda, salt, cinnamon and nutmeg. Resift and set aside.

2. In a separate bowl, using an electric mixer, beat eggs, sugar, sour cream and pineapple until well blended. Gradually beat in dry ingredients. Stir in carrots and walnuts.

3. Spoon into prepared pan. Spread to edges and smooth top with a moist rubber spatula. Let stand for 30 minutes.

4. Bake in preheated oven for 50 to 60 minutes or until a cake tester inserted in the center comes out clean. Let cool in the pan on a rack for 10 minutes. Remove from pan and let cool completely on rack.

Variations

Substitute desiccated coconut for the walnuts.

If you prefer, bake in a 13- by 9-inch (3 L) baking pan and reduce baking time by approximately 10 to 15 minutes.

Pecan Roulade

This rich rolled sponge cake, filled with a knockout Mocha Buttercream, is sure to become the centerpiece of your next dessert buffet. It's great to have one in the freezer for last-minute entertaining.

Tips

For better volume when beating egg whites, make sure the bowl and beaters are completely free of grease. Wash right before using them.

Wrapped airtight, the roulade can be frozen for up to 1 month.

For instructions on toasting nuts, see Techniques Glossary, page 370.

Nutritional value per serving

Calories	351
Fat, total	20 g
Fat, saturated	5 g
Cholesterol	86 mg
Sodium	135 mg
Carbohydrate	36 g
Fiber	2 g
Protein	5 g
Calcium	19 mg
Iron	1 mg

- **Preheat oven to 375°F (190°C)**
- **13- by 9-inch (3 L) baking pan, bottom lined with parchment paper**

2 cups	Mocha Buttercream (see recipe, opposite), chilled for at least 3 hours	500 mL
2 tbsp	pecan flour	25 mL
2 tbsp	cornstarch	25 mL
1/3 cup	unsweetened cocoa powder, sifted	75 mL
1 cup	coarsely chopped pecans, toasted	250 mL
4	egg whites, at room temperature	4
1/4 tsp	cream of tartar	1 mL
1/4 cup	granulated sugar	50 mL
4	egg yolks	4
Pinch	salt	Pinch
2 tbsp	brandy	25 mL
	GF confectioner's (icing) sugar	

1. Prepare Mocha Buttercream at least 3 hours ahead to allow time to chill.
2. In a small bowl or plastic bag, combine pecan flour, cornstarch, cocoa and pecans. Set aside.
3. In a large bowl, using an electric mixer with wire whisk attachment, beat egg whites until foamy. While beating, add cream of tartar. Continue to beat until egg whites are stiff. Gradually add sugar and continue beating until mixture is very stiff and glossy but not dry. Set aside.
4. In a small bowl, using an electric mixer, beat egg yolks and salt until thick and lemon-colored, approximately 5 minutes. Stir in brandy.
5. Fold egg yolk mixture into egg whites. Sprinkle half the cocoa mixture over the whites and fold in gently. Repeat with remaining half. Spoon into prepared pan and carefully spread evenly to the edges.
6. Bake in preheated oven for 7 to 10 minutes, or until top springs back when lightly touched. Let cool in the pan on a rack for 10 minutes.

Tips

For instructions on warming egg whites to room temperature, see Techniques Glossary, page 369.

Wrap airtight and freeze for up to 1 month. Thaw, wrapped, in refrigerator.

7. Dust lightly with confectioner's sugar. Loosen edges of cake with a knife. Turn out onto a clean, lint-free towel set on a cooling rack; carefully remove parchment paper. Starting at the long side, immediately roll up cake in the tea towel. Let cool completely on a rack.

8. Gently unroll cake, being careful not to flatten it, and spread with buttercream. Roll up again and place seam side down on a serving platter. Cover and refrigerate for 30 to 60 minutes, until chilled, or for up to 1 day.

Variation

Substitute an equal amount of thawed orange juice concentrate for the brandy in roulade and buttercream.

Mocha Buttercream

Makes
2 cups (500 mL)

Chocolate and coffee — partners in crime! A perfect filling for Pecan Roulade or frosting for any layer cake.

Nutritional value per 3 tbsp (45 mL) serving	
Calories	194
Fat, total	9 g
Fat, saturated	4 g
Cholesterol	12 mg
Sodium	81 mg
Carbohydrate	26 g
Fiber	1 g
Protein	1 g
Calcium	1 mg
Iron	0 mg

2 cups	GF confectioner's (icing) sugar	500 mL
⅓ cup	unsweetened cocoa powder	75 mL
2 tsp	instant coffee granules	10 mL
½ cup	butter, softened	125 mL
3 tbsp	brandy	45 mL

1. In a bowl, sift together confectioner's sugar, cocoa and coffee granules. Add butter and brandy. Using an electric mixer, beat for approximately 5 minutes, or until light and fluffy.

Variation

To make chocolate buttercream, omit the instant coffee granules.

Raspberry-Filled Jelly Roll

A cookbook would not be complete without a jelly roll recipe. Heather has fond memories of this raspberry-filled treat being prepared by her grandmother every Saturday for lunch.

Tips

For better volume, while beating egg whites, make sure the bowl and beaters are completely free of grease and egg yolk. Wash these, right before using them.

Wrap filled or unfilled jelly roll airtight and freeze for up to 1 month.

- **Preheat oven to 400°F (200°C)**
- **15- by 10-inch (40 by 25 cm) jelly roll pan, lightly greased, then lined with parchment or waxed paper**

1/3 cup	brown rice flour	75 mL
1/3 cup	soy flour	75 mL
2 tbsp	tapioca starch	25 mL
1 tsp	xanthan gum	5 mL
3/4 tsp	GF baking powder	4 mL
1/4 tsp	salt	1 mL
4	egg yolks	4
4	egg whites, warmed to room temperature (see Techniques Glossary, page 369)	4
3/4 cup	granulated sugar	175 mL
1/2 tsp	lemon flavoring	2 mL
	GF confectioner's (icing) sugar	
1 cup	raspberry jam	250 mL

1. In a bowl, sift together brown rice flour, soy flour, tapioca starch, xanthan gum, baking powder and salt. Resift and set aside.

2. In a small bowl, using an electric mixer, beat egg yolks until thick and lemon colored, approximately 5 minutes. Set aside.

3. In a separate large bowl, using an electric mixer beat egg whites until stiff. Gradually add sugar. Continue beating until mixture is very stiff and glossy but not dry.

4. Fold beaten yolks into beaten whites. Add lemon flavoring. Fold in dry ingredients. Spoon into prepared pan. Carefully spread to the edges with a moist rubber spatula. Let stand for 30 minutes. Bake in preheated oven for 10 to 12 minutes or until the top springs back when lightly touched.

5. Dust lightly with confectioner's sugar. Turn out onto a clean tea towel. Carefully remove paper. Starting at the short side, immediately roll up in the tea towel. Let cool on a rack for 15 minutes.

6. Unroll cake and spread with raspberry jam. Roll up again and place, seam-side down, on serving platter. Cover and refrigerate for 30 to 60 minutes before serving.

Nutritional value per serving	
Calories	207
Fat, total	2 g
Fat, saturated	1 g
Cholesterol	74 mg
Sodium	85 mg
Carbohydrate	43 g
Fiber	1 g
Protein	5 g
Calcium	33 mg
Iron	1 mg

Rhubarb Crumb Cake

Makes 12 servings

Looking for more ways to use the first harvest of the season? All summer long, Susan, one of our taste testers, kept requesting more of this one.

Tips

This cake stays moist for lunch or an afternoon snack.

Once frozen, this cake tends to crumble more easily. Freeze it in individual servings, wrapped airtight, then microwave for just a few seconds to warm them up.

Nutritional value per serving	
Calories	217
Fat, total	7 g
Fat, saturated	1 g
Cholesterol	14 mg
Sodium	159 mg
Carbohydrate	38 g
Fiber	2 g
Protein	3 g
Calcium	64 mg
Iron	1 mg

- **Preheat oven to 350°F (180°C)**
- **8-inch (2 L) square pan, lightly greased**

¼ cup	packed brown sugar	50 mL
1 tbsp	orange zest	15 mL
½ tsp	ground cinnamon	2 mL
¾ cup	brown rice flour	175 mL
¾ cup	sorghum flour	175 mL
⅓ cup	tapioca starch	75 mL
¾ cup	granulated sugar	175 mL
¾ tsp	xanthan gum	4 mL
2 tsp	GF baking powder	10 mL
½ tsp	baking soda	2 mL
½ tsp	salt	2 mL
2	eggs	2
⅓ cup	vegetable oil	75 mL
1 tsp	vanilla extract	5 mL
1 tsp	orange zest	5 mL
1 cup	freshly squeezed orange juice	250 mL
2 cups	chopped rhubarb	500 mL

1. In a small bowl, combine brown sugar, orange zest and cinnamon. Set aside for topping.
2. In a large bowl or plastic bag, sift brown rice flour, sorghum flour, tapioca starch, sugar, xanthan gum, baking powder, baking soda and salt. Resift and set aside.
3. In a separate large bowl, using an electric mixer, beat eggs, oil, vanilla extract, orange zest and orange juice until combined. With mixer on low, slowly add dry ingredients and mix just until smooth. Fold in rhubarb and spoon into prepared pan. Spread to edges and smooth top with a moist rubber spatula. Sprinkle with topping. Let stand for 30 minutes.
4. Bake in preheated oven for 50 to 60 minutes or until a cake tester inserted in the center comes out clean. Let cool completely in the pan on a rack.

Variation

Add ¾ cup (175 mL) finely chopped pecans to the topping and ½ cup (125 mL) coarsely chopped pecans to the cake batter.

Sticky Bun Snacking Cake

Makes 8 servings

Traditional sticky buns require a lot of patience as you wait for the dough to rise. This version is ready in no time! Serve it warm.

Tips

For easier pouring, warm the corn syrup in the microwave for 50 seconds on High.

Line the bottom of the lightly greased pan with waxed or parchment paper.

- **Preheat oven to 350°F (180°C)**
- **9-inch (2.5 L) square pan, lightly greased**

Topping

1 cup	coarsely chopped pecans	250 mL
1 cup	halved red and green glacé cherries	250 mL
½ cup	packed brown sugar	125 mL
2 tsp	ground cinnamon	10 mL
¼ cup	melted butter	50 mL

Cake

1¼ cups	brown rice flour	300 mL
½ cup	potato starch	125 mL
¼ cup	tapioca starch	50 mL
½ cup	granulated sugar	125 mL
1½ tsp	xanthan gum	7 mL
1 tsp	GF baking powder	5 mL
1 tsp	baking soda	5 mL
¼ tsp	salt	1 mL
1¼ cups	plain yogurt	300 mL
1 tsp	cider vinegar	5 mL
¼ cup	vegetable oil	50 mL
2	eggs	2
½ cup	corn syrup, warmed	125 mL

1. *Topping:* In a small bowl, combine pecans, cherries, sugar and cinnamon. Add butter and mix well. Spread into pan.
2. *Cake:* In a large bowl, stir together white rice flour, potato starch, tapioca starch, sugar, xanthan gum, baking powder, baking soda and salt. Resift and set aside.
3. In a separate bowl, using an electric mixer or whisk, beat yogurt, vinegar, oil and eggs until combined. Pour mixture over dry ingredients and stir just until combined. Spoon over topping in prepared pan. Spread to edges and smooth top with a moist rubber spatula. Let stand for 30 minutes.
4. Bake in preheated oven for 30 to 35 minutes or until a cake tester inserted in the center comes out clean. Immediately turn upside down on a serving platter and remove pan. Drizzle cake with warm corn syrup.

Nutritional value per serving

Calories	635
Fat, total	24 g
Fat, saturated	5 g
Cholesterol	51 mg
Sodium	361 mg
Carbohydrate	102 g
Fiber	3 g
Protein	6 g
Calcium	134 mg
Iron	2 mg

White Cake

Begin with this light, versatile cake to make desserts that are sure to please. We like to use it to make trifle, cupcakes or to top it with fresh fruit.

Tip

Freeze cakes with no icing to use as a crumb base for cheesecakes or to cut into cubes for a trifle. Freeze individual layers, wrapped airtight, for up to 1 month.

- **Preheat oven to 350°F (180°C)**
- **8-inch (2 L) square pan, lightly greased**

²⁄₃ cup	brown rice flour	150 mL
½ cup	tapioca starch	125 mL
⅓ cup	cornstarch	75 mL
¾ tsp	xanthan gum	4 mL
1½ tsp	GF baking powder	7 mL
½ tsp	salt	2 mL
½ cup	shortening or butter, softened	125 mL
¾ cup	granulated sugar	175 mL
3	eggs	3
¾ tsp	vanilla extract	4 mL
1 tsp	cider vinegar	5 mL
½ cup	milk	125 mL

1. In a large bowl, sift rice flour, tapioca starch, cornstarch, xanthan gum, baking powder and salt. Resift and set aside.

2. In a separate bowl, using an electric mixer, cream shortening and sugar until light and fluffy. Add eggs, one at a time, beating well after each addition. Stir in vanilla extract and vinegar. Stir in dry ingredients alternately with milk, making three additions of dry ingredients and two of milk. Stir just until combined after each addition. Spoon into prepared pan. Spread to edges and smooth top with a moist rubber spatula. Let stand for 30 minutes.

3. Bake in preheated oven for 35 to 40 minutes or until a cake tester inserted in the center comes out clean. Let cool in the pan on a rack for 10 minutes. Remove from the pan and let cool completely on rack.

Variation

For a tiered wedding cake, triple the recipe. Bake one layer in an 8½-inch (21 cm) round pan for 65 minutes, one layer in an 8-inch (20 cm) round pan for 55 minutes and another layer in a 6-inch (15 cm) round for 45 minutes.

Nutritional value per serving	
Calories	241
Fat, total	10 g
Fat, saturated	5 g
Cholesterol	62 mg
Sodium	223 mg
Carbohydrate	34 g
Fiber	1 g
Protein	3 g
Calcium	55 mg
Iron	0 mg

Chocolate Glaze

**Makes
1 cup (250 mL)**

Great for Angel Food Cake, Chocolate Fudge Cake or White Cake (see recipes, pages 297, 302, and 315).

Tip

To eliminate lumps, sift together cocoa, sugar and cornstarch before adding the liquids.

½ cup	unsweetened cocoa powder	125 mL
2 tbsp	granulated sugar	25 mL
2 tbsp	cornstarch	25 mL
⅓ cup	milk	75 mL
¼ cup	corn syrup	50 mL
1 tsp	vanilla extract	5 mL

1. In a small saucepan, sift together cocoa, sugar and cornstarch. Whisk in milk, corn syrup and vanilla extract. Bring to a boil over medium heat, stirring constantly, until glaze boils. Boil for 1 to 2 minutes until thickened and glossy. Cool 5 minutes. Drizzle over cooled cake.

Variation

Use as a chocolate syrup to make chocolate milk.

**Nutritional value
per 2 tbsp (25 mL)
serving**

Calories	62
Fat, total	1 g
Fat, saturated	0 g
Cholesterol	1 mg
Sodium	10 mg
Carbohydrate	14 g
Fiber	1 g
Protein	1 g
Calcium	11 mg
Iron	1 mg

Orange Glaze

Makes
⅓ cup (75 mL)

Don't want the extra calories in a frosting? Drizzle just enough glaze for a tangy sweet orange taste. It complements the flavor of the Applesauce-Date Snacking Cake (see recipe, page 298).

Tip

Sift confectioner's sugar to remove lumps before adding the orange juice.

| ½ cup | GF sifted confectioner's (icing) sugar | 125 mL |
| 2 tsp | frozen orange juice concentrate, thawed | 10 mL |

1. In a small bowl, stir together confectioner's sugar and orange juice concentrate. Drizzle over cooled cake.

Nutritional value per 2 tbsp (25 mL) serving	
Calories	84
Fat, total	0 g
Fat, saturated	0 g
Cholesterol	0 mg
Sodium	0 mg
Carbohydrate	22 g
Fiber	0 g
Protein	0 g
Calcium	0 mg
Iron	0 mg

Cream Cheese Frosting

The only acceptable finish for Pineapple-Carrot Cake (see recipe, page 309) or any carrot cake is Cream Cheese Frosting. Also great over Gingered Pumpkin Snacking Cake (see recipe, page 304).

1	package (8 oz/250 g) cream cheese, at room temperature	1
½ cup	butter, softened	125 mL
2 cups	GF sifted confectioner's (icing) sugar	500 mL
1 tsp	vanilla extract	5 mL

1. In a bowl, using an electric mixer, beat cream cheese and butter until light and fluffy. Beat in confectioner's sugar and vanilla extract. Spread over cooled cake.

Nutritional value per 2 tbsp (25 mL) serving

Calories	67
Fat, total	4 g
Fat, saturated	2 g
Cholesterol	8 mg
Sodium	45 mg
Carbohydrate	8 g
Fiber	0 g
Protein	1 g
Calcium	13 mg
Iron	0 mg

Orange Frosting

**Makes
2½ cups (625 mL)**

We love a chocolate-orange flavor combination. This is great with our Chocolate Fudge Cake (see recipe, page 302), but it suits any kind of cake, from chocolate to white to angel food.

Tip

Check for gluten-free confectioner's (icing) sugar. In Canada, it may contain up to 5% starch, which could be from wheat.

½ cup	shortening or butter, softened	125 mL
4 cups	GF sifted confectioner's (icing) sugar (see Tip, left)	1 L
2 tbsp	orange zest	25 mL
¼ cup	freshly squeezed orange juice	50 mL
2 tbsp	orange liqueur	25 mL

1. In a bowl, using an electric mixer, beat shortening, confectioner's sugar, orange zest, juice and liqueur until smooth and creamy. Spread over cooled cake.

Nutritional value per 2 tbsp (25 mL) serving	
Calories	112
Fat, total	4 g
Fat, saturated	2 g
Cholesterol	5 mg
Sodium	33 mg
Carbohydrate	20 g
Fiber	0 g
Protein	0 g
Calcium	1 mg
Iron	0 mg

Blueberry Dessert Sauce

**Makes
2 cups (500 mL)**

Enjoy this versatile sauce served over cheesecake, angel food cake or pancakes.

Tip

This sauce is great either warm or cold. Small amounts can be frozen to quickly thaw when guests arrive.

2 tbsp	cornstarch	25 mL
1/3 cup	granulated sugar	75 mL
3 cups	frozen blueberries, thawed and drained, juice reserved	750 mL
2 tbsp	freshly squeezed lemon juice	25 mL

1. In a saucepan combine cornstarch and sugar. Slowly add 1/3 cup (75 mL) reserved blueberry juice and lemon juice, stirring constantly. Add blueberries. Cook and stir over medium heat until mixture boils and becomes thick and shiny. Cool, stirring occasionally. Sauce keeps for up to 2 weeks in the refrigerator.

Nutritional value per 1/2 cup (125 mL) serving	
Calories	222
Fat, total	0 g
Fat, saturated	0 g
Cholesterol	0 mg
Sodium	2 mg
Carbohydrate	59 g
Fiber	4 g
Protein	1 g
Calcium	11 mg
Iron	1 mg

Fresh Peach Dessert Sauce

An abundance of peaches in the supermarket inspired this fresh no-cook sauce. Serve over cheesecake or white cake.

4	peaches, peeled and chopped (see Blanch, page 368)	4
1/4 cup	granulated sugar	50 mL
1/2 tsp	freshly squeezed lemon juice	2 mL
2 tbsp	water	25 mL

1. In a bowl, combine peaches, sugar, lemon juice and water. Stir gently to mix. Refrigerate for at least 1 hour.

Variation

Add 1 cup (250 mL) blueberries or coarsely diced plums for a mixed fresh fruit sauce.

Nutritional value per 1/2 cup (125 mL) serving	
Calories	55
Fat, total	0 g
Fat, saturated	0 g
Cholesterol	0 mg
Sodium	0 mg
Carbohydrate	14 g
Fiber	1 g
Protein	1 g
Calcium	0 mg
Iron	0 mg

Lotsa Lemon Sauce

Not too tangy, not too sweet, just perfect! Any excuse is a good excuse to make this recipe frequently.

Tip

Try this lemon sauce drizzled over Gingered Pumpkin Snacking Cake (see recipe, page 304) and Gingerbread (see recipe, page 272).

½ cup	granulated sugar	125 mL
3 tbsp	cornstarch	45 mL
1⅓ cups	water	325 mL
2 tsp	lemon zest	10 mL
⅓ cup	freshly squeezed lemon juice	75 mL
3 tbsp	butter	45 mL

Microwave Method

1. In a bowl, mix together sugar and cornstarch. Add water, lemon zest, lemon juice and butter. Microwave on High, stirring once or twice, for 3 to 5 minutes or until it boils and thickens.

Stove-Top Method

1. In a saucepan, combine sugar and cornstarch. Add water, lemon zest, lemon juice and butter. Heat over medium for 5 to 8 minutes or until it boils and thickens, stirring constantly. Set aside to cool.

Nutritional value per 2 tbsp (25 mL) serving	
Calories	53
Fat, total	2 g
Fat, saturated	1 g
Cholesterol	3 mg
Sodium	20 mg
Carbohydrate	9 g
Fiber	0 g
Protein	0 g
Calcium	1 mg
Iron	0 mg

Nutmeg Rum Sauce

**Makes
1¼ cups (300 mL)**

Serve this delightful sauce over Almond Sponge Cake (see recipe, page 295) or Sticky Date Pudding (see recipe, page 279).

1 cup	packed brown sugar	250 mL
½ cup	2% evaporated milk	125 mL
1 tsp	ground nutmeg	5 mL
½ cup	butter	125 mL
2 tbsp	dark rum	25 mL

1. In a saucepan, combine brown sugar, evaporated milk and nutmeg. Bring to a rolling boil over medium heat, stirring constantly. Reduce heat to low and simmer for 2 to 3 minutes. Remove from heat and add butter and rum, stirring until butter melts. Serve hot.

Variation

Substitute brandy or cold coffee for the rum.

Nutritional value per 2 tbsp (25 mL) serving	
Calories	151
Fat, total	8 g
Fat, saturated	3 g
Cholesterol	12 mg
Sodium	84 mg
Carbohydrate	19 g
Fiber	0 g
Protein	1 g
Calcium	42 mg
Iron	0 mg

Raspberry Dessert Sauce

Mixing fresh and frozen berries gives this sauce a distinct fresh berry flavor. Serve over chocolate or angel food cakes.

Tip

If only unsweetened raspberries are available, add 2 to 3 tbsp (25 to 45 mL) granulated sugar.

2 tbsp	cornstarch	25 mL
1	package (15 oz/425 g) frozen sweetened raspberries, thawed, drained and syrup reserved	1
1 cup	fresh raspberries	250 mL

1. In a large bowl, combine cornstarch and ¾ cup (175 mL) reserved raspberry syrup. Microwave on High, stirring once, for 4 minutes or until thick and shiny or in a saucepan over medium heat on top of the stove, stirring frequently.

2. Gently fold in thawed and fresh raspberries. Refrigerate for 1 hour before serving.

Nutritional value per ½ cup (125 mL) serving	
Calories	113
Fat, total	0 g
Fat, saturated	0 g
Cholesterol	0 mg
Sodium	1 mg
Carbohydrate	28 g
Fiber	5 g
Protein	1 g
Calcium	19 mg
Iron	1 mg

Simple Hot Fudge Sauce

Makes
½ cup (125 mL)

Drizzle this quick sauce over Pear Almond Torte (see recipe, page 292), ice cream, fresh fruit or anything that chocolate improves.

Tips

Timing in the microwave is critical. If you heat the sauce for too long, it could seize.

Stir like crazy. It'll take about 2 to 3 minutes.

Substitute flavored chocolate chips for regular chocolate chips.

| ½ cup | chocolate chips | 125 mL |
| 2 to 3 tbsp | milk | 25 to 45 mL |

1. In a small microwave-safe bowl, microwave chocolate chips and milk, uncovered, on High for 30 seconds, or until partially melted. Stir until completely melted.

Variation

For a richer sauce, substitute half-and-half (10%) cream, whipping (35%) cream or evaporated milk for the milk.

Nutritional value per 2 tbsp (25 mL) serving

Calories	131
Fat, total	7 g
Fat, saturated	4 g
Cholesterol	0 mg
Sodium	3 mg
Carbohydrate	16 g
Fiber	0 g
Protein	2 g
Calcium	8 mg
Iron	0 mg

Toffee Sauce

This buttery sweet sauce is best when served warm. Try drizzling it over ice cream.

Tip

We like to not just drizzle but drench warm Sticky Date Pudding (see recipe, page 279) with this sauce.

½ cup	packed brown sugar	125 mL
½ cup	butter	125 mL
¼ cup	liquid honey	50 mL
¼ cup	2% evaporated milk	50 mL

1. In a small saucepan, combine brown sugar, butter and honey. Heat gently over low heat, stirring constantly, until the sugar dissolves. Simmer for 2 to 3 minutes, or until sauce thickens and bubbles. Stir in evaporated milk and remove from heat.

Storing and Reheating Sauces

- Sauces can be refrigerated for up to 1 week. Reheat in a saucepan over medium-low heat, stirring occasionally, or microwave, uncovered, on High for a few seconds.
- Sauces can be frozen for up to 2 months. They stay soft enough to scoop out in small quantities. Warm in the microwave on Medium (50%) for 1 to 2 minutes.

Nutritional value per 2 tbsp (25 mL) serving	
Calories	129
Fat, total	7 g
Fat, saturated	3 g
Cholesterol	11 mg
Sodium	75 mg
Carbohydrate	15 g
Fiber	0 g
Protein	0 g
Calcium	21 mg
Iron	0 mg

Sweet Treats

continued on next page

Cookie and Bar Tips

- Granulated sugar generally results in crisper cookies than either brown sugar or honey. Equal amounts may be substituted one for the other or a combination of sugars may be used. Experiment to see what you prefer.
- Using butter in a cookie usually causes the dough to spread more, giving a flatter, crisper cookie than when made with shortening. You can substitute or use part of each in a recipe to give the texture you want.
- Bake a test cookie to check the accuracy of your oven's temperature setting. You may need to increase or reduce the temperature slightly or adjust the baking time. This is a good time to check the consistency of the dough. Add 1 to 2 tbsp (15 to 25 mL) sweet rice flour if the dough is too soft, causing the cookie to spread out more than you might like.
- When making cookies, make dough for about 4 to 6 dozen. Bake 1 or 2 dozen and form the remaining dough into logs. Each log should have enough dough to make 1 or 2 dozen cookies. Freeze these logs and, when making more cookies, there is no need to thaw the dough completely. Let a log thaw just enough to be able to slice it in $\frac{1}{2}$-inch (1 cm) circles. Baking a small amount at one time ensures you have fresh cookies without the work of making the dough each time. Dough can be frozen for up to 1 month.
- If the dough is a bit stickier than normal, flour the board and/or your fingertips with sweet rice flour. Use rice flour if it's of normal consistency.
- If dough becomes too soft, refrigerate for at least 15 minutes.
- Shiny baking sheets produce soft-bottomed cookies, while darker pans result in crisper cookies.
- When baked, remove cookies from the baking sheet and place, without overlapping, on a wire rack, to cool completely.
- Store soft cookies in an airtight container so they stay soft and moist. Crisp cookies should be lightly wrapped in a covered, but not airtight container.
- Roll out the dough to a uniform thickness for more even baking. Cut out shapes as close together as possible. Use as little flour as possible when re-rolling dough. Sweet rice flour works well here.
- Store dough wrapped airtight in the refrigerator for up to 5 days or freeze for up to 2 months. Thaw in the refrigerator overnight. Bring to room temperature before using.
- During baking, keep your eyes on the oven, not the clock — 1 to 2 minutes can mean the difference between undercooked and burnt shortbread.
- When using 2 baking sheets, place them in the upper and lower thirds of the oven. Switch their positions halfway through the baking time.
- Layer the baked cookies between waxed paper in an airtight container and store at room temperature for up to 5 days or freeze for up to 2 weeks.

Apricot Coconut Balls

Not too sweet, not too wet, not too dry — but just right for a portable snack at any time of the year. Use these treats like an energy bar for your favorite athlete or on a tray of gluten-free holiday goodies.

Tips

If the fruit mixture is not processed finely enough, the cookie is harder to form and falls apart easily.

Make ahead and store in an airtight container for up to 1 month.

● **Baking sheets, lined with waxed paper**

1 cup	chopped dried apricots	250 mL
½ cup	chopped dried figs	125 mL
½ cup	chopped dried prunes	125 mL
½ cup	chopped dried apples	125 mL
3 tbsp	flavored brandy	45 mL
1 tbsp	orange zest	15 mL
1¼ cups	sweetened desiccated coconut, divided	300 mL
¾ cup	chopped nuts, such as walnuts	175 mL

1. In a glass pie plate, combine apricots, figs, prunes, apples, brandy and orange zest. Cover and let stand for at least 1 hour or overnight.

2. In a food processor or blender, pulse dried fruit mixture until finely chopped. Mix in ¾ cup (175 mL) coconut and nuts. Pulse until nuts are chopped and mixture holds together easily.

3. Shape into ¾-inch (2 cm) balls. Roll in remaining ½ cup (125 mL) coconut. Let stand on prepared pans for 8 hours or overnight.

Variations

Any dried fruit combination works well. Keep the total amount of fruit to 2½ cups (625 mL).

Substitute orange juice for brandy.

Nutritional value per serving (1 cookie)	
Calories	42
Fat, total	2 g
Fat, saturated	1 g
Cholesterol	0 mg
Sodium	14 mg
Carbohydrate	6 g
Fiber	1 g
Protein	1 g
Calcium	7 mg
Iron	0 mg

Chocolate Chip Cookies

Makes 6½ dozen cookies

No point trying to freeze these — the minute anyone knows they are in the house, the cookies disappear.

Tip

For crisper cookies, replace shortening with butter or margarine and substitute half the brown sugar with granulated sugar.

- Preheat oven to 350°F (180°C)
- Baking sheets, lightly greased

1 cup	sorghum flour	250 mL
⅔ cup	whole bean flour	150 mL
½ cup	tapioca starch	125 mL
1 tsp	baking soda	5 mL
1 tsp	xanthan gum	5 mL
½ tsp	salt	2 mL
1 cup	shortening, softened	250 mL
1⅓ cups	packed brown sugar	325 mL
2	eggs	2
1 tsp	vanilla extract	5 mL
2 cups	mini-chocolate chips	500 mL
1 cup	chopped walnuts	250 mL

1. In a bowl or plastic bag, combine sorghum flour, whole bean flour, tapioca starch, baking soda, xanthan gum and salt. Mix well and set aside.

2. In a separate bowl, using an electric mixer, cream shortening and brown sugar. Add eggs and vanilla extract and beat until light and fluffy. Slowly beat in the dry ingredients until combined. Stir in chocolate chips and walnuts. Drop dough by level tablespoons (15 mL), 1½ inches (4 cm) apart on prepared baking sheets. Let stand for 30 minutes. Bake in preheated oven for 8 to 10 minutes or until set. Remove from baking sheets to a cooling rack immediately.

Variations

Substitute white chocolate chips and macadamia nuts for mini-chocolate chips and walnuts.

To bake a dozen cookies at a time or to turn these into slice-and-bake cookies, form the dough into 1-inch (2.5 cm) logs 6 inches (15 cm) in length, and freeze for up to 1 month. To bake, thaw slightly and cut into ½-inch (1 cm) slices. Bake 10 to 12 minutes.

Nutritional value per serving (1 cookie)	
Calories	93
Fat, total	5 g
Fat, saturated	2 g
Cholesterol	6 mg
Sodium	34 mg
Carbohydrate	11 g
Fiber	0 g
Protein	2 g
Calcium	6 mg
Iron	0 mg

Triple-Threat Mocha Chocolate Chip Cookies

Triple the pleasure, triple the fun — but who's counting calories? These fudgy morsels are worth every bite!

Tips

Cookies spread and are still soft when baked; if baked too long, cookies become very crunchy when cold.

For crisper cookies, use ²/₃ cup (150 mL) butter instead of half butter and half shortening.

Make ahead and freeze for up to 2 months in an airtight container.

Nutritional value per serving (1 cookie)

Calories	89
Fat, total	4 g
Fat, saturated	2 g
Cholesterol	8 mg
Sodium	52 mg
Carbohydrate	12 g
Fiber	1 g
Protein	1 g
Calcium	4 mg
Iron	0 mg

● **Baking sheets, lightly greased**

1 cup	sorghum flour	250 mL
²/₃ cup	whole bean flour	150 mL
½ cup	tapioca starch	125 mL
1 tsp	baking soda	5 mL
1 tsp	xanthan gum	5 mL
½ tsp	salt	2 mL
⅓ cup	unsweetened cocoa powder, sifted	75 mL
4 oz	semi-sweet chocolate	125 g
⅓ cup	butter	75 mL
⅓ cup	shortening	75 mL
2 tbsp	water	25 mL
1 tbsp	instant coffee granules	15 mL
2	eggs	2
²/₃ cup	granulated sugar	150 mL
²/₃ cup	packed brown sugar	150 mL
1½ tsp	vanilla	7 mL
1 cup	semi-sweet chocolate chips	250 mL

1. In a large bowl or plastic bag, combine sorghum flour, whole bean flour, tapioca starch, baking soda, xanthan gum, salt and cocoa. Mix well and set aside.

2. In a medium microwave-safe bowl, microwave chocolate, butter, shortening, water and coffee granules, uncovered, on Medium (50%) for 2 minutes. Stir until completely melted. Set aside to cool.

3. In a large bowl, using an electric mixer, beat eggs, sugar and brown sugar for 3 minutes, until smooth. Add vanilla and cooled melted chocolate mixture. Slowly beat in the dry ingredients until combined. Stir in chocolate chips. Drop dough by rounded spoonfuls 2 inches (5 cm) apart on prepared baking sheets. Let stand for 30 minutes. Meanwhile, preheat oven to 350°F (180°C).

4. Bake in preheated oven for 10 to 12 minutes, or until set. Transfer to a cooling rack immediately.

Cranberry Drops

These cookies are a lunchbox favorite! Hermit-like in color and soft in texture, each bite has the tang of fresh cranberries.

Tips

Cool the baking sheet before re-using it to prevent the dough from spreading too much.

Leave cranberries in the freezer until just before adding to the dough. This helps to prevent them from "bleeding" into the cookies.

Freeze raw dough, formed into cookies, for approximately 1 hour then place them in an airtight freezer bag. Freeze for up to 1 month. Bake from frozen for 15 to 18 minutes.

Nutritional value per serving (1 cookie)	
Calories	65
Fat, total	3 g
Fat, saturated	1 g
Cholesterol	6 mg
Sodium	49 mg
Carbohydrate	10 g
Fiber	1 g
Protein	1 g
Calcium	7 mg
Iron	0 mg

- **Preheat oven to 350°F (180°C)**
- **Baking sheets, lightly greased**

1 cup	brown rice flour	250 mL
1/3 cup	yellow pea flour or whole bean flour (see Tips, page 343)	75 mL
2 tbsp	tapioca starch	25 mL
1/2 tsp	baking soda	2 mL
1 tsp	xanthan gum	5 mL
1/4 tsp	salt	1 mL
1/4 cup	shortening or butter, softened	50 mL
3/4 cup	packed brown sugar	175 mL
1	egg	1
3 tbsp	milk	45 mL
1/2 tsp	vanilla extract	2 mL
3/4 cup	cranberries, fresh or frozen	175 mL
1/2 cup	chopped walnuts	125 mL

1. In a bowl, sift brown rice flour, yellow pea flour, tapioca starch, baking soda, xanthan gum and salt. Mix well and set aside.

2. In a separate bowl, using an electric mixer, cream shortening and brown sugar. Add egg, milk and vanilla extract. Beat until light and fluffy. Slowly beat in the dry ingredients until combined. Stir in cranberries and walnuts. Drop dough by rounded tablespoonfuls (15 mL), 2 inches (5 cm) apart on prepared baking sheets. Let stand for 30 minutes. Bake in preheated oven for 12 to 15 minutes or until set. Transfer to a cooling rack immediately.

Variation

Substitute fresh or frozen blueberries for the cranberries.

Cranberry Pistachio Biscotti

Makes 64 cookies

These have the appearance and texture of traditional twice-baked biscotti, but are much easier and faster to make. We like to dip them in a sweet Italian dessert wine, or in coffee.

Tips

Biscotti will be medium-firm and crunchy; for softer biscotti, bake for only 10 minutes in Step 5; for very firm biscotti, bake for 20 minutes.

Store in an airtight container at room temperature for up to 3 weeks, or freeze for up to 2 months.

If you prefer, you can use a 13- by 9-inch (3 L) baking pan instead of the two 8-inch (2 L) pans.

Nutritional value per serving (1 cookie)

Calories	61
Fat, total	2 g
Fat, saturated	0 g
Cholesterol	10 mg
Sodium	9 mg
Carbohydrate	10 g
Fiber	1 g
Protein	2 g
Calcium	14 mg
Iron	1 mg

- Preheat oven to 325°F (160°C)
- Two 8-inch (2 L) square baking pans, foil-lined and lightly greased
- Baking sheets, ungreased

1½ cups	amaranth flour	375 mL
½ cup	soy flour	125 mL
⅓ cup	potato starch	75 mL
¼ cup	tapioca starch	50 mL
1½ tsp	xanthan gum	7 mL
1 tsp	GF baking powder	5 mL
Pinch	salt	Pinch
4	eggs	4
1¼ cups	granulated sugar	300 mL
1 tbsp	grated lemon zest	15 mL
1 tsp	vanilla	5 mL
1½ cups	coarsely chopped pistachios	375 mL
1 cup	dried cranberries	250 mL

1. In a large bowl or plastic bag, combine amaranth flour, soy flour, potato starch, tapioca starch, xanthan gum, baking powder and salt. Mix well and set aside.

2. In a separate bowl, using an electric mixer, beat eggs, sugar, lemon zest and vanilla until combined.

3. Slowly beat in dry ingredients and mix just until combined. Stir in pistachios and cranberries. Spoon into prepared pans. Using a moistened rubber spatula, spread batter to edges and smooth tops.

4. Bake in preheated oven for 30 to 35 minutes, or until firm or tops are just turning golden. Let cool in pans for 5 minutes.

5. Remove from pans, remove foil and let cool on a cutting board for 5 minutes. Cut into quarters, then cut each quarter into 8 slices. Arrange slices upright (cut sides exposed) at least ½ inch (1 cm) apart on baking sheets. Bake for an additional 15 minutes, until dry and crisp. Transfer to a cooling rack immediately.

Variation

Try orange-flavored cranberries and substitute orange zest for the lemon zest.

Crunchy Flaxseed Cookies

These perfect back-to-school lunchbox treats will remind you of oatmeal cookies. We dare you to eat just one!

Tips

We tried this cookie with sprouted flax powder, flax meal, ground flaxseed and flax flour. All were delicious, so you can substitute one for another.

Whole flaxseed can be stored at room temperature for up to 1 year. Ground flaxseed can be stored in the refrigerator for up to 90 days, but for optimum freshness it is best to grind it as you need it.

Nutritional value per serving (1 cookie)	
Calories	70
Fat, total	4 g
Fat, saturated	1 g
Cholesterol	7 mg
Sodium	66 mg
Carbohydrate	9 g
Fiber	1 g
Protein	1 g
Calcium	9 mg
Iron	0 mg

- Preheat oven to 350°F (180°C)
- Baking sheets, lightly greased

⅓ cup	sorghum flour	75 mL
¼ cup	whole bean flour	50 mL
¼ cup	tapioca starch	50 mL
¼ cup	ground flaxseed	50 mL
⅔ cup	cracked flaxseed	150 mL
1 tsp	baking soda	5 mL
1 tsp	xanthan gum	5 mL
¼ tsp	salt	1 mL
½ cup	butter or shortening, softened	125 mL
½ cup	packed brown sugar	125 mL
⅓ cup	granulated sugar	75 mL
1	egg	1
½ tsp	vanilla	2 mL
⅔ cup	buckwheat flakes	150 mL

1. In a medium bowl or plastic bag, combine sorghum flour, whole bean flour, tapioca starch, ground flaxseed, cracked flaxseed, baking soda, xanthan gum and salt. Mix well and set aside.

2. In a large bowl, using an electric mixer, cream the butter, brown sugar and granulated sugar until combined. Add egg and vanilla and cream until light and fluffy. Slowly beat in the dry ingredients until combined. Stir in buckwheat flakes. Roll into 1-inch (2.5 cm) balls. Place 2 inches (5 cm) apart on prepared baking sheets and flatten with a fork or the bottom of a drinking glass.

3. Bake in preheated oven for 10 to 15 minutes, or until set. Remove from baking sheets to cooling rack immediately.

Variations

Make date- or jam-filled sandwich cookies or add 1 cup (250 mL) chocolate chips or raisins to the batter and bake as drop cookies.

Substitute raw hemp powder for ground flaxseed and hemp hearts® for half the cracked flaxseed.

Mini-Thumbprints

Thumbprint cookies, thimble cookies or Swedish tea rings — by whatever name you know them — are so rich that the bite-size morsels melt in your mouth. So tender and delicate, they are not meant to carry for lunch.

Tips

To prevent cookies from crumbling, leave them on the baking sheet for 2 to 3 minutes after you take them from the oven. Then remove them carefully. The one that breaks is your reward for baking.

Nuts must be very finely chopped to generously coat the cookies.

Nutritional value per serving (1 cookie)	
Calories	79
Fat, total	5 g
Fat, saturated	1 g
Cholesterol	7 mg
Sodium	25 mg
Carbohydrate	9 g
Fiber	0 g
Protein	1 g
Calcium	3 mg
Iron	0 mg

- Preheat oven to 350°F (180°C)
- Baking sheets, lightly greased

Cookie

1 cup	brown rice flour	250 mL
⅔ cup	cornstarch	150 mL
⅔ cup	GF confectioner's (icing) sugar	150 mL
⅓ cup	potato starch	75 mL
1 tsp	xanthan gum	5 mL
¾ cup	butter, softened	175 mL
1	egg yolk	1

Coating

2	egg whites, lightly beaten	2
1 tbsp	water	15 mL
1½ cups	finely chopped walnuts	375 mL
½ cup	grape jelly	125 mL

1. *Cookie:* In a bowl or plastic bag, combine rice flour, cornstarch, confectioner's sugar, potato starch and xanthan gum. Mix well and set aside.

2. In a separate bowl, using an electric mixer, beat butter and egg yolk until light and fluffy. Slowly beat in the dry ingredients until combined. With a rubber spatula, scrape the bottom and sides of bowl. Gather the dough into a large ball, kneading in any remaining dry ingredients. Form into ½-inch (1 cm) balls.

3. *Coating:* In a small bowl, combine egg whites and water.

4. Roll cookies in egg white mixture and then in nuts. Place 1 inch (2.5 cm) apart on prepared baking sheets. Using the end of the handle of a wooden spoon, make an indent in the center of each. Bake in preheated oven for 8 minutes then remove from the oven, deepen indent and bake for an additional 6 to 8 minutes or until golden. Let stand for 2 to 3 minutes. Carefully transfer to a cooling rack immediately. Let cool slightly and fill the indent with jelly.

Variation

Instead of jam or jelly, fill the indent with melted chocolate.

Molasses Cookies

Hermit-like in color and flavor — an excellent cookie for packed lunches.

Tips

Keep a close eye on the oven, as these cookies burn easily.

Cookies spread and are still soft when baked; if baked too long, cookies become very crunchy when cold.

Make ahead and freeze for up to 2 months in an airtight container.

Substitute whole bean flour, yellow or green pea flour or garbanzo-fava (garfava) bean flour for the chickpea flour.

- Baking sheets, lightly greased

1²⁄₃ cups	sorghum flour	400 mL
1 cup	chickpea (garbanzo bean) flour	250 mL
¹⁄₃ cup	tapioca starch	75 mL
1 tsp	baking soda	5 mL
1 tsp	xanthan gum	5 mL
¹⁄₂ tsp	salt	2 mL
1 tsp	ground cinnamon	5 mL
¹⁄₂ tsp	ground allspice	2 mL
¹⁄₂ tsp	ground cloves	2 mL
1 cup	shortening or butter, softened	250 mL
2	eggs	2
1 cup	fancy molasses	250 mL
¾ cup	granulated sugar	175 mL
2 tbsp	Orange Marmalade (see recipe, page 35)	25 mL
2 cups	raisins	500 mL
2 cups	chopped walnuts	500 mL

1. In a large bowl or plastic bag, combine sorghum flour, chickpea flour, tapioca starch, baking soda, xanthan gum, salt, cinnamon, allspice and cloves. Mix well and set aside.

2. In another large bowl, using an electric mixer, cream shortening, eggs, molasses, sugar and marmalade. Slowly beat in the dry ingredients until combined. Stir in raisins and walnuts. Drop dough by rounded spoonfuls 2 inches (5 cm) apart on prepared baking sheets. Let stand for 30 minutes. Meanwhile, preheat oven to 350°F (180°C).

3. Bake in preheated oven for 10 to 12 minutes, or until set. Transfer to a cooling rack immediately.

Nutritional value per serving (1 cookie)	
Calories	121
Fat, total	6 g
Fat, saturated	2 g
Cholesterol	8 mg
Sodium	46 mg
Carbohydrate	16 g
Fiber	1 g
Protein	2 g
Calcium	20 mg
Iron	1 mg

Peanut Butter Cookies

Makes
3 dozen cookies

Everybody's absolute favorite cookie! These are just perfect to share with friends of all ages. No need to be separate from the crowd!

Tip

Roll dough into logs $1^1/_2$ inches (4 cm) in diameter. Wrap airtight and refrigerate for 1 week or freeze for up to 1 month to bake later. Thaw slightly and bake for 10 to 12 minutes. You decide the length of the log, depending on the number of cookies you want to bake. Cut partially thawed logs into $1/_2$-inch (1 cm) slices to bake.

- **Preheat oven to 350°F (180°C)**
- **Baking sheets, ungreased**

1 cup	soy flour	250 mL
$1/_2$ cup	packed brown sugar	125 mL
$1/_2$ cup	granulated sugar	125 mL
$1/_3$ cup	cornstarch	75 mL
$1/_2$ tsp	baking soda	2 mL
$1/_2$ tsp	xanthan gum	2 mL
$1/_4$ tsp	salt	1 mL
$1/_2$ cup	butter, softened	125 mL
$1/_2$ cup	smooth peanut butter	125 mL
1	egg	1
$1/_2$ tsp	vanilla extract	2 mL
	Sweet rice flour (optional)	

1. In a bowl or plastic bag, combine soy flour, brown sugar, granulated sugar, cornstarch, baking soda, xanthan gum and salt. Mix well and set aside.

2. In a separate bowl, using an electric mixer, cream butter and peanut butter. Add egg and vanilla. Beat until light and fluffy. Slowly stir in the dry ingredients until combined. With a rubber spatula, scrape the bottom and sides of bowl.

3. Gather the dough into a large ball, kneading in any remaining dry ingredients. Roll into 1-inch (2.5 cm) balls. Place $1^1/_2$ inches (4 cm) apart on the baking sheets. Flatten slightly with a fork dipped into sweet rice flour, if necessary, to prevent sticking. Bake in preheated oven for 10 to 15 minutes or until set. Transfer to a cooling rack immediately.

Variations

Substitute chunky peanut butter for smooth and add $1/_2$ cup (125 mL) chopped peanuts.

For a chewy peanut butter cookie, add an extra egg.

Nutritional value per serving (1 cookie)	
Calories	84
Fat, total	5 g
Fat, saturated	2 g
Cholesterol	8 mg
Sodium	76 mg
Carbohydrate	9 g
Fiber	1 g
Protein	2 g
Calcium	11 mg
Iron	0 mg

Sue's Shortbread

Sue Jennett, of Kingston, Ontario, diagnosed with celiac disease years ago, gave us her recipe for shortbread to share with you.

Tip

As the dough is soft, handle gently when rolling into balls and try not to add extra flour.

- **Preheat oven to 300°F (150°C)**
- **Baking sheets, ungreased**

⅔ cup	brown rice flour	150 mL
½ cup	cornstarch	125 mL
½ cup	GF sifted confectioner's (icing) sugar	125 mL
¼ cup	potato starch	50 mL
2 tbsp	tapioca starch	25 mL
¾ cup	butter, softened	175 mL
	Sweet rice flour (optional)	

1. In a bowl or plastic bag, combine rice flour, cornstarch, confectioner's sugar, potato starch and tapioca starch. Mix well and set aside.
2. In a separate bowl, using an electric mixer, cream butter. Slowly beat in the dry ingredients until combined. With a rubber spatula, scrape the bottom and sides of bowl.
3. Gather the dough into a large ball, kneading in any remaining dry ingredients. Roll into 1-inch (2.5 cm) balls. Place 1 inch (2.5 cm) apart on baking sheets. If desired, flatten with fork dipped into sweet rice flour. Bake in preheated oven for 15 to 25 minutes or until set but not browned. Transfer to a cooling rack immediately.

Variation

Prick with a fork, bake and then sprinkle the tops with a little extra fine sugar while still warm.

Nutritional value per serving (1 cookie)	
Calories	75
Fat, total	5 g
Fat, saturated	2 g
Cholesterol	6 mg
Sodium	41 mg
Carbohydrate	9 g
Fiber	0 g
Protein	0 g
Calcium	0 mg
Iron	0 mg

Buckwheat Date Squares

Makes 16 squares or 8 dessert squares

We both consider these comfort food — we know you will enjoy them either in smaller squares for snacks or in larger pieces for dessert.

Tips

When purchasing chopped dates, check for wheat starch in the coating.

Recipe can easily be doubled and baked in a 13- by 9-inch (3 L) baking pan for 30 to 40 minutes.

Squares can be stored in an airtight container at room temperature for 5 days or frozen for up to 2 months.

Nutritional value per serving (1 regular square)	
Calories	124
Fat, total	4 g
Fat, saturated	1 g
Cholesterol	4 mg
Sodium	93 mg
Carbohydrate	22 g
Fiber	3 g
Protein	2 g
Calcium	18 mg
Iron	1 mg

- Preheat oven to 350°F (180°C)
- 8-inch (2 L) square baking pan, lightly greased

Date Filling

1¼ cups	chopped pitted dates	300 mL
¾ cup	water	175 mL

Crumb Crust

½ cup	pea flour	125 mL
¼ cup	pecan flour	50 mL
¾ cup	buckwheat flakes	175 mL
¼ tsp	baking soda	1 mL
¼ tsp	salt	1 mL
1 tsp	ground cinnamon	5 tsp
¼ cup	butter or margarine, softened	50 mL
½ cup	packed brown sugar	125 mL

1. *Prepare the date filling:* In a saucepan, over medium heat, heat dates and water until the mixture comes to a boil. Reduce heat to medium-low, cover and simmer for 6 minutes, stirring frequently, until mixture is the consistency of jam. Set aside.

2. *Prepare the crumb crust:* In a small bowl or plastic bag, combine pea flour, pecan flour, buckwheat flakes, baking soda, salt and cinnamon. Mix well and set aside.

3. In a medium bowl, cream butter and brown sugar. Slowly beat in the dry ingredients. Mix until crumbly. Firmly pat two-thirds of the mixture into prepared pan. Top with date filling and sprinkle with remaining crumb mixture.

4. Bake in preheated oven for 20 to 30 minutes, or until light golden brown. Let cool completely on a rack. Cut into squares.

Variations

Substitute GF mincemeat or green tomato mincemeat for the date filling. No need to cook the filling first.

Substitute an equal amount of GF oats for the buckwheat flakes.

Butter Tart Bars

Makes
3 dozen bars

A most important Canadian treat, these are a much sought-after addition to any dessert tray. They disappear first.

Tips

The shortbread base tends to crumble if cut while the bars are still warm. Refrigerated overnight, the bars cut more easily.

Omit the nuts and add an equal amount of butterscotch or peanut butter chips or unsweetened coconut.

Nutritional value per serving (1 bar)

Calories	103
Fat, total	4 g
Fat, saturated	1 g
Cholesterol	12 mg
Sodium	49 mg
Carbohydrate	17 g
Fiber	1 g
Protein	1 g
Calcium	10 mg
Iron	0 mg

- Preheat oven to 350°F (180°C)
- 9-inch (2.5 L) square pan, ungreased

Base

1 cup	brown rice flour	250 mL
1/3 cup	tapioca starch	75 mL
1/3 cup	packed brown sugar	75 mL
2 tbsp	potato starch	25 mL
1 tsp	xanthan gum	5 mL
1/2 cup	butter, softened	125 mL

Topping

2 tbsp	cornstarch	25 mL
1/2 tsp	GF baking powder	2 mL
1/4 tsp	salt	1 mL
2	eggs	2
3/4 cup	corn syrup	175 mL
1 cup	raisins	250 mL
1/2 cup	chopped walnuts	125 mL

1. *Base:* In a bowl or plastic bag, combine rice flour, tapioca starch, brown sugar, potato starch and xanthan gum. Mix well and set aside.

2. In a separate bowl, using an electric mixer, cream butter. Slowly beat in the dry ingredients until combined. With a rubber spatula, scrape the bottom and sides of bowl. Press into the bottom of pan. Bake in preheated oven for 10 minutes or until set but not browned. Meanwhile, prepare Topping.

3. *Topping:* In a small bowl, combine cornstarch, baking powder and salt. Set aside.

4. In a separate bowl, using an electric mixer, beat eggs until light and fluffy. Add corn syrup while mixing. With the mixer on low, slowly add dry ingredients and mix just until smooth. Do not over mix. Fold in raisins and walnuts and pour over the hot base. Bake in preheated oven for 25 to 35 minutes or until the center is almost firm. Refrigerate overnight before cutting into squares.

Chocolate-Coated Peanut Blondies

Makes 16 blondies

Blond brownies, or blondies, continue to gain in popularity. Here is a flavor kids of any age will enjoy — perfect for lunches and snacks.

Tips

Spread the melted chocolate chips over the hot blondies with the back of a spoon or a spatula as soon as they come out of the oven.

Don't substitute dry-roasted peanuts, as they may contain gluten.

Substitute GF peanut butter chips for the chocolate chips.

Nutritional value per serving (1 blondie)	
Calories	311
Fat, total	19 g
Fat, saturated	7 g
Cholesterol	43 mg
Sodium	114 mg
Carbohydrate	26 g
Fiber	2 g
Protein	9 g
Calcium	77 mg
Iron	1 mg

● **9-inch (2.5 L) square baking pan, lightly greased**

¾ cup	soy flour	175 mL
⅓ cup	whole bean flour	75 mL
2 tbsp	tapioca starch	25 mL
1½ tsp	xanthan gum	7 mL
1 tbsp	GF baking powder	15 mL
½ cup	butter or shortening, softened	125 mL
½ cup	GF peanut butter	125 mL
⅔ cup	packed brown sugar	150 mL
3	eggs	3
2 tsp	vanilla	10 mL
1 cup	chopped peanuts	250 mL
1 cup	chocolate chips	250 mL

1. In a small bowl or plastic bag, combine soy flour, whole bean flour, tapioca starch, xanthan gum and baking powder. Mix well and set aside.

2. In a large bowl, using an electric mixer, cream butter, peanut butter and brown sugar until well blended. Add eggs and vanilla and cream until light and fluffy. Slowly beat in the dry ingredients until combined. Stir in peanuts. Spoon into prepared pan. Using a moistened rubber spatula, spread to edges and smooth top. Sprinkle with chocolate chips. Let stand for 30 minutes. Meanwhile, preheat oven to 325°F (160°C).

3. Bake in preheated oven 30 to 35 minutes, or until a wooden skewer inserted in the center comes out clean. Spread melted chocolate chips to evenly cover the top. Let cool completely on a rack. Cut into bars.

Variation

Apricot Almond Blondies: Substitute 1 cup (250 mL) chopped dried apricots and ½ cup (125 mL) toasted slivered almonds for the peanuts and ½ cup (125 mL) apricot jam for the chocolate chips.

Crunchy Blondies

Makes 1½ dozen blondies

Full of toffee bits and white chocolate chips, these thin, chewy blond brownies are quick and easy to make.

Tips

We like to sift the dry ingredients when using yellow pea flour because it lumps easily.

Yellow pea flour gives baked products a warm golden color.

- **Preheat oven to 350°F (180°C)**
- **13- by 9-inch (3 L) baking pan, lightly greased**

¾ cup	brown rice flour	175 mL
½ cup	yellow pea flour or whole bean flour	125 mL
¼ cup	tapioca starch	50 mL
2 tsp	GF baking powder	10 mL
2 tsp	xanthan gum	10 mL
¼ tsp	salt	1 mL
½ cup	butter, softened	125 mL
¾ cup	granulated sugar	175 mL
⅓ cup	packed brown sugar	75 mL
2	eggs	2
1 tsp	vanilla extract	5 mL
½ cup	toffee bits	125 mL
½ cup	white chocolate chips	125 mL

1. In a large bowl, sift together brown rice flour, yellow pea flour, tapioca starch, baking powder, xanthan gum and salt. Resift and set aside.

2. In a separate bowl, using an electric mixer, cream butter, granulated sugar and brown sugar. Add eggs and vanilla extract. Beat until light and fluffy. Gradually beat in dry ingredients, mixing just until smooth. Stir in toffee bits and white chocolate chips. Spoon into prepared pan, spread to edges and smooth top with a moist rubber spatula. Let stand for 30 minutes.

3. Bake in preheated oven for 35 to 45 minutes or until a wooden skewer inserted in the center comes out clean. Transfer to cooling rack and let cool completely. Cut into bars.

Variation

Double the toffee bits and eliminate the white chocolate chips or double the white chocolate chips and eliminate the toffee bits.

Nutritional value per serving (1 blondie)	
Calories	198
Fat, total	3 g
Fat, saturated	3 g
Cholesterol	28 mg
Sodium	119 mg
Carbohydrate	31 g
Fiber	2 g
Protein	3 g
Calcium	40 mg
Iron	1 mg

Cinnamon Crisps

Makes 3 dozen bars

Give cinnamon lovers these sweet, crunchy snacks any time!

Tips

The dough is very stiff but still rolls out easily.

Cut bars while warm as they become too crisp to cut when they are cool.

- Preheat 300°F (150°C)
- 15- by 10-inch (40 by 25 cm) jelly roll pan, greased

1²⁄₃ cups	soy flour	400 mL
¹⁄₃ cup	tapioca starch	75 mL
¹⁄₂ tsp	baking soda	2 mL
1 tsp	xanthan gum	5 mL
¹⁄₄ tsp	salt	1 mL
1 tbsp	ground cinnamon	15 mL
1 cup	butter, softened	250 mL
¹⁄₂ cup	packed brown sugar	125 mL
¹⁄₂ cup	granulated sugar	125 mL
1	egg, separated	1
1¹⁄₂ cups	chopped pecans	375 mL

1. In a bowl or plastic bag, combine soy flour, tapioca starch, baking soda, xanthan gum, salt and cinnamon. Mix well and set aside.

2. In a separate bowl, using an electric mixer, cream butter, brown sugar, granulated sugar and egg yolk until light and fluffy. Slowly beat in the dry ingredients until combined.

3. Form the dough into a large disk and place in the prepared pan. Cover with waxed paper. With a rolling pin, roll out the dough to fit the pan. Carefully remove the waxed paper.

4. In a small bowl, beat egg white with a fork just until foamy. Brush on top of dough. Sprinkle with pecans and press them in lightly. Let stand for 30 minutes. Bake in preheated oven for 35 to 45 minutes or until set. Immediately cut into bars. Let cool in the pan.

Variation

Make three kinds of cookies at the same time. Divide dough into thirds. Sprinkle one portion with chopped pecans. Then choose chocolate, butterscotch, peanut butter, raspberry or cinnamon chips for the other two portions.

Nutritional value per serving (1 bar)	
Calories	124
Fat, total	9 g
Fat, saturated	3 g
Cholesterol	11 mg
Sodium	81 mg
Carbohydrate	9 g
Fiber	1 g
Protein	3 g
Calcium	19 mg
Iron	1 mg

Fudgy Brownies

Doubly delicious, these moist, fudgy brownies appeal to the eye as well as the taste of every chocoholic!

Tips

One individually wrapped square of baking chocolate is 1 oz (30 g).

For further instructions on melting chocolate, see Chocolate, page 368.

Keep extra brownies in the freezer. Crumb them and use as a base for cheesecake or cube them for a chocolate trifle.

Nutritional value per serving (1 brownie)	
Calories	176
Fat, total	10 g
Fat, saturated	4 g
Cholesterol	26 mg
Sodium	31 mg
Carbohydrate	19 g
Fiber	1 g
Protein	3 g
Calcium	26 mg
Iron	1 mg

- **Preheat oven to 350°F (180°C)**
- **8-inch (2 L) square pan, lightly greased**

⅓ cup	yellow pea flour	75 mL
2 tbsp	potato starch	25 mL
1 cup	packed brown sugar	250 mL
½ tsp	GF baking powder	2 mL
½ tsp	xanthan gum	2 mL
⅛ tsp	salt	0.5 mL
½ cup	chopped walnuts	125 mL
½ cup	shortening	125 mL
2 oz	unsweetened chocolate	60 g
½ tsp	vanilla extract	2 mL
2	eggs	2

Glaze (optional)

2 tsp	shortening	10 mL
2 oz	white chocolate	60 g

1. In a large bowl or plastic bag, combine yellow pea flour, potato starch, brown sugar, baking powder, xanthan gum, salt and walnuts. Mix well and set aside.
2. In a large bowl, microwave shortening and chocolate on Medium for 3 minutes or until partially melted in a saucepan over hot water. Stir until melted. Add eggs, one at a time, blending after each. Stir in vanilla extract. Slowly add the dry ingredients, stirring until combined. Spread evenly in prepared pan. Let stand for 30 minutes. Bake in a preheated oven for 20 to 25 minutes or until a cake tester inserted in the center still has a little moist crumb adhering to it. Transfer to a rack to cool completely. Let cool for 15 minutes on rack. Meanwhile, prepare glaze, if desired.
3. *Glaze:* In a small bowl, over hot water, partially melt the shortening and chocolate. Remove from heat and continue stirring until completely melted. Spread on warm brownies. Cool completely before cutting into squares.

Variation

Substitute an equal amount of whole bean flour for yellow pea.

Coconut Lemon Squares

Makes 3 dozen squares

Try our delicious simplified version of lemony three-layer squares. The coconut rises to the top during baking to finish the squares with a crisp topping.

Tips

The zest and juice of the fresh lemon enhances the flavor. To get more juice out of it, roll the lemon, brought to room temperature, on the counter or between your hands.

No food processor? Use a pastry blender or two knives to cut the butter into the dry ingredients until the mixture resembles small peas. Add the egg and mix until it forms a soft dough.

Nutritional value per serving (1 square)

Calories	117
Fat, total	6 g
Fat, saturated	3 g
Cholesterol	26 mg
Sodium	41 mg
Carbohydrate	16 g
Fiber	1 g
Protein	1 g
Calcium	12 mg
Iron	0 mg

- **Preheat oven to 350°F (180°C)**
- **9-inch (2.5 L) square baking pan, lightly greased and lined with parchment paper**

Base

¼ cup	brown rice flour	50 mL
¾ cup	cornstarch	175 mL
3 tbsp	tapioca starch	45 mL
1 tsp	xanthan gum	5 mL
¼ cup	packed brown sugar	50 mL
Pinch	salt	Pinch
½ cup	unsweetened shredded coconut	125 mL
½ cup	cold butter, cubed	125 mL
1	egg	1

Topping

4	eggs	4
1½ cups	granulated sugar	375 mL
1 cup	unsweetened shredded coconut	250 mL
2 tbsp	grated lemon zest	25 mL
½ cup	freshly squeezed lemon juice	125 mL
¼ cup	cornstarch	50 mL
1 tsp	GF baking powder	5 mL

1. *Prepare the base:* In a food processor fitted with a metal blade, pulse rice flour, cornstarch, tapioca starch, xanthan gum, brown sugar, salt and coconut. Add butter and pulse until mixture resembles small peas, about 5 to 10 seconds. With machine running, add egg through feed tube. Process until dough just forms a ball. Spread evenly in bottom of prepared pan. Using a moistened rubber or metal spatula, spread to edges and smooth top . Remoisten when dough begins to stick to spatula.
2. Bake in preheated oven for 12 to 15 minutes, or until set. Reduce oven temperature to 325°F (160°C).

Tips

Double the recipe and bake in a 13- by 9-inch (3 L) baking pan. Baking time may need to be increased by 5 to 10 minutes.

Cool squares completely before cutting. To prevent tearing, dip a sharp knife in hot water and wipe with a cloth after each cut.

Make ahead and freeze in an airtight container for up to 2 weeks.

3. *Meanwhile, prepare the topping:* In a bowl, using an electric mixer, beat together eggs, sugar, coconut, lemon zest, lemon juice, cornstarch and baking powder until blended. Pour over the hot base.

4. Bake for 40 to 45 minutes, or until lightly browned and firm to the touch. Let cool completely in the pan on a rack. Cut into squares.

Variation

To turn these into lemon squares, omit the coconut from both the base and the topping.

Cookies Through the Mail

Everyone appreciates receiving a "care package" from home. Here are some tips to help you get it there intact:

1. Select recipes for soft, chewy cookies: they are less likely to crumble. Those baked with sorghum flour travel better than those baked with rice flour.

2. Slice refrigerator cookie dough a bit thicker than usual to avoid breakage.

3. Squares are easier to pack than cookies.

4. Wrap cookies individually or in pairs, with two bottoms sandwiched together. Layer individual cookies in potato chip cylinders with a circle of waxed or parchment paper between them.

5. Place wrapped cookies into individual paper muffin liners. Choose colorful liners for holidays and special occasions.

6. Plan to mail parcels on the same day the cookies are baked.

7. Fill boxes to within 1 inch (2.5 cm) of the top and then add crumpled plastic wrap or bubble wrap to cushion the contents.

8. Pack cookies in several small boxes rather than one large one. Then place the smaller boxes inside a larger box and cushion them with Styrofoam packing peanuts. Seal tightly and mark "fragile."

Hazelnut Apricot Bars

<table>
<tr><td style="background:black;color:white">**Makes
2 dozen bars**</td></tr>
</table>

Imagine the flavors of sweet apricot and creamy white chocolate combined with crunchy hazelnuts — just don't count the calories!

Tips

For further instructions on melting chocolate, see Chocolate, page 368.

If hazelnut flour is not readily available in your area, see Nut Flour, page 370, for instructions to make your own.

- Preheat oven to 325°F (160°C)
- 9-inch (2.5 L) square pan, lightly greased

Base

¾ cup	brown rice flour	175 mL
⅓ cup	hazelnut flour	75 mL
¼ cup	tapioca starch	50 mL
1 tsp	xanthan gum	5 mL
½ cup	butter	125 mL
1 cup	white chocolate chips	250 mL
2	eggs	2
½ cup	granulated sugar	125 mL

Topping

¾ cup	apricot jam	175 mL
1 cup	white chocolate chips	250 mL
¼ cup	sliced hazelnuts	50 mL

1. *Base:* In a bowl or plastic bag, combine rice flour, hazelnut flour, tapioca starch and xanthan gum. Mix well and set aside.
2. In a small saucepan over low heat, melt butter and white chocolate chips, stirring constantly until melted. Set aside.
3. In a separate bowl, using an electric mixer, beat eggs and sugar until thick and creamy, about 5 minutes. Stir in melted chocolate mixture and dry ingredients. Mix well.
4. Spread half the batter in prepared pan with a moist rubber spatula. Set remaining batter aside. Bake base in preheated oven for 20 to 25 minutes or until lightly browned. Cool for 5 minutes.
5. *Topping:* Spread jam over base. Stir white chocolate chips into remaining batter. Drop by spoonfuls evenly over the jam. Spread out gently with moist rubber spatula. Sprinkle with hazelnuts. Bake for 30 to 40 minutes longer or until set. Cool completely, then cut into squares.

Variation

Substitute an equal amount of egg replacer for the xanthan gum. Add ¼ tsp (1 mL) salt.

Nutritional value per serving (1 bar)	
Calories	194
Fat, total	10 g
Fat, saturated	5 g
Cholesterol	22 mg
Sodium	57 mg
Carbohydrate	25 g
Fiber	1 g
Protein	2 g
Calcium	37 mg
Iron	0 mg

Nanaimo Bars

**Makes
3 dozen bars**

Named for the city on Vancouver Island in British Columbia, Canada, these no-bake squares are family favorites in our households.

Tips

A 1-oz (30 g) envelope of custard powder contains $1/4$ cup (50 mL).

One individually wrapped square of baking chocolate equals 1 oz (30 g).

- **9-inch (2.5 L) square pan, lightly greased**

Base

$1/3$ cup	butter, melted	75 mL
1	egg	1
1 tsp	vanilla extract	5 mL
$1/3$ cup	unsweetened cocoa powder	75 mL
2 tbsp	granulated sugar	25 mL
2 cups	hazelnut flour	500 mL
1 cup	unsweetened desiccated coconut	250 mL
$1/2$ cup	chopped walnuts	125 mL

Filling

$1/4$ cup	butter, softened	50 mL
3 tbsp	milk	45 mL
$1/4$ cup	GF custard powder (optional)	50 mL
2 cups	GF sifted confectioner's (icing) sugar	500 mL

Glaze

1 tsp	shortening	5 mL
1 to 2 oz	semi-sweet chocolate, cut into 6 pieces	30 to 60 g

1. *Base:* In a large bowl, blend together melted butter, egg and vanilla. Add cocoa, sugar, hazelnut flour, coconut and walnuts. Stir until combined. Spread evenly in prepared pan. Chill completely.

2. *Filling:* In a separate bowl, using an electric mixer, cream butter. Slowly add milk, custard powder, if using, and confectioner's sugar. Mix until combined. Spread over base and chill.

3. *Glaze:* In a small bowl, microwave shortening and chocolate on Medium for 1 to 2 minutes. Stir until completely melted. Drizzle in ribbons over chilled filling. Refrigerate before cutting into squares.

Variation

For a more traditional thick glaze, melt together 3 to 4 oz (90 to 125 g) semi-sweet chocolate and 1 tbsp (15 mL) butter.

Nutritional value per serving (1 bar)	
Calories	124
Fat, total	9 g
Fat, saturated	3 g
Cholesterol	9 mg
Sodium	32 mg
Carbohydrate	10 g
Fiber	1 g
Protein	2 g
Calcium	17 mg
Iron	1 mg

Pumpkin Date Bars

These quick and easy, lactose-free, moist bars are dotted with dates, nuts and a refreshing touch of orange. No need to frost; simply dust with GF confectioner's (icing) sugar, if desired.

Tips

Check for gluten-free confectioner's (icing) sugar. In Canada, it may contain up to 5% starch, which could be from wheat.

Store in an airtight container at room temperature for up to 5 days or freeze for up to 2 months.

Nutritional value per serving (1 bar)

Calories	80
Fat, total	3 g
Fat, saturated	0 g
Cholesterol	14 mg
Sodium	56 mg
Carbohydrate	11 g
Fiber	2 g
Protein	3 g
Calcium	38 mg
Iron	1 mg

- **9-inch (2.5 L) square baking pan, lined with foil, lightly greased**

¾ cup	soy flour	175 mL
½ cup	packed brown sugar	125 mL
1½ tsp	xanthan gum	7 mL
2 tsp	GF baking powder	10 mL
½ tsp	salt	2 mL
2 tbsp	grated orange zest	25 mL
½ tsp	ground cinnamon	2 mL
½ tsp	ground nutmeg	2 mL
2	eggs	2
½ cup	canned pumpkin purée (not pie filling)	125 mL
2 tbsp	vegetable oil	25 mL
¾ cup	chopped pitted dates	175 mL
½ cup	chopped walnuts	125 mL

1. In a large bowl or plastic bag, mix together soy flour, brown sugar, xanthan gum, baking powder, salt, orange zest, cinnamon and nutmeg. Set aside.

2. In another large bowl, using an electric mixer, beat eggs, pumpkin purée and oil until combined. Slowly beat in the dry ingredients and mix just until combined. Stir in dates and walnuts. Spoon into prepared pan. Using a moistened rubber spatula, spread to edges and smooth top. Let stand for 30 minutes. Meanwhile, preheat oven to 325°F (160°C).

3. Bake in preheated oven for 25 to 30 minutes, or until a cake tester inserted in the center comes out clean. Let cool completely in the pan on a rack. Cut into small bars.

Variations

Substitute an equal amount of dried cranberries for the walnuts.

For a stronger orange flavor, add ½ tsp (2 mL) orange extract.

Rich Cookie Dough

Want to make an assortment of cookies without making dozens of each kind? Start with this basic shortbread-style recipe, divide the dough into portions and make several varieties.

Tips

1 lb (500 g) of butter yields 2 cups (500 mL).

Set butter out on kitchen counter the night before you plan to make this cookie mix.

1 cup	amaranth flour	250 mL
1 cup	GF confectioner's (icing) sugar	250 mL
1⅓ cups	cornstarch	325 mL
4 tsp	xanthan gum	20 mL
1¼ tsp	salt	6 mL
2 cups	butter, softened	500 mL
½ cup	packed brown sugar	125 mL
2	eggs	2

1. In a large bowl or plastic bag, combine amaranth flour, confectioner's sugar, cornstarch, xanthan gum and salt. Set aside.
2. In another large bowl, using an electric mixer, beat butter, brown sugar and eggs just until smooth. Slowly beat in dry ingredients until combined, occasionally scraping the bottom and sides of bowl with a rubber spatula.
3. Divide dough into four portions. For each, select a variation from the recipes on pages 352 to 357.

Nutritional value per serving (1 cookie)	
Calories	55
Fat, total	4 g
Fat, saturated	2 g
Cholesterol	8 mg
Sodium	66 mg
Carbohydrate	5 g
Fiber	0 g
Protein	0 g
Calcium	3 mg
Iron	0 mg

Chocolate Chip Bars

Here's a flavor combination everyone with a sweet tooth will love: chocolate and hazelnuts!

Tips

If batter is slightly sticky, spread with a moistened spatula.

Substitute white chocolate chips or toffee bits for the chocolate chips and macadamia nuts for the hazelnuts.

- **Preheat oven to 350°F (180°C)**
- **8-inch (2 L) square baking pan, lightly greased**

¼ batch	Rich Cookie Dough (see recipe, page 351)	¼ batch
⅓ cup	sorghum flour	75 mL
⅓ cup	whole bean flour	75 mL
¾ cup	chocolate chips	175 mL
½ cup	chopped hazelnuts	125 mL
1 tsp	almond extract	5 mL

1. In a medium bowl, combine Rich Cookie Dough, sorghum flour, bean flour, chocolate chips, hazelnuts and almond extract. Mix well. Press into prepared pan.
2. Bake in preheated oven for 25 to 30 minutes, or until lightly browned. Transfer to a rack. Let cool completely before cutting into bars.

Nutritional value per serving (1 bar)	
Calories	126
Fat, total	8 g
Fat, saturated	3 g
Cholesterol	8 mg
Sodium	66 mg
Carbohydrate	13 g
Fiber	1 g
Protein	2 g
Calcium	8 mg
Iron	0 mg

Crunchy Mocha Cookies

	Makes
	2 dozen cookies

You may think these look like peanut butter cookies, but wait till you taste them!

Tips

The thinner you press the cookies, the crunchier they are when baked.

For a softer cookie, substitute granulated sugar for the brown.

Substitute an equal amount of yellow pea flour for the whole bean flour.

- **Preheat oven to 350°F (180°C)**
- **Baking sheet, lightly greased**

1/3 cup	whole bean flour	75 mL
1/4 cup	sorghum flour	50 mL
1/4 cup	packed brown sugar	50 mL
2 tbsp	unsweetened cocoa powder	25 mL
2 tsp	instant coffee granules	10 mL
1/4 batch	Rich Cookie Dough (see recipe, page 351)	1/4 batch
	Sweet rice flour	

1. In a medium bowl, sift together whole bean flour, sorghum flour, brown sugar, cocoa powder and coffee granules. Add Rich Cookie Dough and combine with a wooden spoon until blended. Roll into 1-inch (2.5 cm) balls. Place 1 1/2 inches (4 cm) apart on prepared baking sheet. Flatten slightly with a fork dipped in sweet rice flour.

2. Bake in preheated oven for 12 to 15 minutes, or until puffed and firm around the edges. Immediately transfer to a rack and let cool completely.

Variations

For coffee-flavored cookies, omit the cocoa.

Roll 1-inch (2.5 cm) balls in finely chopped nuts of your choice.

Nutritional value per serving (1 cookie)	
Calories	79
Fat, total	4 g
Fat, saturated	2 g
Cholesterol	8 mg
Sodium	67 mg
Carbohydrate	10 g
Fiber	1 g
Protein	1 g
Calcium	7 mg
Iron	0 mg

Lemon Hazelnut Snowballs

White as snowballs, melt-in-your-mouth goodness!

Tips

If batter is slightly sticky, dust your hands with GF confectioner's (icing) sugar or sweet rice flour before shaping each cookie.

Layer cookies between waxed paper in an airtight container and store at room temperature for up to 1 week or freeze for up to 2 months.

When entertaining, set each cookie in a decorative miniature paper liner.

- **Preheat oven to 350°F (180°C)**
- **Baking sheet, lightly greased**

¼ batch	Rich Cookie Dough (see recipe, page 351)	¼ batch
1/2 cup	hazelnut flour	125 mL
¼ cup	amaranth flour	50 mL
1/2 cup	chopped hazelnuts	125 mL
2 tbsp	grated lemon zest	25 mL
	GF confectioner's (icing) sugar	

1. In a medium bowl, combine Rich Cookie Dough, hazelnut flour, amaranth flour, hazelnuts and lemon zest. Gather the dough into a ball, kneading in any dry ingredients. Roll into 1-inch (2.5 cm) balls. Place 1 inch (2.5 cm) apart on prepared baking sheet.

2. Bake in preheated oven for 12 to 15 minutes, or until lightly browned. Transfer to a rack. Let cool for 5 minutes.

3. Sift confectioner's sugar into a small bowl and roll balls in confectioner's sugar. Return to rack and let cool completely. If desired, roll in confectioner's sugar a second time.

Variation

Choose any other cookie shape from this section.

Nutritional value per serving (1 cookie)	
Calories	89
Fat, total	7 g
Fat, saturated	2 g
Cholesterol	8 mg
Sodium	67 mg
Carbohydrate	7 g
Fiber	1 g
Protein	1 g
Calcium	13 mg
Iron	0 mg

Lemon Poppy Drops

Our friend Tom insisted we include his favorite cookie — a lemon poppy seed recipe.

Tips

You can keep extra freshly squeezed lemon juice and freshly grated lemon zest in the freezer for up to 6 months.

Substitute orange zest and juice for the lemon.

- **Preheat oven to 350°F (180°C)**
- **Baking sheet, lightly greased**

¼ batch	Rich Cookie Dough (see recipe, page 351)	¼ batch
½ cup	amaranth flour	125 mL
2 tbsp	poppy seeds	25 mL
2 tbsp	grated lemon zest	25 mL
2 tbsp	freshly squeezed lemon juice	25 mL

1. In a medium bowl, combine Rich Cookie Dough, amaranth flour, poppy seeds, lemon zest and juice. Drop by heaping tablespoonfuls (15 mL) $1\frac{1}{2}$ inches (4 cm) apart on prepared baking sheet.

2. Bake in preheated oven for 12 to 15 minutes, or until lightly browned. Immediately transfer to a rack and let cool completely.

Nutritional value per serving (1 cookie)	
Calories	126
Fat, total	8 g
Fat, saturated	3 g
Cholesterol	11 mg
Sodium	71 mg
Carbohydrate	13 g
Fiber	1 g
Protein	2 g
Calcium	7 mg
Iron	0 mg

Orange Pecan Crescents

Makes 2 dozen cookies		

When dipped in chocolate, these shortbread-like crescents will be the first to disappear.

Tips

If pecan flour is not readily available in your area, see Techniques Glossary, page 370, under Nut flour, for instructions on making your own.

If batter is slightly sticky, dust your hands with GF confectioner's (icing) sugar or sweet rice flour before shaping each cookie.

- **Preheat oven to 350°F (180°C)**
- **Baking sheet, lightly greased**

¼ batch	Rich Cookie Dough (see recipe, page 351)	¼ batch
⅓ cup	pecan flour	75 mL
¼ cup	amaranth flour	50 mL
½ cup	chopped pecans	125 mL
2 tbsp	grated orange zest	25 mL

1. In a medium bowl, combine Rich Cookie Dough, pecan flour, amaranth flour, pecans and orange zest. Gather the dough into a ball, kneading in any dry ingredients. Shape into logs 2½ inches (6 cm) long and ½ inch (1 cm) thick, then bend into crescents. Place crescents 1 inch (2.5 cm) apart on prepared baking sheet.

2. Bake in preheated oven for 12 to 15 minutes, or until lightly browned. Transfer to a rack and let cool completely.

Variations

Dip one end of completely cooled cookies in melted chocolate. See Techniques Glossary, page 368, for instructions on melting chocolate.

Add ½ cup (125 mL) dried cranberries to the dough.

While still hot from the oven, roll cookies in GF confectioner's (icing) sugar.

Nutritional value per serving (1 cookie)	
Calories	85
Fat, total	6 g
Fat, saturated	2 g
Cholesterol	8 mg
Sodium	67 mg
Carbohydrate	7 g
Fiber	1 g
Protein	1 g
Calcium	11 mg
Iron	0 mg

Parmesan Rosemary Slices

A savory cracker to go on a cheese and cracker platter.

Tips

Logs can be frozen in an airtight container for up to 1 month. To bake, thaw slightly and cut into slices $1/3$ inch (0.7 cm) thick. Bake for 10 to 12 minutes.

Store baked slices in an airtight container at room temperature for up to 5 days or freeze for up to 2 months.

- **Preheat oven to 350°F (180°C)**
- **Baking sheet, lightly greased**

$1/4$ batch	Rich Cookie Dough (see recipe, page 351)	$1/4$ batch
$1/3$ cup	soy flour	75 mL
$1/3$ cup	freshly grated Parmesan cheese	75 mL
2 tbsp	chopped fresh rosemary	25 mL

1. In a medium bowl, combine Rich Cookie Dough, soy flour, Parmesan and rosemary. Form into a log $1^{1}/_2$ inches (4 cm) in diameter. Wrap in plastic wrap and refrigerate for at least 2 hours, until firm, or for up to 3 days (or freeze for up to 3 weeks).

2. Let stand at room temperature for 20 minutes. Cut log into slices $1/3$ inch (0.7 cm) thick. Place $1^{1}/_2$ inches (4 cm) apart on prepared baking sheet.

3. Bake in preheated oven for 10 to 12 minutes, or until lightly browned. Immediately transfer to a rack and let cool completely.

Variation

Substitute grated Romano or Asiago cheese for the Parmesan.

Nutritional value per serving (1 slice)	
Calories	68
Fat, total	5 g
Fat, saturated	2 g
Cholesterol	10 mg
Sodium	94 mg
Carbohydrate	5 g
Fiber	1 g
Protein	2 g
Calcium	27 mg
Iron	0 mg

Thickener Substitutions

Starches	To thicken 1 cup (250 mL) of liquid	Cooking precautions	Cooked appearance	Tips
Arrowroot	2 tbsp (25 mL)	• add during last 5 minutes of cooking • stir only occasionally • do not boil	• clear shine • glossier than cornstarch	• thickens at a lower temperature than cornstarch • not as firm as cornstarch when cool • doesn't break down as quickly as cornstarch • more expensive • separates when frozen
Cornstarch	2 tbsp (25 mL)	• stir constantly • boil gently for only 1 to 3 minutes	• translucent and shiny	• thickens as it cools • boiling too rapidly causes thinning • boiling for more than 7 minutes causes thinning • add acid (lemon juice) after removing from heat
Potato starch	1 tbsp (15 mL)	• stir constantly	• more translucent and clearer than cornstarch	• lumps easily • thickest at boiling point • thickens as it cools • separates when frozen
Tapioca starch (cassava)	3 tbsp (45 mL)	• add during last 5 minutes of cooking • stir constantly	• transparent and shiny	• dissolves more easily than cornstarch • firms more as it cools • best to use for freezing

Flours	To thicken 1 cup (250 mL) of liquid	Cooking precautions	Cooked appearance	Tips
Amaranth flour	3 tbsp (45 mL)	• browns quickly and could burn if not watched carefully • thickens at boiling point and slightly more after 5 to 7 minutes of boiling • reheats in microwave	• golden brown color • cloudy, opaque • smooth	• nutty, beefy aroma • if too thick, can be thinned with extra liquid • reheats • excellent for gravy
Bean flour	3 tbsp (45 mL)	• thickens after 2 to 3 minutes of boiling • does not thicken with extra cooking	• warm tan color • cloudy, opaque • smooth	• can be used for sauces • brown in hot fat to a golden color
Rice flour (brown)	2 tbsp (25 mL)	• dissolve in cold liquid rather than hot fat or pan drippings • thickens after 5 to 7 minutes of boiling • continues to thicken with extra cooking	• opaque, cloudy • grainy texture • bland flavor	• thickens more as it cools • thickens rapidly when reheated and stirred • stable when frozen
Sorghum flour	2 tbsp (25 mL)	• thickens after 2 to 3 minutes of boiling • does not thicken with extra cooking	• dull • similar to wheat flour	• doesn't thin or thicken with excess cooking • thickens as it cools • reheats well on stove-top or microwave • thickens quickly when extra is added
Sweet rice flour	2 tbsp (25 mL)	• thickens after 5 to 8 minutes of boiling	• shiny, opaque • grainy texture • bland flavor	• thickens

Equipment Glossary

Baking liners. Reusable sheets of nonstick coated fiberglass. Flexible and food-safe, they are used to eliminate the pand dry before storing.

Bundt pan. A tube pan with fluted sides.

Cake tester. A thin, long wooden or metal stick or wire attached to a handle that is used for baked products to test for doneness.

Cooling rack. Parallel and perpendicular thin bars of metal at right angles, with feet attached, used to hold hot baking off the surface to allow cooling air to circulate.

Cornbread pan. A cast-iron corn-shaped pan with detailed construction that shows the kernels and ridges of seven ears of corn. The pan, which measures 11- by $5^1/_2$-inches (28 by 14 cm), can be used to make hot dog buns, cornbread buns or dinner rolls.

Crêpe pan. Smooth, low, round pan with a heavy bottom and sloping sides. It ranges from 5 to 7 inches (13 to 18 cm) in diameter.

Dutch oven. A large deep pot with a tight-fitting lid, used for stewing or braising.

English muffin rings. Available in sets of four or eight $3^3/_4$ inch (8 cm) round, 1 inch (2.5 cm) high, these rings hold batter in place as it bakes.

Griddle. Flat metal surface on which food is cooked. Can be built into a stove or stand-alone.

Grill. Heavy rack set over a heat source used to cook food, usually on a propane, natural gas or charcoal barbecue.

Hamburger bun baking pan. A baking pan that makes six 4-inch (10 cm) hamburger buns.

Hot dog bun baking pan. A baking pan that makes eight 6- by 2-inch (15 by 5 cm) buns to use for hot dogs or mini-submarine sandwiches.

Jelly-roll pan. A rectangular baking pan, 15 by 10 by 1 inch (40 by 25 by 2.5 cm), used for baking thin cakes.

Loaf pan. Metal container used for baking loaves. Common pan sizes are 9 by 5 inches (2 L) and 8 by 4 inches (1.5 L). Danish loaf pans measure 12 by 4 by $2^1/_2$ inches (30 by 10 by 6 cm).

Mandoline. A manually operated slicer with adjustable blades. The food is held at a 45-degree angle and is passed and pressed against the blade to produce uniform pieces of different thickness, either straight-cut or rippled.

Parchment paper. Heat-resistant paper similar to waxed paper, usually coated with silicon on one side; used with or as an alternative to other methods (such as applying vegetable oil or spray) to prevent baked goods from sticking to the baking pan. Sometimes labeled "baking paper."

Pastry blender. Used to cut solid fat into flour, it consists of five metal blades or wires held together by a handle.

Pastry brush. Small brush with nylon or natural bristles used to apply glazes or egg washes to dough. Wash thoroughly after each use. To store, lay flat or hang on a hook through a hole in the handle.

Pizza wheel. A large, sharp-edged wheel (without serrations) anchored to a handle.

Ramekins. Usually sold as a set of small, deep, straight-sided ceramic soufflé dishes also known mini-bakers. Used to bake individual servings of a pudding, cobbler or custard. Capacity ranges from 4 oz or $1/_2$ cup (125 mL) to 8 oz. or 1 cup (250 mL).

Rolling pin. A heavy, smooth cylinder of wood, marble, plastic or metal; used to roll out dough.

Scone pan. A $9^5/_8$- by 1-inch (22 by 2.5 cm) round metal baking pan portioned into eight sections; used to make scones by spooning in a drop batter.

Skewer. A long, thin stick (made of wood or metal) used in baking to test for doneness.

Spatula. A utensil with a handle and blade that can be long or short, narrow or wide, flexible or inflexible. It is used to spread, lift, turn, mix or smooth foods. Spatulas are made of metal, rubber or plastic.

Springform pan. A circular baking pan, available in a range of sizes, with a separable bottom and side. The side is removed by releasing a clamp, making the contents easy to remove.

Thermometers.

• *Instant-read thermometer.* Bakers use this metal-stemmed instrument to test the internal temperature of baked products such as cakes and breads. Stem must be inserted at least 2 inches (5 cm) into the food for an accurate reading. When yeast bread is baked, it should register 200°F (100°C).

• *Meat thermometer.* Used to read internal temperature of meat. Temperatures range from 120°F to 200°F (60°C to 100°C). Before placing meat in the oven, insert the thermometer into the thickest part, avoiding the bone and gristle. (If using an instant-read thermometer, remove meat from oven and test with thermometer. For more information, see Digital instant-read thermometer in Techniques Glossary, page 369.)

• *Oven thermometer.* Used to measure temperatures from 200°F to 500°F (100°C to 260°C). It either stands on or hangs from an oven rack.

Tube pan. A deep round pan with a hollow tube in the center, usually 10 inches (25 cm) in diameter, 16 cups (4 L) volume.

Zester. A tool used to cut very thin strips of outer peel from citrus fruits. It has a short, flat blade tipped with five small holes with sharp edges. Another style of zester that is popular is made of stainless steel and looks like a tool found in a workshop used for planing wood.

Ingredient Glossary

Almond. Crack open the shell of an almond, and you will find an ivory-colored nut encased in a thin brown skin. With the skin removed (see Techniques Glossary, page 368), the almond is called blanched. In this form, almonds are sold whole, sliced, slivered and ground. Two cups (500 mL) almonds weigh about 12 oz (375 g).

Almond flour (almond meal). See Nut flour in The Gluten-Free Pantry, page 13. For instructions on how to make, see Nut flour in Techniques Glossary, page 370.

Almond paste. Made of ground blanched almonds, sugar and egg whites, almond paste is coarser, darker and less sweet then marzipan. Do not substitute one for the other.

Amaranth flour. See The Gluten-Free Pantry, page 12.

Anise seeds. These tiny gray-green, egg-shaped seeds have a distinctive licorice flavor. Anise can be purchased as a finely ground powder. For recipes that call for anise seeds, half the amount of anise powder can be substituted.

Arborio rice. Oval Italian short-grain rice with a distinct nutty flavor and a hard core. It has the ability to absorb large quantities of liquid, and becomes creamy when cooked. Traditionally, it is used for risotto, and we like it for rice pudding.

Arrowroot. Referred to as a starch, as a flour and as arrowroot starch flour. (See also The Gluten-Free Pantry, page 12.)

Asiago cheese. A pungent grayish-white hard cheese from northern Italy. Cured for more than 6 months, its texture is ideal for grating.

Baking chips. Similar in consistency to chocolate chips, but with different flavors such as butterscotch, peanut butter, cinnamon and lemon. Check to make sure they are gluten-free.

Baking powder. Select gluten-free baking powder. A chemical leavener, containing an alkali (baking soda) and an acid (cream of tartar), that gives off carbon dioxide gas under certain conditions.

Baking soda (sodium bicarbonate). A chemical leavener that gives off carbon dioxide gas in the presence of moisture — particularly acids such as lemon juice, buttermilk and sour cream. It is also one of the components of baking powder.

Bean flour. See The Gluten-Free Pantry, page 12.

Bell peppers. The sweet-flavored members of the capsicum family (which include chilies and other hot peppers), these peppers have a hollow interior lined with white ribs and seeds attached at the stem end. They are most commonly green, red or yellow, but can also be white or purple.

Bird's eye chili peppers. Small, very hot chilis that are highly pungent. Use them to add "pure heat" to a meal without very much of the chili favor coming through. The heat level is 9 on a scale of 1 to 10.

Black bean flour. A high-fiber gluten-free flour used mainly in Tex-Mex dishes.

Blueberries. Wild low-bush berries are smaller than the cultivated variety and more time-consuming to pick, but their flavor makes every minute of picking time worthwhile. Readily available year-round in the frozen fruit section of many grocery stores.

Brown rice flour. See Rice flour in The Gluten-Free Pantry, page 14.

Brown sugar. A refined sugar with a coating of molasses. It can be purchased coarse or fine and comes in three varieties: dark, golden and light.

Buckwheat. Also known as saracen corn. Not related, despite its name, to wheat (which is a grain), buckwheat is the seed of a plant from the rhubarb family. Buckwheat flour is dark with a strong pungent flavor and is gluten-free. Buckwheat groats are the hulled seeds of the buckwheat plant. These seeds are soft and white with a mild flavor; when roasted or toasted, the flavor intensifies. Roasted whole buckwheat, called kasha, has a strong nutty flavor and chewy texture. It is low in fat and cholesterol-free.

Buckwheat flakes (oatmeal style). These small brittle flakes have the appearance of small rolled oats with a slightly sweeter flavor and a slightly browner color; they can replace oatmeal in crisps, meatloaves and squares.

Butter. A spread produced from dairy fat and milk solids, butter is interchangeable with shortening, oil or margarine in most recipes.

Buttermilk. Named for the way in which it was originally produced — that is, from milk left in the churn after the solid butter was removed — buttermilk is now made with fresh, pasteurized milk that has been cultured (or soured) with the addition of a bacterial culture. The result is a slightly thickened dairy beverage with a salty, sour flavor similar to yogurt. Despite its name, buttermilk is low in fat.

Caraway seeds. These small, crescent-shaped seeds of the caraway plant have a nutty, peppery, licorice-like flavor.

Cardamom. This popular spice is a member of the ginger family. A long green or brown pod contains the strong, spicy, lemon-flavored seed. Although native to India, cardamom is used in Middle Eastern, Indian and Scandinavian cooking — in the latter case, particularly for seasonal baked goods.

Cassava. See Tapioca starch in The Gluten-Free Pantry, page 15.

Castor or caster sugar. A finely granulated sugar, used in beverages and frostings, that dissolves rapidly due to its smaller crystal size. It is also known as berry or superfine sugar. Regular granulated sugar may be substituted on a one-to-one basis.

Cheddar cheese. Always select an aged, or old, good-quality Cheddar for baking recipes. (The flavor of mild or medium Cheddar is not strong enough for baking.) Weight/volume equivalents are:

4 oz (125 g) = 1 cup (250 mL) grated;
2 oz (60 g) = $1/2$ cup (125 mL) grated;
$1^1/_2$ oz (45 g) = $1/3$ cup (75 mL) grated.

Coconut. The fruit of a tropical palm tree, with a hard woody shell that is lined with a hard white flesh. There are three dried forms available, which can be sweetened or not: flaked, shredded and the smallest, desiccated (thoroughly dried).

Corn flour. A flour that can be milled from the entire kernel of corn. Corn flour and cornstarch are not interchangeable in recipes. Freeze corn flour to prevent molds from developing.

Cornmeal. The dried ground kernels of white, yellow or blue corn. It has a gritty texture and is available in coarse, medium and fine grind. It is the coarser grind of corn flour and cornstarch. Check labels of commercial products for addition of wheat. Maizemeal can be corn or wheat. Its starchy-sweet flavor is most commonly associated with cornbread — a regional specialty of the southern United States.

Cornstarch. See The Gluten-Free Pantry, page 13.

Corn syrup. A thick, sweet syrup made from cornstarch, sold in clear (light) or brown (dark or golden) varieties. The latter has caramel flavor and color added.

Cranberry. Grown in bogs on low vines, these sweet-tart berries are available fresh, frozen and dried. Fresh cranberries are available only in season — typically from mid-October until January, depending on your location — but can be frozen right in the bag. Substitute dried cranberries for sour cherries, raisins or currants.

Cream of tartar. Used to give volume and stability to beaten egg whites, cream of tartar is also an acidic component of baking powder. Tartaric acid is a fine white crystalline powder that forms naturally during the fermentation of grape juice on the inside of wine barrels.

Cross-contamination. The process by which one product comes in contact with another one that is to be avoided. For example, toasters, oven mitts, cutting boards and knives, when used for products containing gluten, still have gluten on them, which is passed on to the gluten-free product. You must either have separate tools or be sure that the gluten is washed off completely before being used by people with gluten sensitivity.

Currants. Similar in appearance to small dark raisins, currants are made by drying a special seedless variety of grape. Not the same as a type of berry that goes by the same name.

Dates. The fruit of the date palm tree, dates are long and oval in shape, with a paper-thin skin that turns from green to dark brown when ripe. Eaten fresh or dried, dates have a very sweet, light brown flesh around a long, narrow seed.

Eggplant. Ranging in color and shape from dark purple and pear-like to light mauve and cylindrical, eggplant has a light, spongy flesh that, while bland on its own, is remarkable for its ability to absorb other flavors in cooking.

Eggs. Liquid egg products, such as Naturegg Simply Whites®, Break Free® and Omega Pro® liquid eggs and Just Whites®, are available in Canada and the United States. Powdered egg whites such as Just Whites® can be used by reconstituting with warm water or as a powder. A similar product is called meringue powder in Canada. Substitute 2 tbsp (25 mL) liquid egg product for each white of a large egg.

Egg replacer. A powder used in place of eggs that acts as a leavening agent. Reconstitute according to package instructions.

Egg substitute. A liquid made from egg whites, or dried egg whites reconstituted according to package instructions.

Evaporated milk. A milk product with 60% of the water removed. It is sterilized and canned, which gives it a cooked taste and darker color.

Fava bean flour. See Bean flour in The Gluten-Free Pantry, page 12.

Feta cheese. A crumbly white Greek-style cheese with a salty, tangy flavor. Store in the refrigerator, in its brine, and drain well before using. Traditionally made with sheep's or goat's milk in Greece and usually with cow's milk in Canada and the U.S.

Fig. A pear-shaped fruit with a thick, soft skin, available in green and purple. Eaten fresh or dried, the tan-colored sweet flesh contains many tiny edible seeds.

Filbert. See Hazelnut.

Flaxseed. Thin and oval, dark brown in color, flaxseed adds a crunchy texture to baked products. Research indicates that flaxseed can aid in lowering blood cholesterol levels. Ground flaxseed (also known as linseed) stales quickly. It acts as a tenderizer for yeast breads. It can be used with or without eggs and adds omega-3 fatty acids and fiber. Flaxseed should be cracked or ground to be digested. Whole flaxseed can be stored at room temperature for up to 1 year. Ground flaxseed can be stored in the refrigerator for up to 90 days, although for optimum freshness it is best to grind it as you need it.

Garbanzo bean flour. See Bean flour in The Gluten-Free Pantry, page 12.

Garbanzo-fava flour. See Bean flour in The Gluten-Free Pantry, page 12.

Garfava flour. See Bean flour in The Gluten-Free Pantry, page 12.

Garlic. An edible bulb composed of several sections (cloves), each covered with a papery skin. An essential ingredient in many styles of cooking.

Ginger. A bumpy rhizome, ivory to greenish-yellow in color, with a tan skin. Fresh gingerroot has a peppery, slightly sweet flavor, similar to lemon and rosemary, and a pungent aroma. Ground ginger is made from dried gingerroot. It is spicier and not as sweet or as fresh. Crystallized or candied ginger is made from pieces of fresh gingerroot that have been cooked in sugar syrup and coated with sugar.

Gluten. A natural protein in wheat flour that becomes elastic with the addition of moisture and kneading. Gluten traps gases produced by leaveners inside the dough and causes it to rise.

Glutinous rice flour. See Rice flour in The Gluten-Free Pantry, page 14.

Golden raisins. See Raisins.

Granulated sugar. A refined, crystalline white form of sugar that is also commonly referred to as "table sugar" or just "sugar."

Guar gum. A white flour-like substance made from an East Indian seed high in fiber, this vegetable substance contains no gluten. It may have a laxative effect for some people. It can be substituted for xanthan gum.

Half-and-half cream. The lightest of all creams, it is half milk, half cream and has a butterfat content between 10% and 18%. It can't be whipped, but is used with coffee or on cereal. To substitute, use equal parts cream and milk or evaporated milk or $7/8$ cup (210 mL) milk plus $1^1/_2$ tbsp (22 mL) butter or margarine.

Hazelnut. Also known as filberts, hazelnuts have a rich, sweet flavor that complements ingredients such as coffee and chocolate. Remove the bitter brown skin before using.

Hazelnut flour (Hazelnut meal). See Nut flour in The Gluten-Free Pantry, page 13. For instructions on how to make, see Nut flour in Techniques Glossary, page 370.

Hazelnut liqueur. The best known is Frangelico, a hazelnut-flavored liqueur made in Italy.

Hemp hearts®. Shelled hemp seeds. Due to their high fat content, hemp hearts should be purchased in small amounts and stored in the refrigerator (can be stored for up to 90 days). Can be eaten raw or added to baking.

Herbs. See also individual herbs. Plants whose stems, leaves or flowers are used as a flavoring, either dried or fresh. To substitute fresh herbs for dried, a good rule of thumb is to use three times the amount of fresh as dried. Taste and adjust the amount to suit your preference.

Honey. Sweeter than sugar, honey is available in liquid, honeycomb and creamed varieties. Use liquid honey for baking.

Kalamata olives. See Olives (Kalamata).

Kasha. See Buckwheat.

Linseed. See Flaxseed.

Maple syrup. A very sweet, slightly thick brown liquid made by boiling the sap from North American maple trees. Use pure maple syrup, not pancake syrup, in baking.

Margarine. A solid fat derived from one or more types of vegetable oil. Do not use lower-fat margarines in baking, as they contain too much added water.

Marzipan. A sweet nut paste made from ground almonds, sugar and egg whites. Used as candy filling and for cake decorations, it is sweeter and lighter in color than almond paste. Do not substitute one for the other.

Mesclun. A mixture of small, young, tender salad greens such as spinach, frisée, arugula, oak leaf and radicchio. Also known as salad mix, spring mix or baby greens and sold prepackaged or in bulk in the grocery produce section.

Millet. The small seed of a cereal grass or grain closely related to corn. With a nutty aroma and taste, it is an excellent source of fiber and a moderate source of protein.

Molasses. A byproduct of refining sugar, molasses is a sweet, thick, dark brown (almost black) liquid. It has a distinctive, slightly bitter flavor and is available in fancy and blackstrap varieties. Use the fancy variety for baking unless blackstrap is specified. Store in the refrigerator if used infrequently.

Nonfat dry milk. See Skim milk powder.

Nut flour (Nut meal). A flour made by finely grinding nuts such as Almond flour, Hazelnut flour or Pecan Flour. To make, see Techniques Glossary, page 370. See also The Gluten-Free Pantry, page 13.

Oats (Gluten-free). Purchase pure, uncontaminated gluten-free oats.

Olives (Kalamata). A large, flavorful variety of Greek olive, typically dark purple in color and pointed at one end.

They are usually sold packed in olive oil or vinegar.

Olive oil. Produced from pressing tree-ripened olives. Extra-virgin oil is taken from the first cold pressing; it is the finest and fruitiest, pale straw to pale green in color, with the least amount of acid, usually less than 1%. Virgin oil is taken from a subsequent pressing; it contains 2% acid and is pale yellow. Light oil comes from the last pressing; it has a mild flavor, light color and up to 3% acid. It also has a higher smoke point. Product sold as "pure olive oil" has been cleaned and filtered; it is very mild-flavored and has up to 3% acid.

Parsley. A biennial herb with dark green curly or flat leaves used fresh as a flavoring or garnish. It is also used dried in soups and other mixes. Substitute parsley for half the amount of a strong-flavored herb such as basil.

Pea flour. See The Gluten-Free Pantry, page 12.

Pecan. The nut of the hickory tree, pecans have a reddish-mahogany shell and beige flesh. They have a high fat content and are a milder-flavored alternative to walnuts.

Pecan flour (pecan meal). See Nut flour in The Gluten-Free Pantry, page 13. For instructions on how to make, see Nut flour in Techniques Glossary, page 370.

Pistachio nut. Inside a hard, tan-colored shell, this pale green nut has a waxy texture and a mild flavor.

Poppy seeds. The tiny round blue-gray seed of the poppy has a sweet, nutty flavor. Often used as a garnish or as a topping for a variety of breads.

Potato flour. See Potato starch in The Gluten-Free Pantry, page 13.

Potato starch (potato starch flour). See The Gluten-Free Pantry, page 13.

Pumpkin seeds. Hulled and roasted green pumpkin seeds have a nutty flavor that enhances many breads. In Mexico, where they are eaten as a snack and used as a thickener in cooking, they are also known as pepitas.

Quinoa. It is the most nutritious grain available, high in protein, calcium and iron content. The small seeds like millet and are naturally coated with a bitter tasting saporin to protect it from birds and insects.

Quinoa flour. See The Gluten-Free Pantry, page 13.

Raisins. Dark raisins are sun-dried Thompson seedless grapes. Golden raisins are treated with sulphur dioxide and dried artificially, yielding a moister, plumper product. Muscat, a grape grown throughout the Mediterranean region, Australia and California, is used for eating and making raisins and wine. Both Muscat and Lexia are large, flat seeded raisins.

Rhubarb. A perennial plant with long, thin red- to pink-colored stalks resembling celery and large green leaves. Only the tart-flavored stalks are used for cooking, as the leaves are poisonous. For 2 cups (500 mL) cooked rhubarb, you will need 3 cups (750 mL) chopped fresh, about 1 lb (500 g).

Rice bran. See The Gluten-Free Pantry, page 14.

Rice flour. See The Gluten-Free Pantry, page 14.

Rice polish. See The Gluten-Free Pantry, page 14.

Sambal oelek (Thai chili paste). An Indonesian flavoring paste made from ground bird's eye chilis, salt, oil and vinegar. Popular in Indonesian/Asian cuisines.

Sesame seeds. Small, flat, oval seeds that have a rich, nut-like flavor when roasted. Purchase the tan (hulled), not black (unhulled), variety for use in baking.

Shortening. A partially hydrogenated, solid, white flavorless fat made from vegetable sources.

Skim milk powder. The dehydrated form of fluid skim milk. Use 1/4 cup

(50 mL) skim milk powder for every 1 cup (250 mL) water.

Sorghum flour. See The Gluten-Free Pantry, page 14.

Sour cream. A thick, smooth, tangy product made by adding bacterial cultures to pasteurized, homogenized cream containing varying amounts of butterfat. Check the label: some lower-fat and fat-free brands may contain gluten.

Soy flour. See The Gluten-Free Pantry, page 14.

Starch. Starch is found in the cells of plants and is insoluble in cold water. When cooked, the granules swell and thicken or gel.

Sugar substitute. For baking, the best choice is sucralose, which is made from processed sugar and remains stable at any temperature.

Sun-dried tomatoes. Available either dry or packed in oil, sun-dried tomatoes have a dark red color, a soft chewy texture and a strong tomato flavor. Use dry, not oil-packed, sun-dried tomatoes in recipes. Use scissors to snip.

Sunflower seeds. Use shelled, unsalted, unroasted sunflower seeds in bread recipes. If only roasted salted seeds are available, rinse under hot water and dry well before using.

Sweet peppers. See Bell peppers.

Sweet potato. A tuber with orange flesh that stays moist when cooked. Not the same as a yam, although yams can substitute for sweet potatoes in recipes.

Sweet rice flour. See Rice flour in The Gluten-Free Pantry, page 14.

Tapioca starch (tapioca flour). See The Gluten-Free Pantry, page 15.

Tarragon. An herb with narrow, pointed, dark green leaves and a distinctive anise-like flavor with undertones of sage. Use fresh or dried.

Vegetable oil. Common oils used are corn, sunflower, safflower, olive, canola, peanut and soy.

Walnuts. A sweet-fleshed nut with a large wrinkled shell.

Wild rice. In its natural state, wild rice is gluten-free, but when found in boxed wild rice/white rice mixes, it's best avoided. For instructions on how to cook, see Techniques Glossary, page 371.

Xanthan gum. A natural carbohydrate made from a microscopic organism called Xanthomonas campestris, this gum is produced from the fermentation of glucose. It is used to add volume and viscosity to baked goods. As an ingredient in gluten-free baking, it gives the dough strength, allowing it to rise and preventing it from being too dense in texture. It does not mix with water, so must be combined with dry ingredients. Purchase from bulk or health food stores. An equal amount of guar gum can be substituted for xanthan gum.

Yeast. A tiny single-celled organism that, given moisture, food and warmth, creates gas that is trapped in bread dough, causing it to rise. Bread machine yeast (instant yeast) is added directly to the dry ingredients of bread. We use this yeast rather than active dry as it does not need to be activated in water before using. Store in the freezer in an airtight container for up to 2 years.

Yogurt. Made by fermenting cow's milk using a bacteria culture. Plain yogurt is gluten-free, but not all flavored yogurt is.

Zest. Strips from the outer layer of rind (colored part only) of citrus fruit. Avoid the bitter part underneath. Used for its intense flavor.

Techniques Glossary

Almonds. *To blanch:* Cover almonds with boiling water and let stand, covered, for 3 to 5 minutes. Drain. Grasp the almond at one end, pressing between your thumb and index finger, and the nut will pop out of the skin. Nuts are more easily chopped or slivered while still warm from blanching. *To toast:* see Nuts.

Almond flour (almond meal). *To make:* See Nut flour.

Baking pan. *To prepare or to grease:* Either spray the bottom and sides of the baking pan with nonstick cooking spray or brush with a pastry brush or a crumpled-up piece of waxed paper dipped in vegetable oil or shortening.

Bananas. *To mash and freeze:* Select overripe fruit, mash and package in 1 cup (250 mL) amounts in freezer containers. Freeze for up to 6 months. Defrost and warm to room temperature before using. About 2 to 3 medium bananas yield 1 cup (250 mL) mashed.

Barbecue by indirect method. To cook with the heat source coming from one or both sides of the food and not from directly beneath it.

Beat. To stir vigorously to incorporate air using a spoon, whisk, handheld beater or electric mixer.

Black beans. *To cook:* For every 1 cup (250 mL) dried black beans, cover with 3 cups (750 mL) cold water. Bring to a boil for 2 minutes; cover and let stand for 1 hour. Drain. Add 6 cups (1.5 L) cold water and boil uncovered until tender, approximately 1 hour.

Blanch. To completely immerse food in boiling water and then quickly in cold water.

Blend. To mix two or more ingredients together thoroughly, with a spoon or using the low speed of an electric mixer.

Bread crumbs. *To make fresh:* For best results, the GF bread should be at least 1 day old. Using the pulsing operation of a food processor or blender, process until crumbs are of the desired consistency. *To make dry:* Spread bread crumbs in a single layer on a baking sheet and bake at 350°F (180°C) for 6 to 8 minutes, shaking pan frequently, until lightly browned, crisp and dry. (Or microwave, uncovered, on High for 1 to 2 minutes, stirring every 30 seconds.) *To store:* Package in airtight containers and freeze for up to 3 months.

Cake crumbs. See Bread crumbs.

Caramelize onions. See Onions.

Cast-iron skillet. *To clean:* Add 2 tbsp (25 mL) salt to a dry cast-iron skillet. Rub with an old toothbrush. Keep replacing salt until it remains white. This usually requires 2 to 3 applications of salt and about 5 minutes.

Chocolate. *To melt:* Chop each 1 oz (30 g) square into 4 to 6 pieces. Place in a heat-proof bowl or the top of a double-boiler over hot water to partially melt the chocolate. Remove from heat and continue stirring until completely melted. Or microwave on High for 1 minute per 1 oz (30 g) square.

Coconut. *To toast:* See Nuts.

Combine. To stir two or more ingredients together for a consistent mixture.

Cream. To combine softened fat and sugar by beating to a soft, smooth creamy consistency while trying to incorporate as much air as possible.

Cream cheese. *To warm quickly to room temperature:* For each 8-oz (250 g) package, cut into 1-inch (2.5 cm) cubes, arrange in a circle on a microwave-safe plate and microwave on High for 1 minute.

Cut in. To combine solid fat and flour until the fat is the size required (for example, the size of small peas or meal). Use either two knives or a pastry blender.

Digital instant-read thermometer. *To test meat for doneness:* Insert the metal stem of the thermometer at least 2 inches (5 cm) into the thickest part of cooked chicken, fish, pork, beef, etc. For thin cuts, it may be necessary to insert the thermometer horizontally. Meatballs can be stacked. *To test baked goods for doneness:* Insert the metal stem of the thermometer at least 2 inches (5 cm) into the thickest part of baked good. Temperature should register 200°F (100°C).

Dredge. To coat a food with flour or bread crumbs before frying, enabling batter to adhere to the food more easily.

Drizzle. To slowly spoon or pour a liquid (such as frosting or melted butter) in a very fine stream over the surface of food.

Dust. To coat by sprinkling GF confectioner's (icing) sugar, cocoa powder or any GF flour lightly over food or a utensil.

Eggs. *To warm to room temperature:* Place eggs in the shell from the refrigerator in a bowl of hot water and let stand for 5 minutes.

Egg whites. *To warm to room temperature:* Separate eggs while cold. Place bowl of egg whites in a larger bowl of hot water and let stand for 5 minutes. *To whip to soft peaks:* Beat to a thickness that comes up as the beaters are lifted and folds over at the tips. *To whip to stiff peaks:* Beat past soft peaks until the peaks remain upright when the beaters are lifted.

Egg yolks. *To warm to room temperature:* Separate eggs while cold. Place bowl of egg yolks in a larger bowl of hot water and let stand for 5 minutes.

Envelope fold. *To make:* Place food off center on double thickness of heavy-duty foil. Bring long end up and over food loosely causing all edges to meet. Seal edges with two to three $1/2$-inch (1 cm) folds. Be sure to pinch the folds tightly so any steam created is sealed in the package. Care must be taken not to put a hole in the package during cooking.

Flaxseed. *To grind:* Place whole seeds in a coffee grinder or blender. Grind only the amount required. If necessary, store extra ground flaxseed in the refrigerator. *To crack:* Pulse in a coffee grinder, blender or food processor just long enough to break the seed coat but not long enough to grind completely.

Fold. To gently combine light, whipped ingredients with heavier ingredients without losing the incorporated air. Using a rubber spatula, gently fold in a circular motion. Move down one side of the bowl and across the bottom, fold up and over to the opposite side and down again, turning bowl slightly after each fold.

Garlic. *To roast:* Cut off top of head to expose clove tips. Drizzle with $1/4$ tsp (1 mL) olive oil and microwave on High for 70 seconds, until fork-tender. Or bake in a pie plate or baking dish at 375°F (190°C) for 15 to 20 minutes, or until fork-tender. *To peel:* Use the flat side of a sharp knife to flatten the clove of garlic. Skin can then be easily removed.

Glaze. To apply a thin, shiny coating to the outside of a baked, sweet or savory food to enhance the appearance and flavor.

Grease pan. See Baking pan.

Griddle. *To test for correct temperature:* Sprinkle a few drops of water on the surface. If the water bounces and dances across the pan, it is ready to use.

Hazelnuts. *To remove skins:* Place hazelnuts in a 350°F (180°C) oven for 15 to 20 minutes. Immediately place in a clean, dry kitchen towel. With your hands, rub the nuts against the towel. Skins will be left in the towel. Be careful: hazelnuts will be very hot.

Hazelnut flour (hazelnut meal). *To make:* See Nut flour.

Herbs. *To store full stems:* Fresh-picked herbs can be stored for up to 1 week with stems standing in water. (Keep leaves out of water.) *To remove leaves:* Remove small leaves from stem by holding the top and running fingers down the stem in the opposite direction of growth. Larger leaves should be snipped off the stem using scissors. *To clean and store fresh leaves:* Rinse under cold running water and spin-dry in a lettuce spinner. If necessary, dry between layers of paper towels. Place a dry paper towel along with the clean herbs in a plastic bag in the refrigerator. Use within 2 to 3 days. Freeze or dry for longer storage. *To measure:* Pack leaves tightly into correct measure. *To snip:* After measuring, transfer to a small glass and cut using the tips of sharp kitchen shears/scissors to avoid bruising the tender leaves. *To dry:* Tie fresh-picked herbs together in small bunches and hang upside down in a well-ventilated location with low humidity and out of sunlight until the leaves are brittle and fully dry. If they turn brown (rather than stay green), the air is too hot. Once fully dried, strip leaves off the stems for storage. Store whole herbs in an airtight container in a cool dark place for up to 1 year and crushed herbs for up to 6 months. (Dried herbs are stored in the dark to prevent the color from fading.) Before using, check herbs and discard any that have faded, lost flavor or smell old and musty. *To dry using a microwave:* Place $1/2$ to 1 cup (125 to 250 mL) herbs between layers of paper towels. Microwave on High for 3 minutes, checking often to be sure they are not scorched. Then microwave for 10-second periods until leaves are brittle and can be pulled from stems easily. *To freeze:* Lay whole herbs in a single layer on a flat surface in the freezer for 2 to 4 hours.

Leave whole and pack in plastic bags. Herbs will keep in the freezer for 2 to 3 months. Crumble frozen leaves directly into the dish. Herb leaves are also easier to chop when frozen. Use frozen leaves only for flavoring and not for garnishing, as they lose their crispness when thawed. Some herbs, such as chives, have a very weak flavor when dried, and do not freeze well, but they do grow well inside on a windowsill.

Leeks. *To clean:* Trim roots and wilted green ends. Peel off tough outer layer. Cut leeks in half lengthwise and rinse under cold running water, separating the leaves so the water gets between the layers. Trim individual leaves at the point where they start to become dark in color and course in texture — this will be higher up on the plant the closer you get to the center.

Mix. To combine two or more ingredients uniformly by stirring or using an electric mixer on a low speed.

Nut flour (nut meal). *To make:* Toast nuts (see Nuts), cool to room temperature and grind in a food processor or blender to desired consistency. *To make using ground nuts:* Bake at 350°F (180°C) for 6 to 8 minutes, cool to room temperature and grind finer.

Nuts. *To toast:* Spread nuts in a single layer on a baking sheet and bake at 350°F (180°C) for 6 to 8 minutes, shaking the pan frequently, until fragrant and lightly browned. (Or microwave, uncovered, on High for 1 to 2 minutes, stirring every 30 seconds.) Nuts will darken upon cooling.

Olives. *To pit:* Place olives under the flat side of a large knife; push down on knife until pit pops out.

Onions. *To caramelize:* In a nonstick frying pan, heat 1 tbsp (15 mL) oil over medium heat. Add 2 cups (500 mL) sliced or chopped onions; cook slowly until soft and caramel-colored. If necessary, add 1 tbsp (15 mL) water or white wine to prevent sticking while cooking.

Peaches. *To blanch:* See Blanch.

Pecan flour (pecan meal). To make: See Nut flour.

Pine nuts. *To toast:* see Nuts.

Pumpkin seeds. *To toast:* See Sunflower seeds.

Quinoa. *To cook:* Rinse quinoa under cold running water in a fine mesh strainer. Bring $1/2$ cup (125 mL) quinoa and 1 cup (250 mL) water to a boil. Reduce heat to low; cover and simmer for 18 to 20 minutes, or until water is absorbed and quinoa is tender. Quinoa is cooked when grains turn from white to transparent and the tiny spiral-like germ is separated.

Raisins. *To plump:* Measure a spirit (usually brandy) into a liquid measuring cup and add raisins; microwave on High for 1 minute and let cool.

Sauté. To cook quickly in a small amount of fat at high temperature.

Sesame seeds. *To toast:* See Sunflower seeds.

Sunflower seeds. *To toast:* Spread seeds in a single layer on a baking sheet and bake at 350°F (180°C) for 6 to 10 minutes, shaking the pan frequently, until lightly browned. (Or microwave, uncovered, on High for 1 to 2 minutes, stirring every 30 seconds.) Seeds will darken upon cooling.

Water bath. Place filled jars, with finger-tightened lids, upright on a rack in a boiling water bath canner filled with enough boiling water so that jars are covered by at least 1 inch (2.5 cm) hot water. Cover canner and return to a full, rolling boil. Boil for time specified in recipe.

Whip. To beat ingredients vigorously to increase volume and incorporate air, typically using a whisk or electric mixer. See also Egg whites.

Whipping (35%) cream (aka heavy cream). *For greater volume:* Chill beaters and bowl in refrigerator for at least 1 hour before whipping.

Wild rice. *To cook:* Rinse 1 cup (250 mL) wild rice under cold running water. Add along with 6 cups (1.5 L) water to a large saucepan. Bring to a boil and cook, uncovered, at a gentle boil for about 35 minutes. Reduce heat, cover and cook for 10 minutes, or until rice is soft but not mushy. Makes 3 cups (750 mL). Store in refrigerator for up to 1 week.

Zest. *To zest:* Use a zester, the fine side of a box grater or a small sharp knife to peel off thin strips of the colored part of the skin of citrus fruits. Be sure not to remove the bitter white pith below.

Library and Archives Canada Cataloguing in Publication

Washburn, Donna, author
    Easy everyday gluten-free cooking : includes 250 delicious recipes / Donna Washburn & Heather Butt.

Includes index.
ISBN 978-0-7788-0462-8 (pbk.)

1. Gluten-free diet—Recipes. 2. Cookbooks. I. Butt, Heather, author II. Title.

RM237.86.W3735 2013   641.5'638   C2013-902263-5

Index